The Regulatory Function of European Private Law

The Regulatory Function of European Private Law

Edited by

Fabrizio Cafaggi

European University Institute, Italy

and

Horatia Muir Watt

Université de Paris 1 Panthéon-Sorbonne, France

Edward Elgar

Cheltenham, UK • Northampton, MA, USA

Published by
Edward Elgar Publishing Limited
The Lypiatts
15 Lansdown Road
Cheltenham
Glos GL50 2JA
UK

Edward Elgar Publishing, Inc.
William Pratt House
9 Dewey Court
Northampton
Massachusetts 01060
USA

A catalogue record for this book
is available from the British Library

Library of Congress Control Number: 2008939740

PEFC
PEFC/16-33-111
CATG-PEFC-052
www.pefc.org

ISBN 978 1 84720 199 7

Typeset by Cambrian Typesetters, Camberley, Surrey
Printed and bound in Great Britain by the MPG Books Group

Contents

Figures and tables

FIGURES

TABLES

Contributors

Mathias Audit Caen University, France
Oliveira Boskovic University of Corsica, France
Fabrizio Cafaggi European University Institute, Italy
Francesco Cardarelli IUSM University, Rome, Italy
Sandrine Clavel University of South Brittany, France
Javier de Cendra de Larragán Maastricht University, the Netherlands
Michael G. Faure Maastricht University, the Netherlands
Hans-W. Micklitz European University Institute, Italy
Horatia Muir Watt University of Paris 1, France
Anthony Ogus University of Manchester, United Kingdom
Gerald Spindler University of Goettingen, Germany
Sophie Stalla-Bourdillon European University Institute, Italy
Vincenzo Zeno-Zencovich University of Rome 3, Italy

Acknowledgements

This book is part of a broader project concerning governance and regulation of European private law. Jointly with 'Making European Private Law – Governance Design', it signals the necessity to look more deeply at the institutional framework in which Europeanization is occurring. The project has been carried out within NewGov. The two books could not have been published without the help and professional assistance of Federica Casarosa and Sophie Stalla-Bourdillon, two young researchers committed to innovative scholarship. We would also like to thankfully acknowledge the support and encouragement of Edward Elgar, the publisher, and Nep Elverd for her essential editorial assistance.

Fabrizio Cafaggi and Horatia Muir Watt

Introduction[1]

This volume is designed to take stock and assess the coherence of the diverse regulatory instruments and approaches which, on a European level, have progressively encroached upon the sphere traditionally recognized as the province of private law.[2] This analysis operates in the context of a multilevel system, where competences of the EU are often shared with those of member states and appropriate and effective transposition is a key feature of the new architecture.[3]

New modes of governance are emerging as a complementary or alternative response to legislative harmonization.[4] The book inquires into the relationship between these new modes of governance and the regulatory functions of European private law.[5]

In order to provide as broad a framework as possible, the chapters in this volume provide both a sectoral (environment, product safety and quality, electronic commerce) and a general (all services) perspective, several of them being devoted to the difficult (and often neglected) cross-border dimension of these fields. Shaping relationships between service providers and their customers, between buyers and sellers, producers and users of products, citizens and polluters, with varied forms of economic and social regulation, now largely overshadow the *ex post*, remedial, market-based arrangements charac-

---

1 This book is the second of a two-volume project concerning governance and regulation of European private law under NEWGOV, a 6th framework project. We are grateful to the publisher, Edward Elgar for supporting the project and to Nep Elverd and the editors who have contributed to its implementation. We also acknowledge the valuable editorial assistance of Federica Casarosa and Sophie Stalla-Bourdillon. Responsibility is ours.

2 Taking stock of the measures and approaches currently used in EC legislation has been largely facilitated by the series of tables drawn up by Hans Micklitz, in 'Regulatory strategies on services contracts in EC law': see Chap. 2 below.

3 See F. Cafaggi and H. Muir Watt, *The Making of European Private Law. Governance Design* (Edward Elgar, 2008).

4 See L.M. Salamon, *The Tools of Government: a Guide to New Governance* (OUP, 2002); G. de Burca and J. Scott, *Law and New Governance in the EU and the US* (Hart, 2006); F. Cafaggi, 'Making European Private Law. Governance Design', in Cafaggi and Muir Watt, above n. 3, pp. 289 ff.

5 See H. Collins, 'The Governance Implications for the European Union of the Changing Character of Private Law', in Cafaggi and Muir Watt, above n. 3, pp. 269 ff.

teristic of private law, which rely primarily upon the courts for their implementation. Indeed, there is little need to emphasize that Community legislation follows a vertical partition in terms of economic sectors, abandoning traditional splits between public/private law. Familiar private law instruments such as tort or contract appear only as a small part of many possible tools harnessed to the pursuit of allocative efficiency or distributive justice, synthetically described as the correction of market failures.[6]

The variety of means available to achieve these goals – which range from traditional public law tools such as state ownership, public franchising or licensing, through the more familiar forms of regulation[7] which rely on semi-private bodies or independent regulatory agencies for standard-making or market controls, to various and still experimental forms of self-regulation by means of voluntary arrangements on the other end of the scale – call for a general framework in order to avoid conflicts, incoherence or redundancy between regulatory approaches.[8] It must be remembered in this respect that the various regulatory tools elaborated by the European institutions are conceived in a Europe-wide context and often take on a cross-border dimension which was not present in these fields until now. To a certain extent, in the wake of traditional public law, regulation seemed to be incompatible with a conflict of laws approach. However, to the extent that regulation and private law instruments are now seriously entwined and no longer territory-specific, it is also time to think about the way in which such tools are implemented in trans-European situations.

I. THE STRUCTURE OF THE BOOK AND SOME POLICY QUESTIONS

The book is divided into four parts concerning services, environment, product safety and electronic commerce. Each section is made up of three contributions: one focusing on the private law dimension, one on the regulatory choices, the third on private international law. The aim is to show that a

---

6 See A. Ogus, 'The Regulation of Services and the Public-Private Divide', Chap. 1 below.

7 See A. Ogus's useful classification of 'traditional' and 'less-traditional' modes of regulation.

8 Hans Micklitz puts us on guard, however, against systemization in the form of general principles, which was indeed emblematic of private law. See too H. Collins, 'The Alchemy of Deriving General Principles of Contract Law from European Legislation: In Search of the Philosopher's Stone' (2006) 2 *European Review of Contract Law* 213.

coordinated if not integrated approach is needed to devise legal instruments at European level to pursue specific policy objectives. The multilevel dimension of European private law rests on the use of combined instruments that operate through choice of law by parties and through harmonized legislation. Within this combination different regulatory strategies have to be employed to perform simultaneously the design of an integrated European market and to provide the responses to its failures. Such an approach should not only be endorsed in academic circles, bridging disciplinary divides among the different approaches, but also and more importantly should be adopted by European institutions to address consistently policy objectives such as consumer protection and market competitiveness.

The endorsement of a coordinated approach does not eliminate the differences between *ex ante* and *ex post* models or between public and private enforcement. But given the changes which have occurred in regulatory theory and practice, it contributes to redesigning the boundaries between the two. The distinction between private and public law can be maintained and perform a useful function only if it becomes a way to describe the difference between two regulatory strategies aimed at designing European and local markets.

Basically, then, three sets of questions arise in connection with the regulatory strategies now practised in the traditional field of private law. The first set calls for analysis of the strategies which lead to the choice of a particular tool or combination of tools within the regulatory arsenal, in order to further a particular economic or social regulatory policy in a given economic sector. Clearly, such a choice, which requires the balancing of diverse and sometimes contradictory values, is no more neutral than is an initial preference for a regulatory approach over recourse to traditional private law instruments. In other words, there may well be a strong need for a coherent strategy of (regulatory) strategies.

The second set of questions concerns the way in which traditional private law arrangements fit into this regulatory picture. No doubt, regulation gains ground wherever private law proves impotent to steer markets, by ensuring adequate competitiveness or by pursuing wider distributive concerns. Recent Community legislation promoting regulatory instruments accredits the idea that private law and regulation are two distinct provinces, which apply 'without prejudice' to one another, the one being content to ensure commutative justice *ex post* in individual situations, while the other, purposive, vertical, sectoral and reliant upon specific remedial arrangements, furthers wider social welfare or economic goals.[9] However, such a partition is questionable, not

9 See the analysis of Article 3.2 of the Unfair Commercial Practices Directive 2005/29/EC, by Collins, above n. 8, p. 214.

only because private law itself has progressively been invested with a regulatory function, creating a risk of overlap, but also because it frequently appears as a complementary tool which allows fine-tuning of specifically regulatory approaches.

Thirdly, a topic frequently neglected in debates on regulation is that of the impact and functional transformation of private international law in various economic sectors.[10] Yet the novel regulatory role and content with which private international law is beginning to be invested by recent Community legislation is potentially most instructive, in that it calls not only for rethinking the public/private partition, but also requires defining the relationship between the conflict of laws and various regulatory instruments linked to the construction of the internal market – most obviously, the country of origin principle. To a certain extent, these contributions provide the link to the twin volume of essays on governance,[11] since private international law has equally been transformed into an instrument of multilevel governance in the sphere of European private law.

II. A STRATEGY OF REGULATORY STRATEGIES?

The available tools for correcting market failures range across the public–private divide.[12] The choice of approach may vary according to the regulatory goal being pursued and is generally hybrid. Thus, as analysed by Anthony Ogus, regulation qualified as 'economic', which is designed to correct insufficient competitiveness in the supply of a service, may take on different forms according to the type of market in which it is called upon to operate. Ordinary competitive markets usually give rise to administrative enforcement of competition law, sometimes completed by private enforcement.[13] More rarely, price control can be justified when competition has proved ineffective, for instance in cases of regulatory capture. Natural monopolies, the object of public ownership in the past, may on the other hand be regulated through authorities or agencies, with a variable role for judicial review, or again through public franchising. Here contractual techniques prevail, although the extent to which they

10 However, see M. Audit, H. Muir Watt, E Patatut, *Régulation et Droit International Privé*, LGDJ 2008, Collection Droit & Economie.

11 See Cafaggi and Muir Watt, above n. 3.

12 A. Ogus, 'The regulation of services and the public–private divide'; Chap. 1 below.

13 See Commission White Paper on Damages Actions for Breach of the EC Antitrust Rules, COM(2008) 165, 2.4.2008; W. Wils, 'The Use of Settlements in Public Antitrust Enforcement: Objectives and Principles' (2008) *World Competition* 335.

are governed by the ordinary rules of private law of contract is variable. Private law may however have a role to play in cases of 'situational monopolies', when the implementation of public competition law is not enough to ensure sufficient competitiveness and regulation through contract is necessary.[14]

As explained by the same author, 'economic' regulation likewise designed to ensure allocative efficiency, must also deal with externalities and informational asymmetries. The array of available public regulatory tools is extremely varied, including prohibition, licensing or prior authorization, quality standards, mandatory disclosure, all potentially accompanied by criminal or administrative sanctions. Private law provides complementary remedies in individual situations through contract law, particularly consumer law in the case of information problems, while tort law tackles the effects of externalities suffered by third parties. Collective redress may complement traditional private law techniques with new remedies which emphasize the regulatory function.[15]

'Social' regulation is linked to distributive justice, whose concerns may be the insufficient resources of part of the population prevented thereby from acceding to essential services, the greater bargaining power of the service provider, or the insufficient financial and educational endowment of consumers to best assess their preferences. Here, public ownership models based on tax-financed subsidies have usually been superseded by privatized models, in which the incumbent supplier may be contractually bound by a universal service obligation or at the least an obligation to ensure that vulnerable groups may enjoy the service at a lower tariff. Regulation may also apply to information, advertising, the provision of cooling-off periods, or consumer rights to withdraw. Tort law may also provide *ex post* situational remedies, in case one party has been seriously disadvantaged.[16]

The array of available regulatory approaches appears however to be ever-widening, to the extent that 'less traditional' methods seem to be given increasing importance. As Hans Micklitz points out, such methods also signal the appearance of new actors, in the form of 'less traditional' regulators, which tend to oust the more established administrative agencies and indeed the courts

---

14 See F. Cafaggi, 'Il diritto dei contratti nei mercati regolati' (2008) *Rivista Trimestrale di Diritto e Procedura Civile* p. 95.

15 See F. Cafaggi and H.W. Micklitz, 'Collective enforcement of consumer law: a framework for a comparative assessment' (2008) 3 *ERPL* 391; C. Hodges, *The Reform of Class and Representative Actions in European Legal Systems: a New Framework for Collective Redress in Europe* (Hart, 2008).

16 See M. Faure, 'Regulatory strategies in environmental liability', Chap. 5 below.

themselves, increasingly bypassed even when private remedies are available through out-of-court settlement procedures.[17] Thus, a clear trend appears towards co-regulation and self-regulation, both as a general rule across the board in the field of services and in specific areas such as environmental protection.[18] Here, as Javier de Cendra de Larragán explains, the use of comitology and groups of experts appears at the same time as new regulatory principles and instruments emerge, such as the precautionary principle, prescriptive standards, risk assessment, impact assessment, emissions trading, subsidies and other financial solutions, voluntary agreements and standardization, eco-labelling, eco-management and not forgetting environmental liability.[19]

The new methods emerge as a (partial response) to different problems, partly implementation fallacies, partly competence deficit, partly burdensome legislative techniques.[20] Self- and co-regulation have been identified as alternatives to legislation,[21] although they should be seen more as complements both at EU and national level.[22]

---

17 H. Micklitz, 'Regulatory strategies on services contracts in EC law'; Chap. 2 below.

18 See on these questions, F. Cafaggi (ed.), *Reframing Self-regulation in European Private Law* (Kluwer, 2006); F. Cafaggi, 'Self-regulation in European contract law' (2007) *European Journal of Legal Studies* 1, available at www.ejls.eu; and C. M. Donnelly, *Delegation of Governmental Power to Private Parties. A Comparative Perspective* (OUP, 2007).

19 J. de Cendra de Lagarrán, 'Regulatory dilemmas in EC environmental law: the ongoing conflicts between competitiveness and the environment'; Chap. 4 below.

20 Emphasis on transposition problems is given by the European Parliament, especially in the Levai Report on Better Regulation in the European Union (2007/2095 (INI) A6-0273/2007), the Gargani Report on the Strategy for the Simplification of the Regulatory Environment (2007/2096 (INI) A6-0271/2007 final), and by the Commission itself. See European Parliament Resolution on Better Lawmaking 2005, 4.9.2007 (2007/2095(INI), Points 48 and 49. The Parliament 'encourages authorities in the Member States to draw up formal transposition strategies, in order to clearly define the roles and responsibilities of the regional and national governments for better and faster transposition [...] Encourages the Commission to publish, where possible, the transposition Guidelines for directives at the same time as the directives themselves, in order to allow national and regional governments to take them into account before starting the transposition process.'

21 See Commission staff working document, 'Instruments for a modernized single market', SEC (2007) 1518, (hereinafter 'Instruments for a modernized single market') annexed to the Communication, 'A Single Market for the XXI Century'.

22 See the Gargani Report, above n. 20 and the European Parliament resolution on simplification at p. 11 after reiterating 'that traditional legislative instruments should continue to be used as a general rule in order to attain the objectives laid down in the Treaty; considers that co-regulation and self-regulation could usefully supplement or replace legislative measures where these methods make improvements of equivalent

The number and variety of methods are not without difficulties. As Hans Micklitz's study shows, standardization is subject to regulatory capture;[23] stake-holders tend to be excluded from co-regulatory arrangements. The increasing rule-making power of private regulators is not paralleled by the growth of accountability mechanisms.[24] Furthermore, the policy considerations which underlie a given choice of instrument are not always transparent.

The Commission has however attempted an interesting, though perhaps in practice not entirely successful, response to this problem through the 2002 'better lawmaking package'.[25] Its aim was to simplify the regulatory environment, to promote dialogue and systematize impact assessment.[26] Impact assessment is promoted to decide among different legislative alternatives and various regulatory strategies, often with similar instruments.[27]

The growing role of impact assessment shows the need for the availability of an accountable method to decide among ever-increasing regulatory alternatives. At the same time there is strong dissatisfaction with current impact assessment especially when it comes to decisions concerning the use of hard and soft law, and those between legislation and self-regulation. The debate about the different weight of these alternatives and the criteria to be used has had strong institutional echoes with different views expressed by the Commission and the Parliament.

In relation to regulation, the use of regulatory impact assessment (RIA) is driven by the awareness of burdensome and often ineffective regulatory strategies. Basically, this means inviting regulators to engage in a balanced

---

broader scope than legislation can provide; stresses that any use of alternative regulatory arrangements should be in compliance with the Inter-institutional Agreement on better lawmaking; points out that the Commission has to lay down the conditions and limits which the parties must observe when employing such methods, and that these should in any event be used under Commission supervision and without prejudice to Parliament's right to object to their use'.

23 See Chapter 2, this volume. See too, within the scope of the World Trade Organization, P. Marquez, 'Standardization and Capture: The Rise of Standardization in International Industrial Regulation and Global Administrative Law' (2007) 7 *Global Jurist* Article 5.

24 See Cafaggi, 'Self-regulation in European contract law', above n. 18.

25 Composed of four communications designed to improve and clarify regulatory techniques: see J. de Cendra de Larragán, 'Regulatory dilemmas in EC environmental law', Chap. 4 below.

26 See 'Inter-institutional Agreement on Better Lawmaking', 16.12.2003, OJ C 321, 31.12.2003, p. 1, and 'A Strategic Review of Better Regulation in the European Union' (COM (2006) final 689); and 'Second Strategic Review of Better Regulation in the European Union' (COM (2008) 32 final).

27 See Commission Guidelines on Impact Assessment and draft revised version 27.05.2008, available at http://ec.europa.eu/governance/impact/consultation/docs/ia_guidelines_draft_text_final_en.pdf.

appraisal of the various available policy instruments. Interests are defined and balanced by experts or high-ranking officials and not by Parliament. Another difficulty attendant upon regulation is precisely the conflicts of values that need to be balanced, on a case-by-case basis but according to general principles compliant with the rule of law. The conflict between competitiveness and environmental protection, analysed by Javier de Cendra de Larragán, is a significant illustration.[28]

(a) The Institutional Debate and its Consequences on European Private Law

The European Parliament has taken stock of these issues with a series of Reports and Resolutions published in 2007.[29] It examines the better lawmaking/better regulation strategy, emphasizing the need for more intense partnership among European institutions and between them and the national ones.[30] The European Parliament (EP) shares the view that impact assessment is a key instrument for evaluating legislative alternatives.[31] It expresses

---

[28] For a general overview see S. Weatherill (ed.), *Better regulation, Studies of the Oxford Institute of European and Comparative Law* (Hart, 2007). In this volume in particular, see J. de Cendra de Larragán, 'Regulatory Dilemmas in EC Environmental Law', Chap. 4 below, showing that stringent regulation may create a brand function/first mover advantage (the 'Porter hypothesis'). But there is a clear need to reduce costs and make use of more imaginative regulatory approaches.

[29] See the Levai Report followed by the European Parliament Resolution on Better Lawmaking, the Gargani Report, followed by the European Parliament Resolution on the Strategy for the Simplification of the Regulatory Environment and the Medina Report on Institutional and Legal Implications of the Use of Soft Law Instruments' (2007/2008 (INI) A6-0259/2007), followed by the European Parliament Resolution on Institutional and Legal Implications of the Use of 'Soft Law' Instruments (2007/2028(INI).

[30] See the Levai Report and EP Resolution on Better Lawmaking: 'G. Whereas better regulation is not exclusively about cutting red tape, reducing the administrative burden, simplifying existing legislation or deregulation but also involves ensuring that the legislative process is engaged with by all relevant governmental and non-governmental actors at all levels and that a close partnership is established between the European institutions and the national, regional and local authorities in order to deliver high-quality regulation.'

[31] See the Levai Report and EP Resolution on Better Lawmaking, where the EP states that it '5. Agrees with the Commission that better lawmaking cannot be achieved without an overall picture of the economic, social, environmental, health and international impact of each legislative proposal; fully supports, therefore, the setting-up within the Commission of an Impact Assessment Board under the authority of the Commission's President in order to monitor the application of these principles in the drafting of impact assessments by the responsible staff of the Commission; 6. Stresses, nevertheless, that, in order to guarantee a minimum level of independent scrutiny in the

concerns about the current practices and it suggests important changes.[32] Furthermore it subscribes to the view that principle-based legislation should be preferred to detailed legislation.[33]

The European Parliament supports the better lawmaking choices but underlines the need for broader involvement of stakeholders and stronger accountability mechanisms.[34] It suggests that while the use of alternatives to

---

drafting of impact assessments, an independent panel of experts should be set up to monitor, by means of spot checks, the quality of opinions delivered by the Impact Assessment Board, and that representatives of interested parties should also be allowed to assist in conducting them; 7. Considers it necessary that the Impact Assessment Board should guarantee the application of a common methodology for all impact assessments, so as to avoid contradictory approaches and to facilitate comparability.'

[32] See EP Resolution on Better Lawmaking where the EP states: '43. Supports the conclusion resulting from the study entitled 'Simplifying EU Environmental Policy' that impact assessments can play an essential role in ensuring better regulation and that the quality of some assessments needs to be improved; urges the Commission to ensure:

- that adequate time and financial resources are allocated for these assessments;
- that impact assessments consider economic, social, environmental and health aspects on an equal footing, in both the short term and the longer term;
- that impact assessments consider not only the costs of measures but also the costs of not addressing the environmental, public health or food issues;
- transparency and input of all relevant stakeholders;
- that the impact assessments are broad enough in scope and that they take into account the different national circumstances in the Member States;
- recognition that impact assessments could also play an essential role in the case of amendments proposed by the European Parliament or the Council having potentially significant impacts . . .'

[33] See the Levai Report and EP Resolution on Better Lawmaking: '17. Is in favour of promoting principles-based legislation and focusing on quality rather than quantity; sees the better regulation debate as an occasion to reflect on legislation as a process designed to achieve clearly defined policy goals by committing all stakeholders to all phases of the process, from preparation to enforcement, and involving them therein.'

[34] See the Levai Report, p. I, and the EP Resolution on Better Lawmaking. The EP in its Resolution states that it: '1. Strongly supports the process of Better Regulation with a view to strengthening the effectiveness, efficiency, coherence, accountability and transparency of EU law; stresses, however, that such a process needs to be based on a number of preconditions:

(i) full and joint involvement of the Council, the Commission and the European Parliament;
(ii) wide and transparent consultation of all relevant stakeholders, including non-governmental organizations;

legislation, namely self-regulation and co-regulation, should be carefully considered by the Commission, democratic scrutiny and respect of the rule of law principle can still be maintained.[35]

After recalling that the contract law project is based on soft law,[36] important concerns were expressed about the use of soft law as a means to circumvent lawmaking power allocation among European institutions.[37] The EP underlines its weak position and that of the ECJ in relation to soft law and

---

(iii) strengthening of the accountability of Community bodies for the regulatory process, and of the general transparency of that process, in particular by opening Council meetings to public scrutiny when the Council is acting in its legislative capacity;
(iv) any assessment aimed at simplification must consider economic, social, environmental and health aspects on an equal footing and should not be limited to short-term considerations;
(v) the simplification process must under no circumstance entail lowering the standards contained in current legislation.'

35 See the EP Resolution on Better Regulation, p. 36. The Parliament 'Encourages the Commission to investigate alternatives to legislation with a view to improving the functioning of the internal market, including self-regulation and the mutual recognition of national rules, while stressing that this should not impede democratic scrutiny by the European Parliament and by Member States' parliaments; underlines that Community regulation must be seen in the context of international competition and global markets . . .' See also EP Resolution on Soft Law, point 12: the EP 'Is of the opinion that standardization and codes of conduct are important elements of self-regulation; considers, however, that standardization must not lead to overregulation and hence constitute an additional burden for small and medium-sized enterprises in particular; believes, therefore, that the legal bases concerned should incorporate built-in safeguards against overregulation.'

36 See EP Resolution on Soft Law, above n. 29. 'W. Whereas, in addition, the European contract law project remains still in the nature of soft law,' and then the EP points out that, '13. Whereas it is legitimate for the Commission to make use of pre-legislative instruments, the pre-legislative process should not be abused nor unduly protracted; considers that, in areas such as the contract-law project, a point must come where the Commission decides whether or not to use its right of initiative and on what legal basis.'

37 See the EP Resolution on Soft Law, above n. 29. 'X. Whereas, where the Community has legislative competence but there seems to be a lack of political will to introduce legislation, the use of soft law is liable to circumvent the properly competent legislative bodies, may flout the principles of democracy and the rule of law under Article 6 of the EU Treaty, and also those of subsidiarity and proportionality under Article 5 of the EC Treaty, and may result in the Commission's acting *ultra vires*. Z. Whereas the better regulation agenda should not be subverted in order to allow the Community executive effectively to legislate by means of soft law instruments, thereby potentially undermining the Community legal order, avoiding the involvement of the democratically elected Parliament and the legal review by the Court of Justice and depriving citizens of legal remedies.'

cautions on its use by the Commission.[38] It emphasizes the need for consultation and suggests the use of Inter-institutional agreement to regulate its use.[39]

More recently the Commission has enacted a Review Package, revising its regulatory approach, focusing on new modes of regulation and their relation with competition.[40]

The Communication stresses the better regulation aspects of the governance dimension.[41] It thus tries to integrate the governance approach, taken by the White Paper, and the better regulation as refined over the last four or five years.[42] It is important to stress that while the governance dimension has been

---

38 According to the EP Resolution on Soft Law: 'J. Whereas where the Community has legislative competence, the proper way to act is through the adoption of legislation by the democratic institutions of the Union, Parliament and the Council, in so far as this still appears necessary having due regard to the principles of subsidiarity and proportionality; whereas it is only by means of the adoption of legislation through the institutional procedures laid down in the Treaty that legal certainty, the rule of law, justiciability and enforceability may be secured, and whereas this also entails respect for the institutional balance enshrined in the Treaty and allows for openness of decision-making. K. Whereas, in general, where the Community has competence to legislate, this precludes the use of "soft law" or "[r]ules of conduct that are laid down in instruments which have not been attributed legally binding force as such, but nevertheless may have certain – indirect – legal effects, and that are aimed at and may produce practical effects", which have been used historically to alleviate a lack of formal law-making capacity and/or means of enforcement and as such are typical of public international law. L. Whereas, where the Treaty expressly provides for them, soft law instruments are legitimate, provided that they are not used as a surrogate for legislation where the Community has legislative power and where Community-wide regulation still appears necessary having due regard to the principles of subsidiarity and proportionality, since this would also constitute a breach of the principle of conferred specific powers, and whereas this applies a fortiori to Commission communications purporting to interpret Community legislation; whereas preparatory instruments, such as green and white papers, also constitute a legitimate use of soft law, in common with notices and guidelines published by the Commission in order to explain how it applies competition and state-aid policy.' So the EP 'Considers that in the context of the Community, soft law all too often constitutes an ambiguous and ineffective instrument which is liable to have detrimental effect on Community legislation and institutional balance and should be used with caution even where it is provided for in the Treaty'.

39 See Medina Report, above n. 29, points 14 to 19, p. 8.

40 See 'A Strategic Review of Better Regulation in the European Union', above n. 26, and later, 'A Single Market for 21st Century Europe' (COM (2007) 724 final) and, in reference to regulatory strategies, see the Commission staff working document 'Instruments for a modernized single market policy', above n. 21.

41 See on these questions Weatherill, above n. 28, in particular S. Weatherill, 'The challenge of better regulation', p. 14; R. Kelemen and A. Menon, 'The politics of EC regulation', p. 175; and E. Olivi, 'The EU better regulation agenda', p. 191.

42 The Commission states that: 'Single market policy should become more evidence-based and impact-driven, more targeted and better enforced, more decentral-

mainly focusing on legitimacy, the better lawmaking emphasizes efficiency and effectiveness.[43] The attempt to integrate the two is based on the need to reach a strategic combination of two different yet not necessarily different goals: stronger legitimacy and greater effectiveness.

The Commission tries to redefine the aims of legislation by using and expanding the Lamfalussy approach.[44] European legislation should be limited to principles and national authorities should become more involved with the lawmaking process beyond implementation.[45]

This development is partly due to the difficulties on implementation and the need to target implementation policies.[46] It has brought out the necessity of better coordination among different policies and the necessity to include across-policies impact assessment.[47] The oversight of an Impact Assessment Board has contributed to target the policies and stage their implementation.[48] These questions should also be considered at transposition level in national systems, where impact assessment is still relatively poor. However it has become clear that RIA can have an adverse impact on regulatory innovation if it is conceived as an instrument to evaluate only strong regulatory modes such

---

ized and network-based, more accessible and better communicated.' See 'Instruments for a modernized single market policy', above n. 21.

[43] See on these questions Weatherill, above n. 28.

[44] This view is shared by EP in its Resolution on Better Lawmaking: '18. Regards the experience of the Lamfalussy procedure in financial markets regulation, and the regulator-market participants dialogue in particular, as a valuable case for a dynamic legislative process; 19. Is of the opinion that the Lamfalussy procedure is a useful mechanism; considers the convergence of supervisory practices to be crucial; welcomes the work of the Level 3 committees in this respect and supports their call for an adequate toolbox; believes that giving supervisors room for manoeuvre can remove much of the burden of technical detail in legislation and produce adequate rules for a dynamic market; stresses, however, that this can never take away the political responsibility as regards the final objectives; insists that legislators should carefully monitor the process and reiterates that Parliament's rights in the legislative procedure should be fully respected.'

[45] See 'Instruments for a modernized single market policy', above n. 21, pp. 8 ff.; but see also Levai Report, above n. 20, p. 7.

[46] See Commission Communication, 'A Europe of results – applying Community law' (COM(2007) 502, 5.09.2007) and 'Instruments for a modernized market policy', above n. 21, para. 2.5, pp. 15 ff. On these questions in relation to European private law, see Cafaggi and Muir Watt, above n. 3, pp. 289 ff.

[47] See 'Instruments for a modernized market policy', above n. 21, para. 3.2, pp. 17 ff.; the Communication, 'Responding to Strategic Needs: Reinforcing the Use of Evaluation' (SEC (2007) 213); and Commission Working Document on the Feasibility of EU Legislation in the Area of Protection of Witnesses and Collaborators with Justice (COM (2007) 693 final).

[48] See 'Second Strategic Review of Better Regulation in the European Union', above n. 26.

as command and control.[49] This is particularly relevant in a field like private law where there is a strong dominance of default rules.

The impact analysis of the principle of proportionality and its application needs to be refined, being still predominantly defined by judicial intervention. The specificity of the principle of proportionality in the area of European private law, especially in relation to the combination between principle and detailed legislation, mandatory and default rules, constitutes a strategic challenge for European law reform.[50]

(b) Focusing on the Multilevel Dimension of Judicial Governance

It is quite clear that the strong divide between lawmaking and implementation disappears when legislation is considered a process rather than a product; the implementation process becomes more articulate, involving horizontal (member state (MS)), vertical (EU) together with diagonal relationships (EU/MS).[51] The Commission strongly supports the development of networks and different forms of administrative cooperation and makes reference to the use of the European Grouping of Territorial Cooperation.[52] Most importantly it recognizes the need to strengthen the national court system by improving the network of national courts and ensuring that they provide effective remedies for breach of single market rules.[53] The current initiatives of judicial governance, involving cooperation of national judiciaries in commercial and civil matters must be redesigned according to these goals.[54]

The use of mutual recognition has defined a flexible complement to legislative harmonization.[55] This multitool approach may have important implications for the harmonization process of European private law but it moves further away from the codification path, at least as conventionally defined.

---

49 See Commission Guidelines on Impact Assessment, above n. 27.

50 See F. Cafaggi, 'Making European private law', above n. 3, pp. 289 ff. part pp. 319 ff.

51 On these developments see Cafaggi and Muir Watt, above n. 3, pp. 328 ff.

52 See Regulation (EC) 1082/2006, OJ L 210, 31.7.2006.

53 See para. 5.5.3, p. 30; and Cafaggi, and Muir Watt, above n. 3, pp. 337 ff.

54 See A. Potocki, 'Les réseaux jurisdictionnels en Europe', in *Liber Amicorum Bo Vestendorf*, C. Baudenbacher (ed.) (2007) p. 141.

55 See the Resolution of the European Parliament on Better Lawmaking, above n. 20, p. 36. The Parliament 'encourages the Commission to investigate alternatives to legislation with a view to improving the functioning of the internal market, including self-regulation and the mutual recognition of national rules, while stressing that this should not impede democratic scrutiny by the European Parliament and by Member States' parliaments; underlines that Community regulation must be seen in the context of international competition and global markets.'

The Commission also emphasizes the correlation between regulation and competition, in particular the role of competition law as a regulatory device to design new markets.

The impact of competition on private law does not only concern regulated fields such as utilities but also areas such as product safety, environmental and consumer protection. It affects contract law and the features of the contractual relationships both in business to business and business to consumer. It contributes to widening the array of remedies in the area of private enforcement.

Different instruments and remedies have been (or are about to be) introduced to ensure the effectiveness of the regulatory strategies. They can have a strong impact on European private law legislation even beyond the domain of consumer protection.

On the one hand, *ex ante* impact assessment can be used to define costs and benefits of specific private law alternatives, such as duty to inform, specific performance versus damages, liability versus validity rules etc. On the other hand, instruments to measure policy effectiveness, such as the consumer market scoreboard that includes the five top indicators, namely complaints, prices, satisfaction, switching and safety, can be applied more broadly to the whole of European private law. These regulatory innovations pose new challenges to law reform concerning European private law to which we now turn.

III. FITTING IN PRIVATE LAW.

How does private law fit into this complex regulatory picture? The coexistence between the many sector, and purposive regulatory techniques and traditional market-based solutions of private law, administered *ex post* by the courts, is not necessarily harmonious, or at least, the articulation between the two approaches requires serious reflection. It appears, incidentally but unsurprisingly, that attempts to elaborate a Common Frame of Reference have encountered this very difficulty.[56] There may, for instance, be problems of overlap. The recent proposal of a horizontal Directive on consumer rights limited to consumer contract law shows the abandonment of a comprehensive project and the focus on the Consumer Acquis as the starting point of a new season of legislative reform.[57]

---

[56] See the interesting account by H. Beale in 'The European Commission's Common Frame of Reference Project: a progress report' (2006) 2 *European Review of Contract Law* 303 and the other essays published in the same issue of the ERCL, 2006.

[57] See Commission Proposal for a Directive on Consumer Rights, Brussels, 8.10.2008 (COM(2008) 614).

The sources of European private law differ quite significantly from those at national level.[58] The function of legislation has changed, moving towards framework principles. The role of national and European regulators has become ever more important in implementation. This in turn triggers judicial review and the emergence of new innovative potential cooperative/competitive partnerships between regulators and judges, to devise private law rules especially in recently liberalized markets.[59]

Furthermore, it is not always clear to what extent the violation of, or the compliance with, regulatory standards may constitute respectively a cause of private action or a defence in individual litigation. Of course, private law itself has to some extent integrated regulatory goals, causing a theoretical debate about the nature of private law.[60] But perhaps more to the point is the impact of the coexistence and interpenetration of private law and regulatory techniques on the relationships traditionally covered by private law. This particular point was explored by several contributors in various regulated sectors.

Conclusions by several contributors converge towards the idea that private law remedies, involving slow, costly, unpredictable, *ex post* court intervention, may be becoming a luxury. However impotent to achieve sophisticated regulatory goals unaided, they may nevertheless retain a certain usefulness by providing complementary incentives for preventing externalities in the form of damages to third parties. Contract is also the form used by self-regulatory techniques, which therefore to a certain extent implement principles developed in the field of private law.[61]

At the beginning of 2008 an academic version of the Common Frame of Reference was made public, following the publication of the first volume concerning the Acquis principles on contract law.[62] These developments

---

58 See F. Cafaggi, 'Introduction', in F. Cafaggi, *The Institutional Framework of European Private Law* (OUP, 2006), p. 3.

59 More often the relationship is conflicting and to some extent competitive but this is also the typical feature of a new phenomenon. In legal systems (e.g. the US) where this coexistence has been in place for a long time, more cooperative relationships tend to substitute for competitive ones. See Cafaggi, above n. 14, p. 95 ff.

60 On the theoretical German debate, see H. Micklitz, 'Regulatory Strategies on Services Contracts in EC law', Chap. 2 below, at n. 40.

61 See H. Collins, *Regulating Contracts* (OUP, 1999). From a different perspective, see F. Cafaggi, 'Self-regulation in European contract law', above n. 18; and C. Scott, 'Regulating private legislation', in Cafaggi and Muir Watt, above n. 3, p. 254.

62 See Draft Common Frame of Reference, Prepared by the Study Group on a European Civil Code and the European Research Group on Existing EC Private Law (Acquis Group), Interim online edition available at http://www.storme.be/DCFRInterim.pdf and the Study Group on the European Civil Code, *Principles of European Law – Commercial Agency, Franchise and Distribution Contracts* (OUP, 2006).

follow the enactment of the Review of the Acquis Communication and the results of the consultation.[63] These endeavours represent two highly relevant attempts to define the common core of European private law, predominantly contracts but also civil liability, unjust enrichment and others.

The first impression is that they have not been able to solve the tensions between the different approaches to European private law at national and European level. First they fail to combine the two main functions of European private law: market design and regulation. They refer to the level of legislation, national and European, and the degree of harmonization, minimum and total, without considering the weight of substantive choices concerning, for example, the relationships between mandatory and default rules.[64] They also adopt a uniform strategy without considering the specificity of information regulation.[65]

Secondly, while they mainly refer to transborder transactions or interactions, they both lack strong coordination with private international law principles, redesigned by Regulations Rome I and Rome II.

Thirdly they fail to address the relationship with the body of private law, predominantly contract and property, developed in regulated markets recently liberalized. Today there is a need for different partitions given that markets have been liberalized and contract law applies to all transactions though with different rules.

Fourthly they do not consider the impact of competition law in typical domains of private law, such as contract and property, which become clear if we only think about unbundling in network industries.

The contributions in this book try to integrate the different perspectives. The proposal of a European Directive on consumer rights in late 2008 represents a turning point, focusing on consumer contract law and trying to build on the principles of the Acquis a set of general rules. The choice of circumscribing the Acquis to consumer contract law, without considering collective redress, poses new questions concerning the internal architecture of the Acquis giving priority to contractual principles.[66] Again, however, the most important issues are left out. Which policy goals lay behind this choice? How has the internal market goal been transformed? What is the relationship between positive and

---

63 See Green Paper on the Review of the Consumer Acquis, Brussels, 08.02.2007 (COM (2006) 744 final).

64 See on these questions H.W. Micklitz and F. Cafaggi, *After the Common Frame of Reference – What Future for European Private Law?* (forthcoming, 2009).

65 See for a different approach S. Grundmann and W. Kerber, 'An optional European contract law code: Advantages and disadvantages' (2006) *European Journal of Law and Economics* 215.

66 See Proposal for a Directive on Consumer Rights, above n. 57.

negative integration policies in the field of consumer contract law? What is the institutional framework to implement the Directive? In particular, what is the relationship between the judiciary and the ever more important role of administrative agencies, often combining consumer protection and competition law? What is the relationship with competition law? Why leave out consumer contract law in a regulated market?

The necessity for coordination between general European private law and sector specific legislation characterizes the overall project. The complementarity between private law devices and administrative law is balanced according to different weights in each field. In environmental protection, for instance, Michael Faure shows, with reference to Shavell's public interest theory, that prevention of environmental harm is undoubtedly the primary province of *ex ante*, regulatory approaches.[67] Emissions limits and emissions trading have proved eminently more efficient than private actions in tort, of which the regulatory effect is marginal. Tort law, which fixes a price for risk creators in case of the violation of certain standards (negligence) or non-achievement of a given result (strict liability), cannot adequately cure the various information asymmetries, problems of insolvency, or underdeterrence in a case where the harm is thinly spread.[68] Potentially, it might nevertheless play a regulatory role through strict liability (at least in the field of the environment, where one party can influence the risk), but such a path is efficient only if a risk-averse injurer can remove the risk through insurance. However, the development of direct first-party insurance, which is no longer triggered by liability, thus avoiding the problems of 'insurer ambiguity' linked to the unforeseeability of judge-made tort law, clearly raises the question of the future of tort law, at least in this field.

The long-term survival of traditional tort law appears equally challenged in the field of electronic commerce. Analysed by Vincenzo Zeno-Zencovich and Francesco Cardarelli,[69] the Electronic Commerce Directive advocates, on the one hand, self-regulation in the form of the adoption of codes of conduct. The path thus chosen is that of voluntary compliance and periodical and independent scrutiny by the various constituencies. Although using contract as a form of constraint, the approach is clearly regulatory, differing from private law where voluntary compliance concerns only default rules. Paradoxically,

---

[67] 'Regulatory Strategies in Environmental Liability'; Chap. 5 below.

[68] See R. Cooter, 'Prices and sanctions' (1984) *Columbia Law Review* 1523; and S. Shavell, *Foundations of Economic Analysis of Law* (Harvard University Press, 2004).

[69] Respectively, V. Zeno-Zencovich, 'E-commerce from a private law perspective'; Chap. 10 below; and F. Cardarelli, 'E-commerce from a regulatory perspective'; Chap. 11 below.

constraint is required here to get rid of monopolies as a form of ransom or toll to be paid for freedom. On the other hand, the novelty of the Directive's regulatory approach lies in the fact that it relies on the equation: no control (by electronic service providers of content)/no liability. Here again, such a principle would appear to go against the grain of tort law, which allocates damages to the wrongdoers and provides both parties with incentives for precautions. The Directive, on the other hand, does not allocate damages, but simply indicates when industries may be liability free. Furthermore, it encourages out-of-court settlement, whereas courts are the prime administrators of tort law. Indeed, it adheres to a minimalist version of governance structures, with little institutional framework. Remarkably, no prior licence is involved, tortious liability is excluded, there are no regulatory agencies nor command and control procedures, which are perceived to be inadequate for a network structure.

The picture which emerges from the examination of the interaction between private law product liability and product safety regulation is analogous. According to Gerald Spindler, analysing Directive 2001/95 on product safety, product safety and product liability are improperly coordinated.[70] Product safety is regulated to a large extent through standards developed by various hybrid bodies and in turn relies on the development of incentives to trigger compliance by producers.[71] Once again, however, the interaction of such standards with tort law remains to be elucidated.[72] Free to impose additional obligations on producers, the courts may, to a certain extent, correct the problems of private or state regulatory capture which inevitably accompanies standardization by non-elected bodies, while offering additional deterrence. Overall, it might seem, therefore, that the incentive structures in this field are well-balanced: public law limits its purport to the definition to essential requirements relating to life and health; technical standard-setting is left to private or semi-private agencies with the veto of public authorities to attenuate the risk of private regulatory capture; tort law fine-tunes and fills gaps. But as Zeno-Zencovich and Cardarelli point out, some sectors remain problematic, since not all damages and risks are covered, this being particularly the case in the field of IT production, where prevention and deterrence are currently set at a sub-optimal level and call out for a better thought out regulatory approach.

---

70 G. Spindler, 'Interaction between product liability and regulation at the European level'; Chap. 8 below.

71 F. Cafaggi, 'Product safety, private standard-setting and information networks'; Chap. 7 below.

72 See F. Cafaggi, 'A Coordinated Approach to Regulation and Civil Liability in European Law: Rethinking Institutional Complementarities', in F. Cafaggi (ed.), *The Institutional Framework of European Private Law* (OUP, 2006), pp. 191 ff.

While these various sectoral analyses confirm the primacy of regulatory, and particularly 'less traditional' regulatory, techniques, overall, tort and contract law are not entirely out of the picture because they have been reinvested to a certain extent with a specifically regulatory function. Contract is often the instrument used in techniques of self-regulation and co-regulation.[73] Even in the field of environment, tort law may provide additional incentives in cases of underdeterrence or regulatory capture. It may also serve a useful role of fine-tuning the principal regulatory instruments[74] or serve to fill the gaps left by regulation, which is impotent to redress situational imbalances.[75]

IV. PRIVATE INTERNATIONAL LAW, REGULATION AND GOVERNANCE

Characterized as a branch of private law in traditional European learning, private international law might have been expected to follow the same declining path as the various national private law rules that it is called upon to allocate, in the context of private, cross-border, litigation. Furthermore, it might be thought to have little reason to cross swords with regulation, given the specificity of its own function and, correlatively, the particular purport of regulation, which is hardly concerned with individual *ex post* 'conflicts justice' any more than with the jurisdiction of the courts in private law litigation. Of course, implementation of regulation is sometimes European-wide, but usually relies, to a variable extent, on national bodies or authorities, whose role is then to cooperate across borders. But these dialogical forms of contact, which may involve negotiation and balancing in cases where national interests diverge, have little to do with the concept of the 'conflict of laws' in private law, which, at least in the European tradition, are themselves far removed from conflicts of substantive interests, since they would appear to involve a primarily aesthetic choice between virtually applicable legal 'systems'. It is comprehensible that, from the outside, the familiar 'quagmire' critique, developed in the wake of interests analysis in the United States fifty years ago, might appear to be relevant still.[76]

However, things are fast and radically changing in this area, under the double pressure of market integration and human rights, as indeed in the other

---

73 See Cafaggi, 'Self-regulation in European contract law', above n. 18.

74 M. Faure, 'Regulatory strategies in environmental liability'; Chap. 5 below.

75 A. Ogus, 'The regulation of services and the public-private divide'; Chap. 1 below.

76 See the critical pages devoted by Zeno-Zencovich and Cardarelli to this point at Chaps. 10 and 11 below.

traditional provinces of private law. These new challenges are inducing a change in the function and structure of what is still called – for want of a better expression – European 'private' international law. Firstly, the conflict of laws has had to define its own scope in relation to the country of origin principle, the designation of the applicable law in commercial relationships covered by the internal market having had to cater for the requirements of mutual recognition. Although mutual recognition concerns public law arrangements (licences, product safety standards, professional qualifications), the increasing difficulty of containing private international law within the traditional category of private law has created significant tensions between the conflict of laws and the country of origin on this point. As Mathias Audit points out, mutual recognition of goods and services is the vector for the extraterritorial application of quality standards applicable in the member state of origin, generating a potential conflict with the level of care imposed by standards of liability in the importing member state.[77] The issue arises as to what extent the conflict of law rules applicable in private litigation are able to mediate such tensions.

Secondly, the field of environmental protection analysed by Oliveira Boscovic demonstrates the radical integration of regulatory objectives into conflict of law and jurisdictional arrangements.[78] To a large extent, those rules are used as a regulatory adjunct to the private attorney-general mechanism, which is in itself a strong invitation to cross the public/private divide. The 2007 Rome II Regulation on the law applicable to extra-contractual obligations contains specific provisions on environmental harm which present the remarkable characteristic of being applicable to 'true conflicts' of environmental policies, including in their regulatory or public law dimension. By contrast, the role left by this instrument to party autonomy, a throwback to a private, facilitative concept of tort law, will enable private actors to frustrate regulatory objectives, and as such deserves severe criticism. The lack of a coherent regulatory strategy is once again apparent.

A third challenge to traditional learning in the field of cross-border relationships concerns cross-border contracts for services within the internal market. Sandrine Clavel draws attention to the extreme difficulty of introducing the balancing skills which, emblematic of regulation, are now required of the courts by the Rome I Regulation on the law applicable to contractual obligations as between conflicting mandatory rules of different states.[79] Here,

---

77 'Impact of the mutual recognition principle on the law applicable to products'; Chap. 9 below.

78 'The law applicable to violations of the environment: regulatory strategies'; Chap. 6 below.

79 'The regulatory function of choice of law rules applying to contracts for services in the European Union'; Chap. 3 below.

proportionality has an important role to play in providing a framework in which courts may assess the need to give room to the specific requirements of the '*lois de police*' of the importing member state. The combining of diverse techniques evokes to some extent the issue of the use of the precautionary principle in private law.

Fourthly and lastly, although the conflict of laws is not, or only partially and recently, constitutionalized in Europe,[80] it also appears, as Sophie Stalla-Bourdillon points out in her chapter on 'Re-allocating horizontal and vertical regulatory powers in the electronic market place: what to do with private international law',[81] that its rules may also involve economic due process considerations, particularly when, in the field of environment or employment relationships, they are used to internalize cross-border externalities in the form of the cost of suboptimal protection which might otherwise weigh upon neighbouring communities. Here, the first links appear with the question of governance dealt with in the twin volume. A more complete picture of the governance role of private international law would, of course, include its importance in maintaining regulatory competition, which brings us back to the question of the relationship between private international law and the country of origin principle and how competition between national systems actually works. In this respect, Anthony Ogus introduces an important distinction between heterogeneous and homogeneous products, meaning laws which, respectively, correspond to conflicting or analogous preferences across the board over the various European legal systems.[82] Competition is likely to lead to convergence when rules are heterogeneous, which is usually the case in facilitative private law. Here, one could imagine that intra-European conflicts might disappear altogether or at least that harmonization of substantive law is justified. On the other hand, in areas where products are heterogeneous, it might be that competition risks generating a race to the bottom. Here, if substantive harmonization is politically impossible, the conflict of laws in its governance function is no doubt the best, if not the only, way to canalize competition. Clearly, here, the public/private divide becomes irrelevant. Thus, with the link between issues of regulatory strategies and governance in mind, the reader of this remarkable set of 'Paris contributions' is invited to explore the transformations that regulation has brought about on the traditional category of 'private law', as to both its function and content.

H. Muir Watt and F. Cafaggi

---

80 See, using the principle of non-discrimination to set aside traditional conflicts methodology, *Wagner*, European Court of Human Rights 28 June 2007, D.2007.2700, note Marchadier; European Court of Justice *Garcia Avello*, 2 October 2003 (aff. C-148/02) *Rev crit DIP* 2004.184, note Lagarde.

81 Chapter 12 below.

82 See 'The regulation of services and the public–private divide'; Chap. 1 below.

PART 1

Utilities

1. The regulation of services and the public–private divide

Anthony Ogus

1. INTRODUCTION

The task I have set myself in this chapter is to explore the justifications for regulating services and how public and private law may, in their different ways, serve that purpose. I then consider the implications that the distinctions between private and public law have for governance in a European context, in particular how they relate to the arguments for harmonizing regulatory principles. First, however, I need to explain what is meant by the 'regulation of services'.

2. WHAT IS THE 'REGULATION OF SERVICES'?

The concept of 'services' is not easy to define. For the purposes of this chapter, I take it to have the broad meaning attributed to it in the programme of the European Commission, leading to the Draft Directive on 'Services in the Internal Market'.[1] This seems to cover almost all forms of trading except the supply of goods, thus including 'a large variety of activities, such as consultancy services, certification services, estate agents, engineering, construction, distribution, tourism, leisure and transport'[2] and normally the subject of a contract between supplier and consumer.

In order to make helpful generalizations about the regulation of these broad ranges of activities, we need to understand the different types of market failure and therefore the forms of regulation to which they have given rise. At the most general level, we can identify four main types of market failure:[3]

1 COM (2002) 401; in its amended form COM (2006) 160 final.

2 COM (2002) 401, p. 5.

3 A. Ogus, *Regulation: Legal Form and Economic Theory* (Hart Publishing, 2004), pp. 30–54.

1. there is insufficient competition in the supply of the service;
2. the consumers of services are affected by significant problems of information, thus making it difficult for them to select particular services to meet their preferences;
3. the services provided generate significant externalities, that is, have consequences for third parties, for example environmental effects;
4. the market does not fail in any of the above ways, but the outcomes are regarded by policymakers as unfair, because they infringe accepted notions of distributional justice.

Regulation justified by failure 1 is often referred to as 'economic regulation' (section 3), to be distinguished from 'social regulation' (section 4) which deals with failures 2 and 3.[4] Failure 4 can apply to both forms of regulation and I deal with it separately (section 5).

3. SERVICES AND ECONOMIC REGULATION

We should here distinguish between two forms of economic regulation: that operating in markets which are, or are intended to be, competitive markets; and that dealing with markets where competition is to some extent restricted.

(a) Ordinary Competitive Markets

The regulatory task here is to establish and maintain a sufficient degree of competition.[5] This is normally undertaken by specialist institutions, for example a Competition Commission, applying principles of public competition (or antitrust) law. In the case of markets, mainly in the energy or utility sector, which were previously private or public monopolies, and subsequently partially but incompletely liberalized, there may be sector-specific competition regulators.[6] In terms of interaction with private law, we should note that those suffering special losses as a result of anti-competitive practices may either be able to enforce the public laws against those guilty of the practice,[7]

---

[4] This distinction, while not universally recognized, features in, for example, OECD policy documents; cf OECD, *Regulatory Reform, Privatisation and Competition Policy* (OECD, 1992).

[5] See, generally, D. Helm and T. Jenkinson (eds.), *Competition in Regulated Industries* (Oxford University Press, 1998).

[6] F. Gilardi, 'Institutional Change in Regulatory Policies: regulation through independent agencies and the three new institutionalisms' in J. Jordana and D. Levi-Faur (eds.), *The Politics of Regulation* (Edward Elgar, 2004), chap. 4.

[7] M. Furse, *Competition Law of the UK and EC* (Blackstone, 1999), chap. 5.

or tort law may confer on them a remedy in private law.[8] So also the general principles of contract law may enable judges to override or refuse to enforce terms of the contract which are anti-competitive by reference to some general principle of *ordre public*.[9]

Price regulation is relatively rare in ordinary competitive markets. Where it exists, this is usually because there is a perception that competition policy has so far been insufficiently effective, as in some jurisdictions with the liberalized energy suppliers (thus more appropriately dealt with in the next section). Sometimes it is a consequence of regulatory capture, the regulated industry being thereby enabled to earn rents (some professional fee regulation falls into this category[10]). Sometimes, as with the housing rented sector, it may be for redistributional purposes.[11]

(b) Insufficiently Competitive Markets

There are some markets where it is economically undesirable to have competition. Technically known as 'natural monopolies', these have the characteristics that there are substantial economies of scale or scope from a single supplier of services over a large range of output.[12] Apart from this, as we have just seen, there are markets which in principle are open to competition between suppliers but which, for some reason or other, fail to achieve the necessary degree of competitiveness. In either case there is a need to regulate, because suppliers will be motivated to engage in the monopolistic pricing of their services (thereby not reflecting marginal cost); and they do not have the incentive to meet consumers' preferences regarding quality.

Traditionally, within Europe, supply in most of the markets affected by natural monopoly, notably energy and transport, has been in public ownership.[13] This regulatory approach was often rationalized on the basis that the lack of a profit motivation, and the political accountability involved, would generate appropriate prices and quality. Although prices and quality controls

---

8 H. Carty, *An Analysis of the Economic Torts* (Oxford University Press, 2001), chaps. 1–5.

9 M. Trebilcock, *The Common Law of Restraint of Trade: A Legal and Economic Analysis* (Carswell, 1986).

10 R. Van den Bergh and Y. Montangie, 'Competition in Professional Services Markets: Are Latin Notaries Different?' (2006) *Journal of Competition Law and Economics*.

11 Ogus, above n. 3, pp. 295–305.

12 R. Baldwin and M. Cave, *Understanding Regulation* (Oxford University Press, 1999), chap. 15.

13 H. Parris, P. Pestieau and P. Saynor, *Public Enterprise in Western Europe* (Croom Helm, 1987).

therefore existed, they were generally applied through internal administrative guidelines rather than by rules which could be the subject of adjudication in the courts.[14]

Under the American tradition, price and quality regulation has been undertaken by a regulatory commission, independent of government, but highly 'legalized', in the sense that its decisions are open to substantive judicial review by the courts.[15] Following privatization, some European jurisdictions have adopted this tradition, but in others the controls have been the responsibility of an agency which is part of, or more closely related to, government, with a reduced role for the judiciary.[16]

As an alternative to price and quality regulation, the problems can potentially be solved through a system of public franchising.[17] The right to supply the services to the market is, on the basis of competitive bidding, awarded by a regulatory agency, which may be more or less independent of government. The idea is that competition for the franchise should induce potential suppliers in their bids to adopt the prices or combination of price and quality which would have emerged if supply in the market had been competitive. Note that the legal form of constraint in this model is essentially that of contract, since the terms of the successful bid normally become terms of an agreement between agency and supplier under which the supplier operates the service. The extent to which ordinary principles of private contract law apply, or the arrangements are rather the subject of a special regime of 'public contracts', varies from one jurisdiction to another.[18]

Independently of its application to franchising arrangements, private law has a significant role in relation to insufficiently competitive markets, and one which is often overlooked by economists. Markets for the supply of services may be competitive in general, but the particular circumstances of a particular transaction may give rise to what has been referred to as a 'situational monopoly': a purchaser has no alternative to dealing with the supplier who happens to be immediately available.[19] A classic example is of a rescuer providing salvage services for a boat in distress. Public competition law is generally ineffective in dealing with problems of this kind; and any solution has to be found

---

14 C.D. Foster, *Privatization, Public Ownership and the Regulation of Natural Monopoly* (Blackwell, 1992), chap. 3.

15 S. Breyer, *Regulation and its Reform* (Harvard University Press, 1982), chaps. 2–3.

16 E. Ferrari (ed.), *I Servizi A Rete In Europa* (Cortina, 2000).

17 Ogus, above n. 3, chap. 15.

18 P. Vincent-Jones, *The New Public Contracting* (Oxford University Press, 2006).

19 M. Trebilcock, *The Limits of Freedom of Contract* (Harvard University Press, 1993), pp. 93–95.

in private law, although for regularly recurring situational monopolies, legislation may prescribe outcomes.

4. SERVICES AND SOCIAL REGULATION

(a) Traditional Regulatory Instruments

There is a range of regulatory instruments to deal with market failure arising from externalities and information problems. The most important can be listed as follows:[20]

- *Prohibition*: services which are particularly dangerous or undesirable may be prohibited by legislation.
- *Licence or Prior Authorization*: an agency is empowered to limit entry to the market to suppliers who can provide evidence of ability to meet quality and other standards (also known as 'entry standards').
- *Quality Standards:* suppliers are allowed to enter the market without prior approval but are subject to ongoing quality standards – these may be applied directly to the operation of the services ('input standards') or else to the performance of the services ('output standards'). Compliance with standards has to be monitored by an enforcement agency, usually that which is responsible for formulating the standards and often a department of government.
- *Mandatory Disclosure*: to meet some externality problems, but primarily to deal with information deficits, suppliers may be required to disclose information concerning the character and quality of the service.

Contravention of these regulatory instruments can lead to the imposition of administrative and/or criminal justice sanctions.

(b) Less Traditional Regulatory Instruments

Particularly in an era of so-called 'deregulation', governments have been searching for modes of regulatory control which are less onerous, more flexible and draw on the knowledge and experience of service providers.[21]

---

[20] Cf Ogus, above n. 3, pp. 150–152.

[21] A. Ogus, 'New Techniques for Social Regulation: Decentralisation and Diversity' in H. Collins, P. Davies and R. Rideout (eds.), *Legal Regulation of the Employment Relation* (Kluwer, 2000), pp. 83–98.

- *Negative licensing*: to save on the very heavy administrative costs of prior authorization systems, it is possible to use the sanction of deprivation of the right to supply in the market as a consequence of serious contraventions of quality standards. This is sometimes called 'negative licensing'.
- *Tertiary/default rules*: to reduce the amount of rigid, prescriptive rules, some regulatory regimes lay down only general objectives, combined with a set of guidelines or rules. These guidelines and rules are not legally binding, but may operate as default rules, in the sense that suppliers are free to adopt their own method of meeting the regulatory objectives, provided that the method can be shown to be at least as effective as that provided by the default rules.
- *Financial instruments*: as we have seen, traditional regulatory instruments are coercive in the sense that compliance is achieved through the threat of imposition of sanctions. An alternative is to induce the desired quality by means of financial incentives, positively by paying to suppliers who meet the desired outcome a grant (or by reducing tax liability); or negatively by imposing a charge or fiscal burden on those who fail to meet it. As my examples suggest, this can often be done as part of existing tax law.
- *Co-regulation/self-regulation*: all the instruments listed in this section involve co-regulation to some degree, in that the supplier plays some part in the formulation of the quality standard which is, in fact, applied. But the idea can, of course, be taken even further by conferring powers of rule-formulation and rule-enforcement on the supplying industry, thus giving rise to self-regulation.

(c) Role of Private Law

Where, as indicated in the last section, systems of co- or self-regulation prevail, then the public regulatory system may well incorporate instruments of private law since the standards in question are likely to arise from private law obligations. Apart from this, remedies are of course available in private law for many of the market failures which have justified social regulation. Taking first information deficits, pre-contractual duties of disclosure are sometimes imposed on suppliers in a contract for services; and in some situations tortious remedies may be available to third parties where suppliers fail to provide, or provide false, information.[22] Failure to fulfil the duty may enable the

---

[22] F. Hanks, M. Bryan and A. Duggan, *Contractual Non-Disclosure* (Longman, 1994).

consumer to resile from the contract; alternatively it may give rise to an action for damages for breach of contract. Then, of course, there is a massive amount of regulated contract law to achieve standards of quality and safety. This normally takes the form of mandatory terms to the contract.[23] Finally, where those problems of quality and safety give rise to major externalities, tort law may provide the relevant third parties with a remedy against the supplier.

The overlap between private and public law can give rise to some legal complexities on which different legal systems give very different answers.

- *Regulatory standards enforceable in private law?* If a service supplier is in breach of a regulatory standard and the consumer in consequence suffers a loss the breach can give rise to a private law claim in contract, if the court can find that it was an implied term of the contract. The position in tort law appears to be more complex, France, Germany, the USA and the UK all adopting conceptually distinct approaches to the question whether the breach automatically gives rise to tort liability.[24]
- *Regulatory standards a defence to actions in private law?* In some, but not all, systems public law may override private law in the sense that compliance with a regulatory standard may be a defence to an action in tort law which prima facie applies a stricter standard. In other systems, this approach would fall foul of constitutional protection of private rights, leaving service suppliers to be governed by divergent public and private law standards.[25]

5. SERVICES AND DISTRIBUTIONAL JUSTICE

In the previous sections I have assumed that the purpose of regulation is to correct market failures in the sense that the law aims at the market outcomes which would have been reached if there had been no such failure. The goal of such regulation is therefore, in principle, allocative efficiency. However, policy-makers may use regulation to achieve non-economic aims, most importantly if they consider that in particular contexts efficient outcomes are, in terms of distributional justice, 'unfair'. In relation to the provision of services, this perception may arise in a variety of circumstances, notably:

23 H. Collins, *Regulating Contracts* (Oxford University Press, 1999).

24 J.A. Jolowicz, *International Encyclopedia of Comparative Law* (Mohr Siebeck, 1972), vol. XI, chap. 13.

25 T.M. Palay, 'Avoiding Regulatory Constraint: Contracting Safeguards and the Role of Informal Agreement' (1985) 1 *Journal of Law, Economics and Organization* 155.

- Where the service (such as health care or education) is essential for the welfare of recipients who have insufficient means to pay the economically determined price for them.
- Where the service provider has greater bargaining power which can be exploited to extract an inequitable portion of the surplus generated by the contract.
- Where the financial and educational endowment of consumers is such that they may not opt for what best meets their longer-term preferences (note that this justification may shade into information problems (above) or paternalism[26]).

(a) Economic Regulation and Distributional Justice

Under the public ownership model, the price controls of utilities often did reflect distributional justice concerns, with taxpayers subsidizing consumers.[27] This is less likely under the privatized model, but here the so-called universal service obligation continues to play a prominent role. The incumbent supplier is generally bound to make the service available, within reasonable limits and at a reasonable cost, to all citizens.[28] This is often done by a tariff which does not vary according to the cost of supply and thus involves low-cost consumers subsidizing high-cost consumers. In some jurisdictions, the regulated contracts between suppliers and consumers enable groups which are regarded as more vulnerable, such as the aged and the disabled, to enjoy more favourable terms,[29] although of course the same outcome can be reached by transfer payments to these groups, independently of the service provision.

(b) Social Regulation and Distributional Justice

There are several ways in which distributional justice can penetrate social regulation. First, conceptions of the educational endowment may influence the level of information, and the means of communication, which suppliers must use. This can lead to regulation of the advertising of the services or of the

---

[26] See further on this, A. Ogus, 'Regulatory Paternalism: When Is It Justified?' in K. J. Hopt, E.Wyrmeesch, H. Kanda and H. Baum (eds.), *Corporate Governance in Context: Corporations, States, and Market in Europe, Japan and the United States* (Oxford University Press, 2005), pp. 303–320.

[27] A. Harrison, 'The Framework of Control' in C. Whitehead (ed.), *Reshaping the Nationalised Industries* (Transaction Books, 1988), pp. 38–40.

[28] Baldwin and Cave, above n. 12, pp. 220–221.

[29] T. Prosser, *Law and the Regulators* (Oxford University Press, 1997), pp. 107–9, 139–140, 188–189.

displaying of the quality and terms of the prospective agreement.[30] Then (though this again overlaps with paternalism) 'cooling-off periods' may be imposed, enabling consumers to resile from certain types of contract.[31] In dealing with risks, particularly of death and personal injury, social regulation may impose relevant controls on suppliers even though consumers can deal with the risk, by prevention or insurance, more cheaply.[32]

(c) Private Law and Distributional Justice

As is well known, private law can, and has been able to, provide some equivalent to many of these regulatory measures. In some areas prices have been controlled through doctrines such as *lésion* or unconscionability.[33] 'Unfair' contractual terms, including exemption, limitation and penalty clauses, have been controlled in important recent legislation.[34] Mandatory contractual terms of standards imposed by tort law have been sometimes formulated to offer protection to consumers of services who are considered in some respect disadvantaged.

6. THE PUBLIC–PRIVATE DIVIDE AND GOVERNANCE IN A EUROPEAN CONTEXT

(a) 'Homogeneous' and 'Heterogeneous' Legal Products

In this section I seek to explore some of the implications of what I have discussed above for governance in a European context. In doing so, I build on some of my earlier work which, in attempting to show how competition between national legal systems can influence legal evolution, posited an important distinction between 'homogeneous' and 'heterogeneous' legal products.[35] My argument was that in the case of those areas and principles of law as to which citizen preferences across the European Union could be assumed to be broadly similar ('homogeneous' legal products), some spontaneous

---

30 Ogus, above n. 3, chap. 7.

31 C. Scott and J. Black, *Cranston's Consumers and the Law* (Butterworths, 3rd edn, 2000), pp. 246–249.

32 Ibid, chaps. 4–6.

33 R. Bigwood, *Exploitative Contracts* (Oxford University Press, 2003).

34 H. Beale et al, *Contract Law* (Hart Publishing, 2002), pp. 513–553.

35 A. Ogus, 'Competition between National Legal Systems: A Contribution of Economic Analysis to Comparative Law' (1999) 48 *International and Comparative Law Quarterly* 405.

evolution towards a common core of principles was desirable and could be anticipated, at least where not thwarted by lawyers seeking to retain artificial national characteristics and thus enhance their own profits. To overcome the latter, I recognized that some European initiative for harmonization or mutual recognition might be necessary. As regards those areas and principles of law as to which preferences were likely to vary significantly between jurisdictions, such an evolution would not, and should not, occur: national law should reflect national preferences, although where those preferences generated externalities in other jurisdictions, some acceptable compromise had to be reached.

In general I identified homogeneous legal products with facilitative law, those parts of mainly contract, property and corporate law which are used for mutually desired outcomes (generating winners and few or no losers) and for which the assumed common preferences are to reach the given outcome with a minimization of legal costs. Heterogeneous legal products were identified with interventionist law (which impacts significantly on losers as well as winners), designed to protect defined interests and/or supersede voluntary transactions. I recognized that this covered:

> tort and regulatory law, but also those aspects of contract, property and corporate law which confer protection on parties assumed to be disadvantaged by processes of free bargaining, for example, consumers, employees, tenants and (in some contexts) shareholders.[36]

Further reflection nevertheless suggests that it is inappropriate to characterize all interventionist law (public or private) as heterogeneous legal products, because even though there may be losses and losers, political preferences are unlikely to differ substantially from one jurisdiction to another. This can be seen when we examine the forms and goals of different regulatory regimes

(b) Economic Regulation

Economic regulation in respect of ordinary competitive markets is interventionist only in the sense that it seeks to control anti-competitive practices; its main purpose is to uphold the competitiveness of markets and, as such, it facilitates trade and commerce. We can thus envisage a common set of European legal principles, the more so since the principal function of the European Union is to operate a single, integrated market. At first sight, the position would seem not to be very different when we turn to insufficiently competitive markets. Here the basic idea would seem to be to achieve the outcomes which would have been achieved if the market had been competitive, whether

[36] Ibid, pp. 412–413.

this outcome is reached by means of price and quality control (aimed at meeting consumer preferences at lowest cost) or through public franchising.

However, some aspects of economic regulation in the latter context may be considered as 'interventionist' or at least as giving rise to varying preferences. Most obviously this applies where issues of distributional justice intrude. It is true that the concept of a 'universal service obligation' is likely to be shared across jurisdictions, but the circumstances in which, and the extent to which, it should operate might vary significantly between jurisdictions, as might the determination of how it is to be financed. Even more delicate are the questions when, on policy grounds, monopolistic supply should be retained and whether it should be in public or private ownership. On the first of these, economic theory might provide objective criteria based on economies of scale and scope,[37] but the application of these criteria is likely to vary according to the geographical and other circumstances of different jurisdictions. As regards the second question, culture and ideology would seem to play a major role in deciding whether services such as education, health, social welfare are to remain a function of the state. As such, it is hard to envisage an integrated or harmonized set of legal principles and arrangements.[38]

(c) Social Regulation

The extent to which social regulation may give rise to heterogeneous legal products depends not only on the nature of regulatory instrument adopted but also on the type of service being regulated. Take, first, mandatory disclosure rules. It might be thought that preferences regarding the level of information and the manner of disclosure (apart from questions of language) are unlikely to vary significantly across the European Union. But that presumption might be rebutted if in a particular jurisdiction there is a particularly strong 'right to know' culture, thus justifying a heavier obligation imposed on service suppliers.[39] Also, though this is less likely, there might be some differences of educational endowment with implications for the level and mode of communicating information.

Regulation governing the quality and safety of services, to deal with externalities as well as information deficits, is more complex. We may recognize a homogeneous preference for a minimum standard of safety (and quality?), justifying some degree of harmonization, but beyond that significant differences may reflect one or more of the following characteristics:

---

[37] A. Kahn, *The Economics of Regulation* (MIT Press, 1988).

[38] G. Majone, 'The European Commission as Regulator' in G. Majone, *Regulating Europe* (Routledge, 1996), chap. 4.

[39] W.F. Korthals Altes et al (eds.), *Information Law towards the 21st Century* (Kluwer, 1992).

- Topographical or climatic conditions, peculiar to individual jurisdictions, or groups of jurisdictions, may impact on the desired level of quality/safety.
- For similar or other reasons, the cost of meeting a given level of quality/safety may vary; so also the trade-off between the regulatory objective and the price to be paid for it may differ across jurisdictions, given in particular varying endowments of wealth and income.
- Non-scientific perceptions of risk are highly subjective and these may vary from one jurisdiction to another, as might the degree of risk aversion, thus justifying higher or lower levels of protection
- Finally, and most obviously, social regulatory regimes may reflect different perceptions of distributional justice so that, for example, policymakers in one jurisdiction may wish to offer a particularly high protection against sickness, injury or death to employees, to the victims of road accidents, or to citizens more generally and exact a higher price accordingly.

(d) Regulatory Private Law

Although it may be the case that many areas of private law are facilitative, thus constituting homogeneous legal products, some areas clearly, as we have seen in earlier sections, have a regulatory purpose in that they override individual preferences and consensual bargaining. The fact that private law instruments, rather than public law instruments, are used for regulatory purposes should not in principle change the arguments outlined above or the implications that they have for harmonization policies. However, account must also be taken of some procedural and technical differences between private and public law.

- Because of its origin in codified legislation or the common law, private law tends to be formulated in terms of general principles. Much of regulatory law is detailed and specific, although in recent years there has been an evolution towards greater generality. General law is more easily transportable and harmonized than specific law.
- Conversely, private law (for historical reasons) is more closely connected with traditional legal culture, which may generate more obstacles to transplantation and harmonization than public law.[40]
- Regulatory law is administered and enforced by procedures which may be highly jurisdiction-specific. Although the same may, to some extent, be true of civil procedural law, there are long-standing arrangements,

---

40 P. Legrand, *Fragments on Law-as-Culture* (Willink, 1999).

through private international law, of accommodating foreign elements; and in recent years there have been efforts within the European Union to harmonize, or at least render compatible, the private international law of Member States.

7. CONCLUSION

In this chapter, I have attempted to articulate the principal economic and non-economic reasons for regulating contracts for services, and to show how private law, as well as public law, has been used to implement these aims. In the latter part of the chapter I have explored the implications of that analysis for the currently topical issue of governance within the European Union. For this purpose I have sought to clarify and expand on ideas I have published elsewhere. In general, one would expect harmonization policies to be more appropriate for 'heterogeneous legal products' but not for 'homogenous legal products'. Although the former are more likely to be identified with public, interventionist law, that is not always the case. Although the latter are more likely to be identified with facilitative, private law, that is not always the case. A deeper understanding of the extent to which the regulation of services might need to reflect differing national preferences provides a firmer base on which to address the harmonization issue.

2. Regulatory strategies on services contracts in EC law

Hans-W. Micklitz

1. PURPOSE AND BACKGROUND

The idea of the chapter is to show how and by what means the European Community is attempting to realize its overall policy to establish and accomplish the internal market for services, and more particularly how this policy which is meant to open up markets affects the contractual relations between the supplier and the customer, whether the latter be a professional or a consumer. This implies that contractual relationships at the primary market for financial services are excluded from the scope of analysis.[1] The European Community relies, as usual, on a piecemeal approach. There is no such thing as a uniform strategy, if one sets aside the internal market rhetoric. Regulation of services is very much following different patterns in different areas of the economic sector. I have chosen a particularly European perspective, as the European Community has become by far the most important regulator. Member States are more or less in a retroactive position. It is still the White Paper on the Completion of the Internal Market[2] which legitimizes the initiatives of the European Commission. European law defines the bottom line of the respective markets for services. National legislators have to implement the European rules. They benefit from a different degree of leeway with regard to shaping contractual relations. However, the chapter does not intend to give a full picture of the Member States' regulatory strategies to confirm or to escape European boundaries. It is first and foremost meant to systemize the existing regulatory strategies applied in the field of services. As such, this chapter is just a first step to provide the groundwork for ongoing research.

In my analysis I rely on previous research. In the area of consumer law I draw on *Europäisches Verbraucherschutzrecht*,[3] which I wrote, together with

1 Heinze, Stephan *Europäisches Kapitalmarktrecht, Recht des Primärmarktes* (Dissertation) (1999, Beck-Verlag, München).

2 COM (1985) 314 final, 23.7.1985.

3 Micklitz, Hans-W. *Europäisches Verbraucherrecht* (2003, Nomos, Baden-

Norbert Reich, with regard to the law of Member States, based on the research done by the European Consumer Law Group.[4] In the area of financial services I refer to a comparative research project which I have undertaken together with Jürgen Keßler.[5] The project focused on investor protection rules in the European Community, Germany, Switzerland, the United Kingdom and the United States. Again together with Jürgen Keßler, I investigated the effects of the EC policy to open up the telecommunications, energy and railway markets on customers in France, Germany, Hungary, Italy, Spain, Sweden and the United Kingdom.[6] Private law relationships between suppliers and customers were at the heart of the analysis. Last but not least, I would like to mention a project on standardization of services which is strongly related to the so-called Services Directive.[7]

The first two parts of the chapter should be understood as taking stock of the existing and envisaged EC rules on services. It seems reasonable to distinguish between vertical regulation and horizontal regulation. The latter covers all sorts of services, the former is bound to a particular type of service. However, the study is not meant to be comprehensive, not even at the EC level,[8] although it covers the major areas currently under discussion (see sections 2 and 3 on types of services vertical and horizontal classification). The third part looks into the instruments which are used to shape particular areas of contractual relations. I here refer to Anthony Ogus's[9] distinction between 'traditional and less traditional regulatory instruments'. The EC regulation under review clearly shows that there is an overall tendency to combine traditional with less traditional instruments, although the latter instruments are gaining more and more importance, in terms of quantity and quality (see

---

Baden). An updated English version published under the title, *The Basics of European Consumer Law* is forthcoming.

4 Available at www.europeanconsumerlawgroup.org.

5 Keßler, Jürgen and Micklitz, Hans-W. *Anlegerschutz in Deutschland, Schweiz, Großbritannien, USA und der Europäischen Gemeinschaft* (2004, Band 15, VIEW Schriftenreihe, Nomos, Baden-Baden).

6 Micklitz, Hans-W. and Keßler, Jürgen unter Mitarbeit von Basler, Mareen, Beuchler, Holger and Bonome-Dells, Romina *Kundenschutz auf den liberalisierten Märkten für Telekommunikation, Energie und Verkehr* (2008, Nomos, Baden-Baden).

7 *Services Standards: Defining the Core Elements and Their Minimum Requirements*: study commissioned by ANEC, 2007. See: http://www.anec.eu/attachments/ANEC-R&T-2006-SERV-004final.pdf.

8 For example postal services are not included.

9 See 'The Regulation of Services and the Public–Private Divide', ch. 1 in this volume. There is much discussion on where, how and why to draw a line between the old and the new instruments, see Trubek, David M. and Trubek, Lousie G. *'Soft Law', 'Hard Law', and European Integration: Toward a Theory of Hybridity* (Univ. of Wisconsin Law School, Legal Stud. Res. Paper Series, Paper No. 1002, 2005). However Ogus and Trubek & Trubek arrive at very similar results.

section 4 ‘Choice of instruments’). The shifting away from traditional instruments to less traditional instruments considerably broadens the set of regulators, public and private, their role and their function in shaping private law relations on services. As regards the distribution of responsibilities, of who is doing what and on what basis of legitimacy, things becomes blurred (see section 5 ‘Traditional and less traditional regulators’). The ground is then prepared to look more closely into who is using the less traditional instruments, mainly co-regulation and self-regulation, the degree to which stakeholders are involved and the possible impact of these new forms on the regulation of service contracts (see section 6 ‘New instruments/new actors’). The seventh part focuses on the substance of the public/private law regulation, firstly – conclusion of contract, formation and advice; secondly the content – affordability, quality and safety; thirdly – rights and remedies (see section 7 ‘The substance of the public/private regulation’). The last part concludes with preliminary observations on the EC regulatory strategies on services (see section 8 ‘Preliminary observations’). A set of tables might hopefully facilitate the understanding of the dispersed rules.

2. TYPES OF SERVICES (VERTICAL CLASSIFICATION)

The European Commission mainly pursues a sector-related vertical approach. Each of the sectors has its own history. Not all sectors involve a different Directorate within the European Commission, instead the competence for the six sectors here at stake is spread over three Directorates – Directorate General for Health and Consumer Affairs (DG SANCO), Directorate General for Energy and Transport (DG TREN) and Internal Market and Services (DG MARKET). The last mentioned is so important and so big in comparison at least with DG SANCO that the subdivisions which deal with financial services, network services and other services (covered by the service directive) come close to constituting a separate Directorate.

Protective Device

Consumer policy dates back to the 1970s. The Directives adopted already appear in the first and second consumer programme.[10] Two of them, on Package Tours and Time Sharing are to be understood as a reaction to a growing new industry which yielded the need for a European-wide solution. The Consumer Credit Directive is inspired by the intention to establish a European market for consumer credit. Common standards should encourage consumers

---

10 OJ C 92, 25.4.1975 and OJ C 133, 3.6.1981.

to engage in price comparison and make better choices. Reality turned out to be different. It remains to be seen whether the now adopted common position[11] will overcome the boundaries of nationally shaped consumer credit markets. The Commission project on European contract law[12] sets a new tone in consumer contract law regulation.

The two Regulations on Air Passengers[13] and Railway Passengers[14] fit relatively well into the picture of transborder mobility and the need for substantive protection of the economic interests of consumers and travellers. Both regulations are designed to grant the passenger basic mandatory rights, just as in consumer law directives. The addressees, however, are not consumers, but passengers, a category which covers businessmen as well as consumers. The Air Passenger Regulation which was revised in 2004 served as a blueprint for DG TREN[15] for shaping the Railway Passenger Rights. The true challenge in the field of transport is the relationship between EC rules and international conventions. The Air Passengers Rights Regulation reaches beyond the Montreal Convention, which has led two business organizations to challenge the competence of the European Community to adopt conflicting European rules. The ECJ, however, confirmed the validity of the Regulation.[16] Otherwise, the air transport industry would have escaped EC law, being bound only to less stringent international rules.

Financial Services

Financial services might cover insurance contracts, investment contracts and banking contracts. The focus lies on insurance and investment directives, with a side glance to the Directive on Payment Services.[17] All these initiatives address the insured, the investor and/or the creditor, be it a consumer or a businessman. They have in common that the European Commission intends to

---

11 14.9.2007, CONSOM 69 Interinstitutional File: 2002/0222 (COD).

12 See COM (2001) 398 final, 11.7.2001, OJ C 255, 13.9.2001, 1; also Grundmann, Stefan and Stuyck, Jules (eds) *An Academic Green Paper on European Contract Law* (2002, Kluwer, Den Haag). The Communication has boosted publication of articles and books on European contract law; see now COM (2006) 744 final on the Revision of the Consumer *Acquis*.

13 Regulation n. 261/2004. See also COM (2000) 365 final, 21.6.2000, COM (2005) 46, 16.2.2006 and COM (2005) 47 final.

14 Regulation 1371/2007, OJ L 315, 31.12.2007, p. 14; see also COM (2004) 144 final, 3.3.2004.

15 OJ L 46, 17.2.2004, 1.

16 Judgment 10.6.2006, Case 344/04, *International Air Transport Association, European Low Fares Airline Association v Department for Transport* [2006] ECR I-403.

17 Directive 2007/64/EC, OJ L 319, 5.12.2007, 1.

open up markets in order to create and enhance European-wide competition between national suppliers. The insured, the investors and the creditors, regardless of whether they are consumers, are to benefit from the increased competition. They are not the primary addressee of the legislation. It is only over time and after having taken the first regulatory steps that the European Community felt the need to focus more directly on the interests of the insured, the investors and the creditors. Despite these common characteristics, each sector has its own historical particularities.

After the failure of early policy initiatives to open up the markets for insurance, the European Commission sued Germany for its rigid prior approval system of insurance contracts, for being out of line with the basic market freedoms. The ECJ's partly favourable judgment[18] triggered a three-step procedure, under which the European Commission managed to open up the market for insurance gradually. However, the Member States resisted any attempt to establish a common set of European rules on insurance contracts.[19]

The spirit in the field of financial instruments is very much the same as in the insurance market. However, the background is different. The two Banking Coordination Directives[20] which allow European-wide activities to operate under one single regulatory regime – the Euro-pass – are only applicable to companies which, inter alia, are providing investment services.[21] The first Directive on Investment Services, 93/22/EEC, closed that gap. The second Investment Directive (Markets in Financial Instruments Directive (MIFID)), 2004/39/EC, pursues a two-fold aim, establishing a fully-fledged Euro-pass and improving investor protection. It is the latter aim – and the means set to implement it – which is of interest here.

In the aftermath of the Single European Act, the European Commission (re)discovered Article 86 ET as a powerful means to challenge Member States' natural monopolies in the telecommunications, energy and railway markets.[22] The Commission managed to open up the markets gradually, however, it was confronted with the challenge of '*services publiques*', or the well-established

---

18 4.12.1986, Case 205/85, *Commission v Germany* [1986] ECR 3755.

19 Reich, Norbert '§ 23.9', in Reich, Norbert and Micklitz, Hans-W. *Europäisches Verbraucherrecht* (2003, Nomos, Baden-Baden), p. 816.

20 Reich, Norbert '§ 3.28', in Reich, Norbert and Micklitz, Hans-W. *Europäisches Verbraucherrecht* (2003, Nomos, Baden-Baden).

21 See also Directive 2006/73, OJ L 241, 2.9.2006, 26 and Regulation 1287/2006 OJ L 241, 2.9.2006, 1.

22 See Telecommunication Directives 2002/19 and 2002/58; COM (2007) 697, 13.11.2007 and COM (2007) 698, 13.11.2007; Electricity Directive 2003/54 and Gas Directive 2003/55, and the (now) third package COM (2007) 528, 19.9.2007, and on electricity and gas COM (2007) 529, 19.9.2007; and finally third railway package, OJ L 315, 3.12.2007, 1.

concept in the Member States that the state has to make sure that all customers have access to public goods. All three markets differ considerably in the degree to which the European Commission has achieved its policy objective, with telecommunications being at the forefront of developments, with energy following suit, whereas the railway market is still rather closed. The means selected to enhance competition so as to benefit the customer are the unbundling of the distribution and of the transmission system.

Services Directive

The Services Directive 2006/123/EC[23] does not fit into this picture. It is in the field of technical standards where the European Community experienced failure in setting aside national barriers to free European trade by way of vertical product related regulation. The 'New Approach on Technical Standards and Harmonization'[24] constituted a breakthrough in EC regulatory policy, the impact of which reached far beyond its limited scope, that is product regulation through technical standardization. The European Commission developed a new regulatory strategy which was designed to overcome the deadlock through a new horizontal harmonization method. It seems as if the Services Directive is also meant to establish a common frame for the 'harmonization' of the remaining services '*d'un seul coup*'. I have set harmonization in quotation marks, because the Services Directive differs from all other vertical regulation on services in that it is not designed to harmonize services. Instead the Directive should be understood as a combination of the country of origin principle designed to establish freedom of services and freedom of establishment and a new approach in regulation, meant to shape the elaboration of contractual rules. As such, in a way it might be misleading to classify the Services Directive as a vertical strategy. However, the Directive has a limited scope of application which has been further narrowed down by exempting labour law and health care services in the finally adopted version.

3. TYPES OF SERVICES (HORIZONTAL CLASSIFICATION)

The European Commission did not rely on a vertical approach alone to set common European rules on contracts for services. Two kind of strategies might be identified, both aiming at a horizontal regulation.

---

23 OJ L 376, 27.12.2006, 32.

24 OJ C 136, 4.6.1985, 100.

Table 2.1 European regulatory framework for services: vertical legislation

Consumer contract law on services	Transport (air and railway)	Financial services (insurance, investment, payment)	Network services for customers	Other services in the Internal Market	Health services (separate initiative)
Consumer Credit 87/102 Common Position	Air Passenger Rights Regulation No. 261/2004, COM (2000) 365 final, COM (2005) 46 and 47 final.	Insurance 92/49 (damage), 92/96 (life insurance)	Telecommunication 2002/19-22 and 2002/58 Now third package, COM (2007) 697 and (2007) 698	Services Directive	No particular rules in secondary community law
Package Tours 90/314	Regulation 1371/2007 on Railroad Passenger Rights; COM (2004) 144 final on rail freight services	Financial Instruments 2004/39 Implementing Directive 2006/73 and implementing Regulation 1287/2006	Electricity 2003/54 and Gas 2003/55 Now third package COM (2007) 528 electricity and gas COM (2007) 529		Commission starts public consultation on patient mobility[1]
Time Sharing 94/47		Directive 2007/64 on Payments Services	Third railway package		

Note: [1] COM (2004) 301 final, 24.4.2004 follow-up to the high-level reflection process on patient mobility and health care developments in the European Union. See now in reaction to the failed effort under the first draft of the service directive to harmonise health services, the new initiative taken by the European Commission at: http://europa.eu/rapid/pressReleasesAction.do?reference=IP/06/1267&format= HTML&aged=0&language=DE&guiLanguage=en.

Consumer Protection Regulation on Services

Usually, the four consumer directives, on Distance Selling, Distance Selling for Financial Services, E-Commerce and Unfair Terms in Consumer Contracts are put into the same box, that of consumer protection. However, contrary to the directives on Consumer Credit, Package Tours and Time Sharing, these four directives lay down horizontal rules on consumer contracts, both for sales contracts and contracts for services. The first three deal with the modalities under which the contract is concluded, be it via direct selling strategies or via distance communication means. The doubling of the distance selling regulation turned out to be the result of hard lobbying by the financial services sector, claiming special treatment due to the particular character of these services. Directive 2002/65/EC, which was adopted five years after Directive 97/7/EC, provides for particular rules on financial services. Ironically enough, the new directive goes even further than its predecessor.[25] Whilst Directive 2002/65/EC closes an important loophole, the two directives together do not fully cover the type of services at stake here, as package tour contracts and transport contracts are exempted from the scope of application. The E-Commerce Directive 2000/31/EC is applicable across all kinds of services, regardless of whether the parties to the contract are consumers or suppliers.

Directive 93/13/EEC, designed to protect consumers, covers all sorts of consumer services, for example credit, package tour and time sharing contracts, as well as transportation, network contracts and all other types of service contracts which come under the scope of the Services Directive – provided the party to the contract is a professional *private* supplier. There has been discussion in legal doctrine regarding the degree to which the directive as it stands covers public suppliers as well, mainly suppliers of energy and railway transportation services.[26] The debate lost impetus due to the privatization policy of the European Community in particular with regard to former natural monopolies.

---

[25] See Micklitz, Hans-W. and Schirmbacher, Martin 'Duties to inform contained in Directive 2002/65/EC concerning the distance marketing of consumer financial services' (2004) *Revue européenne de droit bancaire & financier*, 457–486.

[26] Butters, Beate *Vertragsgerechtigkeit in der öffentlichen Versorgungswirtschaft, Zur Anwendbarkeit der Richtlinie 93/13/EWG über mißbräuchliche Vertragsklauseln in Verbraucherverträgen auf öffentliche Versorgungsbedingungen* (Dissertation) (2003, Beck-Verlag, München); Whittaker, Simon 'Unfair Terms, Public Services and the Construction of a European Conception of Contract' (2000) 116 *Law Quarterly Review*, 95.

International Private Law (IPL)

The Rome Convention was adopted in 1980.[27] It lays down common rules for the applicable law in contracts for goods and services regardless of the addressee, although the Convention provided for particular rules on the protection of the consumer in Article 5. The Rome Convention is currently under review.[28] The European Commission published a first draft on 15 December 2005 which is now subject to a broad discussion.

Thus far, European international private law has suffered from great inconsistencies. The first generation of consumer law directives did not contain rules on the applicable law, such as consumer credit and package tours. The next generation, however, provided for rules which deviated from the Rome Convention – both directives on distance selling. The most recent generation of directives, however, return to the earlier approach, for example with no particular rules on the applicable law, such as the envisaged e-commerce and services directives. The first major aim of the envisaged regulation is to overcome these inconsistencies by defining one and the same rule for consumer contracts – the law of the place where the consumer is habitually resident. However, the regulation as it stands does not cover insurance contracts. Here, the particular rules provided for in the insurance directives should remain. The second major aim is to put international private law rules under the jurisdiction of the ECJ by way of relying on Articles 61/67 of the ET.

The now adopted Regulation 864/2007 on Extra-Contractual Liability, the so-called Rome II regulation,[29] has no predecessor. The Regulation does not distinguish between liability resulting from unsafe goods and liability resulting from unsafe services. The regulation is to apply in situations involving a conflict of laws to non-contractual obligations in civil and commercial matters, with limited exemptions for accountants and trustees. Particular rules are foreseen for product liability and unfair commercial practices. Directive 85/374/EEC on product liability, however, applies to products only. Electricity is regarded as a product. The originally intended directive on liability for the safety of services had to be withdrawn due to strong resistance on the part of the Member States.[30] It remains to be seen whether the European Commission is willing to pick up the issue again, maybe under a new regulatory device.[31]

---

[27] Publication of the consolidated version, OJ C 27, 26.1.1998, 34.

[28] COM (2005) 650 final, 15.12.2005.

[29] OJ L 199, 31.12.2007, 40.

[30] See with regard to the proposal COM (1990) 482 final, OJ C 12, 18.1.1991, 8 and the withdrawal COM (1994) 260 final.

[31] See Magnus, Ulrich and Micklitz, Hans-W. *Liability for the Safety of Services* (2005, Band 21, VIEW Schriftenreihe, Nomos-Verlag, Baden-Baden).

Table 2.2 European regulatory framework for services: horizontal legislation

Horizontal legislation	**Credit, package tour, time sharing**	**Transport (air and railway)**	**Financial services (insurance, investment, payment)**	**Network services forcustomers**	**Other services in the Internal Market**
Distance Selling 97/7	No with regard to package tours.[1] Yes with regard to time sharing contracts[2]	No[3]	No	Yes	Yes
E-Commerce 2000/31	Yes	Yes	Yes	Yes	Yes
Distance Selling of Financial Services 2002/65			Yes, only applicable to these services		
Unfair Terms 93/13	Yes	As far as undertakings are privatized	Yes	As far as undertakings are privatized	As far as undertakings are privatized

Notes:

[1] At least in principle, but see Article 3(2), Distance selling directive, third indent.

[2] Although Article 4(1) of Directive 94/47 provides for concluding the contract in writing, this can also be done by storing the contract on a durable medium: Article 5(1) of Directive 97/7.

[3] Including leasing, as decided by the ECJ. See 10.3.2005, Case 336/03, *Easy Car v Office of Fair Trading* [2005] ECR 1974.

Table 2.3 European regulatory framework for services: applicable law

IPL rules	Time sharing	Distance selling/ unfair terms	Transport (air and railway)	Financial services (insurance, investment, payment)	Network services for customers	Other services
Draft Regulation on Rome I	Particular Intellectual Property Rights (IPR)-rules in the directives, but to be replaced by the consumers habitual residence rule in Rome I	Particular IPR-rules in the directives, but to be replaced by the consumers habitual residence rule in Rome I	EC Regulations applicable on transborder contracts only, but Rome I remains important for complementary contract terms	Excluded from Rome I, particular rules on insurances to be maintained	Covered by Rome I	Covered by Rome I
Rome II Regulation	Yes	Yes	Yes	Yes, but potential exceptions for particular financial services ex art. 1(e) of Rome II	Yes	Yes, but potential exception for accountants ex art. 1(d) of Rome II

4. CHOICE OF INSTRUMENTS IN PUBLIC/PRIVATE LAW

The public/private law divide is not commonly accepted all over Europe. I use the distinction in a very pragmatic way. Public law and public regulatory instruments are mostly all measures which must be taken to establish a competitive European market for the respective services, for setting up single passport regulation on the basis of home country authorizations, on privatization of former natural monopolies, for guaranteeing access to universal services, for separating the transmission system (the net) from the distribution system (the supply of services), and last but not least, on creating single contact points to enhance co-operation between agencies. Private law instruments are directly intervening into the contract for services in the various fields of interests here. It might be argued that regulatory measures regarding the protection of the consumer, the injured, the customer or the investor do not affect the legal character of contract law rules as belonging to private law.[32] It is a common characteristic of all services that the EC legislator combines public and private law means, although the emphasis is put on public law means in the way it is defined here – with the exemption of consumer law which almost entirely focuses on private law.

The differentiation becomes complicated if one looks more closely into the regulatory instruments which are used. *Traditional* instruments in the field of private law are legislative interventions in order to guarantee a certain level of justice in a supposedly unbalanced contractual relationship between a consumer or customer or investor and a supplier by way of mandatory contract law rules. With the exception of the field of services, the European legislator heavily relies on mandatory contract law rules to shape its consumer policy and to supplement its liberalization and privatization policy. In the field of consumer law these mandatory rules laid down minimum standards, thereby leaving it for the Member States to adopt more stringent rules. The European Commission is now striving for full harmonization in consumer contract law, a policy which the Commission has already achieved in other fields where it has taken measures to regulate services.[33]

---

32 There has been an extensive debate in Germany on whether the legal character of civil law changes when it is submitted to regulatory interventions. In particular, scholars from the University of Bremen have been involved in the debate, see Assmann, Heinz-Dieter, Brüggemeier, Gert, Hart, Dieter and Joerges, Christian *Wirtschaftsrecht als Kritik des Privatrechts* (1980, Athenäum Verlag, Königstein).

33 See the Commission paper on a consumer policy strategy 2002-2006, KOM (2002) 208 endg. 7.5.2002; quite critical on this policy shift is Reich, Norbert 'Die Stellung des Verbraucherrechts im "Gemeinsamen Referenzrahmen" und im

There is a tendency in European law on services to shift away from traditional instruments towards *less traditional* instruments, as Anthony Ogus has put it. This category covers default rules and self-regulatory measures in consumer contract law as well as co-regulation, according to the meaning which the European Commission has given to it.[34] It encompasses contract law-making and moulds it along the lines of the new approach in the Services Directive as well as the Lamfalussy procedure in Directive 2004/39 on financial instruments.

At a closer look, the set of services offers a heterogeneous picture. The European Commission has undertaken numerous attempts to enhance the role and function of self-regulation in consumer law. All these efforts, however, must be regarded as a failure as the European Commission did not succeed in substantially influencing the deeply rooted cultural differences in the Member States. Those Member States which traditionally rely on self-regulatory measures could continue their way of implementing EC law, whereas those Member States with no such tradition remain largely unaffected. Two prominent examples might help to underpin these findings: regulation on unfair commercial practices[35] and the role and importance of voluntary dispute settlement procedures.[36] The same is more or less true with regard to co-regulation. The European Commission did not convince Member States in the Council to test new forms of law-making and law enforcement as discussed in various documents in the aftermath of the White Paper on Governance, with the exceptions of the new approach on technical

---

"optionellen Instrument" – Trojanisches Pferd oder Kinderschreck?' in Reich, Norbert and Thévenoz, Luc (eds) *Droit de la consommation – Konsumentenrecht – Consumer Law, Liber amicorum Bernd Stauder.* (2006, Nomos-Verlag, Baden-Baden), pp. 357–382; now in particular COM (2006) 744 final on the Revision of the Consumer *Acquis*.

34 Liikanen, Erkki 'Co-Regulation: a modern approach to regulation' (2000, Brussels), 4 May. *Le Livre blanc sur la gouvernance européenne* COM (2001) 428 final and *Suivi du Livre blanc sur la gouvernance européenne – Pour un usage mieux adapté des instruments*, COM (2002) 278 final, 5.6.2002, *Recours encadré à un mécanisme de corégulation*. See for a deeper analysis, Cafaggi, Fabrizio (ed) *Reframing self-regulation in European private law* (2006, Kluwer).

35 See Henning-Bodewig, Frauke *Unfair Competition Law, European Union and Member States* (2006, Kluwer); Howells, Geraint, Micklitz, Hans-W. and Wilhelmsson, Thomas *European Fair Trading Law – The Unfair Commercial Practices Directive* (2006, Ashgate, Aldershot). See that some Member States would understand unfair commercial practices law as public law, others like Austria and Germany as private law.

36 See J. Stuyck, E. Terryn, V. Colaert, T. Van Dyck, et al. *An analysis and evaluation of alternative means of consumer redress other than redress through ordinary judicial proceedings – Final Report*, Study for the European Commission, available at: http://ec.europa.eu/ consumers/redress/reports_studies/index_en.htm.

standards and harmonization and the Lamfalussy procedure. The former has become an integral part of the Services Directive, the latter is already in action in the field of financial instruments. Both have in common that the law-making process is broken down into different levels of action, where the legislator restricts itself to defining a kind of broader regulatory frame, which is then completed by way of technical standardization organizations (that is technical experts) or through the input of experts from the national regulators (Lamfalussy procedure).

It is certainly too early to comment on the future of the new approach in the Services Directive. The situation is somewhat different with regard to the Lamfalussy procedure. On 10 August 2006 the European Commission adopted Directive 2006/73 and the implementing Regulation 1287/2006 which lays down detailed rules for the implementation, inter alia, of the contract-related provisions in Directive 2004/39 on financial instruments.[37] The first two levels of the Lamfalussy procedure are now completed.[38] The consultation on the third has already been completed. Reading the three pieces of law together, it is obvious that the legal requirements are still rather broad and vague. They need therefore to be concretized at the third level, which means through the regulatory experts. And it is here where the Lamfalussy procedure and the new approach fit astonishingly well together. Experts, technical or regulatory experts, define what the law is. However, the Lamfalussy procedure is much determined by way of regulatory interventions, whereas under the new approach the legislator steps back from laying down detailed rules and leaves the forum to private law-makers.

---

37 OJ L 241, 2.9.2006, 26.

38 See: http://www.cesr-eu.org/index.php?page=consultation_details&id=76.

Table 2.4 European regulatory framework for services: public/private law

	Public law	Private law	Regulatory instruments traditional	Regulatory instruments less traditional	Minimum/ full harmonization
Consumer contract law on services	Commercial practices	Commercial practices, contract law, conflict solution	Comprehensive set of mandatory private law rules. Limited use of country of origin principle	Few default rules, limited impact of self-regulation	Minimum and full
Transport		Contract law and liability	Mandatory rules on transport contracts		Full
Financial services	All financial services: single passport regulation on the basis of home country authorization	Insurance: contract law rules; financial instruments services: conduct of business rules as contract law rules	Insurance: mandatory contract law on particular issues	Financial instruments: rules on conduct of business obligations to be concretized in the Lamfalussy procedure	Full

Network services	Privatization of public monopolies; guarantee of universal services; unbundling		Mandatory rules on universal services (*services publiques*) in network contracts	'Measures' outside universal services in the energy sector[1]	Full
Services	Standardized authorization scheme for the creation of establishments; free access to and free exercise of a service activity; but country of destination retains control powers	Consumer contract law exempted from the scope; pre-contractual information duties	Binding rules on information duties	Co- regulation and self regulation on the quality of services; standardization of services through European standardization institutions	Full

Note: [1] Directive 2003/53/EC and Directive 2003/54 Annex A 'Measures on Consumer Protection', which means according to Article 3(5) and Article 3(3) respectively 'at least household customers', that is to say customers purchasing electricity or gas for their own household consumption.

5. TRADITIONAL AND LESS TRADITIONAL REGULATORS

The shift from *traditional* to *less traditional* instruments is mirrored in the actors which now appear on the European regulatory agenda. Consequently, they might be divided into *traditional* and less *traditional regulators*. Traditionally regulation lies in the hands of the legislator and the executive. The latter might adopt not only general rules but take individual regulatory actions. In the field at hand, there are two European agencies to be mentioned, the European Railway Agency[39] and the European Aviation Safety Agency[40]. Both deal with safety matters and interoperability.[41] They are not involved in the establishment or the completion of the internal market. So far, there is no European regulator in the form of a European agency,[42] not even in the form in which it already exists with regard to pharmaceuticals, agriculture or environmental protection. This does not mean that there is no regulation at the European level beyond the EC legislator. However, it is here where the new regulators show up. Their initiatives and their regulatory interventions in whatever form constitute the institutional framework of European private law.[43] In its third package on telecommunications and energy, however, the European Commission advocates the establishment of an agency for the co-operation of regulators.[44]

Various Forms of Co-operation between National Regulators

The EC policy to establish an internal market for all sorts of services does not only touch upon national substantive law but also on the way in which the law is concretized, shaped, implemented and enforced – and under what responsibility. Most of the areas here under review were traditionally governed by public agencies or public administrations. This is true for transport, financial services and network services. The reasons differ according to the type of

---

39 On the basis of Regulation 881/2004, see http://www.era.europa.eu.

40 http://www.easa.eu.int/home/agenmeas_en.html; see Articles 13, 15, 45, 46 of Regulation 1592/2002.

41 Article 31 of Regulation 1371/2007.

42 See Majone, Giandomenico *Regulating Europe* (1996, London, Routledge).

43 See Cafaggi, Fabrizio 'The Institutional Framework and the Need for European Governance in European Private Law', in Cafaggi, Fabrizio (ed) *The Institutional Framework of European Private Law* (2006, Oxford University Press), 1; Cafaggi, Fabrizio 'Rethinking Private Regulation in the European Regulatory Space', *EUI Working Papers*, Law No. 13 (2006).

44 COM (2007) 530 final, 19.9.2007 (energy) and COM (2007) 699 final, 13.11.2007 (telecommunications).

service. Natural monopolies have led the Member States to entrust particular government departments with regulatory tasks. The European Commission has been and still is fighting hard to get the Member States to set up politically independent public agencies in the energy and the railway sectors.[45] This was less necessary in the field of financial services where the Member States, even with the support of the service sector concerned, established agencies which had to supervise the market and eliminate rogue traders. Here the European Commission could build on a stable network of national regulators. Since the adoption of Regulation 2006/2004 on Consumer Protection Enforcement Co-operation,[46] the European Commission pushes Member States hard to establish a national consumer agency, although Austria and Germany were allowed to involve business and consumer organizations in transborder co-operation.[47] The European Commission seems convinced that public enforcement prevails over private enforcement through business and consumer organizations. So a common policy of the European Commission is built on national regulators in the completion of the internal market. This might partly result from the fact that EC law, at least in the form of directives, can only address and bind Member States.

The way in which co-operation between national regulators is organized differs considerably. Over time, however, the Commission's strategy is relatively easy to identify. Loosely knitted networks are gradually replaced by formal legal structures in which stakeholders no longer have any role to play.

1. The first form is the regulatory committee which is foreseen in Regulation 2006/2004 on Consumer Protection Enforcement Co-operation under reference to the comitolgy procedure.[48] Regulation 2006/2004 marks an important paradigm shift in consumer policy. Directive 1998/27 on injunctions has been understood as an attempt to involve civil society more strongly in consumer enforcement matters. The so-called 'enforcement network' was set up in November 2007 (OJ 28.11.2007, C 286/01). It brings together only administrations and in the long run probably national consumer agencies. The committee is mostly concerned with transborder regulatory actions.

[45] Each Member State has to set up a European Railways Committee (DERC). The Regulatory Body is a body independent from any infrastructure manager, charging body, allocation body or applicant. It is independent in its organization, legal structure, funding and in its decision-making. The legal basis for the creation and competence of the Regulatory Body can be found in Article 10.7 of Directive 2001/12/EC and in Articles 30 and 31 of Directive 2001/14/EC.

[46] OJ L 634, 9.12.2004, 1.

[47] The Netherlands had established a consumer agency by 1 January 2007.

[48] See Article 19.

The Regulatory Committee which will have to be established under the Directive on Services is shaped along the lines of the comitology procedure. It is entrusted with wide-ranging competences in order to give shape to the rather broad requirements which are meant to simplify administrative procedures, to develop further the information requirements, to establish common criteria for defining – for the purposes of professional insurance or guarantees – what is appropriate to the nature and extent of the risk, and last but not least to establish an alert mechanism by means of a network of Member States with the participation of the European Commission. The rulings to be expected might very well affect contract law under the scope of the Directive.

2. The second form is well-established committees in the financial sector which are set up along the lines of the Lamfalussy procedure. The Committee of European Insurance and Occupational Pensions Supervisors (CEIOPS)[49] performs the functions of the Level 3 Committee for the insurance and occupational pensions sectors, following the extension to those sectors of the Lamfalussy procedure, as also applied by the Committee of European Banking Supervisors (CEBS) and the Committee of European Securities Regulators (CESR),[50] respectively, in the banking and capital markets sectors. This role involves advice to the European Commission on the drafting of implementation measures for framework directives and regulations on insurance and occupational pensions ('Level 2 activities'), and establishing supervisory *standards, recommendations and guidelines* to enhance convergent and effective application of the regulations and to facilitate co-operation between national supervisors ('Level 3 activities'). CESR has been involved in the elaboration of the first Level 2 Directive 2006/73. Its recommendations have influenced the concrete shaping of the relevant contract rules.
3. The third form is the two committees set up in the energy sector. The European Regulators' Group for Electricity and Gas (ERGEG)[51] is a body of independent national energy regulatory authorities, which was set up by the European Commission as an advisory group to the Commission on energy issues.[52] It is to give regulatory co-operation and co-ordination a more formal status, in order to facilitate the completion of the internal

---

[49] http://www.ceiops.org/. The Committee of European Insurance and Occupational Pensions Supervisors (CEIOPS) was established pursuant to the European Commission Decision 2004/6/EC of 5 November 2003, OJ L 3, 7.1.2004, 30.

[50] http://www.cesr-eu.org/.

[51] http://www.ergeg.org/.

[52] European Commission Decision of 11 November 2003 (203/796/EC) OJ L 296, 14.11.2003, 14.

energy market. ERGEG provides a platform for co-operation between national energy regulatory authorities, and between these authorities and the Commission. ERGEG is charged with advising and assisting the Commission in consolidating the internal energy market, in particular with respect to preparing draft implementing measures in the field of electricity and gas. The objective is to help ensure a consistent application in all Member States of the Electricity (2003/54/EC) and Gas (2003/55/EC) Directives as well as the Regulation (1228/2003) on cross-border exchanges of electricity. The Decision sets a much stricter framework for co-operation between national regulators and is certainly meant to make more informal networks, such as the Florence Forum, superfluous.[53]

4. The fourth form is initiatives outside the tight regulatory framework of EC law which bring together regulators and stakeholders. The above-mentioned Florence Forum was such an initiative which preceded the establishment of the ERGEG, thereby leaving room for an informal exchange not only between regulators. A similar role to that of ERGEG is played by the Council of European Energy Regulators (CEER).[54] This was created in 2000, when ten national energy regulatory authorities decided to sign a *Memorandum of Understanding for the establishment of the Council of European Energy Regulators*, which led to the establishment of a not-for-profit association. Today it has 26 members. The overall aim is to enhance co-operation among national energy regulators and with the EU institutions. The CEER and the ERGEG share similar objectives. There are strong links between both bodies.
5. The fifth new form might become an agency for the co-operation of energy regulators and an agency for the co-operation of telecommunication regulators. These are to be established for the purpose of complementing at Community level regulatory tasks performed at national level by the competent national regulatory authorities. It remains to be seen whether Member States are willing to give away regulatory powers to the Community level.

Business and Consumer Organizations

Traditionally, business as well as consumer organizations might have a role to play in setting up voluntary regulation, jointly or business on its own with or without consumer participation. At the European level – as well as at national

53 Eberlein, Burkhard 'Regulation by Co-operation: the third way in making rules for the internal energy market', in Cameron, Peter D. (ed) *Legal Aspects of EU-Energy Regulation* (2005, Oxford University Press), 59 et seq., paragraph 4.75.

54 http://www.ceer-eu.org.

level – business organizations are organized sector by sector, being tied together in diverse umbrella organizations.[55] Usually they have no direct and specialized counterpart on the consumer side. Consumer organizations have to cover a broad array of consumer issues. It is an exception to the rule if consumers manage to organize their interests in a particular business sector. If they exist, such formations are the direct result of mass incidents and do not manage to develop a stable infrastructure.[56]

This is why it is not all surprising that the services are organized by sectors, each sector having its own European business organization. The major field of activities of concern to us is the elaboration of business-wide standard contract terms and codes of conduct. Consumers are represented at the European level by the Bureau Européen des Unions de Consommateurs (BEUC)[57] which is the umbrella organization of national consumer organizations and agencies. However, there are two exceptions to the rule and both concern enforcement matters: the International Consumer Protection Enforcement Network (ICEPEN)[58] and the Consumer Law Enforcement Forum (CLEF)[59] which has become the successor of the European Consumer Law Group. Whilst both forums cover consumer services (inter alia), the activities are focused on informal exchange, namely legal training on enforcement matters.

So far the European legislator has made only two attempts to tie business and consumer organizations more closely into its regulatory concept. The Directives on Electricity and Gas encourage the building of countervailing power through 'small and medium-sized consumers'.[60] Medium-sized consumers must be understood as small and medium-sized companies which do not produce energy but which need energy for their own production process. The explicit reference of consumers allows for an understanding under which also final consumers in the sense of the consumer contract law directives are meant. The Services Directive is even more concrete. Here professional bodies, chambers of commerce, draft and consumer organizations are enumerated.[61]

---

55 See for instance, International Air Transport Association (IATA), see http://www.iata.org/index.htm; Community of European Railways and Infrastructure Companies (CER), see http://www.cer.be/content/default.asp; the European Insurance and Reinsurance Federation, see http://www.cea.assur.org/; European Banking Federation, see http://www.fbe.be/Content/Default.asp; and Euroelectric, see http://www.euroelectric.org.

56 Such as the collapse of investment firms and accidents where a large number of people were injured by one single incident etc.

57 www.beuc.org.

58 www.icpen.org.

59 www.clef.org.

60 See Article 3 of the Directives 2003/54 and 2003/55.

61 See Article 26 of the Services Directive.

In both directives, however, the EC legislator addresses the Member States which must in co-operation with the European Commission encourage the enlisted consumer and business organizations to take necessary measures envisaged in the directives. Such a regulatory technique does not allow for clear-cut mandates. In the energy directives, the reference is found in the context of the universal services obligations, in the Services Directive, business and consumer organizations must promote the quality of the services – without any further specifications.[62]

Standardization Institutions and Academic Research Groups

The standardization institutions are in essence business organizations, as they serve the needs of business to develop technical standards for the sake and benefit of everybody. However, the new approach has dramatically changed the outlook of these bodies. The Memorandum of Understanding, concluded between the European Commission and the European Committee for Standardization (CEN)/European Committee for Electrotechnical Standardization (CENELEC) established a fruitful co-operation which is based on mutual rights and obligations.[63] The European Commission subsidizes the work of these bodies and might in return give mandates to the institutions to elaborate standards in areas where the Commission pursues particular objectives, such as increasing consumer safety. The standardization institutions turn into semi-public or semi-private bodies which are no longer tied to industry alone, but which co-operate with the European administration. The Services Directive mentions standardization explicitly, though again through the Member States in co-operation with the European Commission.[64]

Since the adoption of the Commission's Communication on Contract Law,[65] a new player has entered the scene of European regulators: *academic study groups*. Pushed into action by the European Parliament, the European Commission is striving for a Common Frame of Reference[66] which is to be prepared by the so-called *acquis* group and the study group[67] and which will

62 Article 26(3) of Directive 2006/123/EC.

63 See for a deeper analysis, Joerges, Christian, Falke, Josef, Micklitz, Hans-W. and Brüggemeier, Gert *Die Sicherheit von Konsumgütern und die Entwicklung der Europäischen Gemeinschaft* (1988, ZERP-Schriftenreihe, Nomos, Baden-Baden).

64 See Article 26(5).

65 COM (2001) 398 final, 11.7.2001, OJ C 255, 13.9.2001, 1.

66 von Bar, Christian 'Working Together Towards a Common Frame of Reference' (2005) 10 *Juridica International*, 17; Reich, Norbert 'A Common Frame of Reference (CFR) – Ghost or host for integration?', to be published as *ZERP-Discussion Paper* (Zentrum für Europäische Rechtspolitik, University of Bremen).

67 www.sgecc.net/overview.

Table 2.5 European organizations for standardization

	Co-operation, committees, networks	**Academic research groups and standardization institutions**	**Business organizations**	**Consumer organizations**
Consumer contract law on services	Co-operation of national enforcement agencies (Regulation 2006/2004)	*Acquis* group and Study group	BusinessEurope: Confederation of European Business	BEUC International Consumer Protection Enforcement Network (ICPEN); Consumer Law Enforcement Forum (CLEF)
Transport	European Aviation Safety Agency European Railway Agency co-operation of enforcement bodies		International Air Transport Association (IATA); Community of European Railways and Infrastructure Companies (CER)	BEUC
Financial services	Committee of European Insurance and Occupational Pensions Supervisors (CEIOPS); Committee on European Securities Regulators (CESR)	Insurance ECTIL	The European Insurance and Reinsurance Federation; European Banking Federation	BEUC

Network services	Informal network of agencies in energy sector (Florence Forum on Electricity and the Madrid Forum on Gas); European Regulators Group for Electricity and Gas (ERGEG) and Council of European Energy Regulators (CEER); European Regulators Group for Electronic Communication Networks (ERG)[1]		Euroelectric Promotion of *medium-sized* consumers of electricity through aggregation of representation	Florence and Madrid Forum open for consumer organizations; Promotion of *small* consumers of electricity through aggregation of representation
Services	Co-operation and exchange of information via central contact points	CEN/CENELEC, Committee on Consumer Policy of the International Organization for Standardization (ISO/COPOLCO)	Member States in co-operation with Commission shall encourage professional bodies, chambers of commerce, craft associations to promote the quality of services	European consumer voice in standardization (ANEC) Member States in co-operation with Commission shall encourage consumer organizations to promote the quality of services

Note: [1] www.erg.eu.int

soon be available in the form in which it has been submitted to the European Commission. The *acquis* group[68] has, at its name indicates, the task to circumscribe and analyse the existing *acquis communautaire* in European contract law. The work is focusing on European consumer law, the Rome Convention, the Brussels Convention/Regulation and product-related European private law rules.[69] It seems as if the areas of concern here, beyond consumer contract law on services, remained outside its focus of interest. The study group continues the work started 20 years ago in the Lando Commission which culminated in the adoption of the European Principles of Contract Law (PECL) I-III.[70] The broad programme is based on comparative analysis.[71] One of the working groups deals with services. The results were published in 2007.[72]

However, the two study groups are more than mere academic circles where interested lawyers from all over Europe unite in order voluntarily to elaborate European principles of contract law, in the hope that these rules might serve as a common legal ground for the interpretation of transborder contract making in Europe. The European Commission has forged the two groups together in a so-called Network of Excellence. They have a clear political mandate. It might be possible to regard the Commission's project as another variant of the new approach type of law-making: the Memorandum of Understanding being the contract concluded to establish the Network of Excellence, the mandatory requirements being the envisaged Common Frame

68 www.acquis-group.org.

69 The working programme is not publicly available. However it may be derived from a conference held in 2005 whose results are published: Europäische Rechtsakademie Trier (2006), *Special Issue European Contract Law* with contributions from Wilhelmsson, Thomas 'Pre-contractual Information Duties', 16; Schulze, Reiner 'Conclusion of Contract', 26; Poillot, Elise 'Consumer and Contract Law', 36; Howells, Geraint 'Consumer Protection and European Contract Law Harmonisation', 45; Ramberg, Christina 'Electronic Commerce in the Context of the European Contract Law Project', 48; Pfeiffer, Thomas 'Good Faith', 67; Leible, Stefan 'Non-Discrimination', 76; Zoll, Frederyk 'The Future of European Contract Law from the Perspective of a Polish Scholar', 90.

70 Lando, Ole and Beale, Hugh *Principles of European Contract Law, Parts I and II* (2000, Kluwer, Den Haag); Lando, Ole, Clive, Eric, Prum, André and Zimmermann, Reinhard (eds) *Principles of European Contract Law Part III* (2003, Kluwer, Den Haag).

71 Hesselink, Martijn W., Rutgers, Jacobien W., Diaz, Odavia Bueno, Scotton, Manola and Feldmann, Muriel (eds.) *Commercial Agency, Franchise and Distribution Contracts* (2006, Sellier, European Law Publishers and von Bar, Christian (ed.) *Benevolent Intervention into Another's Affairs* (2006, Sellier European Law Publishers). All in all ten volumes are foreseen.

72 Barendrecht, Maurits, Jansen, Chris, Loos, Marco, Pinna, Andrea, Cascao, Rui and van Gulijk, Stéphanie *Service Contracts* (2007, Sellier, European Law Publishers).

of References and the technical standards elaborated by standardization institutions being the set of rules to be elaborated in the tradition of the Lando Commission by European academic research.[73] Such a link to the European Commission is missing in the European Centre on Tort and Insurance Law,[74] which remains a purely academic exercise without political ties.

6. NEW INSTRUMENTS/NEW ACTORS – AND THE EFFECTS ON CONTRACTS FOR SERVICES

The process which will be documented is still in an infant stage. That is why an analysis can only be preliminary. Most of the procedures have just been set up and the guidelines, recommendations and other soft regulatory instruments have been published only recently. However, some tendencies are already clearly emerging.

Differing Regulatory Intensities in Co-regulation

Co-regulation is not a clear-cut concept. This is reflected in the various forms under review here. The Lamfalussy procedure is certainly nearest to traditional regulatory intervention, in the sense that the legislator – Parliament and Council and, later on, the executive (the Commission) – holds the law-making procedure firm in its hands. The management of the third level lies in the hands of the competent committee, CESR (financial instruments) and CEIPOS (insurance and occupational pensions). Although the law-making process has not yet reached the fourth level, Directive 2004/39 (first level) and Directive 2006/73 and the implementing Regulation 1287/2006 (second level) might be paradigmatic for the way in which the competences are shared. Section 2 of Directive 2004/39 dealing with 'Protection to ensure investor protection' (Articles 19 et seq.) starts from a very broad concept. It lays down principles and guidelines and no or very few clear-cut rules. Directive 2006/73, which was meant to give shape to these broad principles, again remains rather broad, see for example, Article 27 of Directive 2006/73 which is to give shape to Article 19(2) of Directive 2004/39. It reads as follows:

---

[73] See for further details, Micklitz, Hans-W. 'Review of Academic Approaches on the European Contract Law Codification Project', in Mads Andenas, Silvia Diaz Alabart, Sir Basil Markesinis, Hans Micklitz, Nello Pasquino (eds), *Liber Amicorum Guido Alpa Private Law Beyond the National Systems* (2007, London, British Institute of International and Comparative Law) 699.

[74] www.ectil.org.

> (The information) shall be accurate and in particular shall not emphasize any potential benefit of an investment service ... without also giving a fair prominent indication of the relevant risk. ... It shall not disguise, diminish or obscure important items, statements or warnings.

Although the subsequent articles provide for a number of specifications with regard to particular types of information, the question remains whether such a provision is really helpful in giving shape to a ruling which is adopted by the European Parliament and the Council. It is very likely that the hard core questions will be resolved at the third and fourth level.

The new approach type of regulation relies much more on shared responsibilities and co-operation between public regulator and private institutions. The results obtained in the field of technical standardization are regarded as a success story.[75] In fact, the new approach has boosted European standard-making through CEN and CENELEC to the detriment of national standardization institutions such as the association française de normalization (AFNOR), the British Standards Institute (BSI) and the Deutches Institut für Normung (German Institute for Standardization (DIN) which have lost influence. Whether the adopted standards satisfy the needs of effective consumer protection against risks to their health and safety has never been systematically and comprehensively evaluated.[76] The Services Directive builds on the new approach type of regulation. The work within CEN/CENELEC and also ISO/COPOLCO, however, has already begun, without yet yielding many results.

The same is true with regard to the Commission project on European contract law.[77] The Common Frame of Reference was completed in 2007, at least in the form it was presented to the European Commission. A set of Principles on European Law on Service Contracts (PELSC) has already been

---

[75] http://ec.europa.eu/enterprise/newapproach/index_en.htm.

[76] As a rare exception to the rule; see Micklitz, Hans-W. and Schieble, Christoph *Legal Study – Exclusion Clauses in Standard Clauses under the EU Low Voltage Directive 73/22/EEC (Children and Disabled People using Electrical Appliances)*, prepared for ANEC (2004).

[77] See COM (2003) 68 final 81–88 and see also Communication from the Commission to the European Parliament and Council, 'European Contract Law and the revision of the *acquis*: the way forward' Brussels, 11.10.2004 COM (2004) 651 final (hereinafter 'ECL and the revision of the *acquis*'), 'The second measure sought to promote the development by private parties of Standard Terms and Conditions (STC) for EU wide use rather than just in one single legal order', p. 6. Wilhelmsson, Thomas 'Coperation and competition regarding standard contract terms in consumer contracts' (2006) *European Business Law Review*, 49 et seq., 59, footnote 37.

elaborated by the study group.[78] However, it has not been merged with the findings of the *acquis* group and has not been agreed by the European Commission. The principles as they stand today contain seven chapters dealing with general provisions, construction contracts, processing contracts (such as repair and maintenance), storage contracts, design contracts, information supply and medical treatment. The services at stake here are not covered. The European Commission puts more and more emphasis on the announced revision of the *consumer acquis*[79] and seems to postpone the political discussion of a Common Frame of Reference.[80]

There is no traditional intervention in the field of transport contracts outside the above-mentioned regulation. The European airports and the European airlines have engaged in a voluntary commitment, however, only in reaction to the Communication of June 2000.[81] The two documents are said – this is highlighted in the documents – to be the result of extensive consultation with consumers, European governments, the European Commission, the airlines, and the airports. The problem is that low cost carriers, in particular, refused to sign the document. It might well be that the European Commission will sooner or later replace these voluntary commitments by binding regulation.[82]

Self-regulation

Outside the field of transport services, there are no major initiatives to be reported which approach contract-making from a European perspective. Standard contract terms or standard contracts are still very much subject to national markets, national regulators and national law.

Participation of Stakeholders

It is a common characteristic in all *less traditional instruments* that stakeholders are not given a formal legal status. Already the new approach on technical standards and harmonization has caused much discussion of the question of whether and to what extent consumer organizations should be legally included in the

---

78 Available on the website of the study group at: http://www.sgecc.net/media/downloads/sgeccservices_contracts.pdf.

79 COM (2006) 744 final.

80 This is certainly a reaction to the meeting of the EU council in London in November 2005, see EU-Council, Resolution of 28–29 November 2005.

81 COM (2000) 365 final, 21.6.2000 and p. 7 of the ECLG Paper on Protecting the Rights of Passengers and Holidaymakers (written mainly by Tonner, Klaus and Schuster, Alex), see: www.europeanconsumerlawgroup.org. See at http://ec.europa.eu/transport/air_portal/passenger_ rights/doc/commitment_airlines_en.pdf.

82 See COM (2005), 46 final, 15.3.2005.

Table 2.6 New models of regulation

	Co-regulation	**Self-regulation**	**Participation of stakeholders**	**Impact on contract law**
Consumer contract law on services	Promotion of European-wide elaboration of standard terms and conditions through Commission, however, withdrawn,[1] Common Frame of Reference and Principles on European Contract Law (PECL)		No guidance under the Communications of the Commission, but consultation of stakeholders on a voluntary basis	Draft Rome I allows for a reference in art. 3(2)
Transport	Airline Passenger Service Commitment; Airports Council International (ACI) voluntary commitment on airport services. Railway passenger rights, monitoring compliance with quality commitments in art. 28 Reg. 1371/2007	Air passenger rights IATA Recommendation 1724	On a voluntary basis	Standard contract terms

Financial services	Lamfalussy procedure in insurances and financial instruments		Consultation within Lamfalussy 2 level; CESR market participants consultative panel	Regulation 1287/2006 and Directive 2006/73 (2nd level) rules on contract related provisions (business conduct/best practice 2004/39, 3rd level rules under preparation
Network services	Measures shall include those under Annex A.[2] Charter on the Rights of Energy Consumers[3]		No particular rules foreseen at EC level; but public guidelines on ERGEG's consultation process[4]	ERGEG launches three best practice propositions on transparency, customer protection and the supplier switching process[5]
Services	Member States in co-operation with the Commission encourage *providers* to take action on voluntary certification quality charters; Ibid; independent assessment of quality and defects of services, in particular comparative trials or		From participation to co-operation, from providing input to state governed rules to developing voluntary rules, on which Member States and the Commission might comment	Direct impact through supplementing voluntary measures, mainly through technical standards elaborated by CEN/CENELEC. Indirect impact through development of 'best practices' and appropriate comparative tests

Table 2.6 continued

	Co-regulation	Self-regulation	Participation of stakeholders	Impact on contract law
	testing and communication of results, *notably by consumer organizations*, Ibid. development of voluntary European standards in art. 26 of Service Dir.			

Notes:
[1] See COM (2005) 456 final, 23.9.2005, p. 11.
[2] Article 3(5) of Directive 2003/54/EC and Article 3(3) of Directive 2003/55/EC.
[3] Towards a European Charter on the Rights of Energy Consumers COM (2007) 386 final, 5.7.2007.
[4] http://www.ergeg.org/portal/page/portal/ERGEG_HOME/ERGEG_PC/ERGEGPUBLIC-CONSULATIONPROPOSAL_ APPROVED.PDF.
[5] http://www.ergeg.org/portal/page/portal/ERGEG_HOME/ERGEG_DOCS/ERGEG_DOCUM-ENTS_NEW/CUSTOMER_ FOCUS_GROUP/PR-06-08_CFG-BestPractices.doc.

standardization process.[83] Today, ANEC[84] has taken over the role of organizing the consumer input, however, without being granted any formal legal status. The Services Directive pursues the same approach. It mentions the importance of standardization of services, it even mentions consumer organizations, but without drawing any conclusion with regard to participation rights in whatever form. The first draft of Regulation 2006/2004 provided for the possibility of stakeholders to be heard in the hearings of the envisaged committee. However, this right did not survive the final agreements in the Council.[85]

The Lamfalussy procedure integrates national governments and national regulators in the law-making process, but does not deal with the role and function of stakeholders. This task has been left to committees set up in the insurance and the investment services, CESR and ERGEG. The former has set up a Market Participants Consultative Panel, which has an advisory function and which comprises representatives from the various business sectors. These are selected and appointed by the European Commission. The Committee chooses the appropriate voices itself. Private investors or their organizations are not regarded as market participants.

The ERGEG has published already, in 2004, Public Guidelines on ERGEG's Consultation Practices. Number 4 says: 'Regulators will, where appropriate, consult the full range of interested parties, including producers, network operators, suppliers and consumers as appropriate'. However, ERGEB has not set up a formal consultative body. Despite the harmonious language, the practical effect of these guidelines is limited. In the end it comes near to the 'normal' consultation procedure which the European Commission initiates whenever it intends to prepare and to take action.

Impact on the Law of Service Contracts

It is striking to see that the European Commission, although it has no stable competence to regulate contract law per se,[86] has found ways and means

---

83 Joerges, Christian, Falke, Josef, Micklitz, Hans-W. and Brüggemeier, Gert *Die Sicherheit von Konsumgütern und die Entwicklung der Europäischen Gemeinschaft* (1988, ZERP-Schriftenreihe, Nomos, Baden-Baden) and more particularly Micklitz, Hans-W. 'Considerations Shaping Future Consumer Participation in European Product Safety Law', in Joerges, Christian (ed), *Workshop on Product Safety and Product Liability in the European Community*, EUI-Working Paper, San Domenico (FIRENZE) (1989), 182–205.

84 www.anec.org.

85 See www.european.consumerlawgroup.org, comments on the regulation on consumer protection co-operation, ECLG 134/2004.

86 Weatherill, Stephen 'European Private Law and the Constitutional Dimension', in Cafaggi, Fabrizio (ed) *The Institutional Framework of European Private Law* (2006, Oxford University Press), 79–107.

through new or less traditional instruments to increase steadily the set of rules which affect directly or indirectly the law of service contracts. Most of the rules which are developed within the co-regulation procedures are not legally binding, with the exception of the level 2 Directive 2006/73[87] and Regulation 1287/2006 on investment services. The vast majority of the rules are soft, in the sense that they do not constitute binding contractual rights and obligations. This will be true for the Common Frame of Reference, although it might require a quasi-legal status,[88] as well as the principles of European contract law to be developed by the *acquis* group and by the study group and to be agreed by the European Commission. For the time being, these rules might certainly gain no more than the status of a formal recommendation.[89] Such a value judgment applies equally to the set of propositions launched by the ERGEG and the standards which will be developed by CEN and CENELC under the Services Directive.

The soft and non-binding character does not preclude these rules from influencing the law of service contracts. The European Commission uses the less traditional instruments in a creative way to build an ever denser net of European (soft) rules which narrows the leeway for national private law regulators, both traditional and less traditional. Theoretically, Member States and the parties to a contract remain free. They may subscribe to this new set of rules or ignore them. In practice, however, these rules, as far as they result from European co-regulation, benefit from a higher repudiation and an increased legitimacy. Therefore indirect pressure for convergence might be high.

7. THE SUBSTANCE OF THE PUBLIC/PRIVATE LAW REGULATION

The crucial difficulty which results from the growing number of European rules launched, issued and adopted by the various regulators is to not lose track. It requires detective skills and stubbornness to dig all the various rules

---

87 OJ L 241, 2.9.2006, 26.

88 If the European Commission really uses the CFR as a toolbox, as it indicated in its Communication; see in particular von Bar, Christian 'Working Together Towards a Common Frame of Reference' (2005) 10 *Juridica International*, 17. The annex contains a list of possible 'tools'.

89 There is much discussion on the way in which such a Code of Reference could be enacted, see van Gerven, Walter 'Needed: A Method of Convergence for Private Law', in Furrer, Andreas (ed.), *Europäisches Privatrecht im wissenschaftlichen Diskurs* (2006, Stämpfli, Bern) 437; Reich, Norbert 'CFR und Sonderprivatrechte im "Europäischen Privatrecht" ' (2007) *ZEuP*, 161.

out of the web. The success is worth the effort. The web reveals more and more rules. All these various regulations, directives, codes, charters, recommendations, programmes etc. will then have to be analysed. It seems as if the legal discipline is very much divided in branches, each dealing vertically with one particular field of services. I would not go as far as claiming the need to systemize all these rules. This sounds as if it is possible to deduce common rules out of this scattered picture.[90] The following survey is meant to show the existing set of rules within a common analytical framework. In this respect, it is no more than a first stocktaking which does not go into detail, but intends rather to give a survey on the European law of service contracts.

Conclusion, Formation and Advice

It belongs to the standard rhetoric of the EC legislator that European law does not intervene in the rules governing the conclusion of contracts. A closer look reveals that the picture is more complicated than that. There are areas where freedom of contract is in fact zero, where suppliers are obliged to conclude a contract on the supply of public goods.[91] But most of the rules could be read so as to focus on the pre-contractual circumstances, by way of transparency rules, of pre-contractual information duties and pre-contractual advice.[92] This goes very much along with the concept of a competitive contract law, which I have developed elsewhere.[93] European contract law rules are said to strengthen the rights of the insured, consumers and customers to receive as much information as possible in the pre-contractual stage so as to be able to compare prices and quality in order to make not only an informed but a best informed decision. European law comes close to an obligation of the supplier to disclose substantial information.[94]

---

90 Optimistic with regard to universal services, see Rott, Peter 'A new Social Contract Law for Public Services – Consequences for Regulation of Services of General Economic Interest in the EC' (2005) 3 *European Review of Contract Law*, 323. For articles which are sceptical, see Christoph Schmid 'The Instrumental Conception of the Acquis Communautaire in Consumer Law and its Implications on A European Contract Law Code' (2005) *European Review of Contract Law*, 211; Collins, Hugh 'The Alchemy of Deriving General Principles of Contract Law from European Legislation: In Search of the Philosopher's Stone' (2006) *European Review of Contract Law*, 213.

91 See COM (2007) 386 final, 5.7.2007, p. 13.

92 See Regulation 1371/2007, Arts 4, 8 and 10 with Annex 1.

93 Micklitz, Hans-W. 'The concept of competitive contract law' (2005) 23 *Penn State International Law Review*, 549–586.

94 Wilhelmsson, Thomas 'Private Law Remedies against the Breach of Information Requirements of EC Law', in Schulze, Reiner, Ebers, Martin and Grigoleit, Hans Christoph, *Informationspflichten und Vertragsschluss im Acquis*

Table 2.7 Public/private regulation: effects on contract rules

	Consumer contract law on services	**Transport**	**Financial services**	**Network services**	**Services**
Access	Access to consumer credit. No EC rules	Particular rules on access to travel information systems	Access to bank account. No EC rules	Access to energy supply and public phone under the universal service doctrine	
Freedom to contract (choice)		Through establishment of competition and unbundling		Through establishment of competition and unbundling; Change of supplier free of charge Charter on the rights of energy consumers – free choice of supplier	Improved choice by way of transborder services (ex art. 20–21 service directive)

Transparency	Contract specific information on price and quality of service	Envisaged: air carrier right to transparency in real time.[1] Envisaged: railway ticket as prima facie evidence for contract[2]	Insurance (no particular rules, but mediator); financial instruments are directed to the *potential* customer	Contract specific information on price and quality of service. Charter on the rights of energy consumers on prices, tariffs and monitoring[3]	Assistance for recipients by way of obtaining information through consumer organizations, in a clear and unambiguous manner (ex art. 21(1)(c) and 22(4) Services Dir.)
Information obligations	Medium related and contract related set of information duties	In particular: right to know the identity of the air carrier;[4] detailed set for railway passengers[5]	Damage: basic information; life insurance: detailed set of information duties; investment services: detailed set of information duties[6]	Contract related set of information duties; charter on the rights of energy consumers	Detailed set of information on request (ex art. 22 Services Dir.)

Table 2.7 continued

	Consumer contract law on services	Transport	Financial services	Network services	Services
Advice	Responsible lending – as information duty[7]		Insurance: no rules (but mediator); financial instruments: know your product, know your customer, agreement in writing[8]		

Notes:
1 COM (2005) 46 final, 16.2.2006 at (47).
2 Art. 4(2) COM (2004) 143 final, 3.3.2004.
3 COM (2007) 386 final, 5.7.2007, p. 12.
4 Regulation 261/2004, ruling that entered into force on 16 July 2006, see press release of DG TREN 18 July 2006.
5 Regulation 1371/2007, Articles 4, 8 and 10 with Annex I.
6 In Articles 19–24 of Directive 2004/39 (level 1) and Articles 27 et seq. of Directive 2006/73 (level 2).
7 Still foreseen in the modified proposal for a Directive of the European Parliament and of the Council on credit agreements for consumers repealing Council Directive 87/102/EEC and amending Council Directive 93/13/EEC, Interinstitutional File, 2002/0222 (COD), 2.10.2006; whether or not this comprises advice is no longer clear under the Common Position, see Arts. 5(6) and 8.
8 Article 19(7) of Directive 2004/39 in combination with the working document and Articles 35 et seq. of Directive 2006/73 (level 2).

Content

Outside anti-discrimination,[95] most of the particular EC rules revolve around quality and safety of the services.[96] Safety seems to be relevant primarily only in transport contracts and in energy supply.[97] The big issue is the regulation of quality of the service which constitutes the major subject of co-regulation and self-regulation.[98] The most developed rules exist in the field of financial services. The four-level mechanism in the Lamfalussy procedure leads, however, to duplications. The Services Directive will probably produce a whole series of technical standards which, sector-related or service-related, define quality standards.[99] The ERGEG is now intensifying its efforts to make propositions on how to define the quality of the service.[100] All these efforts are legally guided by broadly-termed requirements such as fairness, honesty, professional behaviour, transparency and best practice.

It will have to be shown whether the results of co-regulation and enhanced self-regulation meet these standards. A test is possible only if feasible criteria can be deduced from these broadly-termed requirements which allow for independent comparative assessment mechanisms, as Article 26 of the Services Directive puts it. The question remains whether these soft rules, which are meant to harmonize the law *fully* on the particular service in question, will gain supremacy over binding European and national consumer law rules, such as those laid down in Directive 93/13/EEC.[101]

Communautaire (2003, Mohr Siebeck, Tübingen) 245 and now Article 7 of Directive 2005/29 gives a verdict on misleading omissions, see Howells, Geraint, Micklitz, Hans-W. and Wilhelmsson, Thomas *European Fair Trading Law – The Unfair Commercial Practices Directive* (2006, Aldershot, Ashgate), p. 147.

95 See Article 1 of Directive 2000/43/EC OJ L 180, 19.7.2000, 22 and Article 3(1)(h) of Directive 2004/113/EC OJ L 373, 21.12.2004, 37; and Regulation 1371/2007, Chapter V, Arts. 18 et seq. and Art. 28.

96 See respectively, Regulation 1107/2006, OJ L 204, 26.7.2006, 1; COM (2000) 365 final, 21.6.2000, and COM (2005) 46 final, 16.2.2005 at (48).

97 See respectively Regulation 2111/2005 of 14 December 2005, Directive 2004/49/EC, OJ L 164, 30.04.2004, 44, and Articles 5, 6 and 24 of Directive 2003/54 (electricity), Articles 3(2), 6, 26 of Directive 2003/55 (gas).

98 See Articles 21 and 22 of Directive 2003/54 (electricity), Articles 46 et seq. of Directive 2006/73 (level 2).

99 See Article 26 of the Services Directive.

100 Articles 3(3), (7), 4 of Directive 2003/54 (electricity) and in various other references; Articles 3(2), (4), 5, 22 and 27 of Directive 2003/55 (gas). See ERGEG proposition on best practices available at http://www.ergeg.org/portal/page/portal/ERGRG_HOME/ERGEG_DOCS/ERGEG_DOCUMENTS_NEW/CUSTOMER_FOCUS_GROUP/PR-06-08_CFG-BestPractices.doc.

101 I would like to thank Norbert Reich for putting emphasis on the relationship between vertical and horizontal rules in European law, with particular regard to consumer protection.

Table 2.8 *Public/private regulation: content I*

	Consumer contract law on services	Transport	Financial services	Network services	Services
Affordability	Consumer credit?[1]			Energy prices, telephone tariffs.[2] Charter on the rights of energy consumers – protection of vulnerable consumers[3]	
Anti-discrimination					
Quality		Air carrier rules on passengers with reduced mobility. Envisaged transferrability of airline tickets and integrated ticketing. Railway passengers, similar rules. Service quality standards	Financial instruments: best practice and client order handling rules	Security of supply; service to be provided without interruption, ERGEG launched proposition on best practices	Procedural rules on the elaboration of quality standards for services; substance of the quality charter: making it easier to assess the competence of the provider, encourage independent assessment mechanisms

Safety		Operating ban on unsafe carriers; railway safety		Protection of health and safety
Payment modalities	Prohibition of advanced payment in time share contracts[4]			Wide choice of payment modalities.[5] Charter on the rights of energy consumers[6]
Contract terms	In commercial communication making contract terms and general conditions available[7]		Mandatory minimum standards for non-professional clients[8]	Contract conditions shall be provided prior to the conclusion of the contract[9]

Notes:

[1] The question relates to the possible effects of scoring under which the poor pay more, see in this context the European Coalition for Responsible Lending at: http://www.responsible-credit.net/.

[2] See on the existence of such a principle Rott, Peter 'A new Social Contract Law for Public Services – Consequences for Regulation of Services of General Economic Interest in the EC' (2005) *European Review of Contract Law*, 323.

[3] COM (2007) 386 final, 5.7.2007, p. 15 under reference to Article 3(5) of Directive 2003/54/EC and Article 3(3) of Directive 2003/54/EC.

[4] Article 6 of Directive 94/47.

[5] Annex A(d) of Directives 2003/54 and 2003/55.

[6] COM (2007) 386 final, 5.7.2007, p. 12.

[7] Article 10(3) of Directive 2000/31 on e-commerce.

[8] Article 19(7) of Directive 2004/39.

[9] Annex A(a) of Directives 2003/54 and 2003/55.

Table 2.9 Public/private regulation: content II

	Consumer contract law on services	**Transport**	**Financial services**	**Network services**	**Services**
Right to withdrawal and cancellation rights	Consumer credit and time sharing (withdrawal); cancellation (package tour, time sharing)	24 hour cooling-off period for telephone reservations under the 'Airline Passenger Service Commitment'[1]	Right to withdrawal in life insurance contracts[2]	Cancellation right in case of price increase[3]	
Compensation for improper information supply					
Compensation for undue performance	For non-performance and pain and suffering (package tours)[4]	Air carrier: in case of delay and cancellation.[5] Railway: compensation for delays[6]	Liability of investment firms for tied agents[7]	Energy: information on compensation rights	
Joint/subsidiary liability in trilateral contracts	Rules on combined contracts (sale and credit) credit; package tour		Triangle credit card issuer, contracting company and credit card user		

	(liability of operator); financed time sharing contracts				
Compensation for personal injury and belongings		Air carrier liability in the case of accidents.[8] Railway: liability in case of accidents (also hand luggage)[9]			Professional liability insurance and guarantees[10]
Insolvency	Protection against insolvency of tour operator [11]	Envisaged, in the event of bankruptcy of the air carrier [12]	Investor compensation schemes[13]		
Complaint handling		Air carrier dispute settlement on a voluntary basis; railway passengers complaint handling procedure[14]	Financial instruments: promotion of dispute settlement procedures[15]	Energy: dispute settlement 98/257. Charter on the rights of energy consumers[16]	Detailed rules on settlement of disputes[17]

Table 2.9 continued

	Consumer contract law on services	**Transport**	**Financial services**	**Network services**	**Services**
Collective remedies			Financial instruments: in the interests of consumers before courts and administrations by public bodies, and/or consumer and/or business organizations[19]	Charter on the rights of energy consumers refers to Directive 98/27 on injunctions[18]	

Notes:
1 Article 6, http://ec.europa.eu/transport/air_portal/passenger_rights/doc/ commitment_airlines_ en.pdf.
2 Article 30 of Directive 92/96.
3 Annex A(b) of Directives 2003/54 and 2003/55.
4 Article 5 of Directive 90/314 and see Case C-168/00 *Simon Leitner* ECR 2000, I-2631, ECJ.
5 Article 7 of Regulation 261/2004.
6 Article 15 of Regulation 1371/2006.
7 Article 23 of Directive 2004/39.
8 Regulation 2027/97 as amended by Regulation 889/2002.
9 COM (2004), 143 final, 3.3.2004.
10 Article 23 of the Services Directive.
11 Article 7 of Directive 90/314.
12 COM (2005) 46 final 16.2.2005 at (49).
13 Directive 97/9/EC, OJ L 84 26.3.1997.
14 Article 27 of Regulation 1371/2007.
15 Article 53 of Directive 2004/39.
16 COM (2007) 386 final, 5.7.2007, p. 14.
17 Article 27 of the Services Directive.
18 COM (2007) 386 final, 5.7.2007, p. 15.
19 Article 52(2) of Directive 2004/39 leaves Member States the choice between the three potential bodies acting on behalf of consumers.

Rights and Remedies

European law puts much emphasis on rights and remedies. The reason must be found in the early days of the European Community, when the European Court of Justice turned the Treaty of Rome into a genuine legal order, granting rights to suppliers, and later consumers, which prevail over national law that conflicts with the basic freedoms.[102] The European legislator and the European Court of Justice have extended the concept of rights and remedies to secondary EC legislation. This is particularly true with regard to the law on service contracts. There are rights at all ends, the right to withdraw from a contract or at least to cancel the contract in case of undue compliance belongs to the core of EC regulation. And there is a whole series of compensation rights in the field of services which far overreach the existing state of EC law with regard to products. However, European law does not sanction violations of the obligation to supply and/or to disclose information, at least not by contract law remedies.[103]

It is one characteristic of EC contract law that it does not respect the divide between substantive law and procedural law. The different regulations, directives and soft-law instruments contain mostly rules on out of court settlement. This policy of the European Commission fits in very well with the advocacy of less traditional instruments. The law is soft, and so is the enforcement. Collective remedies are scarce. The amazing ruling in Directive 2004/39 has not yet found the attention it deserves.

8. PRELIMINARY OBSERVATIONS ON THE APPLIED REGULATORY STRATEGIES

The overview of the different sectors of EC service regulation confirms once again the instrumental, sector-related approach the European regulator applies. The European regulator, in particular the European Commission, does not care much about regulatory approaches in similar fields which are already operating. The European regulator understands each new sector as a testing ground for new tools, strategies and instruments.

---

102 It is always fascinating to re-read Eric Stein's seminal analysis of the European Court of Justice, 'Lawyers, Judges and the Making of a Transnational Constitution' (1981) 75 *The American Journal of International Law*, 1.

103 Schwintowski, Hans-Peter 'Informationspflichten und effet utile – Auf der Suche nach einem effektiven und effizienten europäischen Sanktionssystem', in Schulze, Reiner et al., ibid. footnote 94 at 267.

This becomes particularly clear in the various forms of co-regulation. For decades the European Commission has been trying to advocate giving self-regulation a stronger place in European law. Co-regulation, broadly speaking, is nothing more than an attempt to combine mandatory legislative requirements with voluntary rule-making through business and consumer organizations. But there is no clear cut concept behind it. It seems as if the European Commission has never discussed what co-regulation really means, to what extent particular tools are appropriate with regard to specific regulatory fields only, or whether it is possible to develop common tools for similar services and what they should look like. The problem is that each new regulatory tool has long lasting consequences on the fabric of law-making once it is established.

There is not even a common policy on the types of committees which are set up, despite the comitology procedure. Since 1985, the year when the new approach was adopted, the question of whether stakeholders should be given a formal status in the development of contract-related rules through codes, recommendations, guidelines or standards has been hanging in the air. The various initiatives to set up informal consultation bodies with no rights or duties yield an artificial European society, in which the European Commission selects and appoints those who may be allowed to provide advice. The open consultation procedure via the publication of communications on which in principle everybody – who knows about the communication – could comment seems a rather reduced form of public input. The legitimacy of law-making through co-regulation is still shaky and far from being resolved.

EC law as it stands today does not explicitly regulate private law matters. However, this is only half the truth. The law-making machinery which is so effectively set into motion by way of the interplay between the legislative, the regulatory agencies and the new actors entering the scene, has boosted the elaboration of all sorts of rules which affect private law on services. The sheer mass of rules and the difficulty of not losing track is reminiscent of law-making in international organizations. Most of these organizations have no regulatory power, a deficit they compensate for by way of constantly adopting new soft law rules. It might be possible to interpret the various forms of co-regulation as a means of circumventing the lack of power within the EU. The problem today is less that there are no rules, but that there are too many rules, whose legal value, however, is – to say the least – uncertain. Most of these rules go back to mandatory though varying European general requirements which are said to harmonize the respective service fully. But is it really the policy that these new regulatory instruments should gain supremacy over binding national law with which they conflict?

To conclude: the regulatory strategies and their impact on the law of service contracts deserve much more attention. The few rules in national civil codes do not reflect the reality in the law on contract of services. There is more research needed on what is really going on in the various areas of services, how the parties interact in law-making and whether the results might receive at least output legitimation.[104] Last but not least, the cascade of rules has to be measured against the imperative general legislative requirements which are at the very beginning of this new law-making process and which set the legal framework for the outcome at the lowest level, where agencies, committees, business and consumer organizations co-operate.

104 Scharpf, Fritz *Governing in Europe, Effective and Democratic?* (1999, Oxford University Press).

3. The regulatory function of choice of law rules applying to contracts for services in the European Union

Sandrine Clavel

INTRODUCTION

Reconsidering the paradigm of the neutrality of international private law,[1] already challenged by the increasing development of internationally mandatory rules through which States intend to impose public policy concerns in the resolution of private disputes, recent scholarship has acknowledged that choice of law rules may endorse a regulatory function.[2] The assumption is that the designation of the law applicable to the resolution of international private litigation might not only be meant to offer private parties an outcome to their dispute, but also to fulfil objectives of a public nature. For several decades now, choice of law rules have been traducing legislators' concerns for the implementation of substantive policies in private law.[3] However, when it

[1] Built on Savigny's teachings, the neutrality of international private law has been pictured as the foundation of the conflict of laws in Europe during most of the twentieth century (Mayer P. and Heuzé V. (2004) *Droit international privé*, Paris; Montchrestien, n°68); However, for a survey of the 'balance movement' between public and private concerns in international private law (IPL), see: Muir Watt H. 'Droit public et droit privé dans les rapports internationaux (vers la publicisation des conflits de lois ?)' (1997) 41 *Arch. Phil. Droit*, pp. 207–214.

[2] Muir Watt H. 'Globalisation des marchés et économie politique du droit international privé', (2003) 47 *Arch. Phil. Droit*, pp. 243–262; Wai R. 'Transnational Liftoff and Juridical Touchdown: The Regulatory Function of Private International Law in an Era of Globalisation' (2002) *Colum. J. Transnat. L* 209.

[3] Through alternative choice of law rules or 'chains' of choice of law rules, pursuing result-selective considerations (for instance, the choice of law rule dealing with maintenance obligations, according to the Hague Convention of 2 October 1973 on the Recognition and Enforcement of Decisions Relating to Maintenance Obligations), or choice of law rules of a unilateral nature (such as Article 310 of the French Civil Code, often presented as a means to guarantee a right to divorce under French law to French citizens and French residents, divorce being considered as an inalienable right in the modern French society).

comes to contract law, the regulatory function of the choice of law rule applying to international contracts is a more recent issue.[4] In the European Union, a particularly topical debate deals with the use of choice of law rules as a tool of integration of the European Market.[5] In other words, is the choice of law rule able to have any influence on the creation of an open space where goods, capital, persons and services could freely flow?

The question is undoubtedly a vital one for the conflict of laws in Europe. The very existence of conflict of laws implies legislative diversity. But legislative diversity is often pictured as an impediment to the creation of the internal market. Therefore, it is only if conflict of laws accept the challenge of offering an efficient (meaning aimed at the creation of the internal market) instrument of co-ordination of the various legislation co-existing in the EU that harmonization, or even unification, will be avoided and thus conflict of laws preserved. Obviously, there lies another important issue, not for the conflicts of laws, but for the EU itself. At present, the EU has to deal with a dominant trend of hostility, and even strong resistance, towards harmonization. Member States, relaying public opinion, want to protect their juridical identity and legislative specificities. The intense debate and often hostile reactions raised by the project of creating a European code of contracts[6] is only one example,

---

4 Conflict of laws in the field of contracts have long been using result-selective rules (in the Rome Convention, choice of law rules are used, for instance, on the matter of formal conditions of the contract), but only to protect private interests, and not to impose public policy concerns.

5 Muir Watt H. 'The Challenge of Market Integration for European Conflicts Theory', in Hartkamp A. et al. (eds), *Towards a European Civil Code* (2004, Kluwer), p. 191; 'Laws & economics: quel apport pour le droit international privé', *in Le contrat au début du XXI° siècle, Etudes offertes à Jacques Ghestin* (2001, Paris, LGDJ), p. 685 at n°11, p. 698; Radicati di Brozolo L.G. 'L'influence sur les conflits de lois des principes de droit communautaire en matière de liberté de circulation' (1993) *Rev. Crit. DIP*, p. 401. The debate is sustained by the new competences on IPL matters, awarded to the EU following the Amsterdam Treaty; on which see: Kohler Ch. 'Interrogations sur les sources du droit international privé européen après le Traité d'Amsterdam' (1999) *Rev. Crit. DIP*, p. 1.

6 In France, the debate has been particularly intense on the desirability of such a Code. For some reactions, of either approbation or on the contrary strong opposition, see: Société de législation comparée *Pensée juridique française et harmonisation européenne du droit* (2003, coll. Droit privé comparé et européen, Paris); Prieto C. 'Une culture contractuelle commune en Europe', in Prieto C. *Regards croisés sur les principes du droit européen des contrats et sur le droit français* (2003, Aix en Provence, PUAM), p. 17 et seq.; Racine J.B. 'Pourquoi unifier le droit des contrats en Europe', (2002) Era-Forum (Académie de droit européen de Trèves), n°2; Fauvarque-Cosson B. 'Droit européen des contrats: première réactions au plan d'action de la Commission' (2003) *Dalloz Chr.* 1171; 'Faut-il un Code civil européen?' (2002) *Rev. Trim. Dr. civ.*, p. 463 et seq.; Jamin Ch. et Mazeaud D. (eds) *L'harmonisation du droit*

among many, of this trend. It is then urgent to find a way not only to authorize Member State legislation to co-exist harmoniously, while removing impediments to the creation of the internal market (horizontal co-ordination), but also to reach an efficient allocation of jurisdiction between Member States and the Community (vertical co-ordination). And conflict of laws, traditionally devoted to the allocation of international jurisdiction, might just be the right tool to achieve both objectives.

This discussion about the regulatory function of the internal market conflict of laws relating to contracts can usefully focus on contracts for services. Not even mentioning the impressive quantity of contracts for services developing in a market where the service industry is prominent,[7] contracts for services offer interesting issues about the pertinence of solutions that are pictured more and more as European principles. The passionate debate drawn by the Draft Directive on services in the internal market,[8] not only in Member States,[9] but

---

des contrats en Europe (2001, Paris, Economica); Witz Cl. 'Plaidoyer pour un code européen des obligations' (2000) *Dalloz Chr.* p.79; Cornu G. 'Un code civil n'est pas un instrument communautaire' (2002) *Dalloz Chr.* 351; Lequette Y. 'Quelques remarques à propos du projet de code civil européen de M. von Bar' (2002) *Dalloz Chr.* 2202. Outside France, see: Legrand P. 'Sens et non-sens d'un Code civil européen' (1996) *Rev. Int. Dr. Comp.* p. 779; Basedow J. 'Un droit commun des contrats pour le marché commun' (1998) *Rev. Int. Dr. Comp.* p. 7.

[7] Service industry represents 69.4% GDP in the internal market (Source Wikipedia at: http://fr.wikipedia.org/wiki/economie_de_l'Union-europenne). It includes activities of an industrial character, of a commercial character, activities of craftsmen and activities of the professions, following the much discussed Draft Directive on services in the internal market (COM/2004/0002 final) where services are defined, according to Article 4 of the Proposal, as 'any self employed economic activity, as referred to in Article 50 of the Treaty, consisting in the provision of a service for consideration'. And Article 50 of the Treaty points out 'activities for remuneration that are not governed by the provisions relating to freedom of movement of goods, capital or persons'. For a general presentation of the various patterns of service contracts in the EU, see: Loos M.B.M. 'Service contracts', in *Towards a European Civil Code*, above n. 5 at 571.

[8] COM/2004/0002 final; and the amended Proposal of the Commission: COM/2006/160 final. On the content of the Draft Directive, see Micklitz H. 'Regulatory Strategies on Services Contracts in EC Law', ch. 2 in this volume. The directive was finally adopted under an amended version, limiting the scope of the home country principle: Directive 2006/123/EC of the European Parliament and of the Council of 12 december 2006 on services in the internal market, Official Journal L 376 27 December 2006.

[9] Heuzé V. 'De la compétence de la loi d'origine en matière contractuelle ou l'anti-droit européen', in *Le droit international privé : esprit et méthodes, Mélanges en l'honneur de Paul Lagarde* (2005, Paris, Dalloz Chr.), p. 396; Garabiol-Furet M.-D. 'Playdoyer pour le principe d'origine' (2006) 495 *Rev. du Marché Commun et de l'UE*, p. 82.

also within the Community institutional framework,[10] reveals that 'principles', such as the home country principle, are far from being uncontested. Moreover, the institutional and scholarly discussion on Services of General Economic Interest (SGEIs)[11] acknowledges that solutions often still need to be found. In such a context, the idea, discussed by the 'services' group, of focusing on utilities is seductive. However, from the conflict of law point of view, it is questionable whether the general principles of solution defined for services contracts should not apply there. This does not mean that all contracts for services always raise similar issues. Undoubtedly, some services, considering their content, might require specific treatment.[12] But utilities markets, the liberalization of which is not yet totally achieved, do not provide enough conflict of law tools to construct an internal market conflict of laws analysis. Our perspective should then be to adopt a global approach of contracts for services, in order to draw, afterwards, some conclusions as to utilities.

In European contract law, two sets of rules co-exist,[13] which present very different features when considering conflict of laws. Some rules are properly 'offered' to private parties to help them organize their contractual relationship. These rules are usually qualified as 'facilitative'. Others are the expression of the will of States to 'intervene' in the contractual relationship, in order to impose certain solutions on the parties. These rules, generally pictured as mandatory, are regulatory tools, be they aimed at addressing market failures (economic regulation) or at protecting specific interests (social regulation). But they belong, although sometimes referred to as semi-public rules, to

---

[10] With the strong opposition of the Parliament, which has – at 1st reading – reduced the scope of the Directive and excluded the country of origin principle to replace it by the 'freedom to provide services' (and see text cited in n. 8).

[11] On which see: Commission Green Paper of 21 May 2003 on services of general interest COM (2003) 270 final Official Journal C 76 25.03.2004; Communication from the Commission to the European Parliament, the Council, the European Economic and Social Committee and the Committee of the Regions of 12 May 2004 entitled 'White Paper on services of general interest' COM (2004) 374 final; Communication from the Commission of 26 April 2006 implementing the Community Lisbon Programme: Social Services of General Interest in the European Union, COM (2006) 177 final. For some reactions, see: UK Parliament, 'Services of general interest' available at: www.publications.parliament.uk/pa/cm200405/; European Association of Craft, Small and Medium-sized Enterprises (UEAPME) 'Protecting services of general interest cannot compromise efficiency', available at www.ueapme.com/docs/press_releases/pr_2005.

[12] For example, services the content of which is juridical; see n. 83.

[13] Grundmann S. 'The Structure of European Contract Law' (2001) 9 *Eur. Rev. Priv. L.* 505, 512–516; Hesselink M. 'The Structure of the New European Private Law', in Moréteau O. and Vanderlinden J. (eds), *La structure des systèmes juridiques* (2003, Bruxelles, Bruyant), pp. 351–373, at 354.

private law,[14] and thus are in the sphere of conflict of laws.[15] For our concern, the important point is that, usually, only regulatory law is internationally mandatory. Consequently, a possible methodology consists in distinguishing, when considering the regulatory function of choice of law rules, between conflicts of facilitative rules and conflicts of internationally mandatory rules. Of course, such an approach is questionable, as choice of law rules usually deal with private law as a whole: when the contract law of a State is designated as the applicable law, both its facilitative rules and its regulatory (that is mandatory) rules apply. But whereas no other State will normally intend to impose the application of its own facilitative rules, one or several other States could try to 'grasp' the cross-border contract, ruled by a foreign law, to subject it to its own regulatory law.

Conflict of regulatory laws, resulting from this confrontation, certainly proposes the most relevant issues when considering the creation of the internal market. Is it to say that conflict of facilitative rules does not deserve any attention? Recent scholarship proves the contrary. This is why we shall try, in part I, to address the interesting issue of the regulatory aspects, for the creation of the internal market, of the resolution of conflict of facilitative rules, before analysing, in part II, how and to what extent rules of conflicts could endorse a regulatory function in conflicts of internationally mandatory rules. As a conclusion, we shall try to reconcile both approaches in terms of facilitative and mandatory rules, to consider whether one given choice of law rule provides a global solution to the question of the allocation of jurisdiction in the European Union. We shall try, moreover, to draw some observations on utilities.

PART I – CONFLICTS OF FACILITATIVE RULES: A REGULATORY STAKE?

Is the existence of divergence between Member States' facilitative rules, applying to services contracts, an impediment to the creation of the internal market? If the answer is a positive one, then either facilitative contract law should be harmonized, and even unified, or the choice of law rule applying to cross-border contracts should remedy the impediment.[16] Notwithstanding the

---

14 Grundmann, above n. 13; Hesselink above n. 13; Mayer P. 'Les lois de police étrangères' (1981) *Journal du Droit International*, p. 277.

15 Because, contrary to public law, their scope is not purely territorial, but usually extraterritorial.

16 The question is particularly topical in the field of contracts for services where no international harmonization of substantial laws exists, contrary to the situation in the

project of creating a European code of contract law,[17] which seems to acknowledge the idea that diverging facilitative rules obstruct the functioning of the internal market,[18] the actual positive position of the EU on the question is that such divergence does not hinder the free flow of services within the internal market.[19] This appreciation has been clearly set by the ECJ in the *Alsthom* case,[20] on the main argument that contracting parties can generally choose the law applying to their contract, and thus may avoid the application of a law, the content of which would obstruct the free movement of services. It is because parties can escape facilitative rules, through choice of law, that these rules avoid scrutiny under fundamental market freedoms.[21] And actually, in Europe, party autonomy is widely admitted. Article 3 of the Rome Convention states that the contract is to be governed by the law chosen by the parties, whereas most directives relating to contracts for services establish party choice.[22] What is interesting, considering that party autonomy explains why facilitative rules divergence does not obstruct the free flow of services, is to consider why party autonomy is so generally admitted with regard to these rules. One convincing explanation lies in the very nature of facilitative rules, usually pictured as neutral. They are rules that States propose to parties for their own good (reduction of transaction costs), having no reason of public interest to intervene; and it is because States have no public interest in the

---

field of sales contracts, where the Vienna Convention provides substantial rules applying to international sales of goods.

17 Communication from the Commission to the Council and the European Parliament on European contract law, 2001/C255/01; and Communication from the Commission to the Council and the European Parliament: a more Coherent European Contract law, an Action Plan, COM (2003) 68 final.

18 Allegedly because of increased transaction costs, resulting from the need to gather information on the content of the applicable law, when foreign, which could result in a competitive disadvantage. See: Communication 2001/C255/01, § 23 and 31; Communication 2003, at n°34; but against this see Heuzé, above n. 9 at 399.

19 Wilderspin M. and Lewis X. 'Les relations entre le droit communautaire et les règles de conflits de lois des Etats Membres' (2002) *Rev. Crit. DIP*, pp. 1 *et seq.* esp. pp. 24 *et seq.*

20 ECJ, *Alsthom Atlantique*, 24 Jan 1991, C-339/89 *Rec.* 1991 I-107.

21 Muir Watt H. 'L'entrave à la prestation transfrontière de services, Réflexions sur l'impact des libertés économiques sur le droit international privé des Etats Membres', *in Droit et Actualité, Etudes offertes à Jacques Béguin* (2005, Paris, LexisNexis), pp. 545–565, at n°21.

22 For instance: Article 3(3) of the Directive 2000/31/EC of 8 June 2000 on certain legal aspects of information society services, in particular electronic commerce (e-commerce; OJ L 178 17/07/2000, p. 1); Draft Directive on Services above n. 7); and implicit. Article 6.2 of the Directive 93/13/EEC of 5 April 1993 on unfair terms (OJ L 095, 21/04/1993, p. 29), Article 12.2 of the Directive 97/7/EC on the protection of consumers in respect of distance contracts (OJ L 144, 04/06/1997, p. 19).

application of their own facilitative rules that they give parties the freedom to escape this application.[23] But what if facilitative rules were to be vested with regulatory functions – as suggested in the present project? In that case, should party choice be maintained, considering the issue of creation of the internal market (see (1) below)? Furthermore, could regulatory concerns of default rules explain that, in certain circumstances and when concerning certain contracts for services, predefined connecting factors substitute for party choice (see (2) below)?

(1) Is Party Choice the Adequate Choice of Law Rule if Facilitative Rules of Contract Law Endorse a Regulatory Function?

The neutrality of facilitative rules, though often presented as a paradigm, has convincingly been challenged.[24] Facilitative contract law could, in reality, hide considerations of a regulatory or interventionist nature. Without going in depth into this analysis, which refers to the regulatory function of substantial private law, it is possible to draw consequences as to the conflict of laws. Because, if the neutrality of facilitative rules explains both the right for the parties to choose the law applying to their contract, and the indifference of the EU towards the existence of diverging legislation (given that it does not impede the free movement of services), then the regulatory function of these rules might just as well challenge both affirmations.[25] Therefore, the choice of law rule dealing with conflicts of 'facilitative' rules within the EU should be designed so that it would allocate legislative jurisdiction in such a way that the creation of the internal market would not be impeded. What should be the content of such a choice of law rule?

In a series of interesting papers,[26] H. Muir Watt comes up with the proposition that party choice could actually be the right choice of law rule, considering the objective of market integration in Europe.[27] The starting point of

---

23 Muir Watt H. 'Concurrence d'ordres juridiques et conflits de lois de droit privé', in *Le droit international privé: esprit et méthodes, Mélanges en l'honneur de Paul Lagarde* (2005, Paris, Dalloz Chr.), pp. 616–633, at n°12.

24 Collins H. 'Regulating contract law', in C. Parker, J. Braithwaite, C. Scott, N. Lacey (eds), *Regulating law* (2003, Oxford, Oxford University Press), p. 23.

25 Muir Watt H., above n. 23.

26 Ibid.; see also: Muir Watt, above n. 5 at 201–202; and 'Choice of law in integrated and interconnected markets: a matter of political economy' (2003) 9 *Colum. Journ. Eur. Law* 383.

27 See, on the positive influence of party choice on the functioning of a common market of services: Radicati di Brozolo L.G., above n. 5 at 411; and also: Grundmann S. 'Internal Market Conflicts of Laws From Traditional Conflicts of Laws to an Integrated Two Level Order', in Fuchs A., Muir Watt H., Pataut E. *Les conflits de lois*

these papers is that party choice constitutes the 'metaphoric expression of the mobility' of market actors. Consequently, party choice promotes competition between legal systems: when legal systems, produced by States in a monopolistic position, do not fulfil the preferences of their constituents, the latter can exit through choice of law and opt out for a legal system that better matches their expectations.[28] Such a competition is a powerful driving force on the path towards market integration in Europe.[29] But the link between legislative competition and market integration will be distinctly analysed, considering the nature of legal products involved in the competition.

When these legal products are facilitative laws, they can be pictured as homogeneous, in the sense that 'there is unlikely to be a significant variation in preferences as between market actors in different jurisdictions'.[30] In this case, it has been convincingly demonstrated that 'competition between jurisdictions should lead to some convergence of legal principles'.[31] In other words, not only does the autonomy principle not obstruct the free movement of services, but it furthermore leads to the approximation of national legislation, through some sort of 'spontaneous' or 'soft' harmonization process. Undoubtedly, there party choice is a useful tool for the creation of the internal market.

Consequences of legislative competition might differ if we admit, following our original proposition, that 'facilitative' contract law endorses a regulatory function. There, it is not certain that competition would lead to harmonization or convergence. Regulatory or 'interventionist' devices constitute heterogeneous products because market actors' expectations may vary.

---

et le système juridique communautaire (2004, Paris, Dalloz Chr.), p. 5, at p. 14, for whom: 'in areas where full party autonomy is realised already in traditional conflicts of laws...traditional conflicts of laws already dispose of the instruments needed for creating an internal market'.

[28] On the general theory of legislative competition, see for example: McCahery J. et al. (eds) *International Regulatory Competition and Coordination* (1996, Oxford, Clarendon Press); on the links between party autonomy and legislative competition: Muir Watt, above n. 23 at n°7; O'Hara E. A. 'Opting Out of Regulation: A Public Choice Analysis of Contractual Choice of Law' (2000) 53 *Vand. L. Rev.* 1551.

[29] Kerber W. 'Interjurisdictional Competition within the European Union' (2000) *Fordham Int'l Law Journ.* 217; Muir Watt, above n. 23 at n°2 on the contrary, deploring the 'anti-European' feature of legislative competition: Heuzé V. 'L'Europe désenchantée' (2005) *JCP Ed. G.* I. 157.

[30] Ogus A. 'Competition between legal systems: a contribution of economic analysis to comparative law' (1999) 48 *Intern. Comp. L. Quaterly* 405, at 410; See also Ogus A. 'The Regulation of Services and the Public/Private Divide', ch. 1 in this volume.

[31] Ogus A., above n. 30.

Thus, the competition between legal systems could lead to specialization,[32] instead of harmonization. As Anthony Ogus puts it very clearly, 'there may be some benefits to firms in establishing in jurisdictions [for our concerns, in choosing laws] with stricter regimes: the higher standards may generate technological improvements to processes which confer competitive advantages on the firms complying with them'.[33] However, competition can still favour market integration. Following W. Kerber,[34] we can admit that market integration is principally wanted because it is perceived as a means to fulfil the preferences of European market actors. This fulfilment will itself be more successful if a competitive system of jurisdiction is adopted in Europe, leading to competitive experimentation processes allowing a high flexibility of economic policies. In other words, competition improves national legal systems and economic policies, and consequently maximizes market actors' satisfaction, in accordance with the very aim of market integration. And party choice, because it promotes legislative competition, thus takes part in the European market integration. So the choice of law rule that is already implemented within the EU can be seen as a regulatory tool, if we agree to rethink its foundations: whereas party choice is usually justified by governments' absence of care about outcomes, it there draws its legitimacy from its ability to allow the selection of the most efficient contract law, considering parties' expectations.

Our conclusion being that party choice is, in any case, an adequate choice of law rule, considering the objective of creation of the internal market, a new question naturally arises: what about choice of law rules substituting predefined connecting factors for party choice?

(2) Do Choice of Law Rules, Relying on Predefined Connecting Factors, Endorse a Regulatory Function in the EU ?

To answer this question, it is necessary to propose a brief typology of choice of law rules applying to cross-border service contracts, in order to assess their potential regulatory function in the resolution of facilitative rules conflicts. But first of all, it is important to remind ourselves of the function of choice of law rule in the classical conflicts of laws theory, where connecting factors are normally designed to serve private parties' interests,[35] and thus mainly promote the solution that is the safer and the more foreseeable for the parties.

---

32 Muir Watt, above n. 23 at n°8; Ogus 'Competition between legal systems', above n. 30 at 415.

33 Ogus A. 'Competition between legal systems', p. 415.

34 Kerber W., above n. 29 at p. 249 et seq.

35 Mayer and Heuzé, above n. 1 at n°68.

Certainly, most choice of law rules that are currently being applied in the EU have been implemented according to this classical theory. But this should not prevent us from analysing whether or not a new foundation can be proposed – as was the case for the autonomy principle. Furthermore, the most recently implemented choice of law rules in EU directives might have already challenged the classical theory to consider the objective of creation of the internal market as a guideline.[36]

Non-voluntary connecting factors have been adopted in choice of law rules relating to contracts for services, either to deal with the absence of choice of law by parties, or because choice of law was properly excluded. When parties have not chosen the law ruling the contract, Article 4 of the Rome Convention states that the applicable law should be the law of the country with which the contract is most closely connected, the contract being presumed to be most closely connected with the country where the party whose performance is characteristic of the contract has his habitual residence. To make it simple, the law of the supplier should normally apply. In a sense, such a rule can be compared with the most discussed one that was contained in Article 16 of the First Draft Directive (2004) on services – and finally deleted from the final text of the Directive[37] – according to which suppliers should be subjected to the law of their home country, with regards to, notably, contract rules (except when there was a party choice, according to Article 17 of the Draft Directive). But there might be a fundamental difference between the two rules, as to their foundations. Whereas Article 4 of the Rome Convention is obviously justified by considerations of a purely private and practical nature, even in its most modern reading,[38] Article 16 of the First Draft Directive was clearly meant to promote market integration,[39] though it was not clear whether the country of

---

36 But see, considering that (at least up until 1993) the choice of law rules implemented in the sectoral directives relating to services did not specifically promote the free flow of services: Radicati du Brozolo, above n. 5 at 408.

37 The country of origin principle, originally applying under Article 16 of the Draft Directive, has been replaced in the final text by the 'freedom to provide services', a provision expressly prohibiting those requirements, imposed by the State in which the service is provided, which could constitute an impediment to the free flow of services.

38 The project of converting the Convention into an EU Regulation (*Proposal for a Regulation of the European Parliament and of the Council on the law applicable to contractual obligations (Rome I)*, COM (2005) 650 final) has been the occasion for a re-reading of the Convention, according to Community features (see, for example, p. 77, the question of the application of Community mandatory rules). However, it does not seem that objectives, other than purely private ones, have been taken into account in the drafting of the Regulation (*Green Paper on the Conversion of the Rome Convention into a Community Instrument*, COM (2002) 654 final, p. 10 on 'the objectives of the rules concerning conflicts of laws as regards contracts').

39 See in particular, recitals 37 and 40.

origin principle should apply to facilitative rules.[40] At this point, however, it is difficult to explain convincingly how the application of the facilitative rules of the law of the supplier could promote the creation of the internal market. Given that parties are offered the option to choose the law of the contract, the subsidiary solution cannot in any way – whatever might be its content – obstruct or promote the free movement of services. Thus, the choice of the law of the supplier can only be based on practical arguments, following the reasoning of the Rome Convention. Further discussion on the regulatory function of the home country principle is justified only when concerning internationally mandatory rules.[41]

Another choice of law rule, applying in the absence of party choice, is related to contracts for services involving consumers. Article 5 of the Rome Convention provides that, when the formation of the contract is in a way connected with the country where the consumer has his residence,[42] the contract is governed by the law of that country. Obviously, this rule has a regulatory function: it is meant to protect consumers.[43] One might wonder, however, about the link between consumer protection and the creation of the internal market. Let us only remark that the protection of consumers is undoubtedly a fundamental feature of the internal market, and that, in the present context, the application of the consumer's residence facilitative law does not hinder, for the reasons already mentioned, the creation of the market. Conciliation of objectives (consumers' protection/market integration) does not raise specific issues.

More interesting could be, for our purpose, the choice of law rules that deliberately exclude party choice, to adopt a given non-voluntary connecting factor. Whereas the consecration of party autonomy has often been explained by governments' lack of interest in private litigation outcomes, the imposition of a rigid connecting factor might, on the contrary, reveal a public objective in the resolution of the conflict of laws.[44] One particularly topical example is to be drawn from the conflicts of laws system implemented in the EU insurance directives.[45] Insurance directives do not totally preclude choice of law, but

40 Nothing seemed to exclude facilitative rules from the scope of the principle; but if the principle is meant to suppress hindrances to the free movement of services, which is not impeded by facilitative rules according to the ECJ, then Member States should be able to dismiss the principle in regard to facilitative rules to apply Article 4 of the Rome Convention, namely the law of the supplier!

41 On which, see Part II of this chapter.

42 Through advertising, signature or receipt of an order.

43 On this objective, see Green Paper on the Conversion of the Rome Convention, above n. 38.

44 For such opinion, see for example Muir Watt, above n. 23 at n°17.

45 Second Council Directive 88/357/EEC of 22 June 1988 concerning direct

they limit its use to a very specific hypothesis.[46] In most situations, the law applying to an insurance contract is the law of the Member State in which the risk is situated.[47] Is there a regulatory explanation to this rule, beyond the purely private interests' concerns? An affirmative answer can be upheld, by introducing data that has not been, so far, dealt with in this chapter: the competitive disadvantage borne by suppliers entering purely domestic contracts, in contrast to suppliers operating at a transnational level within the EU.[48] In the present system of conflict of laws in contracts, party choice is only available in cross-border contracts; hence, while foreign suppliers contracting on a given national market normally have an option as to the law applying to their contract (which could result in a competitive advantage if facilitative rules end up being regulatory[49]), domestic suppliers are compelled to the application of the law of the market in which they operate. The admission of party choice is therefore a source of competitive disadvantage for domestic suppliers. And the same conclusion is to be reached when considering the application of the law of the supplier: if each supplier operates on national markets according to his own law, some suppliers, considering the diversity of legislation, suffer legal constraints that, on the same market, others are free of. In this context, applying the law of the market in which suppliers compete – the law of the market in which the risk is situated in the insurance case – seems to provide a solution to the competitive disadvantage resulting from legislative diversity. The choice of law rule, there, serves the movement of insurance services, by imposing an equivalent burden on all competing suppliers.[50] Therefore, such a rule takes part in the creation of the internal market.

Of course, an option could be to extend party choice even to purely domestic contracts. In an integrated market where legislative diversity would be preserved, such a solution would make sense, as it would truly promote competition between Member States.[51] But party choice may not be the 'holy

---

insurance other than life insurance (OJ L 172, 04/07/1988, p. 1); Directive 2002/83/EC of 5 November 2002 concerning life insurance (OJ L 345, 19/12/2002, p. 1).

46 Article 7.1 of Directive 88/357 (non-life insurance) and Article 32 of Directive 2002/83/EC (life insurance).

47 On the exceptions to this rule, 'so strict that one can barely imagine a single hypothesis of practical application' of these exceptions, see Heuzé V. 'le droit des assurances', in Fuchs, Muir Watt and Pataut, above n. 27 at 249.

48 Actually, the choice of law rule in the insurance directives is also explained by consumers' protection considerations; see Radicati du Brozolo, above n. 5 at 413; less positive: see Heuzé, above n. 47 at 246–247.

49 On which, see p. 77.

50 Heuzé, above n. 47 at 247; on the contrary, judging that this choice of law rule, because it excludes party choice, is in itself a barrier to the free flow, and should therefore be disqualified by the ECJ: Radicati du Brozolo, above n. 5 at 403.

51 See Kerber, above n. 29 at 240–242.

grail' to save the internal market. Indeed, party choice efficiency can only be reached in the absence of market failures. Such market failures exist, and it is (usually) to address these failures that Member States enact regulatory or 'interventionist' laws. So, in a sense, party choice is indissociable from conflicts of regulatory laws, the resolution of which constitutes the main challenge for conflict of laws in the EU.

PART II – CONFLICTS OF INTERVENTIONIST LAWS: A REGULATORY CHALLENGE

Contract law includes, in European countries, an important regulatory part.[52] The reason for this intrusion of concerns of a political nature in private law is to be sought either in economic causes, when market failures are to be addressed, or in distributionist or even paternalistic considerations, when a contracting party is to be protected because that party might, for reasons of insufficient bargaining power or insufficient rationality, enter into an unfair contract.[53] The feature of such interventionist laws, in conflict of laws, is that they are usually imposed as internationally mandatory rules. Because these rules express concerns of public good, States are not ready to accept that parties escape their application through choice of law. Hence, they unilaterally define the scope of their mandatory rules, so that the latter will apply, whatever may be the law of the contract according to the choice of law rule implemented. But, as each State implements its own internationally mandatory rules, cross-border relationships are exposed to be 'grasped' several times, and consequently subjected to 'over-regulation'. This, of course, is a subject of concern in the EU:

> The differences in mandatory rules are the real obstacles to the proper functioning of the Common Market …; this leads to the suggestion that if the functioning of the Common Market must be enhanced, it is not the general rules of non-mandatory contract law that should be harmonised or unified, but rather regulation, ie mandatory rules of general contract law and especially of special contract law. Those seem to be the true impediments to the Common Market.[54]

Actually, Community legislation does not ignore regulation; on the contrary, it has implemented its own regulatory devices, concerning competition law, or

---

52 See above nn. 13 and 14.

53 Ogus A. and Faure M. *Economie du droit: le cas français* (2002, Paris, Panthéon-Assas, LGDJ), p. 143 et seq.

54 Hesselink, above n. 13 at 360.

consumer protection, for instance. So there are in fact two patterns of regulation: on the Community level, and on the national level. As a result, EU conflict of laws is facing a double challenge. Firstly, the scope of Community regulation must be defined (see (1) below); and secondly, Member State regulatory laws must be co-ordinated in order to avoid over-regulation, which hinders the creation of the internal market (see (2) below).

(1) Defining the Scope of Community Regulation

This gives rise to distinct issues, whether the application of such regulation is viewed as compared to Member State regulation, or *vis-à-vis* the law of third States. The co-ordination of Member State regulation and EU regulation does not, in fact, involve the theory of the conflict of laws, because of the hierarchy between these regulations. Co-ordination is, on the one hand, achieved through harmonization, when the EU sets standards of regulation and imposes them upon Member States by means of secondary law. EU standards become part of the laws of Member States, and apply as such. Co-ordination, on the other hand, may be carried out by means of allocation of regulatory authority, either to the Community, or to the Member States, considering *the matter* of regulation, but not the spatial location of the relationship subjected to the ruling. This is the case in competition law.[55]

Conflicts of laws thus appear when considering the application of EU regulation *vis-à-vis* the law of third States. Here, their function is to guarantee that Community regulation might apply whenever there is a political justification to this application. The adequate technique generally relies on *lois de police*, or internationally mandatory rules. The use of plain, bilateral choice of law rules is, on the contrary, disputed. Competition law offers a good example for the terms of the discussion. In the EU,[56] Community competition law applies whenever the anti-competitive effects of a contract are perceived in the Community legal order.[57] The 'law of the effects' rule is undoubtedly a

---

55 Contracts for services, when constituting an abuse by the undertaking of a dominant position, fall under the provisions of Article 82 of the EC Treaty. However, Community law only controls abuses that substantially affect trade between Member States, whereas abuses affecting national markets are left to the jurisdiction of Member State provisions (which actually also deal with abuses affecting trade between Member States). Such a rule, though allocating jurisdiction in so far as it delimits the respective scopes of Community and Member States legislation, is not of the same nature as traditional choice of law rules in IPL.

56 The same rule actually applies in the US: *Hartford Fire Ins Co v California*, 113 S Ct 2891 (1993).

57 *Woodpulp* Case, 27 Sept 1988, 89/85 [1988] ECR 5193, ECJ.

regulatory device of contract law,[58] because it is meant to preserve a state of free competition in the common market, that could be challenged by contracts for services, the content of which induces anti-competitive effects. However, the nature of the 'law of the effects' rule has been disputed. Whereas most scholars picture this rule as a *loi de police*,[59] others have considered that such a rule can be 'bilateralized' in order to shape a choice of law rule, according to which the law applicable to an abuse by the undertaking of a dominant position is the law of the country where the anti-competitive effects of such abuse spread out.[60] It seems that the dominant position is more convincing. EU competition law directly applies whenever competition in the internal market is challenged by a contract, whatever the law actually ruling the contract might be. So we have a 'substantial' law – prohibition of the abuse – which defines its own scope of application – when the competition in the internal market is affected.

The technique of internationally mandatory rules, borrowed from Member States, is however in use elsewhere in the common market. Community regulation pursues objectives that should not be given up mainly because the law of a third State is ruling the contract. This is the case, in particular, for the protection of European consumers. Several sectoral directives lay down that the choice of the law of a third State as the law of the contract should not result in depriving the consumer of the protection granted by Community regulation[61] if the contract has close connection with the EU territory. Beyond the sectoral approach, the introduction of such Community *loi de police* in favour of consumers in the general provisions of the Rome Convention is at present debated, in the context of the conversion of the Convention into a regulation.[62] Hitherto, the application of Community standards is not guaranteed as such by the Rome Convention. Article 5(2) of the Convention states only that 'a choice

---

58 Grundmann, above n. 13 at 511.

59 Idot L. 'Les conflits de lois en droit de la concurrence' (1995) *Journal du droit international*, p. 321, at 323; see also CCI *Competition and Arbitration Law*, 'Rapport introductif' (1993, Paris, CCI), publ. 480/3, at n°10.

60 Toubiana A. *Le domaine de la loi du contrat en droit international privé. Contrats internationaux et dirigisme étatique* (1972, Paris, Dalloz Chr.), biblio. DIP, vol. XIV, spéc. n° 286.

61 Article 6.2 of the directive on unfair terms, Article 12 of the Directive 97/7/EC of 20 May 1997 on the protection of consumers in respect of distance contracts (both quoted above in n. 22); see also: Article 12.2 of the Directive 2002/65/EC of 23 Sept 2002 on distance sales of financial services (OJ L 271, 9 Oct 2002, p. 16).

62 *Green Paper on the Conversion of the Rome Convention*, above n. 38 at p. 18. The Regulation 'Rome I' has since been adopted: Regulation (EC) n°593/2008 of the European Parliament and of the Council of 17 June 2008 on the law applicable to contractual obligation (OJ L 4.7.2008, pp. 6–16).

of law made by the parties shall not have the result of depriving the consumer of the protection afforded to him by mandatory rules of the law of the country in which he has his habitual residence'. Of course, Community minimum standards are normally conveyed by Member State laws. Hence any consumer whose residence is located in the EU territory should be protected by Community minimum standards. But two considerations limit the scope of this protection. On the one hand, it has been seen that Article 5 of the Rome Convention does not apply to all contracts concluded by consumers.[63] And on the other, it is questionable, as regards recent case law in European countries,[64] whether the laws protecting consumers can apply as part of internationally mandatory rules falling under the provisions of Article 7 of the Rome Convention.[65] Consequently, the application of Community regulation in favour of European consumers might not be sufficiently guaranteed, because of 'holes' in the net of protection.[66] This is why the inclusion, in the future Regulation Rome I, of a provision designed to ensure the application of Community minimum standards regarding the protection of consumers, was debated.[67] Finally, this provision has not been included, as such, in the Regulation Rome I adopted on 17 June 2008.

Conflict of laws can thus, especially through the methodology of internationally mandatory rules, guarantee the fulfilment of objectives endorsed by Community regulatory law, such as the protection of consumers or the preservation of competition in the market, when the application of the law of a third State to the contract could result in ruining such objectives.

---

63 See Ogus A. 'The Regulation of Services and the Public–Private Divide', ch. 1 in this volume.

64 The French Cour de Cassation has decided that some of the rules protecting consumers are mandatory within the meaning of Article 7 of the Rome Convention (Civ.1, 10 July 2001, Bull. I, n°210) while the German BGH has excluded the application of the protective German law for consumers as part of mandatory rules of the forum (19 March 1997, *Gran Canaria*, Rev. Crit. DIP, 1998, p. 610, note P. Lagarde).

65 According to which 'when applying under this Convention the law of a country, effect may be given to the mandatory rules of the law of another country with which the situation has a close connection, if and in so far as, under the law of the latter country, those rules must be applied whatever the law applicable to the contract. In considering whether to give effect to these mandatory rules, regard shall be had to their nature and purpose and to the consequences of their application or non-application'.

66 On this problem, see for example: Lagarde P. 'Heurts et malheurs de la protection internationale du consommateur dans l'Union européenne', *Le contrat au début du XXI° siècle, Etudes offertes à J. Ghestin* (2001, Paris, LGDJ), 511–525.

67 See, approving the proposition: Pataut E. 'Lois de police et ordre juridique communautaire', in Fuchs, Muir Watt and Pataut, above n. 27 at 140.

(2) The Most Important Challenge, for the Conflict of Laws in the EU, is Certainly the Co-ordination of Member State Regulation

When they are, as they generally are, internationally mandatory, these 'interventionist' rules can restrict the access of suppliers to the market, and therefore hinder the free flow of services. The negative effects of Member State internationally mandatory rules on the movement of services, and thus on the objective of creation of the internal market, have been picked out both by scholarship[68] and Community case law.[69] Potentially, a cross-border contract can be subjected to the regulatory laws of at least two Member States, the country where the supplier has his residence, and the country where the service is delivered. The risk that one or more regulatory devices apply to a contract, otherwise subjected to a given law designated according to the choice of law rule, is all the more likely because Article 7 of the Rome Convention authorizes the *forum*, not only to apply its own mandatory rules, but also to apply the internationally mandatory rules of any other State claiming jurisdiction over the contractual relationship. How, then, can over-regulation be avoided?

A first option is to substitute Community regulation for diverging Member State regulation, so that, all regulation being the same in content, suppliers will be subjected to similar constraints wherever they conduct their business. Harmonization, which deals almost exclusively with rules that are internationally enforced,[70] is apparently dedicated to such an objective of suppression of diverging Member States' regulation. And it has been observed that almost all the rules that are internationally enforced are harmonized, today, in the EU.[71] However, two problems arise in regard to harmonization of regulatory law. Firstly, it is a fact that harmonization – considering its present approach in the EU – does not suppress all divergences between Member State internationally mandatory rules. As the Community often imposes only minimum standards upon Member States,[72] the latter can still adopt more stringent national laws. Minimal harmonization explicitly allows Member States' regulation to differ from Community regulation. And if so, one might wonder

---

68 Muir Watt, above n. 21; Grundmann, above n. 13 at 515; Hesselink, above n. 13 at 361.

69 ECJ, 25 July 1991, *Sager*, C-76/90 [1991] ECR I-04221; 10 May 1995, *Alpine Investments*, C-384/93, [1995] ECR 1995 I-1141.

70 Grundmann, above n. 13 at 517.

71 Ibid.

72 However, even when harmonization is 'complete', the use of directives leads to national legislation that is not identical, and may be differently interpreted by national courts.

whether harmonization is meant to resolve the question of conflicting internationally mandatory rules. That could only be if Member States were denied the right to apply their own law – when more stringent – to intra-community contracts,[73] with the curious result that, in harmonized areas (at least in areas harmonized on a minimum basis), the substantial law of Member States would in reality be divided into two bodies of rules; one, relaying the EU minimum standards, applying to intra-community contracts,[74] the other – more stringent – applying only to 'really' international contracts and to purely domestic contracts. Such 'reverse' discrimination between domestic and 'Community' suppliers is difficult to admit.[75] But if minimum harmonization does not prevent conflicts of regulatory laws, by imposing a given standard of regulation upon Member States, what is it meant for? This question leads to our second issue, on the desirability of harmonization of Member States' regulatory laws. Scholarship has expressed the idea that regulation could be more efficient when enacted at a national level, because States are, more than the Community, exposed to market pressure.[76] In particular, the competition between States, as a result of a decentralized process of regulation, is pictured as a powerful incentive for States to improve legal products in order to meet the expectations of market actors.[77] Then, harmonization at Community level should only be devoted to dealing with the risk of under-regulation (race to the bottom) that might result from such competition.[78] Minimal harmonization, in this context, is not a means to suppress conflicts of regulatory laws, but only to 'supervise' Member States' regulation in order to avoid the race to the bottom.

But if the conflict of laws cannot – and must not – be excluded by means of harmonization, it is then necessary to seek co-ordination of regulatory laws, that is, for a system allowing the coherent allocation of regulatory authority between Member States. What is needed is a choice of law rule that could organize such an allocation in a way consistent with the objective of integration of the internal market, and at the same time preserve the substantial objectives implemented by internationally mandatory rules.

---

73 In this sense: Grundmann, above n. 13 at 518; and, above n. 27 at p. 22 et seq.

74 Actually, degrees could be admitted, for example when the home country and the host country adopt equivalent rules more stringent than Community standards that could then apply instead of Community minimum standards.

75 The aim would be, then, to compel in any case Member States to adopt only the minimum standards, in order to avoid the creation of a competitive disadvantage for domestic suppliers. Such a method would give substance to the idea, often expressed, that the EU is using more and more 'incentives' that, though non-mandatory by nature, do bind States in practice.

76 Grundmann, above n. 13 at 522.

77 Kerber, above n. 29.

78 Grundmann, above n. 13 at 424; Kerber, above n. 29 at 242.

A preliminary observation to be made, at this point, is that services raise specific issues, when considering the allocation of regulatory authority.[79] It has been demonstrated that the principles worked out as regards products, under *Cassis de Dijon* and *Keck*, cannot apply, as such, to services.[80] The construction made up for products relies on territorial 'compartments': products, subjected to the rules of the country of origin when concerning technical standards, must not be subjected to additional regulatory requirements in the host country, because that would result in a double charge, impeding the free flow of goods.[81] Therefore, mutual recognition must apply: products legally released in their country of origin may freely circulate in all Member States. But this does not mean that products are totally immune from the regulation of the host country. In *Keck*, it has been stated that marketing techniques (how to sell the product) can be ruled by the laws of the State where the product is sold, because this type of ruling does not hinder the access to the market. So the product, subjected at the time of its release to home country requirements as to technical standards, must – once it has entered the market of the host country which cannot subject this entrance to its own regulation on technical standards – submit to local rules regarding selling arrangements.[82] The home country regulation and the host country regulation cannot apply simultaneously, but they apply successively. However, such a scheme does not fit in with services,[83] because of the 'transfrontier nature of the relationship between the supplier and the client'.[84] Whereas the product can be located, and therefore subjected to the law of the place of location, or as in *Keck* to consecutive laws if displaced, the service is, by nature, 'in between' two countries, the country of 'origin',[85] where the supplier has his residence, and the 'host' country, where the client has his residence. Then, both laws are in

[79] Muir Watt, above n. 21 at n°7; Roth W.H. and Andreas M. (Eds) *Services and Free Movement in EU Law* (2002, Oxford, Oxford University Press).

[80] Muir Watt, above n. 21 at n°5 et seq.

[81] These are the lessons learnt from the rulings in the cases of *Cassis de Dijon* and *Keck and Mithouard*.

[82] On this analysis: Snell J. *Goods and Services in EC Law: A Study of the Relationships Between the Freedoms* (2002, Oxford, Oxford University Press).

[83] On the question whether the scheme might nevertheless apply to a certain pattern of services, in particular to services the content of which is juridical, see: Radicati di Brozolo, above n. 5 at 417; Muir Watt, above n. 21 at n°10 et seq.; Muir Watt, above n. 5 at 200.

[84] Muir Watt, above n. 21 at n°7; Muit Watt, above n. 5; see also: Fallon M. *Droit matériel général de l'Union Européenne* (2002, Bruxelles, Bruylant), p. 172.

[85] See, raising the idea that the very notion of home country or country of origin is inconsistent when considering the free flow of services, because the home country could be both the country in which the supplier has his residence, or the one in which the client has his residence, depending on the point of view: Heuzé, above n. 9 at 408.

competition for the ruling of the relationship. Mutual recognition is of no help, and the ECJ, in *Alpine Investments*,[86] has abandoned the double charge criteria, typical of *Cassis de Dijon*, to assess whether the application of the law claiming to rule the service (here, the home country law, but the test can affect either law) did hinder the access of the service to the market.

Following the change of perspective in *Alpine Investments* (substitution of the test of restriction to access to the market for the double charge criteria), it has been observed that the ECJ seems to 'presume' the existence of an impediment, whenever a rule that is internationally mandatory claims to apply against the law of the contract.[87] But it is commonly admitted that internationally mandatory rules are the necessary compensation for party choice.[88] Leaving it up to the law of the contract to rule the relationship in both its default rules and internationally enforced rules would result, when party choice is admitted – as it is generally in contracts – in deregulation, for a party would be able to exclude internationally mandatory rules through choice of law.[89] And the virtue of deregulation, namely the absence of any State regulation, is highly questionable.[90] The solution, then, is to choose a regulatory law imposed upon the parties to rule the contract. There again, choice of law rules constitute a possible resort. Is the objective of integration of the market a guideline in the design of such a rule? A first requirement is undoubtedly dictated by the objective of integration of the market, which is that the contract should be subjected only to one set of regulatory laws. But with regards to identification of the suitable law, the objective of market integration does not propose a useful connecting factor, because the only prescription it seems to impose is that the law that is most favourable to the supplier should apply.[91]

---

86 See above n. 69.

87 Pataut, above n. 67 at 126.

88 Heuzé V. *La réglementation française des contrats internationaux* (1990, Paris, Joly), n°375.

89 On the consequences of choice of forum rules on the application of internationally mandatory rules, see: Radicati du Brozolo L.G. 'Mondialisation, juridiction, arbitrage: vers des règles d'application semi-nécessaire?' (2003) *Rev. Crit. DIP*, pp. 1–36.

90 Brousseau E. 'Les marchés peuvent-ils s'autoréguler?', in *Concurrence et régulation des marchés, Cahiers français* (2003) mars-avril, n°313, pp. 64–70; see also: Treu T. 'What can European governments do for employment policies?', in Blanpain R., Weiss M. (eds), *Changing Industrial Relations and Modernisation of Labour Law, Liber Amicorum in Honour of Professor Marco Biagi* (2003, The Hague, Kluwer), pp. 429–437, esp. p. 431: 'The alternative between regulation and deregulation does not properly represent the present policy options in Europe. The issue is innovation in public policy making and consequently re-regulation.'

91 The solution of the *favor offerentis* – application of the law most favourable to the supplier – has actually been considered as a possible means to promote the free

Following this idea, the application of the law of the country of origin has sometimes been promoted, as if it was necessarily an annoyance for the supplier not to be subjected to his own law.[92] The First Draft Directive on services has implemented such a solution,[93] and thus provoked very hostile reactions.[94] Beyond the discussion on the legitimacy of the country of origin principle when applied to private law,[95] its appropriateness to the favour consideration is questionable, as demonstrated in the *Alpine Investments* case, where the impediment actually resulted from the law of the supplier. Moreover, one must not forget that market integration – be it the primary objective of the Community – is not its only concern, and if it were, that the common market rules do not exclusively operate for the good of the supplier, but also for the good of the clients.[96] Other objectives, such as consumer protection, are also admitted as valuable. Therefore, the conflict of regulatory laws often takes place when a liberal law – in accordance with the objective of creation of the internal market – confronts a stricter law, aiming at the protection of other perfectly legitimate interests.

In international private law, it is admitted that the conflicts of internationally mandatory rules cannot, because of the substantial objectives of these rules, be resolved through plain choice of law rules. The neutral character of the latter does not allow the substantial objectives of the mandatory rules to be taken into account. To decide which mandatory rule should apply, only a case-by-case analysis is conceivable: several elements – relating to the mandatory rules in question – must be compared, such as – following Article 7 of the Rome Convention – the nature of the rule, its object, the closeness of the connection with the contract, the consequences of application or non-application of the

---

flow in the common market: Basedow J. 'The Communitarization of the Conflicts of Laws under the Treaty of Amsterdam' (2000) 37 *Common Market Law Rev.* 687.

92 For instance: Radicati du Brozolo, above n. 5.

93 Article 16 of the Draft Directive laid down, in §1, that 'Member States ensure that providers are subject only to the national provisions of their Member State of origin', and in § 2 that 'paragraph 1 shall cover national provisions relating to access to and the exercise of a service activity, in particular those requirements governing the behaviour of the provider, the quality and content of service, advertising, contracts and the provider's liability'.

94 Heuzé, above n. 9.

95 On which, see: above n. 9; Wilderspin and Lewis, above n. 19; Idot L. 'L'incidence de l'ordre communautaire sur le droit international privé', *Petites Affiches*, 12 Dec 2002, n°248, p. 27, at n°43 et seq.

96 As the ECJ has put it in *Luisi & Carbone* (31 Jan 1984, 286/82 and 26/83, *Rec.* p. 377) and *Cowan* (2 Feb 1989, 186/87, *Rec.* p. 195); on the undue imbalance generated by the country of origin principle when applied to private law, see: Heuzé , above n. 9 at p. 398 et seq.; Wilderspin and Lewis, above n. 19 at p. 33.

rule.[97] The relation between such a method and the method of the balance of interests has often been underscored.[98] And the system of resolution of the conflicts of internationally mandatory rules in the EU certainly has affinities with this reasoning. Considering that each internationally mandatory rule, claiming to apply to an intra-community cross-border contract, is capable of impeding the free movement of services, it has to be assessed, in comparison with the objective of integration of the market it is conflicting with.[99] And it is only if it proves that the public good it intends to protect deserves higher consideration than the integration of the market in itself, and that its intervention is strictly in proportion with the objective it serves, that it will pass the test.[100]

Could there be, instead of a case-by-case assessment, some sort of pre-evaluation of the merits of Member State internationally mandatory rules? Several authors answer this question positively,[101] such as Grundmann, according to whom 'by harmonisation, the directive also selects those reasons which can justify national law which hinders cross border trade and thus in principle, also precludes the others'.[102] To him, whenever harmonization (even minimal) exists, it defines the extent to which the Community may be deemed to accept the 'intervention' of Member States' regulatory laws: national requirements, when more stringent than Community standards, constitute hindrances that cannot be justified for reasons of public good. If harmonization is almost complete as regards internationally mandatory rules, this means that Member States' regulation can never apply to intra-community relationships on the basis of the exception of 'mandatory reasons of public good'. Party choice exclusively finds its compensation in Community regulation applying to contracts for services. However, we have seen previously that such centralization of regulation at Community level is not desirable,

---

97 Mayer and Heuzé, above n. 1 at n°130; Mayer P. 'Les lois de police étrangères' (1981) *Journal du droit international* 277.

98 Idot, above n. 59; Muir Watt, above n. 21 at n°24.

99 On such an analysis of the control of madatory rules as being 'vertical' in the sense that their merits are assessed as regards the Community objective of the free flow of goods and services, and not as regards other Member States' regulation, see: Tebbens H.D. 'Les conflits de lois en matière de publicité déloyale à l'épreuve du droit communautaire' (1994) *Rev. Crit. DIP* 451.

100 As it did in *Alpine*, where the mandatory rule of the home country, though impeding access to the market, has nevertheless been applied for reasons of public good. On the submission of mandatory rules to market freedom under the exception of reason of public good, see: ECJ, 29 Nov 1999, *Arblade*, *Rev. Crit. DIP* 2000, 710, note Fallon.

101 Grundmann, above n. 27 at 22 et seq.; Pataut, above n. 67 at 128.

102 See above n. 27 at 23.

considering that efficient regulation is better achieved at national level. If so, the scheme of 'harmonization as centralized regulation' should not be adopted. Harmonized legislation is not the referent for the evaluation of the legitimacy of Member States' mandatory rules. These rules are to be assessed on a case-by-case basis by the ECJ. The criticism is then that the Community control of Member States' mandatory rules could lead to a 'government of judges', in the absence of any criteria proposed by primary (or even secondary) law for the evaluation of the legitimacy of national rules.[103] This is why a solution, other than balancing interests, could be worked out in the specific context of the EU.

The European Union offers opportunities that other multinational markets do not propose, because it constitutes a supra-national and juridical community, it can therefore claim to achieve an integrated ruling of conflict of laws. If, as a result of harmonization, all Member States' regulation may be deemed 'equivalent', and if the 'reason' for regulation lies in the risks inherent to party choice, parties should then be subjected to *one* Member State's regulation, imposed upon them by a supra-national ruling. In other words, Member States should not be free to define the scope of their regulatory laws, and to have them applied on the basis of Article 7 of the Rome Convention (under scrutiny as to the respect of market freedoms); it should be up to the Community to decide, for a given set of relationships, which Member State regulatory law is applicable, and to exclude conversely the application of all other Member State mandatory rules. This way, an authentic allocation of regulatory authority would be allowed. The scheme has been tried out in the insurance directives: when the law of the contract has been chosen by the parties,[104] only two sets of mandatory rules can apply: one is the law of the place of situation of the risk, and the other the *lex fori*. If we leave aside the application of the *lex fori*, which results from specific justifications,[105] to concentrate on the law of the place of situation of the risk, we notice that the applicable mandatory rules are those of the law that would have been applied, absent of party choice.[106] So it seems that, with this solution, assessment of the connection between the contract and the country the law of which is applicable, is substituted for comparative evaluation of the merits of the laws in conflict. Only the law that has the closest connection with the contract can impose its regulatory devices upon the parties. It is doubtful, however, that such a system can be, at present, implemented in Europe. Firstly, it supposes that all Member State regulation be deemed equivalent. If such equivalence is admitted in the field of public

[103] Mayer and Heuzé, above n. 1 at n°126.

[104] Party choice does not constitute, in these directives, the principal choice of law rule (see p. 72), but it is however available in certain circumstances.

[105] Heuzé, above n. 47 at 249.

[106] See discussion at p. 72.

law,[107] it is highly contested as far as private law – even when regulatory – is concerned.[108] Secondly, it lays down that the country which has 'the closest connection' with the contract be identified. The Rome Convention, as we know, offers presumptions as to the country having the closest connection with different patterns of contracts, the general rule being that the law of the contracting party whose obligation is characteristic of the contract has the closest connection with the latter (the contract). In contracts for services, the law of the supplier is thus applicable. Scholars have sometimes used this observation as an argument to justify the application of the home country principle in conflicts of regulatory laws.[109] But the presumptions of the Rome Convention have been defined in consideration of the interests of private parties.[110] If the test of the closeness of connection is to be used as a criterion for the mandatory application of 'interventionist' laws, can the presumptions of the Rome Convention still be applied as such? This is, of course, questionable. The closeness of connections must be re-evaluated according to public good considerations. It is not easy to determine what should be the adequate criteria for such a purpose. But two considerations are to be taken into account. On the one hand, no resolution of the conflict of regulatory laws can be proposed if no hierarchy is defined between potentially conflicting regulatory objectives: if the correction of information asymmetries or the protection of the consumer impose the application of the law of the consumer, and the free flow of services the application of the law of the supplier, then it is only if priority is given to one of these conflicting objectives that the conflict of laws can be solved.[111] On the other hand, it does not seem possible to imagine a general solution workable in all cases. Considering the diversity of services, the choice of law rules implemented should be sectoral, and defined at least on the basis of various patterns of service contracts. At present, we can doubt that either condition (equivalence of private laws, efficient criteria for the pre-identification of the country whose claims to regulate are the best) is fulfilled.

---

107 For example, concerning authorizations, approvals, or qualification required as a pre-condition for the exercise of a service, for which the home country principle is not contested (Muir Watt, above n. 21 at n°6).

108 Heuzé, above n. 9 at 412.

109 Radicati di Brozolo, above n. 5 at 414.

110 See discussion at pp. 80–81.

111 On the importance and the preliminary character of the conciliation of diverging Community interests for the definition of EU Directives, see: Tebbens H.D. 'Les règles de conflits contenues dans les instruments de droit dérivé', in Fuchs, Muir Watt and Pataut, above n. 27 at 114.

CONCLUSION

If we try to reconcile the approaches in terms both of conflicts of facilitative rules, and of conflicts of mandatory rules, we face an option.

A first scheme leads to a combination of two choices of law rules, one being party choice, and the other a rule dedicated to the co-ordination of regulation. Party choice, in many respects, is a choice of law rule consistent with the objective of creation of an internal market. Where there is party choice, there is no risk of hindrance to the free flow of services, for parties are entitled to set aside the substantial law which constitutes an impediment to their contractual project. But party choice efficiency depends on the absence of market failures. Insufficient competition in the market, information asymmetries and absence of rationality of market actors, are all reasons not to trust party choice as the rule necessarily leading to the maximization of the parties' satisfaction. Therefore, regulation is needed in order to correct the imbalance of the contractual relationship. And to ensure that party choice will not allow parties to be set free from such regulation, the latter is imposed upon the parties, in cross-border contracts, through internationally mandatory rules or *lois de police*. There come the hindrances. By nature, cross-border contracts for services can be subjected to at least two sets of regulations, that of the country of the supplier, and that of the country of the client. In the EU, complete harmonization of regulatory law might be a workable solution, but it is not desirable. And, in the absence of complete harmonization, Member States' regulatory laws must be co-ordinated. Two ways are conceivable to achieve co-ordination. On the one hand, the merits of the rules may be compared through a case-by-case analysis: the issue is to find out whether the claim for jurisdiction is legitimate, considering the nature of the public good in balance with the objective of integration of the market; regulatory authority is to be granted to the State whose claim is more legitimate. On the other, if assurance exists that Member States' regulations are 'equivalent', a choice of law rule could designate *one and only one* Member State's regulation, applying irrespective of the law of the contract. But this choice of law rule should be designed on the basis of considerations of public good, not of private interests. Hence, the general choice of law rules implemented by the Rome Convention do not provide adequate tools, because they lay on pure private interests considerations. It is, besides, questionable whether any general choice of law rule can provide a solution that would work in all cases. The choice of law rule, aiming at the allocation of regulatory authority, can only be sectoral to fit the nature and characteristics of the considered service. Hence, even if the 'home country' principle has, in certain circumstances, a good claim to apply, it cannot, and must not, be proposed as a general principle. Utilities are a perfect illustration of the inadequacy of the home country principle as regards certain contracts for services. The 'principle' cannot apply at present,[112] and it should still not apply, once the liberalization of these markets is achieved. Utilities are deeply territorial by nature: they depend upon infrastructures and networks which only the local State can usefully rule. This is why the regulatory authority should be awarded, for these contracts, to the 'host' country, meaning the country where the service is delivered. Moreover, utilities are provided by big suppliers, which can all the more afford to gather information on the private law of the host country because they can rely on important volumes of contracts in the latter. Hence, suppliers, to compete in a given market, should submit to the laws of this market.

An alternative solution, as party choice cannot work alone, would be to exclude party choice and designate, through a choice of law rule imposed upon the parties, one law which would alone rule the contract in both its facilitative and internationally mandatory rules. Such a scheme has been partially implemented in the insurance directives. However, these instruments – which maintain party choice in certain circumstances – acknowledge how difficult it is, considering European legal traditions, to abandon the rule of free choice by the parties, of the law of the contract. And as long as party choice will be maintained, conflicts of Member State regulatory devices will occur.

---

112 The question of the inclusion of SGEI in the scope of the Draft Directive on services is still debated between the Commission and the Parliament; however, the version of the Directive adopted by the Parliament at first reading excludes the country of origin principle as such (see above nn. 8 and 10).

PART 2

Environmental law

4. Regulatory dilemmas in EC environmental law: the ongoing conflicts between competitiveness and the environment

Javier de Cendra de Larragán

I. THE EC MANDATE TO PROMOTE COMPETITIVENESS AND ENVIRONMENTAL PROTECTION

I.1. The Objectives in the Treaties

The EC Treaty mandates the Community institutions to achieve several objectives, among others to achieve a high level of environmental protection (Arts. 2, 3, and 174–176 EC Treaty), to promote the competitiveness of its industry (Arts. 2, 3, 136 and 137 EC Treaty), and to do so within the overarching aim of achieving sustainable development (Art. 2 EC Treaty).

The protection of the environment and the promotion of competitiveness being fundamental objectives of the EC, both carry equal weight in the elaboration of EC policies and regulation.[1] Article 3 EC refers to the activities of the Community, which include, inter alia, a policy in the sphere of the environment and the strengthening of the competitiveness of Community industry. The rationale of the integration principle set out in Article 6 EC is to make sure that all EC policies integrate environmental protection requirements, including obviously measures destined to promote competitiveness. The integration principle guides policy making and is a criterion for the interpretation of EC law.[2] By virtue of it, the principles of Article 174 EC influence all EC policies,

[1] Wasmeier, M. 'The Integration of Environmental Protection as a General Rule for Interpreting Community Law' (2001) 38 *Common Market Law Review*, 159–177, at p. 163.

[2] Kramer, L., *EC Environmental Law* 5th edn (2003, Sweet & Maxwell, London), at p .21.

so that they need to pursue a high degree of environmental protection. However, integration does not make environmental objectives prevail over other objectives.[3] When two objectives conflict in a particular case, the legislator must seek to achieve a balance between them. Ultimately, the Court will check the conformity of that choice to the EC Treaty applying the principle of proportionality set out in Article 5 EC.[4] When applying the proportionality test, the European Court of Justice awards the Community institutions a wide degree of discretion.[5]

This does not mean however that the Community legislator can simply seek to balance conflicting objectives without paying attention to their relative importance and without checking whether they are really or only apparently in conflict. The Amsterdam Treaty introduced the objective of achieving sustainable development in Community law.[6] This objective appears now in Article 2 of the EC Treaty, in Article 2 of the Treaty on the European Union, and in a more forceful manner in the Treaty establishing a Constitution for Europe.[7] Article I-3 reads in the relevant part:

> The Union shall work for the sustainable development of Europe based on balanced economic growth and price stability, a highly competitive social market economy, aiming at full employment and social progress, and a high level of protection and improvement of the quality of the environment.

This chapter places sustainable development as an overarching objective which includes – and is based on – the three pillars of economic growth, social protection and environmental protection. It therefore reflects better the concept of sustainable development as established in the Brundtland declaration and in several international texts and agreements[8] than the EC Treaty and the Treaty of the European Union do. Thus, it seems to indicate the evolution and maturity of sustainable development as a legal concept. However, the Treaty establishing a Constitution for Europe has not been adopted, following the failures to be ratified in France and in the Netherlands. Under the EC Treaty and the Treaty on the European Union (and the same can be said for the

---

[3] Wasmeier, above n. 1 at p. 163.

[4] Ibid.

[5] Craig, P., De Búrca, G. *EU Law – Texts, Cases, and Materials* (2003, Oxford, Oxford University Press), at p. 373.

[6] Kramer, above n. 2 at p. 8.

[7] OJ C 310 of 16 December 2004.

[8] For an analysis of the foundations of sustainable development in international law, see Cordonier Segger, M-C., Khalfan, A. *Sustainable Development Law – Principles, Practices, and Prospects* (2005, Oxford, Oxford University Press), at pp. 15–23.

EU Constitutional Treaty), sustainable development is not a general principle of EU law, but rather an ideal which seeks, in the long term, to make compatible a good quality of the environment with sustained economic growth and with a high level of employment and of social protection.[9]

This chapter does not focus on the social dimension of sustainable development, but rather on the interaction between the economic and environmental pillars. The short-hand term for sustainable development as regards that relation, within the EU, is 'ecological modernization', arguably a weaker concept.[10] Ecological modernization is a concept which focuses on the positive (inter)relations between economic growth and environmental protection, while leaving outside issues of a pure environmental nature.[11]

I.2. The Link between Competitiveness and the Environment in the EU

The concept of ecological modernization has been used to describe a process of technological reform, a process of policy analysis and a political ideology. Essentially, it expresses the idea that environmental protection and economic growth can go hand in hand. As Revell states,[12] its main tenets are:

- Economic growth can be de-linked from environmental degradation in developed nations.
- There is a growing perception among regulators and society that there are not fundamental conflicts between economic growth and environmental protection, and win-win solutions can be found.
- Science and technology are seen as the principal institutions in finding solutions to environmental problems and thus constitute the key processes of ecological modernization.
- Technological innovation and material and energy efficiency are promoted as economical ways to protect the environment.
- The state plays a key role in encouraging industry to internalize the costs of pollution, more and more so through market based instruments, such as state aid, environmental taxes, emission trading schemes, and voluntary agreements.

---

9 See Kramer, above n. 2 at pp. 9–10.

10 Weale, A., et al. (eds) *Environmental Governance in Europe* (2003, Oxford, Oxford University Press), at p. 89.

11 See Langhelle, O. 'Why Ecological Modernization and Sustainable Development Should Not Be Conflated' (2000) 2(4) *Journal of Environmental Policy and Planning*, 303–322, at p. 313.

12 Revell, A. 'Ecological Modernization in the UK: Rhetoric or Reality?' (2005) 15(6) *European Environment*, 344–361.

By focusing on 'win-win' situations, ecological modernization largely leaves aside conflicts between pure environmental protection and the pursuit of economic interests, thus adopting an anthropocentric approach to the protection of the environment. The protection of natural values is considered from its perspective as a by-product, rather than as an issue as such.[13] Ecological modernization is based on the view that adopting a strong environmental stance in regulation may help the economy to increase its competitiveness, by adopting a first mover advantage. This idea was proposed by Porter and Van der Linde, who argued that since competitiveness at industry level arises from superior productivity, either in terms of lower costs than those of their competitors or in the ability to offer products with a higher value that justify a higher price, international competitive companies are not necessarily those with the cheaper inputs but those with a better capacity to innovate.[14] They consider that properly designed stringent environmental regulation can lead to innovation and improvement which does not negatively affect competitiveness and can even improve it, by giving the so-called first mover advantage.[15] This has been called the Porter Hypothesis. Porter and Esty advanced preliminary empirical evidence supporting a positive link between the quality of a country's environmental regulation and its broader legal and economic context.[16] Their work has been mentioned in several documents prepared by the EC Commission.[17]

However, the Porter Hypothesis is not undisputed, mainly because it focuses on competitiveness at macro level (country level). At this level, competitiveness means a sustained rise in the standards of living of a nation and a level of involuntary unemployment as low as possible.[18] At micro level (industry level), stringent environmental legislation may create winners and

---

13 Unnerstall, H. 'Sustainable Development as a Criterion for the Interpretation of Article 6 of the Habitats Directive' (2006) 16(2) *European Environment*, 73–88, at pp. 83–84.

14 Porter, M.E., Van der Linde, C. 'Towards a New Conception of the Environment – Competitiveness Relationship' (1995) 9(4) *Journal of Economic Perspectives*, 97–118.

15 Porter, M. 'America's Green Strategy' (1991, April) *Scientific American*.

16 Esty, D. and Porter, M.E. 'Ranking national environmental regulation and performance: A leading indicator of future competitiveness', *The Global Competitiveness Report 2001–2002* (2001, New York, Oxford University Press).

17 See for instance the Competitiveness Report of 2004, Commission Staff Working Paper, SEC (2004) 1397, at p. 36. On the other hand, some authors categorically reject the notion of a country's competitiveness, stating that countries do not compete among each other. See Krugman, P. 'Competitiveness: A Dangerous Obsession', *Foreign Affairs*, 73, (2), March/April 1994.

18 Competitiveness Report of 2004, above n. 17 at p. 9.

losers within industry.[19] Thus, even if the EC has to some extent endorsed it from a political and legal perspective, as we will see below, the need to achieve a balance between the positive and negative impacts of (environmental) legislation is still very much needed. The rest of the chapter will focus on the twists and turns of the relationship between the promotion of the environment and of competitiveness in EU policy and law, especially since 2000 which marked the start of the Lisbon Strategy, by looking first at the need for (environmental and competitiveness-related) regulation at EC level, at the situations where conflicts are most likely to arise, and at some features of the approaches chosen to deal with those conflicts.

II. THE RELATION BETWEEN COMPETITIVENESS AND ENVIRONMENT REGULATION

II.1. Need for Regulation at EC Level

The EC Treaty gives the EC institutions competence to enact regulation in a determined number of fields, and at the same time prevents them from regulating directly within other fields where they do not have competence, in accordance with the principle of attribution. The principles of subsidiarity and proportionality in Article 5 EC indicate the breadth and depth of EC legislation within its competences. There are a few reasons why a certain amount of regulation is necessary to bring forward those aims. Since the EU's main objective is to promote the completion of an internal market which, allegedly, will contribute to achieve some of its other aims and objectives, action is needed where the market alone cannot fulfil that role. The outcome of market forces may fail to bring about EC Treaty objectives in a number of situations:

1. Market prices may not reflect the real costs or benefits to society of a certain activity. When this happens, externalities appear. In the case of a negative externality such as pollution, because its harmful effects on the environment or health are not reflected in product prices, consumers will demand too much of those products.
2. In relation to public goods, for example, those which satisfy two conditions: (a) the consumption made by one person does not reduce the amount available to others (non-rival); (b) once it is produced, it is not possible to exclude some people from consuming it (non-excludable). If it

19 Willliams, E., Macdonald, K., Kind, V. 'Unravelling the Competitiveness Debate' (2002) 12(5) *European Environment*, 284–290, at p. 288.

is not possible to charge each person for consumption of the goods, the market will produce too little of those goods or none at all. There are very few pure public goods, and more mixed public goods. Environmental assets and some types of infrastructure can be considered public goods.
3. Missing or weak competition in the market: Article 98 EC mandates the EC and member states to act in accordance with the principle of an open market economy with free competition, favouring an efficient allocation of resources. When there is no competition in the market or only to a low degree, the quantity and quality of goods and services produced might be lower than what is socially efficient, and prices higher.
4. Non-existing or incomplete markets: the market cannot produce some goods and services, or may supply them under over-restrictive conditions, even if society values them, for instance due to lack of information to calculate costs and benefits of supplying them. This is the case of insurance in relation to some types of risks, or providing funding where the potential benefits from it cannot be calculated, and thus extra guarantees or too high interest rates might be required by the financer.
5. Regulatory failures: legislation may be of a poor quality, either because it poorly defines targets and objectives, raising compliance costs beyond what is socially efficient, or because it does not adequately define property rights, thereby raising legal uncertainty. Finally, regulation enacted to achieve one objective may have unintended (negative) effects on other fields.
6. Regulatory capture: the regulator may be influenced by interest groups trying to advance their interests during the legislative process. When some groups have less capacity to do so, it may lead to legislation impacting on them in a way which is not optimal for society.
7. Implementation and enforcement: ensuring adequate and equal levels of both in all member states, with the double objective of ensuring the intended outcome of the legislation while avoiding distortions of the internal market is a further reason to legislate at EC level.

When (some of) these situations arise, regulation will be necessary to help the market deliver the intended objectives.

II.2. Need for (EC) Environmental Regulation

The general justifications for the need to enact regulation dealing with the environment at EC level were traditionally of a (mainly) economic nature, to prevent differing regulations at member state level from creating difficulties in the functioning of the internal market. That reason, with the amendment of the EC Treaty in the SEA, has been coupled with the more political one of achieving a similar degree of environmental protection for all citizens within the EU.[20] Finally, there is arguably a trend for a more ecologically oriented approach to environmental law, where the objective to be pursued is a higher level of protection of ecosystems.[21]

Environmental assets can be considered as public goods not exchanged in the markets, therefore a price for them does not arise. With a growing population and technological capacity, those assets are exploited more intensively than their regenerative capacity would allow for, and thus problems such as extinction of species, extreme pollution of water, air and soil and other problems arise.

In addition, economic activities generate pollution which generates social costs beyond what is socially optimal. In order to reduce that pollution to the optimal level there is a need to internalize the (negative) external costs imposed by polluting activities. Legislation will aim to achieve such internalization, bringing pollution to the optimal (not necessarily and probably not zero) level. As a result, legislation will then raise production costs at least for some producers. While the need for legislation to internalize external costs is theoretically accepted in international and European law, its potential impacts on the competitiveness of industry, especially vis-à-vis international industry not subjected to similar environmental standards, make it very controversial, especially within the WTO law.[22]

II.3. Need for Regulation to Promote Competitiveness

Competitiveness, at company level, is normally defined as the above average and sustained profitability of a company.[23] In order to be in conditions to achieve this, a company requires the presence of four fundamental elements in the market: (1) an open market where it can operate with relative freedom; (2) some type of comparative advantage: an edge over competitors, represented by innovation, better production processes, better management, or reduced costs vis-à-vis competitors; (3) financial leverage; (4) good infrastructure.

---

[20] See for instance, Bell. S. and McGillivray, D. *Environmental Law* (2006, Oxford, Oxford University Press), at p. 194.

[21] See Usui, Y, 'Evolving Environmental Norms in the European Union' (2003) 9(1), *European Law Journal*, 69–87, at p. 85.

[22] See De Cendra, J. 'Can Emissions Trading Schemes be Coupled with Border Tax Adjustments? An Analysis vis-à-vis WTO Law' (2006) 15(2) *Review of European Community and International Environmental Law*, 131–145.

[23] The Commission Competitiveness Reports define competitiveness as 'the ability of an industrial sector to defend and/or gain market share in open, international markets by relying on price and/or quality of goods'. See the Competitiveness Report of 2004, above n. 17 at p. 13.

Some of these elements are not properly (or not at all) provided by the market alone, because they share features of public goods (such as infrastructure), or due to other market failures. Whenever some of those elements are lacking, the ability of companies to compete is reduced. In those cases, as seen above, it can be the task of the regulator to provide for them.

II.4. The Conflicts between Environmental Regulation and Regulation to Promote Competitiveness

The conflict goes both ways: some of the actions carried out by the government to improve competitiveness may have a negative impact on the status of the environment. For instance, the development of infrastructure may have strong negative impacts on the environment. Measures to ensure competition in the market are more ambiguous: they may improve the status of the environment (increasing allocative efficiency is good for the environment) or may damage it (for example when more transport infrastructure is needed or where the EC Treaty rules on competition impede the establishment of monopolies for the collection and treatment of waste).[24]

On the other hand, environmental legislation aimed at tackling specific sources of pollution, normally industry, will impose on industry additional costs, which may or may not reduce their competitiveness. It can actually lower or raise their costs, depending on the specific firm. The type, volume and quality of environmental regulation may also damage the competitiveness of firms. Legislation which does not take account of the specific characteristics of firms may be too costly. Legislation which is far too stringent may raise costs for industry to a point that cannot be justified on the basis of economic or other considerations. Legislation which is of a poor quality, for instance because it is not transparent or is ambiguous, may create legal uncertainty and raise administrative costs for industry. An excessive volume of legislation can increase the costs arising from administrative work beyond what would be economically and environmentally optimal, leading to inefficiencies.

Thus, tensions arise between the two objectives of regulation, between different regulators, between the regulator and those regulated, and within those regulated. These tensions may increase at moments where, for whatever reasons, one of the two objectives is considered more important in the short

[24] For an analysis on EC policies in the competition field and their impact on environmental law, see generally Vedder, H. '*Competition and the Environment: Towards Sustainability?* (2002, Europa Law Publishing, Groningen). See also Boute, A. 'Environmental Protection and EC Anti-Trust Law: The Commission's Approach for Packaging Waste Management Systems' (2006) 15(2) *Review of European Community & International Environmental Law*, at pp. 146–159.

term. In those cases, the legislator may decide to adopt measures which promote the objective perceived to be lagging behind.

Apart from the cases where legislation of poor quality or excessive legislation is responsible for raising administrative costs and legal uncertainty, the cases where real conflicts may appear are: (1) stringent environmental measures which impose high costs on at least some sectors; (2) the need to develop infrastructure, for instance to carry energy or for transportation; (3) the adoption of measures in the field of competition law to promote further the internal market. In these cases, the need to balance conflicting aims may seem unavoidable. And indeed, these are the cases to which now, at a time where the EU is so worried about the competitiveness of the EU economy,[25] the EU is giving special attention: (1) better regulation mainly aimed at improving the quality of legislation and reducing its volume;[26] (2) promotion of innovation and R&D;[27] (3) the need for more infrastructure; (4) reforms in the internal market to create more competitiveness, amongst others, in the energy market.[28]

I will focus on the (potentially negative for the environment) dimension of this relationship. This choice implies leaving aside the analysis of win-win situations advocated within ecological modernization. Indeed, when those actions can be identified, they should always be implemented in their own right. I will also (largely) leave aside the focus on reducing and improving (environmental) legislation to reduce costs to industry, and will focus on the attempts to reduce costs through (a) reducing the stringency of environmental regulation and; (b) using alternative regulatory approaches to regulation that

---

25 The Lisbon Strategy was adopted in 2000 and re-launched in 2005. See below at n. 46.

26 See the Better Regulation Package adopted by the Commission in 2002 on the basis of its Action Plan, set up in Communication from the Commission, 'Action Plan Simplifying and improving the Regulatory Environment', COM (2002) 278 Final. This package was recently updated in the Communication from the Commission to the Council and the European Parliament, 'Better Regulation for Growth and Jobs in the European Union', COM (2005) 97 Final. The link between better regulation and competitiveness was made even clearer by Peter Verheugen, Vice-President of the Commission and Commissioner for DG Industry and Enterprise in a speech entitled 'less red tape = more growth' delivered on 16 March 2006. See IP/05/311.

27 See the amended proposal for a Decision of the European Parliament and the Council concerning the 7th Framework Programme of the European Community for Research, Technological Development and Demonstration Activities, (2007-2013), COM (2006) 364 Final.

28 See the Energy Sectors Enquiry launched by the Commission in June 2005. The Commission has already published an interim report: Communication from the Commission to the Council and the European Parliament 'Report on Progress in Creating the Internal Gas and Electricity Market', COM (2005) 568 Final.

in theory increase efficiency and cost-effectiveness. These represent the hard cases where the commitment of the EU to sustainable development and to the integration of environmental policies into other policies can really be tested, for the other cases are win-win situations which should create no conflicts. However, lack of implementation of win-win situations, for whatever reasons, may lead to higher pressures to reduce the costs created by environmental legislation in order to reach reductions of costs. This approach is economically inefficient and contributes to increase the tensions between the objective of promoting competitiveness and the objective of protecting the environment.

First, I will look at the evolving relationship at the EC political level, then I will look at the process of regulation-making and finally to the instruments used.

III. EVOLUTION OF THE RELATIONSHIP BETWEEN COMPETITIVENESS AND ENVIRONMENTAL PROTECTION IN THE EC SINCE 2000

III.1. The Period until 2000: Focus on Ecological Modernization

As mentioned, the idea of ecological modernization has been the main driver of EC environmental policy, and was already fully endorsed in the 5th Environmental Action Programme (EAP) adopted in 1993.[29] The 5th EAP stated that:

> The perceived conflict between environmental protection and economic competitiveness stems from a narrow view of the sources of prosperity and a static view of competition. Rather than reduce competitive advantage, stringent environmental requirements can actually enhance it by triggering upgrading and innovation.[30]

At the time the 5th EAP was adopted, the EU was struggling to keep up with economic growth, and was lagging behind its main competitors, the US and Japan. In the same year the Commission issued its White Paper on Growth, Competitiveness and Employment.[31] That document was followed by a series of documents aiming to chart the path to increased competitiveness and

---

[29] Pepper, D. 'Ecological Modernization of the "Ideal Model" of Sustainable Development? Questions Prompted at Europe's Periphery'(1999) 8(4) *Environmental Politics,* 1–34.

[30] European Commission, 'Towards Sustainability: Fifth Environmental Action Programme' COM (1993) 465 Final, at p. 31.

[31] European Commission, 'White Paper on Growth, Competitiveness and Employment: The Challenges and Ways Forward into the 21st Century', COM (1993) 700 Final.

economic growth. In 2000, the Lisbon Strategy was launched, with its focus on more growth and employment. The aim was to make the EU the most dynamic and competitive knowledge-based economy in the world capable of sustainable economic growth with more and better jobs, greater social cohesion, and respect for the environment.

III.2. Between 2000 and 2005: Focus on Good Governance and Better Regulation

In the late 1990s, the BSE scandal ('mad' cows), the scandal of the dioxins in chicken feedstuff in Belgium and the corruption in the Santer Commission led to a sense of distrust of the Commission and a loss of credibility of the European project as a whole.[32] This was the main trigger for the launch of the White Paper on Governance.[33] The focus of the White Paper was to recover the trust of citizens in the European project and to bring them closer to the institutions.[34] The White Paper made numerous links to the Sustainable Development Strategy adopted the same year in Gothenburg.[35] The latter sought to establish long-term targets, to ensure that sectoral short-term interests would not prevail, and to focus on the integration between policies and on the internalization of external costs, for instance through a European CO_2 tradable permit system to be established by 2005.[36]

In the White Paper on Governance, the Commission proposed to renew the Community method by following a less top-down approach and making more use of non-legislative instruments. The three keys were better involvement and more openness, better policies and better regulation, and better implementation and enforcement. The last included a greater use of different policy instruments such as regulations, framework directives and co-regulation, simplification of existing EU law and national implementing measures, publication of guidelines on collection and use of expert advice used to regulate, criteria to investigate possible breaches of EU law and criteria for the creation of agencies.[37]

---

[32] Majone, G. and Everson, M. 'Institutional Reform: Independent Agencies, Oversight, Coordination and Procedural Control', in O. De Schutter, N. Lebessis, J. Paterson, (eds), *Governance in the European Union* (2001, Luxembourg: Office for Official Publications of the European Communities).

[33] European Commission, 'European Governance: A White Paper', COM (2001) 428 Final. See Chapter 1 on the justification for the White Paper.

[34] Ibid, at p. 3.

[35] European Commission, 'Communication on a sustainable Europe for a better world', COM (2001) 264 final.

[36] Ibid, at p. 5.

[37] 'European Governance: A White Paper', above n. 33 at p. 5.

Despite the turmoil that preceded the White Paper on Governance and the slow rate of economic growth, the official view as regards ecological modernization was maintained in the 6th EAP issued in 2002:[38]

> The Programme aims to achieve a decoupling between environmental pressures and economic growth whilst being consistent with the principle of subsidiarity and respecting the diversity of conditions across the various regions of the European Union.[39]

Throughout the document it becomes clear that the key procedural strategies are to integrate environmental costs into prices,[40] the insistence on the use of market-based instruments along with legislation,[41] collaborating with citizens, enterprises and other stakeholders and giving them incentives to change production and consumption patterns.[42]

Ecological modernization had then to be integrated within the drive for good governance. The Commission launched in 2002 the better regulation package (see Section IV.1 below).[43] As a whole, the thrust of the package seems to marry well competitiveness and environment protection, placing it firmly within the umbrella of sustainable development and good governance.[44] However, and despite multiple efforts since 1993, and particularly since 2000 through the adoption of the Lisbon Strategy, economic growth and job creation remained low. The 2003 Competitiveness Report acknowledges this, stating that:

> The EU gap in standards of living relative to the US amounts to 30 percentage points of which 25 points can be attributed, in almost equal parts, to a lower employment rate and to a lower hourly productivity in the EU. This suggests that,

38 Decision No. 1600/2002/EC of the European Parliament and of the Council of 22 July 2002, laying down the Sixth Community Environment Action Programme.

39 Ibid, Recital 8 of the Preamble.

40 Ibid, Art. 5.

41 Ibid, Art. 3.

42 Ibid, Art. 3.

43 The Commission issued four communications at the same time on this issue: COM (2002) 275 'European Governance: Better Lawmaking'; COM (2002) 276, Communication from the Commission on Impact Assessment; COM (2002) 277, Communication from the Commission, 'Consultation Document: Towards a Reinforced Culture of Consultation and Dialogue – Proposal for General Principles and Minimum Standards for Consultation of Interested Parties by the Commission'; COM (2002) 278, Communication from the Commission: 'Action Plan Simplifying and Improving the Regulatory Environment'.

44 See Wilkinson, D. et al. 'For Better or for Worse? The EU's Better Regulation Agenda and the Environment', Report by the Institute for European Environmental Policy (IEEP) November 2005, at p. 7.

> to bridge the difference in standards of living between the two regions, the EU will have to rely on an improvement in both employment performance and in the efficiency with which labour is used in the production process.[45]

The strategy to improve competitiveness was based on creating employment and increasing the productivity of labour, which as such are objectives which do not necessarily conflict with the protection of the environment.

In 2005, the Prodi Commission was substituted by the Barroso Commission and the Commission finalized the mid-term review of the Lisbon Strategy and set its strategy for the coming five years.

III.3. After 2005: Forgetting the Porter Hypothesis?

As already mentioned, the Porter Hypothesis states essentially that properly designed stringent environmental regulation can lead to innovation and improvement which does not negatively affect competitiveness and can even improve it. The analysis of the period 1993 to 2005 seems to suggest that the EU institutions had accepted the ideas of Porter about the relation between environmental regulation and competitiveness.

In 2005, the new Commission delivered its ideas to re-launch the Lisbon Strategy with the Communication 'Working Together for Growth and Jobs: A New Start for the Lisbon Strategy'.[46] The document was based on the report prepared by the high level group chaired by Wim Kok.[47] The Communication states:

> The Lisbon strategy gives equal importance to increasing both employment and productivity, through enhanced competitiveness.[48]

Indeed, the focus of the Communication is on increasing the competitiveness of the EU by making Europe a more attractive place in which to invest and work, by increasing investment in research and development (R&D), including in eco-innovation, by creating more and better jobs through employment policies, increased mobility and better use of structural funds, and by improving governance. The Communication makes direct and indirect references to the environment. Directly, the focus is placed on promoting eco-innovation,

---

45 2003 European Competitiveness Report, Commission Staff Working Document, SEC (2003) 1299, at p. 9.

46 Communication to the Spring European Council, 'Working Together for Growth and Jobs: A New Start for the Lisbon Strategy', COM (2005) 24.

47 Document 'Facing the Challenge – The Lisbon Strategy for Growth and Employment', report from the High Level Group chaired by Wim Kok, November 2004.

48 Above, n. 46 at p. 13.

especially in the areas of transport and energy. Research and development will be financed by the EU to promote new technologies, with particular attention to low carbon technologies. The justification for this move supports partially the Porter hypothesis, in so far as it states that investment in environmental technology gives a first mover advantage. Indirectly, the impact on environmental law comes from the approach to better regulation. The starting point for analysis is that existing EU and national regulation is unnecessarily abundant, complex and ambiguous. This, inter alia, raises the costs of compliance for businesses, which sometimes comes from their R&D budget. It impacts more strongly on small and medium-sized enterprises (SMEs), because they do not have the resources to go through the jungle of legislation that affects them. The Commission notes that they constitute 99 per cent of all businesses, employ 66 percent of the working population and suffer too many obstacles coming from the regulatory framework.[49] Thus, there is a general drive to simplify existing legislation, improve the quality of existing and new legislation, and assess better the effect of new legislative and policy proposals on competitiveness, including through the Impact Assessment Instrument.[50] This part of the strategy also follows the Porter Hypothesis. Properly designed, stringent environmental regulation will lead to innovation and improvement of the environment while promoting competitiveness.

The problem seems to arise with the 'stringency' element of the Porter Hypothesis. It is in relation to this part of the Hypothesis that the conflict between different members of the Commission arises, at the micro level. Peter Verheugen, Vice-President of the Commission and Commissioner for Enterprise and Industry has said recently that:

> One of the most stubborn and politically fraught misunderstandings is the apparent conflict between our European policy for growth and employment and our interest in high consumer protection, environmental protection and health policy standards. Unfortunately, this persistent, albeit in my view contrived conflict has cost us a lot of friction over the past two years alone.[51]

Indeed, many of the studies that seek to prove a positive correlation between environmental protection and competitiveness are concerned with competitiveness at macro-economic (country) level.[52] There are a few companies that

---

[49] Ibid, at p. 16.

[50] Ibid, at p. 20.

[51] 'Sustainability and Competitiveness' Meeting of Vice-President Verheugen with the European Parliament's Committee on the Environment, Public Health and Food Safety (ENVI), Speech 06/371, 13 June 2006.

[52] Williams, E., Macdonald, K., Kind, V. 'Unravelling the Competitiveness Debate' (2002) 12(5) *European Environment* 284–290, at p. 286.

will profit from environmental regulation per se, such as those focusing on the production of environmental technologies promoted by new legislation. Other companies will be able to deal with such legislation without incurring large costs. However, there are certain sectors and companies for which an increase in costs, sometimes considerable, will be unavoidable.[53] Especially when differences in the stringency of regulation that impact competitors are large, substantial impacts on competitiveness may arise. The Directorate General for Enterprise endorses this view, when it states that:

> Regulations may promote objectives such as social goals, consumer protection or the quality of environment. At the same time, regulations limit the choices which individuals and enterprises can make; and compliance with regulations usually involves costs. The productivity effects of regulations come as a by-product and are often hard to measure in quantitative terms … *A large number of studies have identified negative productivity effects linked to environmental regulations.*[54] The results are however disputed by others who argue that adjustment to environmental regulations can lead enterprises to discover more cost-effective production methods, with the cost savings offsetting the initial compliance cost of the regulations. Finally, sector- or industry-specific regulations may play an important role in influencing productivity growth in individual industries….[55]

In the 2002 Competitiveness Report, after making a thorough analysis of environmental performance of EU industry, the Commission notes that there has been a significant decoupling of economic growth in manufacturing from intensified environmental impact.[56] However, this has come at a high cost for industry:

> The environmental improvement has come at an important financial cost to manufacturing industry and its customers. Environmental expenditures by EU industry stood in 1998 at some EUR 32,000 million, some 0.4% of GDP or 2.0% of industrial value-added. A drift upwards in environmental protection expenditure has occurred since the early 1980s.[57]

In its 2004 Competitiveness Report, the Commission undertook an overview of the literature analysing the relation between environment and competitiveness,[58] and found that: 'An increasing number of contributions lend support to

---

53 Ibid.

54 Emphasis added.

55 2004 European Competitiveness Report, Commission Staff Working Document, SEC (2004) 1397, at p. 10.

56 2002 European Competitiveness Report, Commission Staff Working Document, SEC (2002) 528, at p. 12.

57 Ibid, at p. 112.

58 Above, n. 55 at p. 37.

the 'Porter Hypothesis … strong environmental performance appears to be positively correlated with competitiveness'.[59]

The trend followed by the Competitiveness Reports indicates that there are, at the same time, appreciation of the Porter Hypothesis together with concern for the costs imposed on industry by environmental regulation. The source of disagreement within the Commission arises not at macro-economic but at micro-economic level, and in the short term rather than in the long term. Indeed, the general aim of improving legislation to make it more efficient is sensible. The manner in which it is done however may spark controversy and disagreement, especially when it implies substituting legislative instruments, such as laws, for soft law approaches, such as market-based instruments not based in law.[60]

The Commission, on the occasion of the new start of the Lisbon Strategy, has put its attention back on the issue of better regulation, but this time with a slightly different angle. Lofstedt argues that the focus of better regulation has narrowed from being a means to promote good governance, competitiveness and environmental protection, to become a means to promote more or less exclusively competitiveness.[61]

It seems necessary to examine this issue more closely, and then to relate it to the most recent action in the environmental field. How does this concern for costs influence the regulation of the environment? A priori, it should bear some influence on the treatment of regulatory costs within the performance of impact assessments for legislative proposals, on the influence of industry and

---

[59] Ibid.

[60] This has been observed in Pallemaerts, M. et al. 'Drowning in Process? The Implementation of the EU's 6th EAP' (2006) IEEP Report, at pp. 42–43. The most recent example of these disagreements concerns the voluntary agreement with car makers whereby they committed to reduce CO_2 emissions per kilometre to 140 grams by 2008/09. In practice, by 2004 European, Japanese and Korean manufacturers had only reduced average CO_2 emissions to 161g/km, 170g/km and 168g/km respectively, and it appears likely that they will not meet the target. How to respond to the shortfall has caused confrontations between Stavros Dimas, the Commissioner for the Environment, and Peter Verheugen. Whereas the former backs stronger action to force car makers additionally towards the EU's more ambitious emissions target of 120 g/km, DG Enterprise disagrees. The approach of Verheugen to this issue had been to set up the High Level Group 'CARS 21', with the idea of analysing the competitiveness of the European automotive industry by screening existing legislation which affects it and setting out a road map for future regulation. Verheugen was criticized for weighting it too much with industry representatives, involving only member states with a significant car industry and excluding Japanese and Korean car makers.

[61] See Wilkinson et al., above n. 44. See also Lofstedt, R. 'The Plateau-ing of the European Better Regulation Agenda: An Analysis of Activities Carried Out by the Barroso Commission', AEI-Brookings Joint Centre for Regulatory Studies, July 2006.

the Directorate General for Enterprise within decision making processes, and on the amount and type of environmental legislation passed. I will have a look at these elements in turn.

IV. BETTER REGULATION, COMPETITIVENESS AND IMPACT ASSESSMENT

IV.1. The Background: the 2002 Better Regulation Package

This package is formed by four communications: COM (2002) 275,[62] COM (2002) 276,[63] COM (2002) 277[64] and COM (2002) 278.[65] It builds on the reactions to the White Paper on Governance relating to the better law making element. Better law making was based on three pillars: (1) simplifying and improving the regulatory environment; (2) promoting a culture of dialogue and participation; and (3) systematizing impact assessment by the Commission. The last would take the form of a general purpose impact analysis tool, which would constitute a decision-making aid while not taking the place of political judgment. It would serve to justify the choice of the right instrument and its intensity, and give more accurate and better structure information on the positive and negative impacts of proposals, having regard to the economic, social and environmental aspects. Finally, it would serve as a means to select, during the work programming phase, those initiatives which are really justified on the basis of proportionality and subsidiarity.

The overall objectives of the whole package were to improve transparency, to achieve better integration between policy sectors through *ex ante* impact assessment, to improve the implementation and transposition of EU measures in member states, the use of alternative policy instruments when justified and permitted by the EC Treaty, and to simplify and clarify the *acquis communautaire*. Most important from the perspective of their impact on environmental regulation are the use of the impact assessment (IA) for future regulation and the simplification and reduction of the volume of existing Community

62 Communication from the Commission, 'European Governance: Better Lawmaking', COM (2002) 275 Final.

63 Communication from the Commission on Impact Assessment, COM (2002) 276 Final.

64 Communication from the Commission, 'Consultation Document: Towards a Reinforced Culture of Consultation and Dialogue – Proposal for General Principles and Minimum Standards for Consultation of Interested Parties by the Commission', COM (2002) 277 Final.

65 Communication from the Commission, 'Action Plan Simplifying and Improving the Regulatory Environment', COM (2002) 278 Final.

legislation through the operations of consolidation, recasting and simplification.[66]

IV.2. The Evolution of the Impact Assessment Instrument

COM (2002) 276 is the Communication on Impact Assessment (IA). It introduced gradually from 2003 a new integrated impact assessment method for all major initiatives, those presented in the Annual Policy Strategy or in the Work Programme of the Commission. It integrated all sectoral assessments concerning direct and indirect impacts of a proposed measure into one global instrument. As such, it allows policy makers to assess the trade-offs and compare different scenarios, something which previous sectoral impact assessments could not do. They are an aid for decision making, not a substitute for political judgment, not least because they generally do not provide clear-cut conclusions or recommendations. The Commission expects that impact assessments will also be introduced in other EC institutions and by member states whenever they have leeway to implement a directive.

The aim of impact assessment is that the Commission bases its proposals on sound analysis and on a balanced appraisal of the various policy instruments available, in order to further sustainable development. It is mainly geared to Directives and Regulations. It is based on two stages: firstly, on a filtering exercise based on a short preliminary assessment of all work programme proposals and secondly, on an extended impact assessment of those proposals likely to have substantial social, economic or environmental impacts. The final outcome of the extended impact assessment can be, for example, a draft Commission proposal submitted for decision by the College of Commissioners (of the European Commission). It will lead to a preferred basic approach and the optimal policy instrument. This could be, amongst others, prescriptive regulatory actions (such as setting air quality standards), co-regulatory approaches, market-based instruments, financial interventions (for example taxation, subsidies, co-financing), voluntary agreements or self-regulation, information, networking or co-ordination activities, framework

---

66 Ibid, at 14. *Consolidation* means grouping together in a single non-binding text the current provisions of a given regulatory instrument which are spread among the first legal Act and subsequent amending Acts. *Recasting* means adopting a single legal Act which makes the required substantive changes, codifies them with provisions remaining unchanged from the previous Act, and repeals the previous Act. Simplification means seeking, with the benefit of hindsight, to make the substance of a piece of regulation simpler and more appropriate to the users' requirements. Legislative Acts which undergo codification, recasting or simplification must be submitted to the legislator for adoption as their structure or substance has been changed.

directives, and the Open Method of Co-ordination (OMC).[67] The main components of the extended impact assessment are the analysis of the issue, the identification of the policy objective, the identification of policy options and alternative instruments, the analysis of the direct and indirect, positive and negative environmental, social and economic impacts – assessing them, as far as possible, in qualitative, quantitative and/or monetary terms – and finally, the analysis of the possible difficulties related to the implementation and the laying down of arrangements for monitoring implementation.[68] The impact assessment is complemented by technical guidelines for impact assessment (see below).

Several analyses carried out show that the use of impact assessment has not been satisfactory. The Commission tried to undertake too many of them at early stages, with different degrees of quality[69] and utilization, and some have been used to lobby the Commission, in particular in relation to the Registration, Evaluation, Authorisation, and restriction of Chemical substances (REACH).[70] However, the Commission issued its own report on the application of the impact assessment, and concluded that the balance was positive but more needed to be done, in particular to refine the method and the procedures to allow for more effective implementation.[71]

In 2005, the document of the Commission which revamped the Lisbon Strategy came back to the issue of better regulation, impact assessment and simplification, as a means to improve competitiveness. A new approach to regulation should seek to remove burdens and cut red tape unnecessary for reaching the underlying policy objectives, and therefore should become a cornerstone for decision making at all levels of the Union.[72] The approach to better regulation in the document does not make express reference to the environment. Environmental protection and sustainable development are mentioned several times in the document, but do not constitute its main focus.

---

67 COM (2002) 276, at p. 9.

68 Ibid, at pp. 13–17.

69 As mentioned by Lofstedt, see above n. 61, who quotes several studies from Ambler et al., namely Ambler, T., Ballantine, B. and Hudig, D. 'Achieving a New Regulatory Culture in the European Union' (2004) European Policy Centre, Brussels; Ambler, T., Chittenden, F. and Obodovski, M., 'How Much Regulation is Gold Plate? A Study of the UK Elaboration of EU Directives' (2004) British Chamber of Commerce, London; Ambler, T., Chittenden, F. and Obodovski, M. 'Are Regulators Raising their Game?' (2004) British Chamber of Commerce, London.

70 Arthur D. Little worked out in detail an impact assessment for the German Industry Association that estimated costs equal to 6.4 per cent of Germany's GDP and 2.35 million job losses. Arthur D. Little 'Economic Effects of the EU Substances Policy: Summary of the Research Project' (2003, Wiesbaden, Arthur D. Little GmbH).

71 Commission Staff Working Paper, 'Impact Assessment: Next Steps – In Support of Competitiveness and Sustainable Development', SEC (2004) 1377, at p. 4.

72 COM (2005) 24, at p. 20.

This was followed by the issue by the Commission, in June 2005, of the revised Impact Assessment Guidelines,[73] updated in March 2006, which replace the 2002, 'Impact assessment in the Commission – Guidelines', and 'A Handbook for Impact Assessment in the Commission – How to do an Impact Assessment.[74] It is interesting to make a comparative analysis of this last document and the 2005 impact assessment guidelines to find out the impact of competitiveness concerns on the manner in which the IA is performed.

The first observation is an easy one to make. Whereas the 2002 version did not mention even once the term 'competitiveness', the 2005 version mentions it eight times. In addition, the 2005 version introduces a new annex called 'assessing impact on growth, competitiveness and jobs'.[75]

The 2002 version starts directly with a mention of the overall goal of achieving sustainable development in Annex 1, 'linking problems to policies'. The question put as an example was: 'is the issue related to some of the unsustainable trends identified in the Commission's proposal for an EU sustainable development strategy?'[76] In contrast, the 2005 version starts, with a chapter entitled 'problems calling for solution', where a link is made between the EC Treaty objectives and the IA and one of the objectives mentioned is 'promoting a high degree of competitiveness and convergence of economic performance'. Equally interesting is the approach to the problem definition set out in the same annex. There is a brief description of two ways to describe a problem: (1) approximating numbers, by using reference sources, using surveys, guessing, using experts; (2) designing a problem tree consisting of three steps: (a) listing the various problems linked to the issue at stake; (b) setting out problems in a hierarchical order, putting causes in the low level and linking them to effects on issues at the higher level; (c) drawing a tree-like structure.

A tree is presented that links the main problems to economic, financial and socio-economic problems. Low competitiveness and low GDP per capita are located at the lowest levels of the tree, and environmental problems at the highest level. Both low competitiveness and low GDP are however directly linked to the environmental problems in a cause-effect relationship, whereas the rest of the problems set at the lowest level follow a more or less long chain of causation before arriving at the top. In addition, inadequate infrastructure

---

73 Impact Assessment Guidelines, SEC (2005) 791.

74 Before, in November 2005, the Council, the Commission and the Parliament agreed on an Inter-institutional 'Common Approach to Impact Assessment' which sets out some basic rules for impact assessment throughout the legislative process.

75 Impact Assessment Guidelines, above n. 73, Annex 9.

76 'A Handbook for Impact Assessment in the Commission – How to do an Impact Assessment', Annex 1, at p. 3.

and the need to develop it, which is presented at the lowest level of the three, does not have a link to environmental problems. This approach already suggests the kind of cause-effect relation assumed between environmental regulation and competitiveness.

Chapter 9 on impacts on growth, competitiveness and jobs is the first chapter of the 2005 guidelines dedicated to specific impacts of legislation. It asks the policy maker to assess policies on a number of elements: impacts on international trade, on competition in the internal market, on firms in terms of investment, operating costs, products and services, on technological development and innovation, on SMEs in terms of the administrative burden, on consumers, on jobs, on third countries, on public authorities and on impacts at the macro-economic level. In addition, Chapter 10 focuses on the costs to administrations of policy proposals.

The 2002 guidelines had an annex entitled 'list of possible impacts'.[77] It listed three topics: economic impacts, environmental impacts, social impacts. The list was quite balanced, with a similar amount of questions for each of the three topics. The 2005 guidelines have Annex 11 entitled 'Assessing non-market impacts, in particular on environment and health'. The Annex has two pages concerned with monetization of non-market impacts, using three techniques to assess the 'willingness to pay' or 'willingness to accept' a particular outcome by people. Those three are: stated preference methods, revealed preference methods and benefit or cost transfer. In addition, Annex 11 states that a life-cycle approach can be used to assess the impacts of certain products on the environment. Annex 12 suggests that a discount rate of 4 per cent is used, which could be lower in cases involving very long horizons, such as climate change.[78]

Annex 6 of the 2002 guidelines focused on public expenditure costs, at a general level establishing some broad outlines to assess cost-effectiveness. Annex 10 of the 2005 guidelines carries the title 'assessing administrative costs imposed by legislation'. Administrative costs are defined as 'the costs incurred by enterprises, the voluntary sector, public authorities and citizens in meeting legal obligations to provide information on their action or production, either to public authorities or to private parties'. Thus, the approach is wider than in the 2002 guidelines, and moreover takes into account, in addition to Annex 9, the costs imposed on businesses. The example given as to what is an administrative cost and what is not is the situation of a company subjected to a regulation on air quality which sets an obligation to keep a register of pollutant emissions

---

77 Annex 5.

78 Reference is made here to the 'Discounting and sustainability: Issues on the choice of discount rate for long-term environmental policy', background paper prepared for the ENVECO meeting, 2–3 June 1999.

and an obligation to meet an air pollution threshold. The cost of the register is an administrative one, while the cost of fulfilling the threshold is not.

IV.3. Some Legal Observations

The change in approach from the 2002 to the 2005 guidelines is beyond doubt in spirit and method. The IA are meant to guide policy makers, but they will not normally come up with definitive conclusions.[79] A level of discretion is therefore allowed. The 'proportionate' analysis introduces discretion in the consideration of costs and benefits within the Impact Assessment.[80] Further political discretion is granted to the College of Commissioners which has to make the final choice. At this level, the newly created Competitiveness Council Commissioners Group (CCCG) has been assigned the task, amongst others, of monitoring the impact on competitiveness of all legislative proposals. The group has been defined as 'a centre of economic integration in the Commission', acting as the 'ultimate forum for reconciling policy interests'.[81]

In the light of the foregoing, the question could be asked whether the current approach to the integrated impact assessment may undermine the role of the precautionary principle as a guidance principle to develop future environmental regulation and whether it can impact negatively on the ambition of future EC environmental legislation.

IV.3.A. In relation to the precautionary principle

In 2004, Lofstedt suggested that the use of the regulatory impact assessment was increasing while the references to the precautionary principle in the better regulation package and indeed in EC policy were decreasing.[82] He further connected this fact to the discussions that were being held at that time in the Commission as regards how many chemicals should be exempted from the proposed chemical legislation that was being submitted to consultation. DG Enterprise wanted more exemptions and DG Environment wanted fewer. The discussions were amplified by the ongoing debate regarding the costs and benefits of the proposed legislation and the very different figures held by different groups, where environmental NGOs highlighted the larger benefits in comparison with costs, while industry focused on the increase in the regula-

---

79 SEC (2005) 791, at p. 44.

80 Ibid, at p. 8.

81 See Wilkinson et al., above n. 44 at p. 17.

82 Lofstedt, R.E. 'The Swing of the Regulatory Pendulum in Europe: From Precautionary Principle to Regulatory Impact Analysis' (2004) 28(3) *The Journal of Risk and Uncertainty*, 237–260, at pp. 251–252.

tory burden. Could the current IA further intensify this effect? Could the outcomes be checked against the precautionary principle?

The precautionary principle is recognized as a principle of environmental law by Article 174 EC. It was developed by the Commission in its Communication on the Precautionary Principle of 2000.[83] There it was considered a risk management tool as part of a risk analysis framework. In principle, although the Communication is not legally binding, the European Court could, applying the principle of equal treatment, ascertain whether the Commission abides by the guidelines that the institutions have laid down for themselves by adopting such a Communication.[84] The Communication establishes the principles of application of the principle, and one of them is the examination of the costs and benefits of action or lack of action. It goes on to state that:

> Examination of the pros and cons cannot be reduced to an economic cost-benefit analysis. It is wider in scope and includes non-economic considerations. However, the examination of the pros and cons should include an economic cost-benefit analysis where this is appropriate and possible.[85]

And further:

> The Commission affirms, in accordance with the case law of the Court that requirements linked to the protection of public health should undoubtedly be given greater weight than economic considerations.[86]

The Court of First Instance, in the *Artegodan* case, defined the precautionary principle:

> as a general principle of Community law requiring the competent authorities to take appropriate measures to prevent specific potential risks to public health, safety and the environment, by giving precedence to the requirements related to the protection of those interests over economic interests.[87]

---

[83] Communication from the Commission on the Precautionary Principle COM (2000) 1.

[84] De Sadeleer, N. 'The Precautionary Principle in EC Health and Environmental Law' (2006) 12(2) *European Law Journal*, 139–172, at p. 142, quoting Case T-13/99 *Pfizer*, para. 119.

[85] Communication from the Commission on the Precautionary Principle COM (2000) 1, at p.18.

[86] Ibid, at p. 19.

[87] Joined Cases T-74/00, T-76/00, T-83/00 to T-85/00, T-132/00, T-137/00 and T-141/00, *Artegodan*, at para. 184.

Thus, the European institutions have to abide, when developing policy proposals, by the precautionary principle as developed in the Commission's communication and as interpreted by the Court of First Instance.[88]

The first question is of course whether EC institutions are obliged to apply the precautionary principle or can ignore it even where risks of serious and irreversible damage are suspected. According to the paragraph of the *Artegodan* case just mentioned, it seems that institutions are required to do so. However, it can be argued that Article 174(2) EC requires authorities to act on the basis of environmental principles. To the extent that these are of an indeterminate character, they offer authorities certain room for manoeuvre.[89] Authorities are allowed not to apply it where the measure would prove to be totally disproportionate to the objective sought.[90] On the other hand, Article 174(2) EC requires authorities to justify their decisions. It is in this way that the Commission has to substantiate why, in a specific situation, it decides not to issue a proposal or to issue one not based on the precautionary principle.[91] It is this justification (or lack thereof) which could be the object of judicial control in accordance with the proportionality principle. On the other hand, where a risk analysis has been performed, and the outcome of the risk management phase is that the application of the principle is not justified, or only to a short extent, in the proposal, could it be argued that in fact the economic analysis has completely overridden the results of the risk analysis? This refers to the problem that economic costs of a regulation are amenable to calculation, whereas the environmental costs and benefits are much less so. A strict application of economic analysis of costs and benefits could indeed risk paralyzing

88 As De Sadeleer notes, in *Pfizer* the CFI did not review the conformity of the decision to ban virginiamicyn with the guidelines laid down in the Communication of the Commission on the grounds that the document was published after the measure in issue was adopted. See De Sadeleer, above n. 84 at p. 142, quoting para. 122 of the *Pfizer* case.

89 De Sadeleer, above n. 84 at p. 165.

90 Ibid.

91 Ibid. Indeed, the REACH proposal as it stands now does not mention the precautionary principle, at least explicitly. It uses instead the term 'risk', to describe the situation that may trigger management measures. The concept as usually understood covers situations of uncertainty and low probabilities of effect, thus enabling the regulator to take precautionary measures. Gerd Winter considers that, in the light of the *Pfizer* judgment, it would be better if REACH would make an explicit reference to the precautionary principle, to make clear that risk management measures of dangerous substances (such as the refusal of authorization, a conditioned authorization and a marketing restriction) do not presuppose full scientific knowledge. See Winter, G. 'Risks, Costs and Alternatives in EC Environmental Legislation: The Case of "REACH"' (2006) 15(1) *Review of European Community and International Environmental Law*, 56–65, at p. 61.

all legal action on risk management.[92] While there is a growing judicial application of the precautionary principle at EC level in the field of health safety (and indeed the *Artegodan* case belongs to this field), its application in the field of the environment is sparse and does not allow conclusions to be reached on this issue, even less at a general level (nor is the aim of this article to go deeper into this issue).

IV.3.B. In relation to the obligation to pursue a high level of protection of the environment

One could imagine that, as a result of the Impact Assessment, the Commission could put forward a proposal for an environmental regulation which has little ambition, or could consider not putting forward a proposal at all, thus renouncing in fact regulating a specific environmental problem.

In the first situation, it seems that it would constitute a case for political rather than legal accountability, as it is accepted that a high level of protection cannot be enforced in court, because it refers to environmental policy and not to each specific measure.[93] Indeed, the Parliament has the results of the IA because the Commission passes them to it, and can judge upon its quality and outcome.[94] If the proposal does go through, but in a rather weak form, the other institutions, with the results of the report at hand, can try to insert amendments to the proposal to make it more ambitious. It could be the case that when the Commission submits a proposal which is not based on a high level of protection, the Parliament could take it to the Court but probably only where the measure would be based on Article 95 EC, not when based on Article 174 EC, because Article 95(3) EC refers to individual measures whereas Article 174 refers to Community policy on the environment.[95] However, as Kramer points out, this possibility is rather theoretical, and so far has never occurred in practice.[96] And indeed, as Nele Dhondt notes,[97] in the *Safety High Tech*[98] and *Bettati*[99] cases, the Court analysed the argument made by a company that

---

92 See on this issue Ackerman, F. and Heinzerling, L. 'Priceless' (2004, The New Press), quoted in De Sadeleer, above n. 84 at p. 171.

93 See Kramer, L. *EC Environmental Law* 5th edn (2003, Sweet & Maxwell, London), at p. 11. See also Epiney, A. 'Environmental Principles', in Macrory, R. (Ed.), *Reflections on 30 Years of EU Environmental Law – A High Level of Protection?* (2006, Europa Law Publishing, Groningen), at p. 28.

94 SEC (2005) 791, at p. 15.

95 Kramer, above n. 93 at pp. 8–9.

96 Ibid.

97 Dhondt, N. *Integration of Environmental Protection into other EC Policies – Legal Theory and Practice* (2003, Europa Law Publishing, Groningen), at p. 148.

98 Case C-248/95 *Safety High Tech* [1998] ECR-I 4301.

99 Case C-341/95 *Bettati v Safety High Tech* (*Bettati* case) [1998] ECR-I 4355.

an EC regulation breached the high level of protection principle, and observed that a high level of protection does not need to be the highest level possible.[100]

On the other hand, and in relation to individual challenges to legislation, she also notes that in the *Fornasar* case,[101] Advocate General Cosmas, in his opinion asserted that the idea of a high level of protection – even though this does not impose an obligation upon the Community legislature to find the highest level of protection possible – does bind the Community legislature in the sense that if a Community rule does not correspond with this qualitative criterion it constitutes a reason for annulment of the rule.[102] In fact, in the case at stake, which referred to Directive 91/689/EEC on hazardous waste, he considered that it violated the high level of protection principle. However, he did not believe that the Court should examine which level of protection would be high enough because it does not have the necessary scientific and technical data to do so.[103]

As regards the second case, it has to be recalled that the Commission has the monopoly on taking initiatives for legal action, although Article 175(3) EC can be interpreted as putting a legal (or at least political) obligation on the Commission to undertake action. However, it is for the Commission to decide on the form, objective and content of its proposal and what preparatory work has to be undertaken. When the outcome of the IA would recommend no action at all, even if it was tabled in an action programme, no legal accountability can follow, unless in the extreme case of a total lack of justification from the Commission, according to Article 230 EC.

It follows that the balance between environmental protection and competitiveness is primarily a political one, and the law remains behind the policy maker when dictating which outcomes should arise.[104]

IV.3.C. The attitude towards environment – competitiveness of the European Parliament and of the Council

The Commission is the formal initiator of regulation. However, and under the co-decision procedure, the most used in relation to environmental issues, the European Parliament has a fundamental role as co-legislator. And indeed it is accepted that it normally adopts a stronger stance towards the environment

100 *Safety High Tech*, above n. 98 at para. 49 and *Bettati* case, above n. 99 at para. 47.

101 Case C-318/98 *Fornasar* [2000] ECR I-4785.

102 Opinion of Advocate General Cosmas in case C-318 *Fornasar*, ibid, at para. 32.

103 Ibid, para. 45.

104 See also Kramer, above n. 93, at p. 19.

than the Commission and the Council.[105] On the other hand, the Parliament has also defended the views of industry in those cases where the Commission had disregarded them in its proposals.[106] It is generally agreed that the powers of the European Parliament in the co-decision procedure have presented a range of opportunities for environmental activities to influence legislation that they would not have otherwise.[107] In addition, through inter-institutional cooperation processes,[108] the Parliament has early participation in the regulatory processes, for instance by taking part in the high level groups, such as in CARS 21 (a regulatory system for the car industry). Further, recently EU governments and the European Parliament have reached an agreement allowing MEPs for the first time to block implementing decisions adopted through so-called 'comitology' procedures. The agreement follows increasing controversy over comitology, often concerning environment-related decisions[109] and amends Article 5 of Decision 1999/468/EC on comitology.[110]

---

105 See Burns, C. 'The European Parliament: the European Union's Environmental Champion?', in Jordan, A. (Ed.) *Environmental Policy in the European Union – Actors, Institutions and Processes* (2005, Earthscan, London)), 87–105. See also Liefferink, D. and Andersen, M.S. 'Strategies of the "Green" Member States in EU Environmental Policy-Making', in ibid at p. 61.

106 During the first reading of the proposed new air quality EU legislation, the Parliament has made the Commission angry by voting to allow member states to postpone compliance with existing limit values on air pollutants for up to four years beyond 2010, and even longer periods for certain pollutants. The vote of the MEPs was criticized by the Commission, which has argued that it will expose populations to 'excessive and avoidable' pollution levels. Air quality legislation is strongly lobbied by industry because it imposes emission limits on their operations which strongly raise their production costs. See ENDS Europe Daily 2171, 26 September 2006.

107 Burns, above n. 105 at p. 99.

108 The Inter-institutional Agreement (IIA) on Better Law-Making (OJ C 321, 31.12.2003, p. 1), agreed in December 2003 by the three EU institutions (Parliament, Council and Commission,) establishes a global strategy for better lawmaking throughout the entire EU legislative process in the context of the co-decision procedure. Its main elements include improving inter-institutional co-ordination and transparency, providing a stable framework for 'soft law' instruments that should facilitate their future use, increasing the use of impact assessment in Community decision-making, and having Parliament and the Council modify their working methods to accelerate the adoption of simplification proposals.

109 See ENDS Europe Daily 2130, 4 July 2006.

110 Council Decision of 28 June 1999 Laying Down the Procedures for the Exercise of Implementing Powers Conferred on the Commission, OJ L 184, 17.7.1999. Comitology is the system for delegating implementing powers to the Commission in conjunction with national representatives, enabling technical decisions regarding a piece of EC legislation to be amended without undergoing the whole legislative procedure.

As regards the Council, within it member states try to ensure that their views prevail in EC environmental law. 'Green' member states have developed a number of strategies to have stringent environmental law adopted.[111] Currently, the focus on competitiveness however may may make the Council more willing to protect competitiveness from the cost-impacts of new environmental legislation.[112]

As regards the immediate future, there is a chance that an increasing attention to competitiveness concerns reduces the number and ambition of new environmental legislation. I will look therefore at some of the regulatory strategies and the type of regulation advanced by the Commission in recent years.

V. THE MAKING OF ENVIRONMENTAL LAW

V.1. Regulatory Strategies for the Environment

In the light of the above-mentioned considerations, it is interesting to note that in the last annual work programme of the Commission (where it states its future legislative proposals), there are only three legislative proposals in the field of the environment.[113] Also, there is a higher reliance on co-regulation and self-regulation. Co-regulation is used where a Directive sets the bare minimum and the standards are left to standardizing bodies, in accordance with the new approach. When used in national legislation that implements an EU directive, ECJ case law has clearly stated that those standards have to be explicitly prescribed in legislation that is binding, because only then can citizens exert their rights.[114] Self-regulation is also being used in directives, such as the directive on eco-design of energy-using products.[115] This directive promotes

---

[111] See Liefferink and Andersen, above n. 105 at 50–66.

[112] See for instance the Presidency Conclusions of the European Council Meeting of March 2006, where it states that 'At Community level, significant progress has been achieved, notably through the Commission's thorough and balanced impact assessments of new proposals and their strengthened competitiveness dimension, as well as the rolling programme of simplification', at p. 8.

[113] Communication from the Commission to the European Parliament, the Council, the European Economic and Social Committee and the Committee of the Regions, 'Unlocking Europe's Full Potential – Commission Legislative and Work Programme 2006', COM (2005) 531 Final.

[114] See for instance Cases 361/88, 1991 ECR I-2567 and C-59/89, 1991 ECR I-2607 (TA-Luft).

[115] Directive 2005/32/EC of the European Parliament and of the Council of 6 July 2005 establishing a framework for the setting of eco-design requirements for energy-

voluntary agreements and other modes of self-regulation as it provides that the Commission is to refrain from taking mandatory implementing measures where its policy objectives can be achieved 'more quickly or at lesser expense' through other instruments. The use of self-regulation is also evident within Integrated Product Policy (IPP), based almost exclusively on soft-law.[116]

The Commission is relying more and more on High Level Groups to get ideas on how to regulate. These groups may be very influential for the process of legislating, by providing preliminary figures to the Commission, and indeed by ensuring that their concerns are met. Whereas this is a good sign, there is an obvious risk of regulatory capture. This is important in the light of the impact assessments, because one potential outcome is that the proposed legislation does not go through. The discussions within these groups are not transparent, as the minutes are not published.[117]

The recourse to committees also helps to find cost-efficient solutions to problems that arise in the implementation of EU legislation at national level. For instance, the committee set up under Directive 2003/87/CE on emissions trading[118] is looking at possible ways to reduce the burden that the emissions trading scheme imposes on small installations, which according to all member states and numerous observers makes neither environmental nor economic sense (as they emit a very small fraction of the overall volume of emissions while lacking capacity to profit from the scheme).[119] There is also a higher reliance on the open method of co-ordination in the environmental field.[120] Some examples are the Environmental Technologies Action Plan (ETAP), for instance in regard to subsidies to support clean technologies, and the IMPEL Network for the implementation and enforcement of environmental law.[121]

There is a preference, at least theoretically, for market based mechanisms;

---

using products and amending Council Directive 92/42/EEC and Directives 96/57/EC and 2000/55/EC of the European Parliament and of the Council, OJ L 191, 22.7.2005, 29-58.

[116] Indeed that is the approach adopted in the document launching IPP. See the Communication from the Commission to the Council and the European Parliament, 'Integrated Product Policy – Building on Environmental Life-Cycle Thinking', COM (2003) 302 Final.

[117] Wilkinson et al., above n. 44 at p. 20.

[118] Article 23 of Directive 2003/87/EC.

[119] See for instance Egenhofer, C., et al. 'The EU Emissions Trading Scheme: Taking Stock and Looking Ahead' (2006, CEPS, Brussels), at p. 12.

[120] On the potential of the Open Method of Co-ordination (OMC) within the environmental field, see Brink, P., et al. 'Exploration of Options for the Implementation of the Open Method of Coordination (OMC) for Environmental Policy', Report prepared by Ecologic and the IEEP, October 2005.

[121] Holzinger, K., Knill, C. and Schäfer, A. 'Rhetoric or Reality? New Governance in EU Environmental Policy' (2006) 12(3) *European Law Journal*, 403–420.

however, empirical studies have recently shown that their application in practice within the European Union is not widespread, due to lack of political support, the need for unanimity in the Council for the introduction of environmental taxes, and the use of environmental regulations as a means of harmonization within the EU.[122]

V.2. Some Recent Patterns in Environmental Regulation

In line with its greater emphasis on economic growth and job creation, the EU is advocating more intensely the use of market-based instruments at EU and member state level. The concern for competitiveness carries with it the desire to increase the flexibility of the means of compliance with standards set up by regulation, which is considered to reduce compliance costs while applying the polluter pays principle. Market-based instruments have been used in EC law in the following areas:

- Environmental taxes and charges, and deposit-refund schemes.
- Emissions trading.
- Subsidies, subsidy reform, support schemes and green purchasing.
- Voluntary agreements.
- Others, such as eco-labelling, eco-management, and environmental liability.

I will put forward a few examples of the recent use of some of them in EC law.

V.2.A. Taxation

The rationale of using taxes in the environmental field is to internalize the costs of pollution into prices of products. The original idea was put forward by Pigou in 1932.[123] Within the EU, the main developments have taken place at national level.[124] However, also at EU level there are some examples of their use for environmental protection purposes. Recent examples include the Community framework for the taxation of energy products and electricity, set up in Directive 2003/96/EC.[125] This Directive, which applies from 2004 onwards, sets minimum rates of duty for transport fuels. Several member

---

122 Ibid, at pp. 413–419.

123 Pigou, A.C. *The Economics of Welfare* 4th edn (1932, London).

124 See the Report 'Market-Based Instruments for Environmental Policy in Europe', European Environment Agency, Technical Report No. 8/2005.

125 Council Directive 2003/96/EC of 27 October 2003 restructuring the Community Framework for the taxation of energy products and electricity, OJ L 283 31.10.2003.

states are required to introduce new taxes levied on coal, natural gas and electricity, whereas other member states are not obliged to introduce taxes, because their level of taxation is already higher than the levels set by the Directive.

A second example is the recent political agreement achieved for the so-called new '*Eurovignette*' Directive,[126] amending Directive 1999/62/EC on the charging of heavy goods vehicles for the use of certain infrastructures.[127] It will now allow charging for road use taking into account not just costs of infrastructure but also congestion and environmental issues. Member states are free to choose how to implement the system and what levels to impose, but there is no obligation to introduce charges.[128]

The main difficulties to introduce more (environmental) taxes at EU level are twofold: (a) the need to achieve unanimity in the Council in accordance with Article 175(2)(a); (b) although the use of taxation in the environmental field is in the recent political agenda of the EU,[129] the current concern about economic growth and job creation which is attracting considerable attention from policy makers is, as shown above, moving the focus away from integration of environmental concerns into other EU policies to the integration of competitiveness concerns in environmental policies.[130] Indeed, also at national level, the main obstacle to the widespread use of taxes is the potential or perceived risk of loss of international competitiveness due to the impact of the tax on prices. Tax exemptions and reductions for, for example, energy intensive industries are common. As they can constitute state aid, they will be examined by the EC Commission under Article 87(1) EC, and under the 2001 guidelines on state aid for environmental protection.[131] Those guidelines establish under which conditions exemptions may be authorized. The main requirement is to assess whether distortions of competition are created and

---

126 Directive 2006/38/EC of the European Parliament and of the Council of 17 May 2006 amending Directive 1999/62/EC on the charging of heavy goods vehicles for the use of certain infrastructures, OJ L 157 9.6.2006.

127 For an analysis of this topic at EU and national level, see Rodi, M. 'Motorway Tolls and Sustainable Transport Policy', in Somsen, H., Etty, T.F.M., *The Yearbook of European Environmental Law* (2006, Oxford, Oxford University Press), 1–26.

128 Directive 2006/38/EC, Article 7.10 (a).

129 European Commission, 'Integrating Environmental Considerations into Other Policy Areas – A Stocktaking of the Cardiff Process', Commission Working Document, COM (2004) 394 Final.

130 See the Report, 'Market-Based Instruments for Environmental Policy in Europe', above n. 124 at p. 69.

131 European Commission, 'Community Guidelines on State Aid for Environmental Protection' 2001/C37/03.

whether they are offset by real environmental benefits. The Commission has authorized a number of reductions and exemptions under specific conditions, such as voluntary agreements concluded between sectors and the national authorities.[132]

V.2.B. Emissions trading at EU level

As regards emissions trading, the economic rationale lies in the allocation of property rights on the use of the environment as a way to solve the over-exploitation of environmental assets. The idea was first put forward by Dales.[133] At its basic, it sets an absolute cap on emissions, which is then divided into tradable allowances which are allocated within certain industrial sectors at the level of each installation. Each operator thus receives a certain number of allowances representing some quantity of emissions each, coupled with the obligation to surrender at the end of certain period a number of allowances that equals the actual emissions. Each operator can decide whether to reduce emissions below the allocated allowances and sell the remaining to other installations operating in the market, to emit only up to the amount of allowances received, or to emit more and purchase the allowances needed to cover those extra emissions in the market. Thus, cost-effectiveness in reaching the overall cap is theoretically achieved. The EU introduced the European Union emissions trading scheme (EU ETS), by Directive 2003/87/EC.[134] It was introduced to help the EU to comply with its target under the Kyoto Protocol to the United Nations Framework Convention on Climate Change (UNFCCC). The EC Commission supported the introduction of an emissions trading scheme, especially after the failure to introduce an EU-wide carbon tax, and also, albeit more cautiously, so did European industry. The scheme is based on six principles: it is a cap-and-trade system (meaning that an absolute cap on emissions, which cannot be surpassed, is set); it focuses initially on emissions of CO_2 from large emitters; it is being implemented in phases, with the possibility to cover more gases and sectors; the manner in which allocation takes place is open to change (currently allowances are mainly given by member states for free on the basis of historical emissions); includes a strong compliance framework; and is EU-wide but foresees links with the (future)

---

[132] Ibid, at p. 54.

[133] Dales, J.H. *Pollution, Property and Prices: An Essay in Policy-Making and Economics* (1968, University of Toronto Press).

[134] Directive 2003/87/EC of the European Parliament and of the Council of 13 October 2003 establishing a scheme for greenhouse gas emission allowance trading within the Community and amending Council Directive 96/61/EC, OJ L 275, 25.10.2003.

international emissions trading scheme under the UNFCCC and with regional schemes.[135]

Even if its performance cannot (yet) be judged, the fact is that the scheme has not achieved reductions so far.[136] The main reason is that member states are responsible for the allocation of emissions to industry, and so far remain cautious about setting stringent reductions which could damage the competitive positions of national industries.[137] This is also confirmed by the fact that most member states allocated all allowances for free in the first trading period (from 2005 to 2007), and continue to do so in the second trading period (2008–2012), thus rejecting the possibility given in the directive to allocate 5 and 10 per cent of the allowances in each period.[138] In addition, most of the reductions achieved come from the energy sector, which in most countries is not open to international competition, whereas those industries which are subject to international competition are generally awarded more generous allocations.[139] NGOs have criticized the national allocation plans submitted by member states to the Commission for the second trading period, extending from 2008 to 2012, and have warned that if the Commission does not reduce the volumes allocated by member states, the scheme will not achieve any reduction in the level of emissions.[140]

V.2.C. Subsidies

Subsidies have traditionally been used for economic or social reasons, for instance to support industries in difficulties, to help develop essential infrastructure or to protect domestic producers from international competition.[141] Their use for environmental purposes is more recent and a less well-established policy. This policy normally focuses on two issues: first, removing environmentally harmful subsidies, such as those giving incentives to fish, use

---

135 EU Emissions Trading: An Open Scheme Promoting Global Innovation to Combat Climate Change, European Commission, November 2004.

136 See 'The Environmental Effectiveness of the EU ETS', Ilex Energy Consulting, October 2005, at p. 38. For the second trading period, the European Commission has suggested that the number of emission allowances in the second phase (2008–2012) be on average 6 per cent lower than the first phase (2005–2007). However, the UK's cap was reduced only by 2.9 per cent and Germany's by 3.4 per cent. Poland, however, increased its cap by 17 per cent.

137 See Grubb, M., Azar, C. and Persson, U.M. 'Allowance Allocation in the European Emissions Trading System: A Commentary' (2005) 5(1) *Climate Policy*, 127–136, at p. 133.

138 As stated in Article 10 of Directive 2003/87/EC.

139 See for instance the draft National Allocation Plan 2008–2012 of Spain, at p. 40.

140 See ENDS Europe Daily 2174, 29 September 2006.

141 See 'Market-Based Instruments for Environmental Policy in Europe', above n. 124 at p. 101.

roads, or consume energy produced from fossil fuels above the level that is environmentally and economically optimal; second, supporting the development of 'green' markets and technologies. Some claim that if all external costs were internalized into prices, subsidies would not be necessary, while others maintain that they are nevertheless needed in order to rectify market failures. At EU level, they have been used in the agricultural sector, in the fisheries sector, in the industry sector, in the transport sector, in environmental support schemes and in green public procurement.[142] In all these sectors, it is possible to find examples of environmentally beneficial subsidies and of environmentally harmful subsidies.

Action undertaken in three fields of action at EC level comprises:

- The 'greening' of the Common Agricultural Policy (CAP), by replacing production subsidies with income support, and shifting the emphasis towards rural development. After the 2003 CAP reform,[143] the concept of 'conditionality' was fully introduced, and now, in order to receive EU funds, it is necessary to meet a number of environmental and animal welfare standards.
- The reform of the EU fisheries subsidies regime which began in the early 1990s. In the further reform which took place in 1999, a stronger environmental element was included in the relevant EU regulations that determine the framework for aid.[144] Even if this has resulted in more chances to use funds to promote sustainable development, still much of the aid is designed to increase supplies of fish, improve the economic performance of vessels and strengthen competitiveness in global markets.[145]
- Thirdly, the Commission is reviewing its state aid guidelines to reduce the number and amount of environmentally harmful subsidies. This strategy is part of the priority actions of ETAP, launched by the Commission in 2004 to foster the market for clean technologies.[146]

---

142 Ibid, at pp. 102–113.

143 Council Regulation 1782/2003/EC of 29 September 2003 establishing common rules for direct support schemes under the common agricultural policy and establishing certain support schemes for farmers and amending Regulations 2019/93/EEC, 1452/2001/EC, 1453/2001/EC, 1454/2001/EC, 1868/94/EC, 1251/1999/EC, 1254/1999/EC, 1673/2000/EC, 2358/71/EC and 2529/2001/EC, OJ L 270, 21.10.2003.

144 Regulation 1260/1999/EC and Regulation 1263/1999/EC.

145 Pallemaerts, M., et al. 'Drowning in Process? The Implementation of the EU's 6th Environmental ACTION Programme' (2006) IEEP Report for the European Environmental Bureau, at p. 51.

146 COM (2004) 38.

In general, concern about the competitiveness of industry is an important driver for the use and type of subsidies, also in the environmental field.[147]

V.2.D. Voluntary agreements

There is also an increase in the use of voluntary agreements within directives, where it is stated that only where these do not achieve their objective, recourse will be made to binding standards. This is the case of, as mentioned above, the directive on eco-design of energy-using products and the directive on waste electrical and electronic equipment, adopted in 2002 (the WEEE Directive).[148] The latter formally allows member states to implement certain parts of it in national legislation through voluntary agreements.[149] Indeed, this is a surprising twist in legislative technique. The Commission had promoted the use of voluntary agreements for some time, but by late 2001 only 12 had been agreed upon. Further, the Commission and the Council had encouraged member states to conclude voluntary agreements as a means to implement Community directives.[150] Now, harmonization at EU level has replaced some of those voluntary agreements at national level by voluntary agreements at EU level, such as in the case of the end-of-life vehicles directive and the packaging and packaging waste directive.[151]

VI. LEGISLATION FOR THE DEVELOPMENT OF INFRASTRUCTURE

A final and brief mention has to be made of EC law which aims to promote the development of infrastructure with the double objective of completing the internal market and of promoting the competitiveness of businesses.[152]

---

147 See 'Market-Based Instruments for Environmental Policy in Europe', above n. 124 at p. 115.

148 Directive 2002/96/EC of the European Parliament and of the Council of 27 January 2003 on waste electrical and electronic equipment (WEEE), OJ L 37, 13.2.2003.

149 Ibid, Article 17.3 allows member states to implement through agreements Articles 6.6, 10.1 and 11 on eco-management systems, facilitation of information to consumers, and information for treatment facilities, respectively.

150 Commission Recommendation 96/733, OJ L 333/69 and Council Resolution of 7 October 1997, OJ C 321/6.

151 See Heldeweg, M. 'Good Environmental Governance in the EU: Lessons from Work in Progress?', in Curtin, D.M. and Wessel, R.A. (eds), *Good Governance and the European Union – Reflections on Concepts, Institutions and Substance* (2005, Intersentia-Metro, Antwerp), 175–214, at p. 191.

152 COM (2005) 24, at p. 20.

According to Article 6 EC, this legislation has to integrate environmental requirements in order to promote sustainable development. However, a tension is frequently perceived between both objectives, and a topical issue in EC environmental law is that integration is far from achieved within the transport sector.[153] Some attention is required to the development of energy and transport infrastructure of European importance. Title XV of the EC Treaty regulates trans-European networks. Article 3(o) EC mentions, as one EC objective, to encourage the establishment and development of those networks. Article 154 EC states that the Community is to contribute to the development of networks in the areas of transport, telecommunications and energy infrastructure. Article 155 EC gives the Commission the task to establish guidelines which, inter alia, will identify projects of common interest. The Commission pressed member states in 2005 to start work on 45 'quick start' cross-border projects for transport and energy,[154] and the Council adopted the Commission proposal for a revision of the Trans-European Energy (TEN-E) Guidelines on 24 July 2006.[155] The guidelines reflect the three main objectives of Europe's energy policy, namely sustainability, competitiveness and security of supply. The objective is to boost and to accelerate the implementation and construction of connections and to increase the incentives for private investors. The guidelines present a number of projects of European interest, which are the projects of highest priority. The original proposal of the Commission[156] intended to prepare the EU for enlargement, and to ensure security of supply, against the backdrop of the blackouts that occurred in the EU in the summer of 2003. The Commission would identify priority projects, would have the competence to designate a co-ordinator for priority axes or priority projects and could attribute a declaration of European interest to cross-border priority projects.[157] The Commission noticed that the lack of progress on infrastructure priority projects was correlated to obstacles in the authorization procedures relating to the routing and the environmental consequences of the projects, which could delay the approval of those projects by five to ten years.[158] Thus, to streamline those procedures, the declaration of European interest was created. Article 7 stated that priority projects will be those which: (a) shall have a significant impact on the competitive operation of the internal

---

[153] For an analysis of the integration of environmental requirements in EC energy and transport policy, see above n. 97, especially chapters VI and VII.

[154] See Dhondt, above n. 152 at p. 20.

[155] MEMO/06/304, 24 July 2006. 2747th Session of the European Competitiveness Council.

[156] COM (2003) 742 Final.

[157] Ibid, Explanatory Memorandum of the Proposal, at p. 3.

[158] Ibid, at p.7.

market, and/or (b) shall strengthen the security of supply in the Community. Article 8 stated that a selection of priority projects which are of cross-border nature or which have significant impact on cross-border transmission capacity are declared to be of European interest. Article 8.7. stated that:

> Five years after the completion of a project declared to be of European interest or of one of the sections thereof, the Member States concerned shall carry out an assessment of its socio-economic impact and its impact on the environment, including its impact on trade between Member States, on territorial cohesion and on sustainable development.

ShuYu Zhang has criticized this as being contrary to the prevention principle and unacceptable under Council Directive 85/337/EC (the Environmental Impact Assessment Directive), and its amending Directive 97/11EC.[159] Article 2(1) states that the assessment needs to be done before consent is given for projects falling under Annex I. For projects falling under Annex II, member states are to determine whether an assessment is needed through the thresholds or criteria set by them or on a case-by-case basis. Many of those cross-border projects will relate to criterion 20 of Annex I and to criterion 3 of Annex II.[160]

Thus by reversing the order of the impact assessment and the construction, the TEN-E guidelines put competitiveness and the completion of the internal market before environmental protection requirements for projects of European interest.

VII. CONCLUSIONS

The EC legislator is committed to pursuing a large number of objectives under the paradigm of sustainable development. However, it is unrealistic to assume that all of them can be pursued to the same extent at all times; rather, a direction must be set whereby all of them may be satisfied, but at some point one will need more support than others. Moreover, today it seems already clear that the objective of the Lisbon Agenda was over-ambitious; the competitiveness of the EU

---

159 Zhang, S. 'The Proposed EU Energy Security Package vis-à-vis EU Law' (2004) 13(6) *European Environmental Law Review*, 170–176, at p.172.

160 Criterion 20 of Annex I EIA Directive refers to 'construction of overhead electrical power lines with a voltage of 220 kv or more and a length of more than 15 km'. Criterion 3 of Annex III refers to '(a) industrial installations for the production of electricity, steam and hot water (projects not included in Annex I); (b) industrial installations for carrying gas, steam and hot water; transmission of electrical energy by overhead cables (projects not included in Annex I)'.

economy has not improved substantially, and the same generally applies to the protection of the environment.[161]

Currently the EU struggles with issues of economic growth and job creation. Promoting them requires the implementation of a number of measures, a number of which, such as those to increase labour productivity or to simplify and rationalize legislation, are not necessarily at odds with environmental protection. It seems inefficient to put the political focus on the conflicts between both objectives rather than on identifying the specific measures which promote one of them without harming the other. Labour productivity can be improved partly through better legislation without watering down its environmental stringency. Job creation can be on those sectors which are environmentally friendly and away from the most damaging ones. The structural adjustments must be faced with courage and analytical consistency, giving due attention to the distributional impacts, which so far has not really been the case.[162]

It might be legitimate to focus temporarily on measures promoting job creation and economic growth while seizing all chances possible to improve marginally the protection of the environment, through the full implementation of the better regulation package, and in this process it is necessary to ensure that there are no substantive reductions in environmental protection. The 2005 IA guidelines need to be applied carefully and systematically, otherwise they may result in downplaying the environmental objective.

As regards substantive environmental improvements, it is possible to work in that direction through the more extended use of market-based mechanisms that seek to internalize prices to the full, as long as the distributional impacts are duly taken into account. This is possibly the best way to proceed, fully in accordance with the better regulation initiative.

---

161 'The European Environment – State and Outlook 2005', European Environment Agency, at p. 210.

162 See Kriström, B. in Serret, Y. and Johnstone, N. (eds), *The Distributional Effects of Environmental Policy* (2006, OECD and Edward Elgar), 79–136.

5. Regulatory strategies in environmental liability

Michael G. Faure

1. INTRODUCTION

The question what the particular task of private law is in remedying environmental damage has in recent years been discussed extensively in the literature. Economists, starting from the idea that, in a situation where transaction costs are prohibitive and hence private bargaining cannot provide efficient solutions, stress that private law may be one of the instruments to be used to address the market failure caused by environmental damage. Indeed, the traditional way in which economists would approach environmental issues is usually by stressing the fact that there is a reason for law to intervene given the market failure constituted by the externality resulting from the environmental damage. Law in general should then, stated very basically, have as a goal that the marginal social costs caused by the externality should be taken into account by the decision maker. The environmental damage should, in other words, be internalized.

Lawyers have, with different wordings of course, also pointed at various benefits of private law in remedying environmental damage. Although they tend to attach less belief than economists to the preventive function of liability rules, legal doctrine also has often stressed that it is important to impose the costs due to environmental damage upon polluters since this may provide them incentives to abate environmental pollution. Often legal principles (even incorporated into international conventions) have been used to justify this idea. Well known in this respect is of course the 'polluter pays' principle.

The goal of this chapter is to sketch how, following this legal and economic literature, private law can play a role in the governance of environmental risks. This is a very broad and seemingly abstract question and it would take several books to answer it. Given the necessary limits of this chapter, that is of course not possible. Therefore in this chapter to some extent the main results of the legal and economic literature that has addressed the role of private law in remedying environmental damage will be presented. These issues have, moreover, not been dealt with in the abstract (for example just by analysing them within the context of economic models). Quite often the effectiveness or efficiency of specific environmental liability regimes has been critically reviewed. Thus in this chapter the way in which private law tackles environmental problems will be looked at both from the economic literature, and also by addressing tendencies in some member states and of course within the European Union. Since Europe finally adopted in 2004 a European Directive on remedying environmental damage some attention will have to be given to that document as well.

By addressing the role of private law in remedying environmental damage I will limit myself necessarily to one instrument of private law, being environmental liability, in other words tort law. Of course other instruments of private law could be thought of as well. Property rules and legal instruments related to property law (like nuisance law) are in many legal systems used as remedies in the fight against environmental pollution as well. And in some cases contract solutions may provide a remedy as well. However, the main instrument of private law in legal practice is undoubtedly liability law. Therefore I will mainly focus on that instrument.

The approach that will be taken in this chapter is by using on the one hand the knowledge acquired from the rich literature addressing environmental liability from a so-called law and economics perspective, but on the other hand by also looking at some developments within Europe. Thus the chapter will to some extent be positive, in the sense that it will mainly describe some evolutions in the way some member states (and Europe) have been using private law in remedying environmental damage. At the same time the economic literature especially will be used to come to some policy conclusions with respect to the way in which private law should probably be used in remedying environmental damage. As far as economics is used to address these policy issues the chapter is therefore unavoidably normative as well.

A great number of various topics within environmental liability could theoretically be addressed given the enormous richness of this literature as it has been developed during the past decades. However, since we have to select we will focus on those issues that are crucial in analysing what the role of environmental liability can be in preventing and compensating for environmental damage. Those two questions will therefore be the crucial ones. The question will indeed be addressed whether environmental liability is able (and to what extent) to *prevent* environmental damage and whether it can also provide *compensation*. At the same time the limits of environmental liability in providing both prevention and compensation will be addressed as well.

Especially within the context of a project interested in various regulatory approaches and tools, a focus on private law and more particularly liability is interesting since it has always been considered as a 'market solution'. Even in the context of the discussion of new so-called 'economic' environmental policy instruments, the importance of liability rules to guide the behaviour of potential polluters is often mentioned. However, many have of course rightly pointed at the fact that in comparison the role of private law in preventing environmental harm will often be limited. Most of the preventive behaviour will probably be the result of regulatory tools. Still this merits some attention to the question whether liability can play an additional role in backing up a regulation.

Within the context of a project on strategies and governance in European private law the question also needs to be briefly addressed whether there is any justification for a 'Europeanization' of the way in which private law deals with environmental liability. Again this is a question which has been addressed in economic literature. From a legal perspective the question has apparently been answered in the positive, given the fact that Europe has issued an important directive dealing with environmental damage. Nevertheless it still is interesting, also with a view to jurisdictions other than Europe, to address the question what the precise functions of harmonization in this area could be.

Of course, as mentioned already, this chapter merely aims at providing a '*tour d'horizon*' of the issues at stake in environmental liability. It therefore necessarily builds on earlier research and is rather meant to give an overview of where legal and economic research in this domain stands today, as well as evolutions at the policy level.

On the basis of these starting points, after this introduction (section 1) the following issues will be addressed: first the question will be asked whether and how tort law can assist in preventing environmental damage (section 2). Necessarily then the question will be addressed why in practice it is mainly regulation that exercises this preventive function (section 3) and whether there still can be a complementary role for liability law in addition to regulation (section 4). Next the issue of compensation has to be addressed whereby unavoidably the compensatory role of tort law and its limits has to be addressed briefly (section 5). Immediately it will be shown that, without a backup by a financial security such as liability insurance, tort law provides little by way of a guarantee of compensation. However, liability insurance also has its limits in providing compensation especially in the area of diffuse environmental damage (section 6). Therefore many have addressed alternatives for liability insurance in providing compensation for environmental damage. An interesting alternative, since it again builds on a private initiative, is the tendency to use environmental damage insurance instead of liability insurance (section 7). Although all of these approaches fit into 'private law' the question of course also needs to be addressed whether there is any role for government, even when sticking to the private law solution. Can government be of any help, for example in providing facilitative strategies to improve the functioning of the liability system instead of immediately turning to regulatory solutions (section 8)? Of course the question how harmonization is viewed both from a legal and from an economic perspective needs to be addressed as well (section 9). A final section (section 10) will address the challenging question whether there is indeed a role and future for private law in protecting the environment. Since this is a broad and ambitious agenda it has once more to be stressed that many of these topics can be touched upon briefly in this general overview. For in-depth analysis of the specific issues the reader will be referred to the literature mentioned in the references.

2. PREVENTIVE ROLE OF TORT LAW

One of the regulatory functions of private law is, at least from an economic perspective, within the context of environmental harm, to provide incentives to risk creators aimed at prevention. The way liability rules aim at prevention can moreover be considered as a market oriented approach or, if one wants, as the use of soft law instead of hard law. Indeed, the way tort law functions in providing these incentives is that it fixes a price for a specific violation of norms (negligence) or for reaching a certain consequence (strict liability), but it generally leaves it up to the parties to find the optimal mode to prevent environmental harm. We will have a quick look at how this regulatory function of environmental liability is seen from an economic perspective (2.1), then the functioning of the two major liability rules, negligence and strict liability, will be addressed (2.2) and a brief word will be spent on actual policy in the European Union in this domain (2.3).

2.1 Economic Principles of Accident Law

The economic analysis of law in general and of accident law more specifically starts from the belief that a legal rule and more particularly a finding of liability will give incentives to potential parties in an accident setting for careful behaviour.[1] Thus, economists tend to stress the deterrent function of tort law. Lawyers on the other hand sometimes mention this deterrent function as well, but tend to attach more value to the compensation goal of accident law. This 'victim protection' argument is discussed in the law and economics literature as well.[2] In that respect it is, however, often stressed that the best form of

---

1 For excellent overviews of the role of liability and insurability as 'engineering instruments' see Endres and Staiger 1996, pp. 79–93; Wagner 1999, pp. 1441–1480; Monti 2001, pp. 51–79 and Gimpel-Hinteregger 1994, pp. 19–58.

2 Schwartz showed that rules of tort law may serve both the aims of deterrence and corrective justice (Schwartz 1997, pp. 1801–1834).

victim protection is to avoid victimization in the first place. Of course, no one will argue that prevention of accidents is not a way of victim protection as well. This difference in accent between both approaches is also characterized as an *ex ante* versus an *ex post* vision. Whereas lawyers tend to be more interested in the accident problem *ex post*, where there is a victim who needs to be compensated, economists look at the accident problem in an *ex ante* perspective by asking the question how an *ex post* finding of liability will influence *ex ante* the incentives for care-taking of potential parties in an accident setting.

Of course, the differences in approach between lawyers and economists are not really that black and white. There are lawyers who stress the deterrent function of tort law as well[3] and some economists pay attention to compensation issues by stressing that accident law should also aim at an equitable loss spreading.[4] Moreover, lawyers also argue that tort law should lead to duties of care, which aim at prevention.

From an economic perspective the main goal of liability rules is the minimization of what was called by Guido Calabresi, the primary accident costs:[5] the costs of accident avoidance and the expected damage. Indeed, from a social point of view accidents do not only cause costs from the moment an accident occurs and harm is suffered; potential parties in an accident setting, both injurers and victims make investments in care to avoid the occurrence of an accident. Sometimes costs of care-taking are very clear and visible. We can refer for instance to the investments made by firms to reduce environmental pollution by investing in water-cleaning equipment or the investment to install safety controls to avoid product defects. But also the mere fact that in a traffic accident case both injurers and victims are limited in their freedom of movement, for instance because they have to drive or work carefully, is considered as a cost by economists. A difference is further made between so-called unilateral accidents in which only the care taken by one of the parties (the injurer) can influence the accident risk on the one hand and bilateral accidents in which the behaviour of both parties can influence the accident risk on the other hand.[6] In a bilateral accident situation the goal of accident law should therefore be to give incentives to minimize the total costs of care-taking by the potential injurer and the potential victim and the expected damage that will occur in case of an accident.

Economists use classic cost/benefit analysis to determine what the level of care is that will lead to such minimization of the social costs of accidents. Not surprisingly, this can be found where the marginal costs of care-taking equal

---

3 See Koziol 1997, pp. 8–13.
4 See Veljanovski 1981, pp. 125–150.
5 See Calabresi 1961, pp. 499–553 and Calabresi 1970.
6 This distinction has been made by Shavell 1987, p. 7.

the marginal benefits in accident reduction.[7] Indeed, since care-taking has its price as well, a legal rule should not give incentives to avoid every possible accident that could occur, but only accidents that could be avoided by investments in care, of which the marginal costs are lower than or equal to the marginal benefits in accident reduction. It might well be that extremely high care could well additionally contribute to a reduction of the accident risk but the marginal costs of care-taking in that case might well be much higher than the additional benefit in accident reduction. Investments in care would in that case be inefficient and scarce resources would be spoiled.[8] These levels of care where marginal costs of care-taking equal marginal benefits in accident reduction are referred to in the literature as optimal or efficient care levels.[9]

2.2 Strict Liability versus Negligence

After having defined the regulatory function of liability rules, being that from an economic perspective liability rules should provide incentives to risk creators to take optimal care, the next question (which has been extensively addressed in the literature) is which liability rule may provide these appropriate incentives and can, in other words, be considered as fitting in a regulatory strategy optimally to prevent environmental damage. The two legal rules distinguished in this respect are on the one hand the classic fault or negligence rule, such as for example the one incorporated in Article 1382 of the the French Civil Code and on the other hand the strict liability rule. The basic difference is that under a fault or negligence regime the risk creator is only due to compensate the victim when his behaviour falls short of a certain level of due care, to be determined by the court. Strict liability on the other hand lays a duty upon the injurer to compensate the victim irrespective of his behaviour. A strict liability rule only requires that there is a causal relationship between the activity of the injurer and the damage of the victim.

Economic literature holds that if a negligence rule is adopted, the injurer will take optimal care, provided the due care required in the legal system is equal to the optimal care as defined in the model.[10] This can be easily understood. If the judicial system sets the due care standard correctly, the injurer can avoid liability by taking due care. Thus he will have to take care to avoid the accident, but if he does so he can avoid paying the expected damage. Since the

---

7 Ibid.

8 This finding only holds in a risk neutral setting. In a case of risk aversion, higher investments in care might well be efficient since a reduction of accident risk will in that case also remove the disutility of risk from a risk averse person.

9 See Landes and Posner 1981, p. 870 and Polinsky 1983.

10 Shavell 1987, p. 8 and Calabresi 1975, p. 658.

optimal care standard was defined as exactly that level of care where the marginal costs of care equal the marginal benefits in accident reduction, taking less than the due care standard will not be worthwhile for the individual injurer since it will increase his total expected costs. Thus a negligence rule will lead to an efficient outcome as long as the legal system defines the due care as equal to the optimal care of the model.

Also a strict liability rule will lead to the optimum in a case where only one party can influence the accident risk. The reason is quite simple. A strict liability rule basically states that the injurer has to compensate in any case no matter what care he took. It is sometimes argued that this will lead the injurer to take excessive precautions or to take no care at all since he is liable anyway. Neither of these statements seems true. By making the injurer strictly liable, the social decision is in fact shifted to the injurer. In a unilateral accident case it simply means that he has to bear all the social costs of accidents, namely his own costs of care-taking and the expected damage.[11] Therefore, he will take exactly the same decision, namely to minimize his total expected accident costs. We discussed in the model that this could be reached at the optimal care level. Therefore, the injurer will take optimal care since this is the way to minimize his total expected costs. Spending more on care would increase his costs of care-taking inefficiently and spending less on care would increase the expected damage inefficiently.

This leads to the conclusion that in this particular setting where we only considered the influence of the injurer's care on the accidents, both negligence and strict liability will provide incentives to take optimal care. Of course important nuances to this difference can be added. For instance the administrative costs of applying both rules differ. The strict liability rule seems to have the disadvantage that a legal case will follow with every accident since the injurer is always bound to compensate. Court costs can therefore be expected to be high. On the other hand, the negligence rule seems to have high information costs for the judge since he will have to determine in a particular case what the marginal costs and marginal benefits of care-taking were.[12]

The analysis of course can be much more refined, for instance if one goes into the bilateral accident situation. In that case, a contributory or comparative negligence defence has to be added to a strict liability rule to give victims an incentive as well to take optimal care. In other words, since victims would be fully compensated under strict liability, some defence should be added if the victim can equally influence the accident risk. Otherwise the victim would lack the incentives for prevention.

---

11 Polinsky 1983, p. 39; Shavell 1987, p. 11 and p. 8.

12 Brown 1973 p. 343; Calabresi 1975, p. 666, footnote 22 and Shavell 1987, p. 9.

The advantage of the negligence rule in that case is that the victim will anyway assume that he has to bear the loss, so he will always have an incentive for taking optimal care. The simple reason is that a fully informed victim (which is obviously a strong assumption) will be aware of the fact that the injurer will take due care to avoid liability. Hence the victim is left with his loss and will automatically have incentives for prevention, even if no defences are added. A further refinement can be found when attention is given to factors other than care that can influence the accident risk. In the literature, attention, has especially been paid in that respect to the influence of the activity level.[13]

How does this test apply to the issue concerned in this chapter, being environmental liability? Environmental pollution can in most cases certainly be considered a unilateral accident, that is to say an accident whereby only the injurer can influence the accident risk. In this case we noted that the economic model predicts that the advantage of the strict liability rule is that it will give the injurer an incentive both to adopt an optimal activity level and to take efficient care. Since the victim cannot influence the accident risk, strict liability seems to be the best solution to give the potential polluter optimal incentives for accident reduction in those cases.[14]

There may, however, obviously be cases where other parties than the polluter could influence the risk of environmental degradation. These are not always the victims in the traditional sense. One can imagine cases where, for example, public or private actors would be responsible for managing a natural resource area. It might be desirable in those cases that liability also aims at giving them appropriate incentives to take those preventive measures. In that case environmental pollution would constitute a bilateral risk on the condition that one considers that third party a victim.[15] However, since, in the example given, the influence of the polluter is probably still far more important than the influence of the other parties, the outcome does not change: a strict liability rule still is warranted to give the party who has most influence on the accident risk (the polluter) the incentive to take preventive measures. It is, however, important to remember that in bilateral cases a defence should always be added to victims as well. Moreover, if parties other than the polluter can also influence the accident risk, they might be held liable as well for the amount in which they contributed to the loss. That is, however, not an argument against the strict liability of the polluter.

---

13 See Adams 1989; Diamond 1974, pp. 107–164; Shavell 1980, pp. 1–25.

14 See for an application to nuclear liability; Faure 1995a, pp. 21–43.

15 Although it is then probably more a case where more parties can influence the accident risk (and should therefore be given appropriate incentives) since the actors in the example given cannot be considered traditional victims who suffer the loss personally (see also Niezen, Raaijmakers and Tervoort 2000, p. 171).

So, if we apply the criteria of Shavell determining the choice between negligence and strict liability to the environmental case, there seem to be strong arguments in favour of an introduction of strict liability. In many cases environmental pollution will be truly unilateral in the sense that only the injurer's activity can influence the accident risk, which constitutes a strong case for strict liability.[16]

There is another important aspect of the difference between negligence and strict liability which should be mentioned. This concerns the fact that the application of negligence requires high information costs from the judge, who will have to set the due care standard. The information necessary to weigh costs and benefits and to fix the optimal care may not be readily available to the judge. Strict liability shifts all costs to the injurer, who will then have to define the optimal care level. If one therefore assumes that, as may be the case with environmental harm, the information on optimal precaution is more easily available to industry than to the judges, this constitutes an argument for strict liability. Note that obviously in some cases there may be an information advantage with the regulator. This is, as we will discuss below, an argument in favour of regulation, but not necessarily against strict liability. This information advantage may therefore constitute an additional argument in favour of strict liability for environmental harm.

One should, however, remember that this finding only holds in all the models, such as the one which has been developed by Shavell, which start from an assumption of risk neutrality. If risk aversion is introduced and the potential injurer is risk averse, Endres and Schwarze correctly argue that strict liability is only efficient if in some way risk can be removed from the risk averse injurer, for example through insurance.[17] Moreover, we assume that the judge has accurate information on the amount of the damage. If courts err in assessing damages, strict liability will lead to underdeterrence.[18]

2.3 Environmental Liability in European Private Law

Of course a discussion of the regulatory function of liability rules within the context of a project on European private law should also pay some attention to

16 In some cases it will be the victim's activity that caused the harm, e.g. if the victim knowingly came to the nuisance. This may then lead to a denial of a claim for compensation. See in that respect the discussion on the coming to the nuisance doctrine, by Wittman 1980, pp. 557–568.

17 See Endres and Schwarze 1991, pp. 1–25.

18 If, in other words, courts can more easily observe the socially desirable level of precaution than the exact amount of external harm, a negligence rule should be favoured. This point has been made by Cooter 1984, pp. 1343–1523.

recent developments in this respect at the policy level. The question of course more particularly arises as to what extent the preference for strict liability (at least in unilateral accident cases) can also be found back in legal practice. First of all it can be held that the move towards strict liability for environmental damage can be discovered in many legal systems in Europe. This is more particularly the case when it concerns liability for soil pollution.[19] Indeed, one can point at developments in legislation and case law in many countries which indicate a general trend towards strict liability. Strict liability rules could already be found in many international conventions, for example in the civil liability convention of 29 November 1969 with respect to oil pollution damage[20] and also in the nuclear liability conventions (of Paris and Brussels), which equally impose a strict liability on the licensee of a nuclear power plant. Strict liability has also been introduced in the legislation of many countries. For instance section 7 of the 1995 Environmental Act in the UK imposes strict liability for soil pollution.[21] Also chapter 32 of the 1998 Swedish Environmental Code provides for a strict joint and several liability regime and a duty to compensate for those whose activity would cause bodily injury, material damage and pecuniary losses. Chapter 10 of the same environmental code equally imposes a strict liability rule for soil contamination. Also the 1990 German Environmental Liability Act introduced a strict statutory liability.[22] In other countries the move towards strict liability did not result from formal changes in legislation, but from developments in case law. This is for instance the case in France where a broad interpretation of Article 1384, first line of Article 1384 of the Civil Code led effectively to a strict liability for example for polluted soils.[23]

---

19 For an overview, see Faure and Grimeaud 2003, pp. 68–122.

20 Faure, M. and Wang, H. (2006), 'Economic Analysis of Compensation for Oil Pollution Damage', *Maritime Law and Commerce*, 179–217.

21 For more details on the UK soil pollution regime, see McIntyre 1996, pp. 67–74. For an overview of environmental law in the UK, see Jones 1999. For an overview of the liability system for environmental damage in the UK, see also the 1996 McKenna Report, *Study of Civil Liability Systems for Remedying Environmental Damage* (Report for the European Commission, McKenna & Co (now Cameron McKenna), Mistre House, 160 Aldersgate Street, London EC1A 4DD, UK) and the 2001 Clarke Report for the European Commission, *Update Comparative Legal Study* (update on the Mckenna Report): posted at: http://europa.eu.int/comm/environment/liability/legalstudy.htm.

22 For an overview of environmental law in Germany, see Pape and Schillhorn 1999. See also the 1996 McKenna Report, above n. 21 and the 2001 Clarke Report for the European Commission, above n. 21. See also Hager 1993, pp. 41–44.

23 For a critical discussion of French tort law from an economic perspective, see Faure 2001a, pp. 169–181.

This European-wide tendency towards strict liability now also seems to have reached the European Union with its Directive 2004/35/CE of 21 April 2004.[24] Of course this is not the place to discuss the contents of the directive in any detail. It only seems interesting to verify to what extent the approach in the directive follows the lessons from economic analysis enabling environmental liability to exercise its regulatory function.

3. REGULATION

3.1 Environmental Liability versus Regulation

It is not difficult to argue that although environmental liability undoubtedly has an important task as a regulatory instrument to prevent environmental damage, it also has serious inherent limitations. Given these limitations some scholars therefore qualify the public law approach as 'the preferred approach' to prevent environmental damage.[25] However, it would intellectually of course not be correct to qualify the fact that liability law cannot be applied to many cases of environmental damage as a shortcoming or limitation of tort law. The limitation of this instrument is that it of course can only be used when there is an identifiable victim and injurer and when a causal relationship can be established between an activity of the risk creator and the damage of the victim. If the injurer cannot be identified or the cause of the environmental damage cannot be established, liability law can indeed not be applied to this particular type of damage. However, this can hardly be considered as a 'shortcoming' of liability law; it simply means that the conditions for the application of liability law are not fulfilled. However, this does justify the conclusion that, if one wants to attain prevention of environmental harm, instruments other than liability law will have to be used.

Law and economics has paid a great deal of attention to the question whether safety in society can best be attained through liability rules or through regulation. An important contribution in this respect comes from Steven Shavell who examined the choice between liability rules and regulation in a thorough way.[26] Both liability rules and regulation can be used to reach the same goal, being an optimal prevention of environmental harm. However, the way in which both instruments are used is totally different. If tort law is used, the risk creator remains free to choose the way in which environmental

---

24 Official Journal L143/56 of 30 April 2004.

25 See Bergkamp 2001, p. 208.

26 Shavell 1984a, pp. 357–374; Shavell 1984b, pp. 271–280 and Shavell 1987, pp. 277–290.

damage can be prevented. Tort law assumes that the preventive function of liability rules will give incentives to the potential risk creator to introduce optimal preventive mechanisms. This is the case either because this is the optimal way for the potential risk creator to prevent the damage (under strict liability) or because it is a way to prevent having to pay compensation to the victim (under a negligence rule). Under regulation the government will *ex ante* impose the use of a particular preventive mechanism. Non-compliance with this preventive mechanism will also be enforced and can lead to the imposition of administrative or criminal sanctions. Regulation is thus considered as an *ex ante* system aiming at prevention, whereas liability rules mainly intervene *ex post* after the damage has occurred. The criteria advanced by Steven Shavell that influenced safety regulation and liability are to be found in 3.2, 3.3 and 3.4.

3.2 Information Asymmetries

Information deficiencies have often been advanced as a cause of market failure and as the justification for government intervention through regulation.[27] Also, for the proper operation of a liability system, information on for example the existing legal rules, the accident risk and efficient measures to prevent accidents, is a precondition for an efficient deterrence. According to Shavell, the parties in an accident setting generally have much better information on the accident risk than that possessed by the regulatory body.[28] The parties themselves have, in principle, the best information on the costs and benefits of the activity that they undertake and of the optimal way to prevent accidents. This 'assumption of information' will, however, be reversed if it becomes clear that some risks are not readily appreciated by the parties in an accident setting. This may be a problem more particularly if costs are external. These cannot always be easily assessed by the parties involved.

3.3 Insolvency

If the potential damages can be so high that they will exceed the wealth of the individual injurer, liability rules will not provide optimal incentives. The reason is that the costs of care are directly related to the magnitude of the expected damages. If the expected damages are much greater than the individual wealth of the injurer, the injurer will only consider the accident as

---

[27] See the basic article by Stigler 1961, p. 213 and see Schwartz and Wilde 1979, pp. 630–682 and Mackay 1982.

[28] Shavell 1984a, p. 359.

having a magnitude equal to his wealth. He will take, therefore, only the care necessary to avoid an accident equal to his wealth, which can be lower than the care required to avoid the total accident risk.[29] This is a simple application of the principle that the deterrent effect of tort liability works only if the injurer has assets to pay for the damages he causes. If an injurer is protected against such liability, the problem of underdeterrence arises.[30]

Safety regulation can overcome this problem of underdeterrence caused by insolvency.[31] In that case, the efficient care will be determined *ex ante* by regulation and will be affected by enforcement instruments which induce the potential injurer to comply with the regulatory standard, irrespective of his wealth.

Therefore, a problem might still arise if the regulation were also enforced by means of monetary sanctions. Again, if these were to exceed the injurer's wealth, the insolvency problem would remain. Hence, if a safety regulation is introduced because of a potential insolvency problem, the regulation itself should be enforced by non-monetary sanctions.[32]

3.4 Underdeterrence of Tort Law

Some activities can cause considerable damage, but even so a law suit to recover these damages may never be brought. If this were the case, there would of course be no deterrent effect of liability rules. Therefore, the absence of a liability suit would again be an argument to enforce the duty of efficient care by means of safety regulations rather than through liability rules.[33] There can be a number of reasons why a law suit is not brought, even though considerable damage has been caused.

Sometimes an injurer can escape liability because the harm is thinly spread among a number of victims. As a consequence, the damage incurred by every individual victim is so small that there is no incentive to bring a suit. In particular, this problem will arise if the damage is not caused to an individual but to common property, such as the surface waters in which each member of the population has a minor interest. In addition, a long time might have elapsed

---

29 Ibid., p. 360.

30 Shavell 1986, pp. 43–58. Above we mentioned that insolvency causes a problem especially under a strict liability rule, but less so under negligence. See Section 5.2 at pp. 152–153.

31 If insurance were to come into the picture it could overcome the problems of underdeterrence, provided that the moral hazard problem, caused by insurance, could be cured.

32 Shavell 1985a, pp. 1232–1262.

33 Shavell 1984a, p. 363.

before the damage becomes apparent; in this case much of the necessary evidence may be either lost or not obtained. Another problem is that if the damage only manifests itself years after the activity, the injurer might have gone out of business.

A related problem is that it is often hard to prove that a causal link exists between an activity and a type of damage.[34] The burden of proof of a causal relationship becomes more difficult with the increasing passage of time since the damaging incident took place. Often a victim will not recognize that the harm had been caused by a tort, but might think that his or her particular ailment, for example cancer, had a 'natural cause', associated with general ill health. For all these reasons, a liability suit might not be brought and hence safety regulation is necessary to ensure that the potential polluter takes efficient care.[35]

3.5 Empirical Evidence

For these reasons it is clear that some form of government regulation of environmental pollution is necessary. To reformulate: this shows that liability rules alone cannot suffice to prevent environmental harm, but there might be other, publicly imposed, instruments than the command and control type regulation which can be used to reach this goal. Taxes are obviously such an alternative. But these also are publicly imposed and can hence be considered as 'regulation'.

Although it is difficult to examine whether environmental regulation is generally also effective in reducing environmental harm, some studies have attempted to examine the effectiveness of safety regulation in controlling environmental harm. These studies do not address the specific quality of every environmental law, but examine whether regulation has generally been more important in reducing environmental harm than liability rules. Dewees demonstrated that in North America the quality of the environment has improved substantially as a result of regulatory efforts, not so much in response to legal action in tort.[36]

This empirical evidence of the success of regulation, compared to tort law, has been stressed in the book by Dewees, Duff and Trebilcock.[37] They hold that the large regulatory effort to improve the environment has met with

---

[34] See Landes and Posner 1984, p. 417 and Kunreuther and Freeman 2001, pp. 304–305.

[35] For alternatives to liability suits, see Bocken 1987, pp. 83–87 and Bocken 1988, pp. 3–10.

[36] Dewees 1992a, pp. 446–467 and Dewees 1992b, pp. 139–164.

[37] Dewees, Duff and Trebilcock 1996.

considerable success when measured by the reduction of emissions, but that it is more difficult to argue that the environmental regulations of the 1970s in the US equally had a considerable influence on the ambient environmental quality. Moreover, they also stress that while environmental regulation is a determining factor in pollutant emissions and ambient concentrations, other non-regulatory factors such as economic growth and even the weather also influence environmental quality.[38]

4. NECESSITY TO COMBINE LIABILITY AND REGULATION

We just stressed that according to Shavell's criteria there is a strong argument to control the environmental risk through *ex ante* regulation (or taxes). However, in individual cases there can still be damage to the environment. Then again, liability under tort comes into the picture and the question has been addressed in the literature how regulation influences the liability system and vice versa. The complementary relationship between tort law and regulation has been examined in detail by Rose-Ackerman,[39] Faure and Ruegg,[40] Kolstad, Ulen and Johnson[41] and recently by Arcuri[42] and Burrows.[43] Rose-Ackerman also compared US and European experiences in using regulation versus tort law in environmental policy.[44]

The first point which is often stressed is that the fact that there are many arguments in favour of *ex ante* regulation of the environment, does not mean that the tort system should not be used any longer for its deterring and compensating functions. One reason for still relying on the tort system is that the effectiveness of (environmental) regulation is dependent upon enforcement, which may be weak.

In addition, the influence of lobby groups on regulation, to which public choice theory has rightly pointed, can to some extent be overcome by combining safety regulation and liability rules. Moreover, safety regulation, for example emission standards in licences, can become outdated fast and often lacks flexibility, which equally merits a combination with tort rules. Hence, from the

---

38 Ibid., pp. 307–323.

39 Rose-Ackerman 1992a, pp. 223–243; Rose-Ackerman 1992b, pp. 118–131 and Rose-Ackerman 1996, pp. 13–39.

40 Faure and Ruegg 1994, pp. 39–60.

41 Kolstad, Ulen and Johnson 1990, pp. 888–901.

42 Arcuri 2001, pp. 39–40.

43 Burrows 1999, pp. 227–242.

44 Rose-Ackerman 1995b, pp. 312–332 and Rose-Ackerman 1995a.

above it follows that although there is a strong case for safety regulation to control the environmental risk, tort rules will still play an important role as well.[45] This obviously raises the question whether compliance with regulation will affect the liability issue. We will address this point in the next section.

These interdependencies between regulation and tort law raise a number of interesting questions that have been extensively addressed in the literature, but that will not be addressed in this chapter for the reason that these complementarities have been addressed by Anthony Ogus in Chapter 1 of this volume.

5. COMPENSATION: THE LIMITS OF ENVIRONMENTAL LIABILITY

As we mentioned when discussing the preventive versus the compensatory role of tort law, we noticed that economists tend to stress the deterrent function of tort law whereas lawyers tend to attach more value to the compensation goal of liability rules. This belief that tort law may have a compensatory function as well plays an important role in legal literature and has largely influenced the choice between strict liability and negligence, which was addressed above from an economic perspective.

5.1 Negligence versus Strict Liability

The reason that is often advanced in legal literature in favour of strict liability is that strict liability will help the victim to obtain compensation since he or she is released from the heavy burden of proving fault under the negligence rule.[46] However, from a deterrence point of view victim compensation is not as such a goal of accident law. The duty of the injurer to compensate his victim is only an instrument to reach deterrence efficiency. Moreover, the victim compensation argument to introduce strict liability for environmental pollution is not that convincing in all cases. Indeed, many legal systems qualify every violation of a statutory or regulatory norm as a civil fault. Most industries are subjected to extensive safety regulation. Hence, in these systems the victim only has to prove the violation of one of these regulations to establish a fault. If, in addition, the victim can prove a causal relationship with the loss suffered, he or she will be able to claim compensation. In many accident cases

45 For a different analysis, leading to the same result that liability and regulation should be combined, see Schmitz 2000, pp. 371–382.

46 For an overview of all legal arguments in favour of strict environmental liability, see Jones 1997, pp. 11–27.

this burden of proof will therefore not be as heavy as has been argued. It is, therefore, at least questionable whether a strict liability rule substantially improves the situation of the victim in comparison with an already existing broadly interpreted civil fault regime. It should also not be overlooked that under the general fault regime of tort law no limitations apply and the victim is entitled to full compensation. In many of the cases where strict liability was first introduced, more particularly in the international conventions concerning nuclear accidents and oil pollution,[47] financial caps and other limitations on the victim's rights were introduced. The alleged compensating benefit of the strict liability in those cases is therefore doubtful.

Obviously arguments in favour of strict liability could also be based on distributional differences. These are more particularly distributional arguments which can often be found in the legal literature. Indeed, an important difference between strict liability and negligence is obviously that if the negligence rule works perfectly, the injurer will take the care that the legal system requires from him and will therefore not be held liable. A perfectly working negligence rule will therefore give appropriate incentives to the injurer, but not provide compensation to the victim. A strict liability rule is a rule which in principle guarantees compensation to the victim (if one disregards the insolvency issue, which we shall discuss below). It is precisely because of this distributional difference that many lawyers favour the strict liability rule. Remember, however, that from an economic perspective in bilateral cases strict liability is efficient only if a defence is added (contributory or comparative negligence) to give the victim incentives as well for effective prevention.

5.2 Insolvency

In sum, one should be careful with merely advocating strict liability because it would provide a better compensation to victims for the reasons (1) that these advantages are not always that obvious and (2) that the strict liability rule only guarantees compensation if we assume (unrealistically) a full solvency of the risk creator. Thus, tort law can never fulfil its compensatory goals if one were to stick to a negligence rule (the economic model showed that under negligence the injurer will in principle take due care and hence avoid having to pay compensation to the victim). Moreover, even if one were to shift (as we have seen in many countries) to strict liability, this shift only guarantees compensation to the victim if solvency guarantees are added as well. If these solvency

[47] See with respect to nuclear accidents, Vanden Borre 2001; Faure and Skogh 1992, pp. 499–513; Deprimoz 1995, pp. 1–24; and see with respect to civil liability for marine oil pollution, Faure and Heine 1991, pp. 39–54; and see for recent evolutions, Brans 1994, pp. 61–67 and pp. 85–91.

guarantees are not added, strict liability may even cause a problem of underdeterrence.

Under strict liability the injurer will consider the accident as one which is equal to his total wealth and will therefore only take the care necessary to avoid an accident with a magnitude equal to his total wealth. If that wealth is lower than the magnitude of an accident, he will take less than the optimal care and therefore a problem of underdeterrence arises under strict liability.

Insolvency is less of a problem under negligence since under that rule the injurer will still have an incentive to take the care required by the legal system as long as the costs of taking care are less than his individual wealth. Taking due care remains indeed a way for the injurer to avoid having to pay compensation to the victim. If there would thus be a potential accident setting whereby the magnitude of the loss may be higher than the injurer's wealth (which can often be the case in environmental liability) this constitutes an argument in favour of negligence rather than strict liability.

Indeed, strict liability is efficient only if an injurer is always held to pay fully for the consequences of the accident. If the injurer were insolvent or if the judge were to underestimate the amount of the damage underdeterrence would follow.[48] Therefore, the negligence rule is better if the judge can adequately set the optimal level of care, even if there is uncertainty concerning the precise amount of the damage. If on the other hand, the judge can fix the amount of the damage with certainty (and the injurer is able to pay) but there would be error concerning the optimal care level, a strict liability rule would be the preferred rule.[49]

5.3 Environmental Liability Directive

From this perspective one could also formulate a serious criticism of Directive 2004/35 of 21 April 2004. The economic literature has indeed stressed, as we just mentioned, that strict liability can only exercise both its preventive and its compensatory function if the insolvency risk can be cured. It is therefore important to stress that if one assumes that insolvency may arise a remedy has to be found which can provide the injurer with adequate incentives. History has unfortunately shown that even companies with limited financial means may cause huge environmental damage and may thereafter be judgment proof. Moreover, the insolvency risk may even arise with larger companies since almost all (larger) companies are organized as legal entities and therefore

48 Cooter and Ulen 2000, pp. 316–318.

49 Cooter 1984, p. 1523.

enjoy the benefits of the limited liability of the corporation. It is precisely because companies enjoy limited liability that some authors have argued that a serious underdeterrence may arise.[50]

A problem in this respect is that Directive 2004/35 does not solve the insolvency problem. Article 14 merely states in respect of financial security:

> Member states shall take measures to encourage the development of financial security instruments and markets by the appropriate economic and financial operators, including financial mechanisms in case of insolvency, with the aim of enabling operators to use financial guarantees to cover their responsibilities under this directive.

This is a dangerous approach since the directive introduces strict liability for many activities. If this strict liability is not accompanied by a mandatory financial guarantee or insurance, underdeterrence may arise. Moreover, it seems clear that environmental liability, given the serious insolvency risk, cannot exercise its compensatory function unless a regulatory intervention has taken place to impose a duty to seek financial coverage. Hence the question has to be addressed whether insurance or other financial instruments are able to provide compensation.

6. COMPENSATION OF ENVIRONMENTAL HARM: LIABILITY INSURANCE

Of course many studies have addressed the issue of to what extent liability for environmental damage can be insured against. Attention in this literature has more particularly been given to the question under which conditions environmental damage can be considered insurable.[51] It is of course not possible to repeat or even summarize the contents of this extensive body of literature within the scope of this chapter. However, we would like to focus on some of the main conclusions of this literature which basically show some of the problems that arise in providing insurance cover for environmental liability. A further insight into some of these problems may lead to a better understanding of why particularly the liability risk concerning environmental damage is often considered as 'hard to insure' by insurers. Studying these problems may make

---

50 See Hansmann and Kraakman 1991, p. 1879 and see Cortenraad 2000.

51 For a summary of this literature see Faure 2007, pp. 73–102 and Faure and Hartlief 2003, p. 260. For a summary see Kunreuther and Freeman 2001, pp. 305–306. See e.g. Abraham 1988, pp. 949–951; Katzman 1988, pp. 89–90; Cousy 1995, pp. 235–237 and Rogge 1997, pp. 3–6.

it easier to understand why insurers increasingly seek different solutions from liability insurance, precisely because they consider some of these alternative arrangements better insurable (this will be addressed in section 7). What are the issues that particularly endanger the insurability of the liability risk for environmental damage?

6.1 Predictability of the Risk

Obviously for every insurance scheme, including environmental liability insurance, it is crucial that the insurer possesses accurate information on the likelihood that the event will occur (the probability) and on the possible magnitude of the damage once the accident does occur. These expectations on probability and magnitude of the loss are essential for the insurer to be able to calculate a fair premium. Added to this are the so-called loading costs (for, among other things, administrative expenses) and, depending on the market structure, a profit margin, so that this will constitute the premium to be paid by the insured.

In this respect environmental liability insurance is obviously not different from any other type of insurance; for these general principles we can hence refer to the insurance economics literature. However, it is important to stress that to make accurate premium calculation possible, one crucial element in insurance is, as we have just indicated, precise information on the probability that a certain loss will occur and the possibility to make a more or less accurate estimate of the potential magnitude of the damage. This is not only necessary in order to make an accurate estimation of the premium to be charged, but also to calculate the magnitude of the reserve to be set aside in case the accident for which insurance coverage was sought, occurs.

A conclusion of this simple introduction to the working of liability insurance is that an insurer needs information concerning the probability (p) that a certain event (the fact that the insured will be held liable) will occur and he or she will need information on the possible magnitude of the damage (D). The multiplier of these (p x D) constitutes the fair premium in actuarial terms. The reason the insurer can take over this risk is the law of large numbers: a larger group of insurers with a similar risk can be brought together in a risk group and thus risk spreading becomes possible.

If the insurer ideally has *ex ante* perfect information on the *predictability* of the probability and the magnitude of the damage, we call the particular risk insurable. It is precisely on the basis of statistics that the insurer will acquire information on the likelihood that the risk will occur with a particular insured; statistics may also provide information on the possible magnitude of the damage. Both these requirements may, however, be a problem in the case of environmental (liability) insurance. Several elements may negatively influence the *ex ante* predictability of the risk.[52] The *ex ante* information on the predictability of the risk is often low, given the relatively new character of environmental risks. Reliable statistics may sometimes be missing both with respect to the probability of the event occurring and with respect to the damage.[53] Hence, there may not be a 'law of large numbers' to be applied. This obviously is not only a problem for environmental insurance, but occurs in every case where insurers are confronted with new risks, where reliable data may be missing.

The predictability of the liability risk is obviously a crucial element to guarantee the insurability of environmental liability. The question therefore arises whether the predictability of the liability risk can be increased, even in the absence of reliable statistics, or whether 'hard to predict risks' should be judged as uninsurable. The literature has indicated that uncertainty concerning the probability or the damage is of course an element which the insurer can – in principle – take into account *ex ante*. If there is uncertainty, because of a lack of reliable statistics, this should not necessarily lead to the conclusion that a particular risk is uninsurable. We are then dealing with the concept referred to as 'insurer ambiguity' addressed by Kunreuther, Hogarth and Meszaros.[54] They argue that the insurer can react to this uncertainty concerning either the probability of the event or the magnitude of the damage by charging a so-called risk premium to account for this unpredictability. Hence, an insurer can in principle also deal with a 'hard to predict' event, by charging an additional premium. Although theoretically the additional risk premium is hence the answer to insurer ambiguity, in practice the insurer will at least need some information to make more than an educated guess concerning the risk premium to be charged. Moreover, given the fact that an insurer is to be found in a competitive environment, market forces may well force the insurer to engage in liability insurance even when an appropriate risk premium cannot be charged.

The conclusion at the normative level is that the policy-maker should obviously make the scope of liability *ex ante* as clear as possible. In other words: the legislator should try to avoid legal uncertainty which may endanger insurability.[55]

---

52 Monti rightly points out that there may be both factual and legal uncertainty (Monti 2001, pp. 59–62).

53 Rogge 1997, p. 4.

54 Kunreuther, Hogarth and Meszaros 1993, pp. 71–87.

55 See Monti 2001, pp. 59–62.

6.2 Capacity

We have already mentioned that a requirement for insurability is that the insurer should have *ex ante* information on the predictability of the risk and on the magnitude of the damage. So far we have dealt with the importance of the predictability of liability. However, the magnitude of the harm may also constitute a problem.[56] There may be uncertainty as far as the possible magnitude of the harm is concerned. The insurer may react to this uncertainty by providing for an adequate reserve to be able to provide coverage for the environmental damage once it occurs. However, in many cases the expected loss may exceed the possibilities of the individual insurer. In that case the insurer can use various traditional insurance techniques to cope with this capacity problem. One possibility is to insure a similar risk jointly with a few insurers (so-called co-insurance); another possibility is reinsurance. One other solution which is often used in case of environmental liability insurance is pooling of capacity by insurers. In many countries insurers have shared risks in mutual pools on a non-competitive basis to be able to provide coverage, also for risks with a relatively high potential magnitude. This is typically the case for the nuclear risk.

Generally legal doctrine has pointed to the fact that the possibilities to insure large risks have increased as a result of changes in the insurance industry. One effect of creating a European internal insurance market has been that the size of insurance markets (and hence the capacity) has considerably increased.[57] Notwithstanding all of these possibilities to increase the capacity, the liability risk may be such that it can reach the limits of insurability.

6.3 Risk Differentiation as Remedy for Moral Hazard and Adverse Selection

As is well known from economic theory, insurance can always be endangered as a result of moral hazard or adverse selection. The appropriate remedy for both phenomena is risk differentiation. It follows from the economic principles of liability insurance that an adaptation of the policy conditions to the individual risk is essential to control both moral hazard and adverse selection. George Priest has claimed that the adverse selection problem has caused an insurance crisis in the United States and that it can only be cured by an appropriate differentiation of risk.[58] If the insurance policy requires preventive

---

[56] See Rogge 1997, pp. 3–4.

[57] Cousy 1995, pp. 227–241.

[58] Priest 1987, pp. 1521–1590. Priest has been criticized by Viscusi, who claims that there were other reasons for the product liability crisis in the US than adverse selection on its own (Viscusi 1991, pp. 147–177).

action from the insured party and provides for a corresponding reward in the premium, this should give optimal incentives to the insured for accident reduction. Thus risk pools should be constructed as narrowly as possible so that the premium reflects the risk of the average member of that particular pool.[59]

Considering the current practice of many European insurers, especially as far as the liability risk of enterprises is concerned, one is struck by the fact that so little use is made of the possibilities of risk differentiation. In that respect we specifically refer to the insurance of the risks of enterprises in the Netherlands where premiums merely depend on the turnover of a company and almost no individual differentiation takes place.[60] Up to now, one lump-sum premium has been charged for a whole variety of risks from environmental liability to occupational health. Such a global tariff for a whole variety of different risks obviously does not correspond to the economic need for individual risk differentiation. This system might have worked in a legal system where liability law was not used as the main source for compensating victims. But now that governments in Western Europe are increasingly withdrawing from social security systems, victims may need to use the tort system more often.[61] This will inevitably force insurers into more effective risk differentiation.

The insurer can of course rely on existing mechanisms to control the 'ecological reliability' of the insured. In this respect one should not forget that most insureds in the case of environmental risks are licensed operators. Hence, an absolute minimum would be that the insurer checks whether the insured operator in fact possesses a valid licence. In addition the insurer could expressly require in the policy conditions that the operator follows the conditions of the licence and could even make insurance coverage dependent upon that.[62] In other words, the insurer could make use of the fact that a decision concerning the way to reduce environmental harm has already been made by the administrative agency and possibly been laid down in the administrative licence. This is, by the way, current practice in Belgian environmental liability insurance. Many insurance policies stipulate that there would be no coverage in a case where the damage resulted from a violation of regulatory norms.[63]

Obviously, we should refer to the argument made above that following regulatory standards is, from a perspective of tort law, often merely a minimum. If socially efficient care is higher than the regulatory standard the potential polluter may be held liable, even in case of regulatory compliance. However, from the insurer's perspective it seems useful to rely at least on

---

59 Abraham 1988, pp. 949–951.
60 See Faure and Hartlief 1996a, pp. 140–150.
61 See Faure and Hartlief 1996b, pp. 254–259.
62 See also Kunreuther and Freeman 2001, p. 316.
63 Rogge 1997, pp. 28–29.

regulatory standards, even though they may not always constitute the optimal norm and even though the insured may be held liable even though regulatory standards were met. Compliance with regulatory standards is, in other words, a minimum which an insurer could require. But other techniques should be used as well to control whether the insured could have taken more cost-effective prevention measures than the ones required by regulation.

Notwithstanding all these instruments which the insurer theoretically posseses to check the ecological liability of a firm, there is of course one element of uncertainty that can hardly be excluded by an insurer, which is the legal uncertainty following from the liability system. Although the ecological performance can be monitored, for example through eco-audits and other instruments, the insurer will not know *ex ante* how the judiciary may interpret for example the specific duty of care of a risk creator. Given the relatively new character of environmental liability many insurers still consider that the precise content of the scope of environmental liability is still uncertain. This not only endangers the predictability of the risk (see 6.1), but of course makes an adequate risk differentiation more difficult as well. There are more particularly several tendencies in legislation and case law concerning environmental liability which often cause nightmares to insurers: shifting the risk of causal uncertainty, joint and several liability as well as retroactive liability.

6.4 Shifting the Risk of Causal Uncertainty

A major problem with environmental damage, and also with so-called toxic torts,[64] is that an exposure to some environmental harmful activity may cause a certain disease, but the particular disease may have been caused through other causes as well. In these cases the identity of the victim is certain, but there is uncertainty about who the injurer is. Indeed, the victim may well have got the disease from some background risk and not from the presence of, say, a nuclear power plant.[65] Such questions have indeed arisen both in Belgium and in the United Kingdom. Causal uncertainty played a role in the famous British Sellafield case, where an English court had to decide on the causal relationship between childhood leukaemia and the nearby presence of a nuclear power plant at Sellafield.[66] Similarly, Belgian courts have been confronted with the question of whether the physical complaints of inhabitants of the community of Mellery in the Walloon Region were caused by emissions from a nearby waste site.[67]

64 Trauberman 1983, pp. 177–296.
65 Estep 1960, pp. 259–304; Van 1994, pp. 109–118 and Van 1995, pp. 145–154.
66 Gardner 1990, pp. 423–434.
67 For a discussion of that case, see Lavrysen 1995, pp. 219–243.

The danger of shifting the burden of causal uncertainty to the enterprise is that the insurer of the specific employer or producer will be required to compensate for damage which, on the whole, had probably not been caused by the insured party.[68] In many countries an all or nothing approach is followed to causal uncertainty or a so-called threshold liability. That means that when the probability that the activity caused the loss is higher than a certain threshold (usually 50 per cent)[69] the risk taker will have to compensate for the total loss. In other cases the burden of proof is shifted to the enterprise which will then mean that the enterprise will have to prove that the activity did not cause a particular damage, for instance cancer. In those cases the enterprise may end up paying to a large extent for damage that could never have been caused by its activity.

This perverse result could be avoided through a proportionate liability rule, such as a market share liability in product liability cases. This proportionate liability rule has been defended by several American scholars and is also defended in the economic analysis of law.[70] The negative consequences of causal uncertainty could then be limited. A proportionate liability rule is less rigorous than the all or nothing approach of the reversal of the burden of proof.[71] The proportionate liability rule would indeed mean that all victims can claim a proportion of their damage equal to the amount by which the power plant contributed to the loss. Thus the exposure to liability of the enterprise corresponds precisely with the amount to which the power plant contributed to the risk.[72]

Unless a proportionate liability rule is followed, it is not possible to cover a risk if that would mean that the insurer would not only cover the damage of its own insured parties but also the damage that might possibly have been caused by another party. These tendencies lead to a liability of enterprises for risks that they have not caused themselves (in the case of causal uncertainty) or for risks that were not foreseen at the time when the tort was committed (in the case of retrospective liability). They are largely caused by a hidden redistributive agenda: the wish to provide victim protection no matter what it may

---

68 Also Abraham 1988, pp. 959–960 and Katzman 1988, pp. 89–90. See also Bergkamp 2000a, pp. 154–155.

69 It is often expressed that it must be 'more probable than not' that the activity caused the damage.

70 Rosenberg 1984, pp. 851–929; Shavell 1985b, pp. 587–609. The Dutch Attorney General Hartkamp defended a market share liability in the DES case (Hartkamp 1992, pp. 241–258). In addition Spier pleaded in favour of a proportionate liability for latent diseases in his inauguration address (Spier 1990), as did Akkermans (1997) in his dissertation.

71 See Brüggemeier 1991, pp. 88–91.

72 Robinson 1985, p. 798.

cost. These tendencies may be far more problematic from an insurability point of view than the shift towards strict liability itself. Indeed, whereas strict liability as such is insurable, this is no longer true if retrospective liability is introduced or the risk of causal uncertainty is shifted to the enterprise.

Also these features, which deviate from the principle that an injurer can only be held liable for the damage he or she has caused, may lead to difficulties when it comes to insuring environmental liability. Several of these deviations can, however, be noticed precisely in the area of environmental liability.

6.5 Joint and Several Liability

One is an area which is closely related to the issue of causal uncertainty just discussed. It is the tendency to hold joint tortfeasors jointly and severally liable for all the damage to which their behaviour might have contributed. The reasons for doing so are well known. For the victim it is often difficult to prove a clear causal link with the actions of one particular polluter. This may sometimes lead to alleviations of the burden of proof or to holding several insurers jointly and severally liable. The often debated superfund regime under the Comprehensive Environmental Response, Compensation, and Liability Act (CERCLA) is an example of such a joint and several liability regime.

The effects of a joint and several liability are obviously also that the risk of insolvency is shifted to the injurer who will be sued by the victim. Indeed, joint and several liability means that the victim can claim full compensation from one injurer which then can exercise a redress against the other parties which contributed to the loss in proportion to their contribution. If, however, the other parties were all insolvent, the one injurer which was the defendant will have to compensate for the total loss, also for the losses it has not caused. In addition, the risks of uncertainty concerning the causal link are, under joint and several liability, also shifted to the one injurer which is sued in the particular case. The victim can suffice with suing just one of the many potentially liable insurers and claim full compensation. If the one injurer does not succeed in proving that others contributed to the loss, the damage will ultimately fall on the one injurer.

From an insurance perspective, joint and several liability may be dangerous for the simple reason that the insurer is then no longer merely insuring the risk posed by its individual insured (which it can still control), but also the risk caused by all the others.[73] The welfare losses resulting from such a system of joint and several liability may be large. This mutual monitoring may *ex ante* not always be possible and the transactions costs involved (also in the systems

---

[73] See Cousy 1995, p. 235.

of redress) can be huge. Hence, on balance it is doubtful that joint and several liability will have positive incentive effects. The insurance effect is obviously, as the case of causal uncertainty illustrated, that an insurer will be held liable for the risks that its insured never caused. This tendency towards joint and several liability seems therefore to endanger the insurability.[74]

6.6 Retrospective Liability

There are, moreover, some other specific features of environmental liability insurance discussed in the literature which make it difficult to apply traditional insurance principles to environmental liability. One of these aspects, often stressed, is that liability insurance traditionally provides for coverage of accidents, meaning a sudden event, whereas in environmental liability there is often a long time lapse between the emission and the occurrence of the harm. Moreover, many of the pollution cases are not sudden events, but evolve gradually. This causes many technical problems, for example relating to the question when the damage actually occurred. These and other questions relating to the application of insurance principles on environmental liability are extensively discussed in the literature.[75] One particular aspect of the potential long time lapse between the wrongful event and the damage is that this may result in retrospective liability. Retrospective liability is not only inefficient as far as giving incentives for accident prevention is concerned, but also leads to uninsurability.[76]

Let us, before showing why retrospective liability is insurable, once more come back to the requirement of foreseeability as a basis for insurability. We have already briefly discussed this in the context of predictability. It is important to stress that, apart from exceptional situations, there should be no reason to argue that there is uninsurability of environmental liability as long as the present-day insurer can see a growing liability threatening its position and can adjust its policy conditions accordingly.

The question whether a change in the liability regime therefore leads to uninsurability when this is applied in a retrospective manner can be relatively easily answered.

At first sight one could argue that this certainly is the case. If the insurer were not aware that the behaviour of this insured party might potentially have been considered wrongful, no premium would have been charged for this risk,

---

74 Monti 2001, p. 58. And see Bergkamp 2000a, p. 154 who argues that under joint and several liability civil liability becomes unpredictable and hence uninsurable.

75 See, e.g. Bocken 1992, pp. 284–327; Bocken 1993; Bocken and Ryckbost 1991 and see Cousy 1995, pp. 237–239.

76 For formal proof of this statement, see Faure and Fenn 1999, pp. 487–500.

no preventive measures would have been required in the policy conditions and no reserves against losses would have been set aside. Indeed, insurance assumes that the insurer covers future risks which are at least to some extent foreseeable. Insurance requires some degree of predictability. However, the mere fact that insurers of, say, industrial waste disposal sites in the 1960s have – as a matter of fact – not foreseen that the activities of their insured parties could lead to a liability in the future, does not make this event totally unforeseeable. The potential of a change in the scope of liability is an uncertain element which the insurer can – in principle – take into account *ex ante*. We are dealing here with the concept of 'insurer ambiguity' addressed by Kunreuther, Hogarth and Meszaros.[77] If insurers could foresee the likelihood of a possible change in the liability system, they could react to uncertainty by estimating the probability that this event would occur and charge an additional risk premium to account for this legal uncertainty. In sum, in an *ex ante* perspective one can argue that nothing is totally unforeseeable or unpredictable; insurers can in principle cope with 'hard to predict' events such as the introduction of retrospective liability by charging an additional premium. However, in an *ex post* perspective this message is not very helpful for insurers which, at the time, did not take this risk into account and now have to provide cover to enterprises for risks which the insurers considered apparently unforeseeable. Hence, no additional premium was charged and no reservations were made, which explains why the retrospective liability now laid down, say, for soil clean-up costs, leads to major problems for insurers.[78] There is, hence, no problem of the uninsurability of retrospective liability as such, but only the simple fact that insurers did not take these risks into account when the policy was drawn up.

From the above it follows that real retroactive liability, where any change in the law was not foreseeable, will pose problems for insurers. Also insurers argue in their publications that liability for past pollution is uninsurable.[79] Our theoretical analysis supports this claim. However, the problem of a long time lapse between the wrongful event (for example the emission of a toxic substance) and the damage will obviously often happen in environmental insurance.

6.7 Summary

We have tried to sketch briefly some conditions of insurability and relate them to the literature on environmental liability insurance. The lesson from this

77 Kunreuther, Hogarth and Meszaros 1993, pp. 71–87.

78 See Zeckhauser 1996, p. 5, who argues that retrospective liability may affect the predictability of risks; and see Abraham 1988, pp. 957–959.

79 For Belgium, see e.g. Rogge 1997, p. 6.

literature seems to be that environmental damage can in principle also be covered through liability insurance. However, many conditions need to be fulfilled in order to apply classic liability insurance to environmental damage. From a theoretical perspective one could notice that the predictability of the liability risk may be difficult, given the many uncertainties in the legal system. In many countries the content of the environmental liability regime is still so uncertain that the liability risk is still hard to predict for injurers. That uncertainty will of course hardly be removed with Directive 2004/35/CE given the fact that its scope of application is rather limited and that it comes on top of national law dealing with the same issue. Uncertainties that would exist in national law thus remain. Also the potentially large scope of environmental disasters may outweigh the capacity of an insurer, even when remedies like pooling, co-insurance and reinsurance are used.

Insurers particularly seem to fear the 'difficult-to-predict' nature of environmental liability since it may endanger their possibilities of an adequate risk differentiation. The latter is again necessary to cure the problems of moral hazard and adverse selection. Insurers more particularly dislike the environmental liability risk since it has what is often referred to as a 'long-tail' character. They fear to provide cover today for damage with a cause in a very distant past. It is precisely this long-tail character of many environmental risks that according to insurers endangers the predictability and thus the 'manageability' of the environmental liability risk.

The core problem is undoubtedly that environmental damage is not a classic accident, being a sudden event which is the normal object of liability insurance. Environmental damage has to the contrary a gradual nature. This can lead to important problems in the insurance context related for example to the question when liability precisely was created.

Moreover insurers will be confronted often with the risk that courts, being confronted with a case of environmental damage, will often seek the deep pockets of risk creators or (preferably) their liability insurers. This may lead to a shift in the burden of proving causation, to imposing joint and several liabilities and even to applying liability rules in a retrospective manner. Insurers have often argued that especially these characteristics of many environmental liability regimes may endanger the insurability of environmental liability. We have shown that from a theoretical and insurance technical perspective there is some support for this claim.

Within the perspective of the central line of this chapter, where we examine whether liability insurance could fulfil a compensatory function, we have to conclude that this is only the case to a limited extent. It is precisely because of the reasons we have discussed that in practice many alternatives to liability insurance have been developed of which it is thought that they might better be able to provide financial cover (and thus guarantee compensation) than traditional liability insurance. Some of these alternatives are still rather novel in the sense that there is not much experience with them yet. This is for instance the case for the use of capital markets and new financial instruments to cover environmental risks; with others there is already more experience. This is for instance the case with risks sharing agreements. The oil pollution risk has for many years been covered through the so-called Protection and Indemnity clubs (P&I clubs) which function as a mutual insurance company.[80] One particular alternative to liability insurance which seems particularly interesting is the shift away from liability insurance towards first-party and direct insurance schemes. These are particularly interesting since insurers have in some countries, more particularly in the Netherlands, advocated the use of these first-party and direct insurance schemes, arguing that any of the problems that arise in covering environmental liability play less of a role when environmental damage is covered on a first-party basis. Hence this new tendency, which seems to receive attention in many other countries as well, deserves some attention.

7. ALTERNATIVE COMPENSATION MECHANISM: ENVIRONMENTAL DAMAGE INSURANCE

7.1 Theory

There is another alternative which may compensate victims of environmental damage, which is now sometimes advocated, and that is first-party insurance. Liability insurance is a third-party insurance, whereby the insurer covers the risk that its insured (the potentially responsible party) will have to compensate a third party. A first-party insurance is a system whereby the compensation is awarded directly by the insurer to the victim. Whether such a first-party insurance can be considered as an efficient alternative for third-party liability cannot be answered in general terms. It depends to a large extent on the details of such a system and more particularly on the question whether the first-party insurance is combined or not with the liability of the potentially responsible party.

The underlying principle in a first-party insurance is that the insurance undertaking – in principle – pays as soon as damage occurs, provided that it can be proven that the particular damage has been caused by the insured risk.

---

[80] For an overview of alternatives to liability insurance, see Faure 2004, pp. 455–489.

Payment by the insurance undertaking occurs irrespective of the fact whether there is liability. The arguments advanced in the literature in favour of first-party insurance are that the transaction costs would be lower and that risk differentiation might be a lot easier.[81] The reason is simply that with first-party insurance the insurer directly covers the risk of damage with a particular victim or a particular site. The idea is that it is therefore much easier for the insured to signal particular circumstances which may influence the risk to the insurer. The problem with liability insurance is that the insurer is always insuring the risk that its insured (the potential injurer) will harm a victim (a third party) of which the properties are unknown *ex ante* to the insurer. Moreover, under liability insurance there are lots of uncertainties, for example how the judge will interpret this specific liability of the insured. In the ideal world of first-party insurance the insurer directly covers the victim, e.g. the risk. The insurer can therefore directly monitor the risk and in principle provide a much better risk differentiation.

Obviously lots of practical questions arise when it comes to the application of the ideal model of first-party insurance to environmental harm, such as damage to biodiversity or soil pollution. One question is under what kind of circumstances the insurance will be triggered if liability is not required. Does damage suffice and, if so, how is damage to be described? Moreover, also in a first-party insurance scheme the question will have to be answered as to who finances the system. In an ideal theoretical world, it would be the victim who finances a first-party insurance. That would obviously constitute a major difference from liability insurance. Immediately one can understand that there would be opposition to a first-party insurance scheme since under this condition it might violate the polluter pays principle. However, one could also imagine a first-party insurance scheme whereby it is the one who possesses the particular site (which could be the polluter, but that might not necessarily be the case) who pays the premium. In that hypothesis one usually refers to it as 'direct' insurance instead of first-party insurance.

Finally, also under a first-party insurance scheme, the relationship to liability law will have to be clarified. One question is whether a first-party insurance system would replace the liability system. That would obviously be a far-reaching solution whereby the liability system would be totally set aside. It would mean that the victim would receive compensation directly from the insurer simply by proving that a certain damage has been caused. But then inevitably the question would arise as to how potentially responsible parties would still have incentives for prevention without a liability system. Therefore one can assume that a first-party insurance system would not replace liability

---

81 This argument is especially advanced by Priest 1987, pp. 1521–1590.

law. But that then raises the question whether there would be an accumulation of liability and first-party insurance and whether that can be considered as efficient.

Moreover, the question arises as to what amounts would be paid under first-party coverage. Usually the amounts paid in first-party insurance are lower than the full compensation which is in principle awarded under tort law.[82]

This shows that although first-party insurance might seem very attractive at first sight at the theoretical level, since it might better enable a narrowing of risk pools, still a lot of questions arise. It is probably best to examine these questions by looking at a practical example where a first-party insurance of polluted sites has been implemented.

Before doing so it is probably important to stress that this exposé of first-party insurance is not merely theoretical, but does indeed have a certain practical relevance. Indeed, the general liability committee of the *Comité Européen des Assurances* (CEA) has executed a study on first-party legal obligations for clean-ups and corresponding insurance covers in European countries.[83] This study shows that although the insurance situation between European countries still differs to a large extent, first-party insurance coverage seems to be available in several member states.[84] In one country, namely the Netherlands, the insurers have deliberately chosen to provide coverage of polluted sites on a first-party basis. The idea is that the first-party coverage should replace the traditional environmental liability insurance. Hence, it seems sensible to take a closer look at the insurance situation in the Netherlands.

7.2 First-party Insurance for Polluted Sites in the Netherlands

7.2.1. Dissatisfaction with existing coverages

The starting point for the concern of the Dutch insurers was the fact that all the theoretical problems which we discussed in section 6 concerning the insurability of environmental liability had also played a major role in Dutch environmental practice. This had to do with the fact that environmental risk is the example of a 'long-tail risk' whereby the insurer today could be confronted with events which occurred in the distant past and would lead to liability of the insured now. Insurers held that this generally endangered the predictability of the risk.

---

82 Note, however, that under liability insurance the coverage provided will be linked to certain limits as well.

83 CEA, Study on first-party legal obligations for clean-ups and corresponding insurance covers in European Countries, Paris, CEA, 21 October 1998.

84 See the summary tables in the CEA study, above n. 83 at 32.

Most of these problems were hence related to the fact that environmental harm does not constitute a sudden event, as is the case with most 'traditional' accidents insured under liability insurance.

The Dutch insurance market therefore used to have the environmental risk covered through a variety of insurance policies, of which the most important were:

- the liability insurance policy (AVB)[85] for sudden risks and for occupational health risks which were related to the environment;
- the environmental liability insurance (MAS) for risks of a more gradual nature, excluding personal injury;[86]
- fire insurance for clean-up costs after fires (although the precise coverage of that policy was debated).

This environmental liability insurance was provided by an environmental pool, referred to as MAS.[87] In this MAS 50 (re)insurers work together to cover the environmental liability risk. The MAS was hence constructed as an environmental pool, although the individual insurers connected to the MAS contracted individually the MAS policy under their own label.

There was, however, a lot of criticism of that system, which can be summarized as follows.

First of all the whole division of coverage between the AVB and the MAS was based on the idea that the AVB would cover the sudden risks and the MAS would cover the risks of a more gradual nature. As is well known, in practice it was not always possible to make a clear distinction between sudden and gradual risks, which led to uncertainties concerning the scope of the coverages of both policies. This was obviously the result of the fact that the Dutch insurers did not decide to exclude the environmental risk altogether from the traditional liability insurance of companies (AVB).[88]

The environmental liability policy (MAS) was considered to be rather complicated and had a very complicated procedure towards accepting insureds. The policy was also rather expensive and hence difficult to sell.

A further problem was that neither the general environmental liability policy (AVB) nor the environmental liability insurance policy (MAS) provided any coverage for damage caused to the insured's own site. This caused a problem for insureds since according to the case law of the Dutch Supreme Court companies could be held liable also for pollution of their own

85 Aansprakelijkheidsverzekering bedrijven.

86 See on that policy, Wansink 1985, p. 98.

87 Milieu-aansprakelijkheidsverzekering Samenwerkingsverband.

88 For further details on these difficulties, see Wansink 1997, pp. 451–460.

site. In addition, the fact that pollution caused to the site of the insured was not covered inevitably again caused uncertainty concerning the scope of coverage. One could imagine cases where polluted groundwater went from the site of the insured to a neighbouring site. This would cause problems since the pollution of the site of the neighbour would be insured whereas the pollution of the insured's own site would not.

Furthermore, there were more uncertainties concerning the question whether clean-up costs were covered under the fire insurance policy. The fire insurance policy covers the clean-up costs after fire as well as any environmental damage that occurred, but only on condition that there was a prior fire. In the fire insurance policy no account was taken of the fact that after a fire serious soil and water pollution could also occur. It was not always clear whether the soil clean-up costs resulting from the fire were also covered under the fire insurance.

Finally there were obviously all the traditional problems related to environmental liability, such as the question whether specific damage was indeed caused as a result of an insured risk. Also case law concerning environmental liability extended in a way which was hardly foreseeable for insurers. Hence, the liability risk was increasingly considered unpredictable and thus uninsurable as far as environmental harm was concerned.

7.2.2 Environmental damage insurance: main features

This led the Dutch insurers association to present in 1998 a new product, the environmental damage insurance (MSV[89]). This policy has been available since 1 January 1998 and takes a radically different approach from traditional environmental liability insurance.[90]

This new environmental damage policy provides for various new elements. First of all it provides integrated coverage of all the environmental damage which occurs on or from the insured site. A prerequisite is that it concerns pollution of the soil or of the water. The integrated coverage means that the new environmental damage insurance replaces the traditional pollution insurance (for sudden pollution) in the AVB and the liability insurance of the MAS (for gradual pollution).

The whole idea is that this coverage constitutes a direct insurance. In other words, the insured site is insured, even when the costs of clean-up have to be met for the site of a third party. Coverage takes place as soon as the insured site is polluted as the result of the insured risk, irrespective of the fact that the insured could be held liable for the damage or not. In some cases the third

89 Milieuschadeverzekering.

90 For a good description of the new policy, see Wansink 1999, pp. 77–82 as well as Janssen 1998, pp. 111–112 and Drion 1998, pp. 19–21.

party (the victim), moreover, receives a direct action on compensation on the basis of the environmental damage insurance policy. The trigger for compensation under this policy is therefore no longer tort law, but the insurance policy as concluded between the insured and the insurance company. This therefore typically is a first-party insurance or, as it is called in the Netherlands, a direct insurance. It is a direct insurance to the extent that it also benefits third parties. It is indeed not the third-party victim who purchases insurance (although the insured may be the victim), but someone who has responsibility for a site on or from which water or soil pollution may occur. The policy thus benefits third-parties as well, at least when this is provided in the policy.

Obviously the environmental damage insurance cannot set aside tort law, but the main advantage according to Dutch insurers is that the coverage is not triggered on the basis of liability. The advantage from the victim's point of view is obviously that coverage can be provided more rapidly and probably at lower transaction costs than through the court cases which are necessary as a result of liability law.

The environmental damage insurance as provided by the Dutch Insurers Association consists of several categories with different coverages. This obviously shows that first-party insurance better enables an optimal risk differentiation since every insured will be able to purchase insurance coverage according to its own preferences. The damage on the insured location itself is insured. This at least provides coverage for clean-up costs and this is rather broadly defined. Also costs for the repair of damage are included.

The insured remains in principle fully liable, although the third party (beneficiary) which would be protected under the new MSV policy could claim directly on the policy and would hence in principle not have an interest in using liability law. However, it might be that the insured has taken too limited coverage and that in that particular case the third party would still (have to) use liability law. In that case the liability itself is not covered (and an insolvency risk remains), but the MSV policy provides for legal aid assistance in a number of specific cases. This is the case if the sum which is insured under the MSV coverage is sufficient to pay for the clean-up costs incurred by the government. The same applies in the case where a third party would choose the liability law instead of direct action under the MSV policy.[91]

7.3 Assessment

The main feature of the new environmental damage insurance provided in the Netherlands is obviously that it is no longer a liability insurance, but only a

[91] See Wansink 1999, p. 81.

first-party (or direct) insurance. The advantage for the insurer (and for the insured) is that the difficult road of liability law is excluded. Whether liability law will still be used is uncertain. Third parties could still use liability law, although it is obviously easier for victims to use the direct action provided under the MSV policy, at least in those cases where it is provided for.[92] There is, however, one important weakness which unavoidably remains, namely the fact that the environmental damage insurance is not compulsory. Hence, there may be situations where companies in the Netherlands have purchased no insurance coverage at all or situations where only a basic coverage was taken on for damage on the particular site, but not to a sufficient amount so that all damage suffered by third parties would be covered. In those cases, third parties claiming against the party responsible might still be confronted with an insolvent polluter. Moreover, the new MSV regime is exclusive, meaning that the coverage for (sudden) soil and/or water pollution has now been removed from the liability insurance policy. This means that if an insured only had taken an MSV coverage for the insured site and a loss occurred to a third party on another site, this third party would probably use liability law against the polluter. In that particular case the polluter cannot call on its general liability insurance (AVB) since the environmental risks have now been completely removed from that policy as a result of the entering into force of the MSV.[93]

But that can obviously hardly be considered a weakness of the system of first-party insurance: the insured obviously does not get more than he pays for. Since the MSV is a general policy with a lot of options for the insured, premiums and amount of coverage can vary. The type of costs which are insured are, however, identified in the general policy and according to the CEA study on first-party insurance the total amount of coverage available under this new environmental damage insurance in the Netherlands would be 25 million Dutch guilders (11 344 505 Euros).

7.4 Evaluation

According to information provided by the Dutch Insurance Association, this new product works remarkably well. It claims that the interest of enterprises in this new environmental damage insurance is much larger than in the traditional environmental liability insurance. Whether this new product is actually yet a success is more difficult to judge. There is, however, undoubtedly growing interest from industry for this new environmental damage insurance. The

---

[92] The direct action of the third party must indeed be explicitly accepted by the insured.

[93] Wansink 1999, pp. 81–82.

fact that a wider financial security for environmental damage is provided in the Netherlands as a result of this product should definitely be considered as positive. Moreover from the victim's (mostly the government) perspective, the fact that the environmental damage insurance provides for direct action for victims should be considered as a positive as well. It also shows that it seems possible to provide financial security for environmental damage without many of the insecurities and dangers inherent in an environmental liability insurance system.

Moreover, the advantage for the insured is that under this environmental damage insurance, damage caused to its own site is also covered, which was obviously not the case under liability insurance.[94] However, some company lawyers have been critical of this new insurance product. They argue that in practice insurers are so stringent in providing coverage that effectively only the very good risks would be able to receive coverage.[95] Hence, they claim that one cannot blindly argue that environmental damage insurance is a remedy for all insurability problems concerning environmental risks.

If, at a policy level, one were therefore to conclude that a strict liability system should be combined with some form of guarantee that financial security is available, one should at least leave the option open to industry to provide this financial security via environmental damage insurance. The Dutch example shows that this first-party type coverage seems able to meet that end.[96] Moreover, the example seems to be being followed in other countries as well.[97]

8. REGULATORY STRATEGIES TO SUPPORT PRIVATE SOLUTIONS

So far we have looked at private versus public solutions to environmental liability and this both from the perspective of prevention and compensation for environmental harm. As far as prevention was concerned we stressed that although the main role in preventing environmental harm will lie with regulation, there is

94 Cousy 1995, p. 240.

95 Niezen 1998, p. 114.

96 Bergkamp also argues strongly in favour of first-party and against environmental liability insurance (Bergkamp 2000b, pp. 112–114).

97 Ranson reports that in Belgium too a 'direct' environmental insurance is to be offered which would also cover gradual pollution (but would exclude ecological damage). See Ranson 2000, p. 68. The new policy would also cover, like the Dutch example, remediation costs. It is to be offered by AIG and would provide coverage of up to 1 billion BEF (24 789 352.48 Euros) (see Kerremans 1999, pp. 537–583).

still a task for environmental liability as well, especially to back up regulatory norms. As far as compensation is concerned we mainly addressed the role of private legal instruments, being tort law, liability insurance and alternatives like first-party and direct insurance. However, also as far as compensation is concerned, the dividing line between private law and regulatory solutions is not always that clear since, as far as promoting compensation is concerned, governments could play a role as well. The question indeed rises whether government can be of help providing facilitative strategies to improve the functioning of the private legal system. Again, this is an issue that has been addressed at great length in economic (and other) literature. Within this chapter, which aims merely at providing a *tour d'horizon* of the issues at stake, we just want to summarize this literature briefly by indicating what types of facilitative strategies could be followed and what the advantages and possible drawbacks of some of these strategies are.

8.1 Compulsory Insurance?

In the theoretical analysis provided in section 2 we made it clear that although there may be arguments in favour of strict environmental liability in cases where environmental harm can be considered unilateral, strict liability may cause underdeterrence in the case of insolvency. Hence, we have to consider carefully the risk that a potential polluter would simply choose a 'hit and run' strategy whereby he or she would pollute, irrespective of strict liability, since the strict liability rule could not affect him or her if he or she were insolvent. This risk of an 'orphaned' polluted site is obviously one reason why liability rules alone cannot suffice as a deterrent. Regulation is needed in that respect as well as has been shown in section 3. In this section we will address the question whether insurance, as presented in section 6, could remedy this risk. In section 6 we have explained how liability insurance generally works and which conditions have to be met to make the environmental liability risk insurable. The question however arises as to whether the benefits of liability insurance as sketched out in section 6 are so large that they warrant the introduction of compulsory liability insurance.[98]

One reason that could be advanced for introducing compulsory insurance would be information problems. These might arise in the case where the potential injurer cannot make an accurate assessment of the risk he or she is exposed to nor of the benefits of the purchase of insurance. An underestima-

98 If we refer to compulsory liability insurance here, this should be read as any scheme whereby the potentially responsible parties are forced to take out financial security. This may also take the form of a bank guarantee or a mandatory participation in a funding pool.

tion of the risk would in that case lead to the wrong decision of the injurer not to purchase liability insurance. The legislator could remedy this information problem by introducing a general duty to insure. This information problem is probably a valid argument to introduce a generalized duty to insure for motor vehicle owners. Maybe the average driver of a car underestimates the benefits of liability insurance. If there were no information problem and the legislator nevertheless introduced a duty to insure because this would be 'in the best interest' of the insured, this would of course be mere paternalism.

Moreover, the problem with this information argument is that it is merely a reason to introduce regulation aiming at the provision of information (see section 8.3 below), but not necessarily an argument to introduce compulsory insurance. The major disadvantage is that one is not sure of the attitude towards risk of the various risk takers. For some, compulsory insurance may not increase their utility and thus not be beneficial.

Another reason to introduce compulsory liability insurance is the argument often used by lawyers, namely the insolvency argument. The argument goes that the magnitude of the harm will often exceed the individual wealth of an injurer, whereby a problem of undercompensation of victims will arise. Lawyers would, hence, push forward compulsory insurance as an argument to guarantee effective compensation to the victim. This – more distributional – argument obviously may play a role in the context of environmental liability insurance as well. If an injurer were to be found judgment proof and hence a polluted site 'orphaned', the costs would be borne by society.

It is, however, also possible to make an economic argument that insolvency will lead to underdeterrence problems which might be remedied through liability insurance. Indeed, this so-called 'judgment-proof' problem has been extensively dealt with in the economic literature.[99]

Insolvency may pose a problem of underdeterrence. If the expected damage largely exceeds the injurer's assets, the injurer will only have incentives to purchase liability insurance up to the amount of its own assets. The injurer is indeed only exposed to the risk of losing its own assets in a liability suit. The judgment-proof problem may therefore lead to underinsurance and thus to underdeterrence. Jost has rightly pointed to the fact that in these circumstances of insolvency, compulsory insurance might provide an optimal outcome.[100] By introducing a duty to purchase insurance coverage for the amount of the expected loss, better results will be obtained than with insolvency whereby the

[99] More particularly by Shavell 1986, pp. 43–58.

[100] Jost 1996, pp. 259–276. A similar argument has been formulated by Polborn 1998, pp. 141–146 and by Skogh 2000, pp. 521–537. Skogh has also pointed out that compulsory insurance may save on transaction costs.

magnitude of the loss exceeds the injurer's assets.[101] In the latter case the injurer will indeed only consider the risk as one where it could at most lose its own assets and will set its standard of care accordingly. When the injurer is, under a duty to insure, exposed to full liability the insurer will obviously have incentives to control the behaviour of the insured. Via the traditional instruments for the control of moral hazard the insurer can make sure that the injurer will take the necessary care to avoid an accident with the real magnitude of the loss. Thus Jost and Skogh argue that compulsory insurance can, provided that the moral hazard problem can be cured adequately, provide better results than under the judgment-proof problem. This is probably one of the explanations why, for instance, compulsory insurance was introduced for traffic liability. Uninsured and insolvent drivers who have little money at stake which they may lose compared to the possible magnitude of accidents they may cause, may have little incentive to avoid an accident. Insurers might better be able to control this risk and could force the injurer to take care under the threat of being shut out of the insurance. Thus the insurer comes under a duty to insure the licensor of the activity.

Indeed, this economic argument shows that insolvency may cause potentially responsible parties to externalize harm: they may be engaged in activities which may cause harm which can largely exceed their assets. Without financial provisions these costs would be thrown on society and would hence be externalized instead of internalized. Such an internalization can be reached if the insurer is able to control the behaviour of the insured. As we have shown above, when discussing how risk differentiation can be applied to environmental liability insurance, the insurer could set appropriate policy conditions and an adequate premium. This shows that, if the moral hazard problem can be cured adequately, insurance leads to a higher deterrence than a situation without liability insurance and insolvency.

However, there are also serious drawbacks to introducing a duty to insure. One problem is that governments may become too dependent upon the insurance market. One should realize that if one makes the availability of insurance coverage a prerequisite for the operation of an enterprise, insurance undertakings in fact become the licensor of the industry, which may be questionable from a policy point of view.[102] In fact the insurer becomes the 'environmental policeman'.[103]

A second issue is that compulsory insurance should only be introduced when competitive insurance markets can provide a sufficiently differentiated

101 See also Kunreuther and Freeman 2001, p. 316.

102 See Rogge 1997, p. 40.

103 See Monti 2001, p. 65. See also Bergkamp 2000b, pp. 112–114 who argues heavily against compulsory insurance.

offer of insurance policies. From a policy view point it also seems highly problematic to make liability insurance compulsory in concentrated insurance markets. Indeed, in that case the inefficiencies in the insurance market would be reinforced by making the purchase of insurance compulsory.

A further problem is that the policymaker should equally realize that today liability insurance coverage for environmental harm is still a relatively young and inexperienced branch. In this respect we can refer to fact that risk differentiation in environmental liability insurance in Europe still stands at the beginning of its possibilities and that far more possibilities exist to relate policy and premium conditions in an appropriate way to the ecological reliability of firms. Hence, one can really question whether today insurance firms are yet able to differentiate environmental liability risks in such a way that one can argue that moral hazard can be controlled optimally on competitive insurance markets. The cure to these problems is obviously not to make a poorly functioning insurance system compulsory.

It shows, however, one probably important conclusion from this discussion on compulsory liability insurance. Although it may be important from a theoretical perspective to introduce a duty for the permit holder to secure appropriate means, it seems more appropriate to look for a flexible system whereby the licensing administrative authorities could judge in individual cases whether the obligation to provide financial security has been met. Such a system, whereby it is left to the administrative authorities to decide the form and amount of the financial obligation, seems more flexible and entails fewer of the risks and dangers of a generalized system of compulsory liability insurance.

There is some, although limited, experience in European countries with compulsory insurance. Compulsory insurance was introduced in the German environmental liability Act of 1990.[104] Also, in chapter 33 of the Swedish environmental code, compulsory insurance has been introduced. Remarkably, as we have already mentioned above (in section 5.3), Directive 2004/35CE did briefly address the issue of financial security in Article 14 but left it to member states to take measures to encourage the development of financial security instruments. Given the fact that the directive at the same time introduces a strict liability for a great many activities, this solution seems rather weak.

8.2 Compensation Funds?

A question that inevitably arises when issues of environmental damage are discussed is whether traditional liability law, combined with insurance, is at all

---

104 The insurability policy used is discussed by Lang 1996, pp. 169–183. For an overview of the German system, see Richardson 2000, pp. 61–62.

able to provide compensation for environmental damage. Issues of fault or negligence have been avoided in many legal systems by a trend towards strict liability. However, we have already indicated that strict liability alone will of course not guarantee compensation for environmental damage, given the insolvency problem. This will create a demand for insurance. However, it is well known that many problems may arise with the insurance of environmental damage.[105] Therefore in many legal systems the question has been asked whether compensation for environmental damage should be provided through compensation funds. Well known in this respect is of course the United States Superfund, introduced through CERCLA, which has led to a lot of criticism.[106] Also in several European legal systems pleas can be heard in favour of installing compensation funds to cover environmental damage. In the Netherlands this has been proposed in the literature.[107] In addition the idea is now increasingly being introduced in policy documents in the various member states formulating proposals for the reform of environmental law. In this respect we can point to the Interuniversitary Commission for the Revision of Environmental Law in the Flemish Region that proposed the introduction of a compensation fund in the Flemish Region,[108] and also to a Dutch study performed on behalf of the Ministry of the Environment proposing the introduction of an environmental compensation fund in the Netherlands.[109] Hence, there are ample reasons to take a closer look at the phenomenon of compensation funds.

One cannot escape the impression that often – especially at the political level – funds are advocated as a miracle solution for all problems of environmental damage although no clear definition is given of the specific funds. This can be misleading since the term 'fund' is often used for a variety of private or public financial arrangements that may be quite different.[110]

From an economic perspective there are not many reasons why if both are – in theory – available, a compensation fund would provide better protection

---

105 See generally on the limits of insurability; Faure 1995b, pp. 454–462 and the discussion in section 6 of this chapter.

106 Interesting papers analysing Superfund can be found in Revesz and Stewart 1995.

107 See Kottenhagen-Edzes 1992, pp. 297–298; Hulst 1993; Knottenbelt 1990; Van 1994, pp. 109–118 and Van 1995, pp. 145–154.

108 See Interuniversitaire Commissie voor de Herziening van het Milieurecht in het Vlaamse Gewest 1995, pp. 943–985 and Bocken, Lambrecht, Boes, De Nauw, Faure and Lavrysen 1996, pp. 31–32.

109 Gilhuis and Verschuuren 1994, p. 3. For comments, see Hulst 1995, pp. 167–173 as well as De Putter and Verschuuren 1995, pp. 96–99.

110 An overview of various types of environmental funds is provided in Faure and Hartlief 1996c, pp. 321–326.

against insolvency than the private insurance markets. One could assume that an insurer is better able to differentiate risks since an insurer is specialized in risk differentiation and risk spreading. Insurers therefore possess techniques to determine in what way their insured contribute to the risk. Obviously this assumes that the insurance markets are competitive. In the absence of competition on insurance markets, either the supply of insurance coverage could be too limited or premiums could be excessively high, which could justify a preference for a compensation fund.[111] But if insurance markets are competitive, insurers can be assumed to be better able to deal with classic insurance problems such as moral hazard and adverse selection than the administrators of a compensation fund. One cannot see as a matter of principle why a government agency that would run a compensation fund would have better information on risks than an insurer. This might, however, be different if highly technical risks are involved where operators of certain facilities are in a much better position than the insurance company to monitor each other. This point has been made for instance concerning the compensation for nuclear damage. One could argue that a risk-sharing agreement between nuclear plant operators could lead to optimal monitoring between the operators since they possess much better information on prevention, and good and bad risks than an insurance company would.[112] Also in maritime insurance the Protection and Indemnity Clubs, which we have already discussed and which are based on a mutual risk sharing between tanker owners, play a crucial role.[113]

So far we have outlined that in general there are very few reasons to expect that a compensation fund would provide better compensation than a private insurance market. This does not mean, however, that there may be no role at all for compensation funds with respect to environmental damage. However, most fund solutions typically refer to the situation that a polluter cannot be identified or is insolvent.[114] A compensation fund may well be used to guarantee compensation in case of insolvency of the injurer or the insurer. In that case a fund does not replace the liability and insurance system, but only intervenes in a particular case when the injurer or the insurer were found to be insolvent. This combined use of the liability system, insurance and a guarantee fund for the insolvency risk has the advantage that the incentives of the liability system will remain untouched and that the fund will only have to intervene in the event of insolvency.[115]

111 Faure and Van den Bergh 1995, pp. 65–85.
112 See Faure and Skogh 1992, pp. 499–513 and Faure 1995a, pp. 21–43.
113 See Coghlin 1984, pp. 403–416.
114 See e.g. Smets 1997, pp. 223–248.
115 This combined approach is also proposed by Monti 2001, pp. 65–68.

However, the question arises whether such a fund could at all be used separately from compulsory insurance (in the broadest sense). Indeed, if insolvency of the injurer is the problem one fears, it seems more logical to discuss the introduction of a duty to insure instead of immediately advancing a fund solution.

Many phenomena that include a private or public compensation scheme for environmental damage are referred to as 'fund' solutions. We took a brief look at some of these solutions, comparing them to traditional liability and insurance. Generally insurance seems better able to control risks and can be provided at lower costs. It seems therefore more appropriate to use traditional liability and insurance as far as possible and to use funds only in cases where insurance markets fail and there is reason to believe that funds would be able to provide adequate compensation. In that respect a guarantee fund comes to mind to provide coverage if an insurance company were to go out of business. However, it does not seem useful to introduce a guarantee fund without a corresponding duty to insure.

8.3 Other Approaches

Of course governments could do more to facilitate the provision of compensation and the well functioning of private law and insurance markets than merely introducing a duty to ensure or a compensation fund. First of all government could structure liability law in such a way that insurability is promoted. Thus shifting the risk of causal uncertainty to the injurer and introducing retrospective or joint and several liabilities should be avoided. There are, in addition, also examples of governments which actively intervene to provide financial guarantees themselves on which potential risk creators can call. Too often one has the impression that when insurance or financial markets do not function optimally the government immediately intervenes with public funds. It seems perhaps that there is a need to investigate whether other facilitative strategies could be used to promote the functioning of private law and insurance markets.

In that respect one can also point at the importance of an effective competition policy. There have indeed been some examples (more particularly as a result of pooling in nuclear liability insurance and marine insurance for oil pollution damage where a very close co-operation between insurers took place) whereby the compatibility with insurance policy was doubtful. It may be clear that insurance markets can only function effectively and offer a wide spectrum of differentiated insurance policies when this is supported by an effective competition policy. However, in some cases it may equally be needed for insurers to co-operate, for example to acquire information on specific new (environmental) risks. In those cases this co-operation can increase the insurability of particular risks. The same may in some cases be true with pooling as well. In some cases pooling of risks between insurers can create insurance markets (for example for large catastrophic risks) where without the pooling the risks may simply be uninsurable. In all of those cases where co-operation is necessary to increase the insurability of the risk, competition authorities will nevertheless have to be extremely careful and watch that this co-operation does indeed lead to the desired benefits for society and does not create the adverse effect of rather reducing than increasing the insurability of particular risks.

Finally one can also point at the importance of information strategies. Indeed, we have already indicated that particular risk creators (or potential victims) may be insufficiently informed of the environmental risks that they are exposed to. It could then be considered as a task of government to provide informational strategies whereby both injurers and potential victims are informed of the risks they are exposed to, of the availability of insurance or other financial means to provide protection against these risks and of the benefits this may generate. Hence, these facilitative information strategies may cure an information asymmetry and can thus equally remedy a potential market failure.

At the same time one equally has to warn that as soon as governments are asked to intervene there is always the danger that private interest may play an important role. As a result of private interest one can for instance notice that with the argument that this should promote insurability in some areas of environmental liability (notably oil pollution and nuclear liability), many governments have (as a result of international conventions) put a financial cap on the liability of risk creators. These financial caps or limits are largely considered inefficient (since they lead to underdeterrence) and of course limit the available compensation to the victim.[116] This example shows that one has to be very careful that governments are not captured by business interests and as a result create inefficient regulatory solutions (like financial caps) under the pretext that this will promote insurability of risks.

9. HARMONIZATION

9.1 Starting Point

A crucial question is whether there should be any harmonization of the issues addressed in this chapter and more particularly of environmental liability.

[116] For critical analysis of financial caps, see inter alia Faure 2003, pp. 194–206.

Again this question can be addressed taking into account the rich economic literature that has been dealing with the subsidiarity principle and its application to environmental harm. This is also an issue that has been dealt with extensively in the economic literature.[117] We can thus largely refer to this literature and briefly summarize the way in which economists would view the federalism debate, applied to environmental liability.

The starting point for economists is that a competition between legal orders will lead to a locative efficiency in the provision of legal rules if certain specific conditions are met. From this starting point it is argued that, from an economic point of view, decentralization should be the starting point. Thus the central question becomes: why centralize? Although decentralization thus has the preference (since the decision maker as close as possible to the citizens will have the best information on what is optimal for the citizens concerned) several criteria for centralization are advanced as well.

9.2 Transboundary Externality

A first reason for centralization is the transboundary character of an externality. If governments were able to externalize damage to the territory of another state an optimal internalization of that damage would not occur. This argument can certainly play a role with respect to many environmental problems. These are undoubtedly often transboundary.[118] It is, however, difficult to apply this argument to the case of environmental liability. Many pollution cases giving rise to liability are confined within the borders of one country. Moreover, even if there is transboundary pollution, other remedies could be applied (for example international private law) that do not go as far as total harmonization. It is particularly difficult to argue that, for example, liability for soil pollution could fall within this rationale since most of the soil pollution cases (with a few exceptions) are confined within national borders. Moreover, this argument would only be a reason to harmonize issues of transboundary pollution.

9.3 Race for the Bottom

A second economic rationale to centralize the regulation of environmental problems is the risk of destructive competition, referred to as the 'race for the bottom' between countries that could emerge to attract foreign investments

---

117 See for instance Van den Bergh, Faure and Lefevere 1996, Faure 2001b, pp. 263–286 and Faure and de Smedt 2001, pp. 217–237.

118 See also Oates and Schwab 1988, pp. 333–354. They argue that as long as the effects of pollution are confined within the borders of the relevant jurisdictions, local authorities will make socially optimal decisions of environmental quality.

with low environmental standards. As a result of this, a prisoner's dilemma could arise, whereby countries would fail to enact or enforce efficient legislation. It would mean that local governments would compete with lenient environmental legislation to attract industry.[119] The result would be an overall reduction of environmental quality below efficient levels. This should correspond with the traditional game–theoretical result that prisoners' dilemmas create inefficiencies. Centralization could be advanced as a remedy for these prisoners' dilemmas.

The 'race for the bottom' argument has had several supporters as well as opponents in North American scholarship. Law and economics scholars tend to stress the benefits of competition between states and point at the dangers of centralization,[120] whereas some legal scholars tend to attach more belief to the 'race for the bottom' rationale for centralization in environmental matters.[121] In Europe these issues are rarely discussed in the context of the 'race for the bottom' but are discussed in the European Community dogma of 'levelling the playing field to avoid distortions of competition'. This somewhat confuses the debate.

Empirical evidence to uphold this 'race for the bottom' rationale is rather weak. Repetto argues that pollution control costs are only a minor fraction of the total sales of manufacturing industries.[122] Moreover, Jaffe, Portney and Stavins[123] argue that empirical evidence shows that the effects of environmental regulations are 'either small, statistically insignificant or not robust to tests of model specification'. They argue that the stringency of environmental regulations might have some effect on new firms in their decision to locate for the first time, but that this will not induce existing firms to relocate. They equally argue that other criteria such as tax levels, public services and the unionization of labour force have a much more significant impact on the location decision than environmental regulation. This empirical evidence has been somewhat contradicted by Xing and Kolstad,[124] who argue that the laxity of environmental regulations in a host country is a significant determinant of foreign direct investment by the US chemical industry. The more lax the regulations, the more likely the country is to attract foreign investment, so

119 For a discussion of this theory, see Rose-Ackerman 1992b, pp. 169–170.

120 See especially with applications to environmental law, Revesz 1992, pp. 1210–1254 and Revesz 1996, pp. 2341–2416.

121 See Esty and Geradin 1998, pp. 5–46 and see Esty and Geradin 1997, pp. 265–336 in which they provide an interesting overview of the various legal instruments to deal with harmonization and apply this in the NAFTA and in the European context. See also Trebilcock and Howse 1999, pp. 5–37.

122 Repetto 1994.

123 Jaffe, Portney and Stavins 1995, pp. 132–163.

124 Xing and Kolstad 1995.

Xing and Kolstad argue. This somewhat weakens the evidence presented by Jaffe, Portney and Stavins[125] as far as the location of new firms outside the US is concerned.

All these arguments apply to the area of environmental liability as well. It is doubtful that within Europe member states would be able to engage in a game in which they would strive for low level environmental liability in order to attract industry. There is no proof of such a destructive competition towards lower liability standards and this risk is, moreover, not very realistic. Indeed, as indicated, one can doubt whether environmental liability plays a significant role in attracting or repulsing business to or from a given state. Other elements may be far more important than the level of environmental liability in location decisions of businesses. Moreover, if environmental liability were to have any effect as far as the race for the bottom is concerned, it is even more likely that states would wish to protect victims of environmental pollution instead of corporate interests. Indeed, a lenient environmental liability legislation may well run counter to the states' interests since it would limit the possibilities, for example to recover soil clean-up costs from liable polluters. If there is any effect at all one can therefore expect a 'race for the top' rather than a 'race for the bottom' in the area of environmental liability. This would enable states to recover for example costs for clean-up of (domestically) polluted soils, also from foreign polluters.

9.4 Harmonization of Conditions of Competition

There is a third, although not strict economic, argument advanced in the European harmonization debate, being that the harmonization of conditions of competition would be necessary to create an integrated European market. Thus differences in legal rules would endanger the creation of the integrated market.

This argument seems particularly weak. From an economic point of view, the mere fact that conditions of competition differ does not necessarily create a 'race for the bottom' risk. There can be differences in marketing conditions for a variety of reasons, and if the conditions of competition were indeed totally equal, as the argument assumes, there would also be no trade according to the theory of specialization.

Also, Europe has developed an elaborate set of rules, which guarantee, inter alia, a free flow of products and services[126] and thus contribute to market inte-

---

[125] Jaffe, Portney and Stavins 1995, pp. 132–163.

[126] See Articles 28–30 of the Treaty of the European Union (the 'old' Articles 30–36).

gration without the necessity to harmonize all rules and standards.[127] In this respect one can think of the case law of the European Court of Justice with respect to the free movement of goods versus environmental protection.[128] This shows that the goal of market integration can be achieved via (other) less far-reaching instruments than total harmonization[129] which can equally remove barriers to trade.

The same applies for the area of environmental liability. It is very possible to create a common market without a total harmonization of all legal rules. The goal of market integration should not necessarily be achieved via this far-reaching instrument of total harmonization. This would only justify for example general safety standards that aim at avoiding pointless incompatibilities which could create barriers to trade and distortions of competition within the internal market. That argument can, however, not justify a harmonization of rules of private law such as environmental liability. Finally, attempts which have been undertaken so far to harmonize rules of private law, for example in the area of product liability, have not been proved to be able to achieve a total harmonization of marketing conditions.[130]

9.5 Reduction of Administrative Costs

There is a third economic argument in favour of harmonization, which would be based on a reduction of administrative costs. This argument is often advanced by European legal scholars pleading for harmonization of private law in Europe, and is based on the argument that differences in legal systems are very complex and only serve Brussels law firms.[131] This argument cannot be examined in detail here.[132] It is obviously too simple to state that a harmonized legal system is always more efficient than differentiated legal rules because of the transaction costs savings inherent in harmonized rules.[133] This

---

127 See generally on the potential conflict between free trade and environmental protection, Esty 1999, pp. 190–209.

128 For an overview of this case law, see Lefevere and Faure 1995, pp. 93–107 and Trebilcock and Howse 1999, pp. 21–28.

129 See also Esty and Geradin 1998, pp. 5–46 and see Esty and Geradin 1997, pp. 265–336 in which they provide an interesting overview of the various legal instruments to deal with harmonization and apply this in the NAFTA and in the European context (see specifically pp. 296–299); and Ogus 1994, pp. 177–179.

130 See Faure 2001b, pp. 263–286 and see Faure 2000, pp. 467–508.

131 This is one of the arguments made by the Danish scholar, Lando in favour of harmonized private law; see Lando 1993, pp. 473–474.

132 It is further developed and criticized in a paper by R. Van den Bergh; see Van den Bergh 1998, pp. 129–152.

133 For a discussion of this theory, see Rose-Ackerman 1992b, p. 172 who argues

argument neglects the fact that there are substantial benefits from differentiation whereby legislation can be adapted to the preferences of individuals.[134] Moreover, given the differences between the legal systems (and legal cultures) in Europe, the costs of harmonization may be huge – if not prohibitive – as well.[135] The crucial question therefore is whether the possible transaction costs savings of harmonization outweigh the benefits of differentiated legal rules. There is little empirical evidence to support the statement that transaction costs savings could justify a European harmonization of all kinds of legal rules. Moreover, the transaction costs savings are likely to be relatively small.[136]

It is very doubtful whether the transaction costs argument could play a role in justifying a harmonization of environmental liability. That would only be the case if the regime were to be exclusive in the sense that it replaces national law and thus reduces existing differences. Directive 2004/35/CE, however, makes it clear that it leaves national law unaffected.[137]

The transaction costs argument could, however, play a role to justify the so-called negative harmonization, which aims at a co-ordination of for example product standards to prevent states from hindering a free flow of products and services.[138] This type of co-operation between states can reduce transaction costs, but does not necessitate a homogenization of process standards, which is often the goal in environmental law.

The conclusion therefore is that the economic arguments to harmonize environmental rules with respect to problems which are not transboundary are relatively weak. Nevertheless, many European directives deal with problems (for example drinking water or bathing water) which are not typically transboundary and for which the European competence is therefore difficult to fit into the economic framework.

---

that uniform federal regulation may reduce search costs and tends to produce a more stable and predictable jurisprudence.

[134] Mendelsohn 1986, p. 301.

[135] That point has especially been made by Legrand (Legrand 1997, p. 111).

[136] See Van den Bergh 1998, pp. 146–148.

[137] See Article 16 of the directive which provides: 'This directive shall not prevent Member States from maintaining or adopting more stringent provisions in relation to the prevention and remedying of environmental damage, including the identification of additional activities to be subject to the prevention and remediation requirements of this directive and the identification of the additional responsible parties.'

[138] The free flow of services was the result of directives issued as a consequence of the so-called 'Single Market Initiative'. See Vogel 1995. See on the need to harmonize product safety, M. Faure 2000.

10. CONCLUDING REMARKS

The final question that of course has to be addressed within the framework of this ambitious project is what the particular regulatory function of environmental liability can be in the context of European private law on the basis of the analysis we have provided. Of course we should repeat that it is only possible to provide a partial and very cautious attempt to answer this question, given the fact that we merely addressed the regulatory function of environmental liability from a law and economic perspective and by drawing on the basis of some experiences in member states and in Europe. Notwithstanding these limits, a few conclusions can be formulated concerning the role of environmental liability in remedying environmental damage. To some extent one can hold that tort law is probably more a minor, luxury phenomenon than an instrument that would be capable of providing compensation to accident victims at any price. Indeed, Hartlief held in his inauguration address that the thresholds for tort liability are so high that it should be considered as a luxury system (in the sense that it is also the only system that guarantees full compensation).[139] Even though the regulatory function of tort law in this domain of environmental harm may thus be limited (both as far as prevention and compensation is concerned), one can still argue that environmental liability (and thus private law) does have an added value.

Addressing the issue of prevention it is not difficult to argue that the primary regulatory instrument to reach prevention of environmental harm is undoubtedly public law or regulations. Shavell's public interest theory of regulation seems to obtain large support from legal practice in many European countries and at the EU level: most of the preventive measures that are required from potential polluters to reduce environmental risks are determined by regulations such as emission limit values which can be found in environmental permits. However, we argued that even as far as prevention is concerned private law and more particularly environmental liability undoubtedly plays a complementary role. This role is more particularly that environmental liability can still provide additional incentives for prevention in cases where the deterrent effect of regulation fails. Even though the intensity of regulation in the area of environmental protection is undoubtedly very intense, there are still always potential situations where the regulatory authority has (perhaps as a result of capture by private interest) defined inefficiently lenient environmental standards or has simply failed to issue norms with respect to a particular situation (for instance because that type of harm could not be foreseen when an environmental permit was granted). Particularly for these types

139 Hartlief 1979.

of situations the knowledge that even though public regulations have been followed (which has to be seen as a minimum) the injurer can still be held liable, will undoubtedly offer a complementary deterrent effect. Moreover, where lawyers are traditionally rather suspicious and even critical of a potential role of tort law in preventing damage, they seem to attach much more belief to the preventive function of liability rules in the area of environmental harm, probably because these rules are largely addressed to professional risk creators. Hence there is at least a (limited but not unimportant) added value of environmental liability in providing complementary incentives for prevention in cases where regulation fails.

Also as far as compensation is concerned environmental liability can have an added value for the simple reason that it is the only regime that guarantees complete indemnification of the victim. The major weakness of environmental liability is that a liability without solvency guarantees does not offer any security that compensation will effectively take place. Therefore this added value of tort law (complete indemnification) has to be combined with other mechanisms in order to guarantee that environmental liability can also exercise this regulatory function of providing compensation to victims of environmental harm. Liability insurance could be such a mechanism, although the application of the classic liability insurance to environmental harm leads to several problems, as has been held by many in the literature. Environmental risks are still relatively new; therefore reliable statistics on accident frequency and potential scope of the damage are still lacking. Moreover, environmental damage is such a vague notion that the predictability is often difficult. To this can be added that the conditions for environmental liability in (national) case law are still in full evolution. That makes it rather difficult for a liability insurer to estimate what the probability may be that his insured injurer would be held liable to a third party for environmental damage. To this can be added the risk that new liability rules would be applied with retrospective effect in all situations and that the risk of causal uncertainty would be shifted to the risk creator, or that he could be held jointly and separately liable also for damage that is (at least partially) caused by others. All of these elements make it easy to understand that insurers consider environmental liability a difficult to insure risk. Some of the evolutions we outlined are considered by some insurers as so serious that they consider the environmental liability risk as uninsurable. In some countries insurers have already been withdrawing from the liability insurance market. This withdrawal of insurers from the environmental liability market can seriously endanger the functioning of environmental liability in providing compensation for environmental harm. Without a solvency guarantee it may be clear that environmental liability also cannot exercise its regulatory function in compensating environmental harm.

Therefore in some countries, for example the Netherlands amongst others, insurers have moved to another system of coverage. This is no longer based on environmental liability, but on a direct insurance of the particular site. It is held that direct insurance would be better able than liability insurance to provide an effective differentiation of risks. But notwithstanding the advantages we also indicated that questions still arise concerning this direct insurance. One of the problems is that of course (as is always the case with first-party insurances) the conditions of coverage will be determined in the insurance policy. These conditions will, understandably, try to limit the risk for the insurer in order to keep the risk insurable. Another problem is that the entire Dutch insurance market switched to direct insurance. As a result of this it is no longer possible to get insurance mainly on the basis of environmental liability. This shows that serious questions can be asked as far as the competitiveness of insurance markets is concerned. Environmental liability can only exercise its regulatory function in compensating harm when a wide variety of differentiated policies are offered in a competitive insurance and financial market among which potentially responsible partners can choose. One cannot escape the impression that in some cases a too strong co-operation between insurers limits the offer of insurance policies, precisely as competition theory would predict.

The importance of the availability of insurance or alternative methods of coverage is, as we have shown, not only important to guarantee compensation to the victim. In the case of insolvency there is also the risk that environmental liability cannot exercise its regulatory function of prevention since insolvency may lead to underdeterrence. Hence, the law and economic literature strongly supports pleas in favour of a duty for potential responsible parties to seek financial coverage to meet their obligations. A problem, however, is that it is doubtful whether today's European insurance markets are sufficiently developed to be able to execute an outright duty to insure. Thus it seems more pragmatic to provide competent authorities with the possibility to demand financial guarantees from potentially responsible parties, for example in environmental permits. This individualized approach has the advantage that the competent authority can take into account the individual situation of the particular potential polluter.

REFERENCES

Abraham, K. (1988), 'Environmental Liability and the Limits of Insurance', 88 *Columbia Law Review*, 957–959.

Adams, M. (1989), 'New Activities and the Efficient Liability Rules', in M. Faure and R. Van den Bergh (eds.), *Essays in Law and Economics. Corporations, Accident Prevention and Compensation for Losses*.

Akkermans, A. (1997), *Proportionele aansprakelijkheid bij onzeker causaal verband.*

Arcuri, A. (2001), 'Controlling Environmental Risk in Europe: The Complementary

Role of an EC Environmental Liability Regime', *Tijdschrift voor Milieuaansprakelijkheid* (*TMA*), 39–40.

Bergkamp, L. (2000a), 'The Proper Scope of Joint and Several Liability', *TMA*, 154–155.

Bergkamp, L. (2000b), 'The Commission's White Paper on Environmental Liability: A Weak Case for an EC Strict Liability Regime', *EELR*, 112–114.

Bergkamp, L. (2001), *Liability and Environment*, The Hague/London, Kluwer Law International 208.

Bocken, H. (1987), 'Alternatives to Liability and Liability Insurance for the Compensation of Pollution Damages', *TMA*, 83–87 and (1988) *TMA*, 3–10.

Bocken, H. (1992), 'La réparation des Dommages causées par la Pollution au Droit Belge. La Situation en 1992', *Tijdschrift voor Belgisch Burgerlijk Recht*, 284–327.

Bocken, H. (1993), L'Assurance Responsabilité Civile pour Dommages causées par la Pollution, in *Les Assurances de l'Entreprise, Actes du Collogues tenu à l'Université Libres des Bruxelles les 2 et 3 décembre 1993*.

Bocken, H., W. Lambrecht, M. Boes, A. De Nauw, M. Faure, L. Lavrysen (1996), 'The Flemish Draft Decree on Environmental Policy: An Outline', in H. Bocken, D. Ryckbost (eds.), *Codification of Environmental Law. Proceedings of the International Conference*, pp. 31–32.

Bocken, H. and D. Ryckbost (1991) (eds.), *Verzekering van Milieuschade, Insurance of Environmental Damage*.

Brans, E.H.P. (1994), 'Liability for Ecological Damage under the 1992 Protocols to the Civil Liability Convention and the Fund Convention and the Oil Pollution Act of 1990', *TMA*, 61–67 and 85–91.

Brown, J.P. (1973), 'Toward an Economic Theory of Liability', *Journal of Legal Studies* (JLS), 343.

Brüggemeier, G. (1991), 'Liability for Water Pollution under German Law: Fault or Strict Liability', in J. van Dunné (ed.), *Transboundary Pollution and Liability: The Case of the River Rhine*, pp. 88–91.

Burrows, P. (1999), 'Combining Regulation and Liability for the Control of External Costs', 19 *IRLE*, 227–242.

Calabresi, G. (1961), 'Some Thoughts on Risk Distribution and the Law of Torts', *Yale Law Journal*, 499–553.

Calabresi, G. (1970), *The Costs of Accidents, A Legal and Economic Analysis*.

Calabresi, G. (1975), 'Optimal Deterrence and Accidents', 84 *YLJ*, 658.

Coghlin, T.G. (1984), 'Protection and Indemnity Clubs', *Lloyd's Maritime and Commercial Law Quarterly*, 403–416.

Cooter, R. (1984), 'Prices and Sanctions', 84 *Columbia Law Review*, 1343–1523.

Cooter, R. and Th. Ulen (2000), *Law and Economics*, 3rd edition, pp. 316–318.

Cortenraad, W.H.F.M. (2000), *The Corporate Paradox. Economic Realities of the Corporate Form of Organization*.

Cousy, H. (1995), 'Recent Developments in Environmental Insurance', in F. Abraham, K. Deketelaere and J. Stuyck (eds.), *Recent Economic and Legal Developments in European Environmental Policy*, pp. 227–241.

Deprimoz, J. (1995), 'Régime Juridique des Assurances contre les Risques Nucléaires', *Juris. Classeur*, 1–24.

De Putter, P. and J. Verschuuren (1995), 'Een milieuschadefonds in Nederland?', *MenR*, 96–99.

Dewees, D. (1992a), 'The Comparative Efficacy of Tort Law and Regulation for Environmental Protection', *GPRI*, 446–467.

Dewees, D. (1992b), 'Tort Law and the Deterrence of Environmental Pollution', in T.H. Tietenberg (ed.), *Innovation in Environmental Policy, Economic and Legal Aspects of Recent Developments in Environmental Enforcement of Liability*, pp. 139–164.

Dewees, D., D. Duff and M. Trebilcock (1996), *Exploring the Domain of Accident Law; Taking the Facts Seriously*.

Diamond, P. (1974), 'Single Activity Accidents', *JLS*, 107–164.

Drion, P.J.M. (1998), 'Milieu onder één dak: milieuschadeverzekering' (MSV), *Verzekeringsrechtelijke Berichten*, 19–21.

Endres, A. and R. Schwarze (1991), 'Allokationswirkungen einer Umwelthaftpflichtversicherung', *Zeitschrift für Umweltpolitik und Umweltrecht* (ZUU), 1–25.

Endres, A. and B. Staiger (1996), 'Ökonomische Aspekte des Umwelthaftungsrecht', in M. Ahrens and J. Simon (eds.), *Umwelthaftung, Risikosteuerung und Versicherung*, pp. 79–93.

Estep, E. (1960), 'Radiation Injuries and Statistics: The Need for a New Approach to Injury Litigation', *Michigan Law Review (*MLR), 259–304.

Esty, D. (1999), 'Economic Integration and the Environment', in N. Vig and R. Axelrod (eds.), *The Global Environment*, pp. 190–209.

Esty, D. and D. Geradin (1997), 'Market Access, Competitiveness and Harmonization: Environmental Protection in Regional Trade Agreements', 21 *Harvard Environmental Law Review* (HELR), 265–336.

Esty, D. and D. Geradin (1998), 'Environmental Protection and International Competitiveness. A Conceptual Framework', 32/3 *Journal of World Trade* (JWT), 5–46.

Faure, M. (1995a), 'Economic Models of Compensation for Damage Caused by Nuclear Accidents: Some Lessons for the Revision of the Paris and Vienna Conventions', *European Journal of Law and Economics* (EJLE), 21–43.

Faure, M. (1995b), 'The Limits to Insurability from a Law and Economics Perspective', *Geneva Papers on Risk and Insurance* (GPRI), 454–462.

Faure, M. (2000), 'Product Liability and Product Safety in Europe: Harmonization or Differentiation?', 53 *Kyklos*, 467–508.

Faure, M. (2001a), 'Tort Liability in France: An Introductory Economic Analysis', in B. Deffains and Th. Kirat (eds.), *Law and Economics in Civil Law Countries*, pp. 169–181.

Faure, M. (2001b), 'Regulatory Competition versus Harmonization in EU Environmental Law', in D. Esty and G. Geradin (eds.), *Regulatory Competition and Economic Integration*, pp. 263–286.

Faure, M. (ed.) (2003), *Deterrence, Insurability, and Compensation in Environmental Liability. Future Developments in the European Union.*

Faure, M. (2004), 'Alternative Compensation Mechanisms as Remedy for Uninsurability of Liability', *The Geneva Papers on Risk and Insurance*, vol. 29, no. 3, 455–489.

Faure, M. (2007), 'Shift Toward Alternative Compensation Mechanisms for Environmental Damage?', in M. Faure and A. Verhey (eds.), *Shifts in Compensation for Environmental Damage*, Vienna, Springer, pp. 73–102.

Faure, M. and P. Fenn (1999), 'Retroactive Liability and the Insurability of Long-tail Risks', *IRLE*, 487–500.

Faure, M. and D. Grimeaud (2003), 'Financial Assurance Issues of Environmental Liability', in M. Faure (ed.), *Deterrence, Insurability and Compensation in Environmental Liability. Future Developments in the European Union*, Vienna, Springer, 68–122.

Faure, M. and T. Hartlief (1996a), *Ontwikkelingen in de werkgeversaansprakelijkheid voor beroepsziekten: aanleiding voor een nieuwe AVB-polis?*, A&V, 140–150.

Faure, M. and T. Hartlief (1996b), 'Towards an Expanding Enterprise Liability in Europe? How to Analyse the Scope of Liability of Industrial Operators and their Insurers', *Maastricht Journal of European and Comparative Law* (MJ), 254–259.

Faure, M. and T. Hartlief (1996c), 'Compensation Funds versus Liability and Insurance for Remedying Environmental Damage', *Review of European Community and International Environmental Law*, 321–326.

Faure, M. and T. Hartlief (2003), 'Insurance and Expanding Systemic Risks', Paris, *OECD*, p. 260.

Faure, M. and G. Heine (1991), 'The Insurance of Fines: The Case of Oil Pollution', *GPRI*, 39–54.

Faure, M. and M. Ruegg (1994), 'Standard Setting through General Principles of Environmental Law', in M. Faure, J. Vervaele and A. Weale (eds.), *Environmental Standards in the European Union in an Interdisciplinary Framework*, pp. 39–60.

Faure, M. and G. Skogh (1992), 'Compensation for Damages Caused by Nuclear Accidents: A Convention as Insurance', *GPRI*, 499–513.

Faure, M. and K. de Smedt (2001), 'Should Europe Harmonize Environmental Liability Legislation?', *Environmental Liability*, vol. 5, 217–237.

Faure, M. and R. Van den Bergh (1995), 'Restrictions of Competition on Insurance Markets and the Applicability of EC Anti-Trust Law', *Kyklos*, 65–85.

Gardner, M. (1990), 'Results of a Case-control Study of Leukaemia and Lymphoma Among Young People Near Sellafield Nuclear Plant in West Cumbria', *British Medical Journal*, 423–434.

Gilhuis, P. and J. Verschuuren (1994), 'Een milieuschadefonds in Nederland; een onderzoek naar de mogelijkheden', *Publicatiereeks Milieubeheer*, 3.

Gimpel-Hinteregger, M. (1994), *Grundfragen des Umwelthaftung*.

Hager, G. (1993), 'Umwelthaftungsgesetz: The New German Environmental Liability Law', *EL*, pp. 41–44.

Hansmann, H. and R.H. Kraakman (1991), 'Toward Unlimited Shareholder Liability for Corporate Torts', 100 *YLJ*, 1879.

Hartkamp, G. (1992), *Tijdschrift voor Consumentenrecht* (TvC), 241–258.

Hartlief, T. (1997), *Ieder draagt zijn eigen schade*, inauguration address, Deventer, Kluwer.

Hulst, E. (1993), *Grondslagen van Milieuaansprakelijkheid.*

Hulst, E. (1995), 'De werkelijkheid rondom een algemeen milieuschadefonds, een commentaar', *TMA*, 167–173.

Interuniversitaire Commissie voor de Herziening van het Milieurecht in het Vlaamse Gewest (1995), *Voorontwerp Decreet Milieubeleid*, pp. 943–985.

Jaffe, A., S. Portney and R. Stavins (1995), 'Environmental Regulation and the Competitiveness of US Manufacturing: What Does the Evidence Tell Us?', *Journal of Economic Literature* (JEL), 33, 132–163.

Janssen, C.A. (1998), 'Aansprakelijkheid voor milieuschade en financiële zekerheid naar toekomstig recht: nieuwe oplossingen. Nederlands Recht', in L.F. Wiggers-Rust and K. Deketelaere (eds.), *Aansprakelijkheid voor milieuschade en financiële zekerheid*, pp. 111–112.

Jones, B. (1997), 'Deterring, Compensating and Remedying Environmental Damage: the Contribution of Tort Liability', in P. Wetterstein (ed.), *Harm to the Environment: The Right to Compensation and the Assessment of Damages*, pp. 11–27.

Jones, B. (1999), 'Environmental Law in the United Kingdom', in N.S.J. Koeman, (ed.), *Environmental Law in Europe*.

Jost, P.J. (1996), 'Limited Liability and the Requirement to Purchase Insurance', *IRLE*, 259–276.
Katzman, M. (1988), 'Pollution Liability Insurance and Catastrophic Environmental Risk', *Journal of Risk and Insurance* (JRI), 89–90.
Kerremans, H. (1999), 'Aansprakelijkheid voor milieuschade en verzekeringsmogelijkheden', in *Milieuzorg in de onderneming I, Juridische, Fiscale en Organisatorische Aspecten*, pp. 537–583.
Knottenbelt, J. (1990), *Produktaansprakelijkheid.*
Kolstad, Ch.D., Th.S. Ulen and G.V. Johnson (1990), 'Ex Post Liability for Harm vs. Ex Ante Safety Regulation: Substitutes or Complements?', 80 *American Economic Review* (AER), 888–901.
Kottenhagen-Edzes, P.A. (1992), *Onrechtmatige daad en milieu. Het gebruik van het privaatrecht bij het voorkomen van milieu-aantasting en het verhaal van milieuschade.*
Koziol, H. (1997), *Österreichisches Haftpflichtrecht.*
Kunreuther, H. and P. Freeman (2001), 'Insurability, Environmental Risks and the Law, in A. Heyes (ed.), *The Law and Economics of the Environment*, pp. 304–316.
Kunreuther, H., R. Hogarth and J. Meszaros (1993), 'Insurer Ambiguity and Market Failure', *Journal of Risk and Uncertainty*, 71–87.
Landes, W. and R. Posner (1981), 'The Positive Economic Theory of Tort Law', *Georgia Law Review* (GLR), 870.
Landes, W. and R. Posner (1984), 'Tort Law as a Regulatory Regime for Catastrophic Personal Injuries', *JLS*, 417.
Lando, O. (1993), 'Die Regeln des Europäischen Vertragsrecht', in P. Müller-Graff (ed.), *Gemeinsames Privatrecht in der Europäischen Gemeinschaft*, pp. 473–474.
Lang, R. (1996), Die neue Umwelt-Haftpflichtversicherung nach dem HUK-Modell', in M. Ahrens and J. Simon (eds), *Umwelthaftung, Risikosteuerung und Versicherung*, pp. 169–183.
Lavrysen, L. (1995), 'Judicial Responses in the Nineties to Dutch (and German) Shipments of Waste to Belgium in the Eighties', *MJ*, 219–243.
Lefevere, J. and M. Faure (1995), 'Introduction to European Environmental Law', in T. Kegels (ed.), *Shipping Law faces Europe: European Policy Competition and Environment*, pp. 93–107.
Legrand, B (1997), 'The Impossibility of "Legal Transplants" ', *MJECL*, 111.
Mackaay, E. (1982), *Economics of Information and the Law.*
McIntyre, O. (1996), 'The UK Environmental Act 1995: Section 57: A Contaminated Land Regime at Last!', 4 *EL* 4, 67–74.
Mendelsohn, R. (1986), 'Regulatory Heterogeneous Emissions', 13 *Journal of Environmental Economics and Management* (JEEM), 301.
Monti, A. (2001), 'Environmental Risk: A Comparative Law and Economics Approach to Liability and Insurance', *European Review of Private Law* (ERPL), 51–79.
Niezen, J. (1998), 'Nieuwe milieuschadeverzekering – geen panacee', *MenR*, 114.
Niezen, G.J., M.J.G.C. Raaijmakers and A.J.S.M. Tervoort (2000) (eds.), 'Aansprakelijkheid voor milieuschade in de Europese Unie' in *Ongebonden Recht Bedrijven*, p. 171.
Oates, W.A. and R.M. Schwab (1988), 'Economic Competition Among Jurisdictions: Efficiency Enhancing or Distortion Inducing?', 35 *Journal of Public Economics*, 333–354.
Ogus, A. (1994), *Regulation, Legal Form and Economic Theory.*
Pape, K.A. and K. Schillhorn (1999), 'Environmental Law in the Federal Republic of Germany', in N.S.J. Koeman (ed.), *Environmental Law in Europe.*

Polborn, M. (1998), 'Mandatory Insurance and the Judgement-Proof Problem', *IRLE*, 141–146.
Polinsky, A.M. (1983), *Introduction to Law and Economics*.
Priest, G. (1987), 'The Current Insurance Crisis and Modern Tort Law', *YLJ*, 1521–1590.
Ranson, D. (2000), 'Verzekering van milieuaansprakelijkheid', *M&R*, 68.
Repetto, R. (1994), *Trade and Sustainable Development*, UNEP, Environment and Trade Series.
Revesz, R. (1992), 'Rehabilitating Interstate Competition: Rethinking the "Race for the Bottom" Rationale for Federal Environmental Regulation', 67 *New York University Law Review* (NYULR), 1210–1254.
Revesz, R. (1996), 'Federalism and Interstate Environmental Externalities', 144 *University of Pennsylvania Law Review* (UPLR), 2341–2416.
Revesz, R.L. and R.W. Stewart (1995), *Analysing Superfund, Economics, Science and Law*.
Richardson, B.J. (2000), 'Financial Institutions for Sustainability', *EL*, 52–64.
Robinson, G. (1985), 'Probabilistic Causation and Compensation for Tortious Risk', *JLS*, 798.
Rogge, J. (1997), *Les assurances en matière d'environnement*.
Rose-Ackerman, S. (1992a), 'Environmental Liability Law', in T.H. Tietenberg (ed.), *Innovation in Environmental Policy, Economic and Legal Aspects of Recent Developments in Environmental Enforcement and Liability*, pp. 223–243.
Rose-Ackerman, S. (1992b), *Rethinking the Progressive Agenda. The Reform of the American Regulatory State*.
Rose-Ackerman, S. (1995a), *Controlling Environmental Policy: the Limits of Public Law in Germany and the United States*.
Rose-Ackerman, S. (1995b), 'Public Law versus Private Law in Environmental Regulation: European Union Proposals in the Light of United States Experience', 4 *Review of European Community and International Environmental Law* (RECIEL), 312–332.
Rose-Ackerman, S. (1996), 'Public Law versus Private Law in Environmental Regulation: European Union Proposals in the Light of United States and German Experiences', in E. Eide and R. van den Bergh (eds.), *Law and Economics of the Environment*, pp. 13–39.
Rosenberg, D. (1984), 'The Causal Connection in Mass Exposure Cases: A "Public Law" Vision of the Tort System', *HLR*, 851–929.
Schmitz, P.W. (2000), 'On the Joint Use of Liability and Safety Regulation', 20 *IRLE*, 371–382.
Schwartz, A. and L. Wilde (1979), 'Intervening in Markets on the Basis of Imperfect Information: A Legal and Economic Analysis', *University of Pennsylvania Law Review* (UPLR), 630–682.
Schwartz, G. (1997), 'Mixed Theories of Tort Law: Affirming both Deterrence and Corrective Justice', 75 *Texas Law Review* (TLR), 1801–1834.
Shavell, S. (1980), 'Strict Liability versus Negligence', *JLS*, 1–25.
Shavell, S. (1984a), 'Liability for Harm versus Regulation of Safety', *JLS*, 357–374.
Shavell, S. (1984b), 'A Model of the Optimal Use of Liability and Safety Regulation', *Rand Journal of Economics* (RJE), 271–280.
Shavell, S. (1985a), 'Criminal Law and the Optimal Use of Non-monetary Sanctions as a Deterrent', *Columbia Law Review*, 1232–1262.
Shavell, S. (1985b), 'Uncertainty over Causation and the Determination of Civil Liability', *JLE*, 587–609.

Shavell, S. (1986), 'The Judgement Proof Problem', *IRLE*, 43–58.

Shavell, S. (1987), *Economic Analysis of Accident Law*.

Skogh, G. (2000), 'Mandatory Insurance: Transaction Costs Analysis of Insurance', in B. Bouckaert and G. de Geest (eds.), *Encyclopedia of Law and Economics*, pp. 521–537.

Smets, H. (1997), 'COSCA: A Complementary System for Compensation of Accidental Pollution Damage', in P. Wettenstein (ed.), *Harm to the Environment: The Right to Compensation and the Assessment of Damage*, pp. 223–248.

Spier, J. (1990), *Sluipende schade*.

Stigler, G. (1961), 'The Economics of Information', *Journal of Political Economics* (JPE), 213.

Trauberman, J. (1983), 'Statutory Reform of "Toxic Torts". Relieving Legal, Scientific and Economic Burdens on the Chemical Victim', *Harvard Environmental Law Review* (HELR), 177–296.

Trebilcock, M. and R. Howse (1999), 'Trade Liberalization and Regulatory Diversity, Reconciling Competitive Markets with Competitive Politics', 6 *European Journal of Law and Economics* (EJLE), 5–37.

Van, A. (1994), 'Statistisch bewijs van causaal verband, Discussion of High Court of Justice 8 October 1993 (Sellafield Claims)', *TMA*, 109–118.

Van, A. (1995), *Onzekerheid over daderschap en causaliteit*.

Van den Bergh, R. (1998), 'Subsidiarity as an Economic Demarcation Principle and the Emergence of European Private Law', *Maastricht Journal of European and Comparative Law* (MJECL), 129–152.

Van den Bergh, R., M. Faure and J. Lefevere (1996), 'The Subsidiarity Principal in European Environmental Law: An Economic Analysis', in E. Eide and R. Van den Bergh (eds.), *Law and Economics of the Environment*.

Vanden Borre, T. (2001), *Efficiënte preventie en compensatie van catastroferisico's. Het voorbeeld van schade door kernongevallen*.

Veljanovski, C.G. (1981), 'The Economic Theory of Tort Liability – Toward a Corrective Justice Approach', in P. Burrows and C.G. Veljanovski (eds.), *The Economic Approach to Law*, pp. 125–150.

Viscusi, W.K. (1991), *The Dimensions of the Product Liability Crisis*, JLS, 147–177.

Vogel, D. (1995), *Trading Up: Consumer and Environmental Regulation in the Global Economy*.

Wagner, G. (1999), 'Haftung und Versicherung als Instrumente der Techniksteuerung', *Versicherungsrecht* (VR), 1441–1480.

Wansink, J.H. (1985), 'De nieuwe milieuaansprakelijkheidsverzekering', *M&R*, 98.

Wansink, J.H. (1997), 'Hoe plotseling en onzeker is de verzekeringsdekking voor millieuaansprakelijkheidsrisico's?', in J. ten Kate et al (eds.), *Miscellanea. Jurisconsulto vero dedicata, Essays offered to Prof. Mr. J.M. van Dunné*, pp. 451–460.

Wansink, J.H. (1999), 'Verzekering en milieuschade als gevolg van vervoer/opslag van gevaarlijke stoffen ', *TMA*, 77–82.

Wittman, D. (1980), 'First Come, First Served: An Economic Analysis of "Coming to Nuisance" ', *JLS*, 557–568.

Xing, Y. and C. Kolstad (2002), 'Do Lax Environmental Regulations Attack Foreign Investment?', *Environmental and Resource Economics*, 21, 1–22.

Zeckhauser, R. (1996), '19th Annual Lecture of the Geneva Association and Catastrophes', *GPRI*, 5.

6. The law applicable to violations of the environment – regulatory strategies

Oliveira Boskovic

Can the conflict of laws rule in the field of environmental liability fulfil a regulatory function? The question is surprising for a continental lawyer. Although the growing importance of the regulatory function of private law, largely based on the decline of the classical distinction between private and public law has been demonstrated,[1] the problem remains largely unexplored in private international law.[2]

The idea of regulation seems absent in the traditional reasoning of European private international law systems. When designing a conflict of laws rule in the European tradition, private law considerations are generally preferred to state interests and goals traditionally qualified as belonging to public law.[3] Even when this is not the case, policies which are taken into account are generally municipal policies of the law of the forum.

For several reasons, the law of environmental liability seems particularly suitable to show that this perspective is not the only possible one. First of all because many environmental disasters have an international dimension. Secondly, because a truly transnational or at least European policy exists in this field. And last but not least because harmonization of substantive law is still limited,[4] leav-

---

1 See H. Muir Watt (2004) 'Les aspects économiques du droit international privé', RCADI t 307, p. 268.

2 See however, R. Wai (2002) 'Transnational liftoff and juridical touchdown: the regulatory function of private international law in the era of globalisation', 40 Col J Trans Law, p. 209.

3 This is true at least since the second half of the twentieth century. On the cyclical movement which affects the place of public law and private law considerations amongst the foundations of the conflict of laws theory, see H. Muir Watt (1997) 'Droit public et droit privé dans les rapports internationaux (Vers la publicisation des conflits de lois?)' Archives de philosophie du droit, p. 207.

4 See for example, Paris and Vienna Conventions of 29 July 1960 and 21 May 1963 on civil liability for nuclear damage, Brussels Convention of 29 Nov 1969 on civil liability for oil pollution damage, London Convention of 3 May 1996 on liability and compensation for damage in connection with the carriage of hazardous and noxious substances by sea. It is significant that even within the European Union civil

ing place for conflict of law rules[5] and calling for a uniform rule at least at the European level. Of course regulation in this field is essentially assumed by public law rules and this situation is approved by some academics who emphasize the limited usefulness of private law rules in this field.[6] However the latter and namely liability law rules continue to play a secondary but undeniable role, which necessarily leads to the question of the applicable law.

And yet the question of the law applicable to civil liability in relation to violations of the environment has been perceived as an autonomous question only in recent years. At the international or European level there are no specific rules for jurisdiction[7] in matters relating to environmental liability. As far as choice of law is concerned, the enrolment of this question on the agenda of the Hague Conference in 1992 ended in failure eight years later. For a long time, the only specific provision to be found was a provision in the 1987 Swiss statute on private international law. Then similar provisions appeared in various versions of the draft convention and later in the Rome II Regulation n° 864/2007 on the law applicable to non-contractual obligations. Article 7 of the Regulation provides: 'the law applicable to a non-contractual obligation arising out of environmental damage or damage sustained by persons or property as a result of such damage shall be the law determined pursuant to Article 4(1), unless the person seeking compensation for damage chooses to base his or her claims on the law of the country in which the event giving rise to the damage occurred'.

In the light of these developments one must wonder in what way the choice of law rule can contribute to environmental regulation and to the achievement of transnational and European goals of environment protection. This is the question of choice of the choice of law rule. But the difficulties do not end at

---

liability for violations of the environment is not governed by uniform rules. The European lawmakers limited themselves to particular categories of accidents, concentrating more on prevention than on liability and compensation. Of course, on 21 April 2004, Directive 2004/35/EC 'on environmental liability with regard to the prevention and remedying of environmental damage' was adopted by the European Parliament and Council. But this directive does not give private parties a right of compensation towards environmental tortfeasors. Moreover, it is not applicable to damage to persons, to property, or to economic loss resulting from violations of the environment. Hence, it represents a public law approach.

[5] On the contrary some writers argue that private international law is not fit to cater for the very specific needs of civil liability for environmental torts and that the time is ripe for EC action at the substantive level. See F. Munari and L. Schiano di Pepe (2005) 'Liability for environmental torts in Europe: choice of forum, choice of law and the case for pursuing effective legal uniformity' Rivista di diritto internazionale privato et processuale, p. 607.

[6] L. Bergkamp (2001), *Liability and Environment* (Kluwer Law International), particularly pp. 208–210.

[7] For these matters, Art. 5(3) of Council Regulation 44/2001/EC, relating to jurisdiction in matters relating to tort and delict, is applicable.

this point. In order to understand fully the possible role of the choice of law rule in environmental regulation one must examine the way it is implemented. Consequently, the original question of the regulatory function of the choice of law rule may be addressed by examining in a very classical manner the choice of the choice of law rule and its implementation.

(I) CHOICE OF THE CHOICE OF LAW RULE

A preliminary question on the applicability of the conflict of laws method as a whole must first be asked. Supposing that liability for violations of the environment needs to be treated as an autonomous question, should one reason in terms of conflict of laws or should laws relating to the protection of the environment be promoted to the status of overriding mandatory rules? Given the importance recently acquired by the protection of the environment and the promotion of the right to a healthy environment to the status of a quasi-human right, the question is worth examining. It is well known that several constitutions and international declarations affirm the right to live in a healthy environment.[8]

However, even though the application of overriding mandatory rules in non-contractual matters is more and more accepted, their role must remain secondary.[9] Moreover, such rules are in principle applicable, automatically, regardless of the fact that other rules could more easily support a given policy.[10]

For all these reasons, it is preferable to answer negatively the preliminary question we asked and to continue reasoning in terms of conflict of laws.

Within a classical conflict of laws reasoning the most important question is the opportunity of a specific choice of law rule. In other words, was there a need for specific choice of law rule for liability in relation to violations of the environment or is the general rule applicable to non-contractual obligations sufficient, as legislators and academics seemed to think for a long time? If the former

---

8 For example, 1970 Declaration of the Council of Europe on the development of the natural environment in Europe; Final Stockholm Declaration of the 1972 United Nations conference on the environment; 1989 UNESCO Declaration on peace in the spirit of men; 1992 Rio Declaration of the United Nations Conference on the environment and development.

9 Their intervention is particularly necessary in contractual matters. Expressing this opinion, see P. Mayer, 'Lois de police' Rép. Dalloz, 1998, No. 26.

10 In a conflict between an overriding mandatory rule of the forum and a foreign overriding mandatory rule the former will always prevail. It is true that the application of these rules could be subordinated to the examination of their contents. Important writers analyse Art. 5 of the Rome Convention in this manner. See P. Mayer and V. Heuze (2004) *Droit international privé*, Montchrétien, n° 128.

is right, as the present writer thinks it is, the question of the most adequate connecting factor naturally arises. The opportunity of a specific choice of law rule and the choice of the connecting factor will consequently be examined.

(A) The Opportunity of a Specific Choice of Law Rule

The problem is often obscured by the vagueness of the terms used. The words used by texts and writers do not always refer to the same reality. Before envisaging the solutions it is hence useful to try to clarify the terms of the problem.

(1) The terms of the problem

The difficulty comes from the idea that the opportunity of a specific choice of law rule depends on the definition one adopts of liability in relation to violations of environment. Three points are subject to discussion: the definition of the term liability, of parties that can be held liable and, above all, of the compensatable damage. This last aspect needs some further explanation.

The question is, should the choice of law rule apply only to ordinary damage caused to persons or to property resulting from a violation of the environment, or should it encompass what may be called pure ecological damage, in other words damage caused to the environment itself?

One must start by specifying that this question of compensatable damage should logically enter into the scope of the law applicable to liability. In other words, once the law applicable to liability has been designated, this law governs, among other questions, the question of compensatable damage. All international instruments on the law applicable to non-contractual obligations proceed in this way. Why should one proceed differently in matters relating to environment? Why should the compensatable damage be defined before designating the applicable law?

Two reasons could be advanced. First of all, compensation of pure ecological damage is not neutral. From an economic and political point of view a lot is at stake. It is therefore understandable that prior to any attempt at international unification of choice of law rules this point needs to be defined.[11]

---

[11] It is significant that the explanatory report accompanying previous amendments brought by the European Parliament and aimed at suppressing the specific provision for violations of the environment justified this amendment by the uncertainty of the notion and observed that if a specific choice of law rule was however to be judged necessary, a definition of terms would have to be undertaken prior to its elaboration. This has been done to some extent by Recital 24 of the Regulation, which explains: '"Environmental damage" should be understood as meaning adverse change in a natural resource, such as water, land or air, impairment of a function performed by that resource for the benefit of another natural resource or the public, or impairment of the variability among living organisms'.

Secondly, there seemed to be a tendency to think that the opportunity of a specific choice of law rule depended on the adopted definition of the compensatable damage in the sense that a specific choice of law rule was needed only for pure ecological damage. Damage caused to persons or property resulting from a violation of the environment is not, in this view, specific enough to justify a special choice of law rule.

Of course, it is true that pure ecological damage raises specific questions. But, if the choice of law rule is to play a regulatory role, it appears that a specific one is needed both for ordinary damages resulting from a violation of the environment and for pure ecological damage. This assertion is easily explained. The general choice of law rule for non-contractual obligations is traditionally designed in such a way that it cannot fulfil the specific regulatory function in matters relating to the environment. It is based on the idea that the situation should be localized as exactly as possible in order to find the right balance between the rights and obligations of the parties. Therefore, it cannot contribute to carrying out environmental policies and improving the level of protection of the environment.

In the light of this observation the opportunity of a specific choice of law rule raises no doubts.[12] It would apply to ordinary damage (to persons and property) resulting from a violation of environment. But should this special choice of law rule apply also to pure ecological damage? Logically the answer should be affirmative. But if one takes into account the connecting factor and puts into question its appropriateness, a doubt appears. We will come back to it when examining the connecting factor.

The problem having been laid out, it is interesting to examine the different solutions envisaged by various draft Conventions and the Regulation concerning our subject matter.

(2) The solutions

First of all one needs to recall that, the protection of the environment being a relatively recent preoccupation, the question of the opportunity of a specific choice of law rule for violations of the environment has only been raised recently. The first provision to be found seems to be Article 138 of the 1987 Swiss statute on private international law.

---

[12] One can even observe, as the note published by the Permanent Bureau of the Hague Conference in 2000 did, that a specific choice of law rule for these matters would represent a concrete implementation of Principle 22 of the Stockhom Declaration of 1972 and Principle 13 of the Rio Declaration of 1992, calling on States to develop national and international rules on liability and compensation for environmental damage. Secondly, the note observes in an interesting way that such a specific rule could contribute to the rapprochement which is increasingly desired between public international law and private international law.

Even though it remained isolated for a long time, this first choice of law rule specific to violations of the environment contributed to a general awareness of the specificity of the problem and probably played a part in the decision of the Hague Conference to list the question on its agenda. Unfortunately, the initiative ended in failure.[13]

However, it is notable that several national codifications of private international law, although adopted in the 1990s, at a time when the question of a specific choice of law rule had already been raised, remain totally silent on this point. This is the case with the Italian, English and German reforms of private international law none of which contain a specific rule.

And yet, among academics, the inappropriateness of the general choice of law rule for non-contractual obligations was highlighted and the need for a specific rule was exposed as early as 1990 and sometimes even a decade earlier. For example, Professor Jessurun d'Oliveira[14] proposed a specific choice of law rule precisely in the name of goals pursued by environmental law, namely the redress of damage caused by pollution to the benefit of the general community.

Today this call seems to have been finally heard. A specific choice of law rule first appeared in the proposition for an international convention on the law applicable to non-contractual obligations elaborated by the European Group for Private International Law (EGPIL) in 1998[15] and now in the Rome II Regulation.

The latter provisions seemed to go further than the former since they aim to apply to obligations resulting from a violation of the environment, which is a more encompassing term than 'damage caused to persons and property resulting from a violation of the environment', which was the wording of the European Group's proposal. Consequently, pure ecological damage seemed to enter into the scope of these rules. But, strangely enough, while introducing these specific rules, their very proponents seemed to explain them above all in terms of balance between the rights and duties of the parties, that is in terms of private law considerations. Policy, State interests and regulation seemed to have played no role.

And yet, one must observe, and American observers already have,[16] that the provision relating to violations of the environment is difficult to explain if one sets aside these considerations. The connecting factor it chooses, which is

---

13 In 2000 the Permanent Bureau decided to maintain the question on its agenda, but without priority.

14 'La pollution du Rhin et le droit international privé' in *La pollution du Rhin, Aspects juridiques, économiques et techniques* (1978).

15 (1998) Revue critique de droit international privé, p. 802.

16 S. Symeonides (2004) 'Tort Conflicts and Rome II: A View from Across' in *Festschrift für Erik Jayme,* München, p. 935.

extremely favourable to the establishment of liability, seems to have been chosen not only to protect the victim as such, but also in order to promote interest in European countries in deterring pollution and protecting environment. Hence, it had to be welcomed.

Indeed, in the absence of a specific provision relating to violations of the environment, damages resulting from violations of the environment would be governed by the general choice of law rule for non-contractual obligations which designates the law of the place where the damage occurred or threatened to occur notwithstanding the possible application of the escape clause. This place would hence be decisive: if the damage occurred in a country with a low level of protection, it could not be compensated.

The specificity of liability for violations of the environment and the necessity to design a choice of law rule able to contribute to environmental regulation were not acknowledged.[17] Hence, the initiative of the European Commission which rejected the amendment tending to suppress the specific choice of law rule for violations of the environment and reintroduced this rule into the proposal, must be fully approved. A specific choice of law rule for violations of the environment is a good solution.

However one question remains. What connecting factor could contribute in the most appropriate manner to environmental regulation? We must now turn to it.

(B) The Choice of the Connecting Factor

One must examine the connecting factor in the absence of a choice of the applicable law made by the parties, the possibility to choose the applicable law and last but not least the influence of what is now referred to as rules of conduct and safety.

(1) The connecting factor in the absence of choice made by the parties

In the absence of choice, one must search for the most appropriate connecting factor, meaning, from our perspective, the connecting factor able to contribute to achieving the goals pursued by environmental law. It has been said that a specific choice of law rule for violations of the environment was justified precisely by the need to obtain not only the best balance between the rights and obligations of the parties, but also to promote goals relating to environmental

---

[17] One must also mention the European directive on services imposing the application of the law of origin of the operator even in matters concerning the environment. This directive could come into conflict with the specific choice of law rule for violations of the environment. As such it has been unanimously criticized.

regulation[18] which could not be promoted by the general choice of law rule in non-contractual matters. In private international law when one seeks to promote a particular goal the usual technique is the alternative choice of law rule or unilateral options allowing the person whom the legislator wants to favour to choose the applicable law. Choice of law rules in matters relating to family law or, closer to our subject, the choice of law rule applicable to the direct action against the insurer, enacted in Article 9 of the 1971 Hague Convention on the law applicable to traffic accidents, come to mind. And yet, both the proposal of EGPIL and the earliest version of the proposal for the European regulation on the law applicable to non-contractual obligations, chose a fixed connecting factor, that is the law of the country where the damage occurred or threatened to occur. One must pause to think about the opportunity of such a solution. From the viewpoint of EGPIL whose proposal was limited to damage caused to persons and property resulting from a violation of the environment, without applying to pure ecological damage, this connecting factor could be justified. Focused on private law preoccupations, the proposal sought to localize the situation as exactly as possible. By choosing this specific connecting factor, it avoided the application of the law of the common habitual residence of the parties, which is completely irrelevant in matters of environmental liability.

Moreover this connecting factor was a simple presumption, which could be disregarded if it appeared that the obligation was more closely connected with another country.

However this connecting factor could be criticized for not expressing any particular bias towards the compensation of damage in matters relating to the environment and hence no ambition to promote the protection of the environment.

Article 8 of the European Commission's proposed draft Rome II Regulation on the law applicable to extra-contractual obligations was even more questionable. Although the provision was apparently meant to apply both to ordinary damage and to pure ecological damage, it still designated the law of the country in which the damage occurred, this being a fixed rule and no longer a presumption. It has been criticized by some writers who emphasized the fact that it presented no specificity in comparison with the general rule.[19] This criticism must be moderated since the specific choice of law rule for violations of the environment avoided the application of the law of the common habitual residence of the parties, which would otherwise apply. This

---

18 Goals such as the prevention of accidents and adequate compensation.

19 C. Nourissat and E. Treppoz (2003) 'Quelques observations sur l'avant-projet de proposition de règlement du Conseil sur la loi applicable aux obligations non contractuelles Rome II', Journal du Droit International, p. 7.

in itself is a specificity justifying a special choice of law rule. The common habitual residence has no localizing value for ordinary damage and even less, obviously, for pure ecological damage. From this point of view the solution appeared to be justified. But, in spite of arguments favourable to its application, this connecting factor was not intended either to favour the victim and improve his or her chances of success or to promote a better protection of the environment.

It is precisely this failure that motivated the new Article 7. This provision which is applicable both to ordinary damage and to pure ecological damage designates the law of the place of the damage, but gives the victim the possibility to opt for the law of the place of the event giving rise to the damage.

This option granted to the injured party seems satisfactory both in the light of the importance of the protection of the environment and of the extent of damage, even ordinary damage, resulting from its violations. The explanatory report presented by the Commission in 2003, large parts of which remain in the 2007 version, made it clear that this option was granted not so much in order to favour the victim as such, but in order to promote the interests of European countries and the European Union as a whole in deterring pollution and enhancing environmental protection. The report explains that the polluter pays principle, the principle of preventive action and the need for a high level of protection based on the precautionary principle that flows from Article 174 of the EU Treaty justify the use of the principle in discriminating in favour of the victim. It also explains that applying exclusively the law of the place where the damage is sustained in so far as it means that a victim established in a country with a low level of protection would not benefit from the higher level of neighbouring countries, would be contrary to the underlying philosophy of the European substantive law of the environment and the polluter pays principle. Similarly, one can observe that if the solution[20] aimed to protect only the interests of the victim as such, it should have logically been extended to other cross-border torts, which has not been done.

Finally it appears that the choice left to the victim is a good solution. It enables the choice of law rule to play a part in environmental regulation. But the question is whether it should apply equally to ordinary damage and to pure ecological damage. In this latter case it may give rise to opposition. Pure ecological damage is a collective damage caused to nature itself and hence to future generations. Since a no-pollution society is impossible, compensation of pure ecological damage is the result of a difficult balance between economic and ecological considerations. Many legal systems do not provide

---

[20] Namely, the choice given to the victim.

for it. In this context it may seem reasonable to say that only the State whose resources have been damaged is entitled to decide whether this damage is compensatable. Moreover, preserving natural resources and means used by States for the redress of ecological damage present a strong public law dimension. For all these reasons it could appear that the law of the injured environment, that is to say, the law of the place of the harm is the only one which can legitimately govern this question.[21] The respect for State sovereignty could be another argument in favour of this solution.[22]

However, the final version of the Rome II draft seems to adopt a very different approach. It applies to 'non-contractual obligations resulting from a damage to the environment or damage caused to persons or property resulting from such a damage'. The wording clearly includes pure ecological damage. And yet it has been said that a choice is granted to the injured party between the law of the place of conduct and the law of the place of harm. This means that a law other than the law of the place of the harm could come to govern the compensation of pure ecological damage. One wonders whether this means that associations for the protection of the environment, in countries which grant them the right of action, could choose the law of the place of the harmful conduct although the law of the place of the damage does not provide, or provides with more strict conditions, for the compensation of pure ecological damage. Of course such a situation will be quite rare in practice since it is probable that a country which does not provide for compensation of pure ecological damage will not grant right of action to associations. Yet, as a matter of principle the solution is questionable.

Whatever the right answer on this point may be, one question remains. If one acknowledges the need for a special choice of law rule based on the idea of preference for the victim and designed to promote the protection of the environment, should the choice be limited as previously explained or should the panel of laws that can be chosen by the victim be enlarged? The law of the habitual residence of the defendant, which may sometimes prove to be relevant, comes to mind. It is significant that, in order to justify the choice granted to the victim between the law of the place of harm and the law of the place of conduct, the report states the need to encourage 'operators established in countries with

---

21 Expressing this opinion, see C. Von Bar (1997) *Environmental Damage in Private International Law*, 268 RCADI, p. 303.

22 Of course, this solution could theoretically contribute to a race to the bottom in the sense that States could try to attract companies by adopting the lowest standards of environment protection. However, besides the fact that the relevance of this argument has never been proven in an empirical manner, the existence of a choice granted to the victim concerning the compensation of ordinary damage seems sufficient to prevent such a risk.

a low level of protection to abide by the higher levels of protection in neighbouring countries'. And the country of the place of the harmful conduct does not necessarily coincide with the country in which the defendant is established. To take the simplest example, the defendant may have factories in countries other than the country in which it is principally established. Hence a question arises: should the claimant be able to chose the law of the principal establishment of the defendant? It is true that such a solution would be contrary to the rule, traditional in private international law and asserted under Article 23 of the Rome II Regulation, according to which when the defendant has several establishments, where the event giving rise to the damage occurs or the damage is sustained in the course of operation of a subsidiary, a branch or any other establishment, the establishment takes the place of the habitual residence. It is also true that such a solution would maybe give too much freedom of choice to the victim. In any case, it is a path that needs to be mentioned and explored.

Whether one wants to go that far or not, it appears that an alternative choice of law rule or an option granted to the victim, according to whether one prefers to grant choice to the judge or to the victim, is the right solution for these matters. It ensures both an adequate protection for the victim and the promotion of general goals of environmental law. The only remaining hesitation concerns the opportunity of its application to pure ecological damage.

But choosing this connecting factor is not sufficient. There is a trend in modern private international law to allow parties to choose the applicable law. The appropriateness of such a solution in matters of violations of the environment must now be examined.

(2) The possibility to choose the applicable law

On this question EGPIL's proposal and the several versions of the Rome II draft are almost unanimous. A general rule, applicable to all non-contractual obligations, allows the parties to choose, in general after the dispute has arisen, the law applicable to the non-contractual obligation. It is specified that this choice must either be explicit or emerge clearly from the circumstances of the case and that it may not affect the rights of third parties. What is at stake here is true party autonomy, in other words a bilateral choice made by the parties, which must be distinguished from the option granted to the victim, that has been examined up to now.

In the final version it is also stated that when all the parties exercise a commercial activity the choice may be contained in an agreement freely negotiated before the event causing the harm occurs.

Last but not least, a provision analogous to Article 3§3 of the Rome Convention is designed to prevent the parties escaping from mandatory rules of the internal law which should normally apply in cases where all the elements of the situation (except the choice of law) are located in a country other than the one whose law is chosen (see Articles 14.2 and 3).

In the absence of any particular exclusion, it seems that these rules[23] concerning the possibility to choose the applicable law equally concern violations of the environment. Hence, one must raise the question of their usage. Several problems come to mind.

The first and most important question from the viewpoint we have taken is to ask whether party autonomy is an adequate method for a choice of law rule aiming not only to achieve a satisfactory balance between rights and obligations of the parties but also to promote environmental regulation and protection of the environment.

The justification for party autonomy usually put forward is '*libre disponibilité des droits*'. Parties are free to renounce their rights under domestic law, by way of consequence they may choose the applicable law under private international law. The problem is that the right to compensation for pure ecological damage can obviously not be renounced. And even as far as ordinary damage is concerned, if one admits that the choice of law rule plays a regulatory function, allowing the parties to choose the applicable law is obviously not the best way to achieve the pursued goals. Similarly, one can observe that third parties' rights, reserved by the choice of law rule, would seem to be always affected in matters concerning the environment.

Finally, even if this first obstacle is disregarded and party autonomy admitted, the second question would be, should we opt for unlimited party autonomy? Such a solution seems very undesirable. What could at most be admitted is a choice in favour of the law of the forum, which is often suggested by writers, namely because it facilitates legal action. But it immediately appears that such a possibility would add very little to the option already granted to the victim, especially if this option was to be extended to the law of the habitual residence of the defendant.

The conclusion is clear: party autonomy is not the right solution. It should be excluded in matters concerning violations of the environment. In order to cover fully the question of the most appropriate connecting factor at the prospect of the regulatory function of the choice of law rule relating to violations of the environment, one question remains to be examined. It is the influence of what is now referred to as rules of conduct and safety.

(3) The influence of rules of conduct and safety

Article 17 of Rome II contains a provision prescribing to take into account, whatever the applicable law may be, the rules of safety and conduct which were in force at the place and time of the relevant event.

---

[23] Article 4 of the Rome II Regulation.

The rule is not new. It is inspired by analogous provisions from the Hague Conventions on the law applicable to traffic accidents[24] and to products liability[25] as well as by various national conflict systems.[26]

First of all, it can be observed that the exact meaning of 'taking into account as an element of fact' remains quite vague. Above all, the consequences of this provision in matters of violation of the environment make one wonder. Can the fact that the perpetrator of the harmful conduct complied with the rules of the country of tortious act, which are less demanding than, for example, the ones in force in the country where the damage occurred, allow him to escape all liability? What about a permit granted by the authorities of the same country? Can it have the same effect? The answer should be negative. An affirmative one would be contrary to the letter and the spirit of the option granted to the injured party and would lead to very disappointing results not only for the victim, but also and above all for environmental protection.[27]

By way of consequence a regret must be expressed as to the absence of exclusion of Article 14 in matters of violation of the environment.

In a nutshell, it appears that a judicious choice of a specific choice of law rule with adequate connecting factors leads to satisfactory results not only from the point of view of the parties, but also from the point of view of environmental regulation. Once the choice of law rule has been designated, the question of its implementation must be addressed.

(II) THE IMPLEMENTATION OF THE CHOICE OF LAW RULE

Two questions come immediately to mind, namely the question of the scope of the applicable law and the question of public policy.

---

24 Article 7 of the Convention on the Law Applicable to Traffic Accidents, 4 May 1971.

25 Article 9 of the Convention on the Law Applicable to Products Liability, 2 October 1973.

26 Article 142(2) of the 1987 Swiss Act on private international law; Art. 45(3) of the Portugese Civil Code; §33.1 of the Hungarian statute on private international law.

27 In the famous *Mines de Potasses d'Alsace* v. *Bier* case, Case 21/76, [1976] ECR 1735, the Rotterdam court and the Hague Court of Appeal admitted the existence of liability in the application of Dutch law without giving any effect to the French permit. Similarly under French domestic law administrative permits and authorizations are not sufficient to escape liability. On this point, see M. Prieur (2004) *Droit de l'environnement* (Dalloz), n° 1163.

(A) The Scope of the Applicable Law

This question of the scope of the applicable law, which is very classical in private international law, consists in asking, once the applicable law has been designated, which issues it will govern. In matters we are concerned with, these issues can be grouped around two ideas: liability and compensation.

(1) Liability

Concerning the problem of the very existence of liability, the most important question concerns the determination of persons entitled to compensation. This problem, and also the issue of indirect victims (*victimes par ricochet*), is a classical problem of conflict of laws in matters of non-contractual liability. It is usually decided that it enters within the scope of the *lex causae*, law applicable to the non-contractual obligation. But in matters of violation of the environment this problem is particularly difficult. This is because in these matters, more than elsewhere, one is confronted with the problem of 'collective actions', instituted in defence of a collective public interest.

Concerning essentially pure ecological damage, in a context where Nature as such has no legal personality, its compensation raises the problem of persons entitled to bring a legal action and the problem of admissibility of such actions. This question has raised a lot of controversy under domestic French law.[28] From our point of view the problem is which law will govern these issues. Very concretely, the decision whether a particular association for environmental protection will be able to bring an action will turn on this point.

Traditionally, this question is governed both by the law of the forum and by the law of the association.[29] Of course, as with all rules designating two laws, this solution tends to restrict the number of admissible actions.

Moreover it seems that when actions instituted by associations are used to protect general public interests, as is the case in our subject matter, the procedural aspect of the question weighs less. Each State must decide which general interests it wants to protect and to whom it wants to entrust the task of enforcing them.

---

[28] See for example, M. Prieur, above note 27 at n° 1151 who expresses the opinion that the role of associations could be fundamental and that an evolution in this direction is inevitable.

[29] Mayer and Heuzé, (2004) *Droit international privé*, Montchrétien, n° 497, A. Huet, Jurisclasseur Droit International, fascicule 582-10, n° 54 et seq. However, it is remarkable that the 1993 Lugano Convention of the Council of Europe on civil liability for damage resulting from activities dangerous to the environment explicitly provides for the possibility of legal actions instituted by an association and submits the admissibility of these actions to the lex fori.

However, having in mind the goals we would like the choice of law rule to promote, it would be possible to introduce a system analogous to the one that already exists in matters of consumer protection. By virtue of the 1998 directive on injunctions for the protection of consumers interests, every Member State designates entities qualified to bring this type of action. These entities may commence proceedings for compensation for damage which occurred in the country in which they are established before the courts of all Member States. An analogous system could work in matters relating to the environment.

In this respect, it is difficult to deduce something definite from Article 15 of the Regulations. It provides that the law applicable to the non-contractual obligation will apply to the issue of persons entitled to compensation for damage sustained personally. Collective actions are not provided for. But, the list established by Article 15 is not closed. Other issues, not expressly provided for, may be governed by the lex causae.[30] Hence, the new provision allows no certainty.

The second difficulty concerns persons who can be held liable and namely the problem of liability of parent companies for violations of the environment committed by their subsidiaries. This problem, which is extremely important in practice, comes down to the question, can one impute a harmful conduct to the mother company?

In principle, the determination of persons who can be held liable comes into the scope of the *lex causae*, law applicable to liability. Hence, logically, this law should govern the issue of liability of parent companies. One writer[31] expressed a similar view. He submitted that the harmful conduct committed by the parent company, which will as a rule be an omission, occurs at the place 'where the abstract danger created by this omission turns into a concrete danger'. This is no other than the place where the subsidiary committed the environmentally harmful action. In this way, liability of the parent company and liability of the subsidiaries would often be governed by the same law.

However it appears that, in reality, in law the sole fact that the parent company entirely controls the subsidiary is not sufficient to give rise to liability of the parent company, in the absence of an identifiable fault.

(2) Compensation

Concerning compensation several questions arise: the first is knowing whether preventive actions come into the scope of the applicable law. This question is nowadays resolved in a satisfactory manner by the various drafts which have

---

[30] In favour of the application of the lex causae to the admissibility of legal actions instituted by associations, see C. Von Bar, above note 21 at p. 358.

[31] C. Von Bar, above note 21 at p. 393.

been examined. Unanimously they refer to the place where the damage has occurred or threatens to occur. Preventive actions are hence envisaged.

The second question concerns actions against insurers. The one which raises a question of private international law is of course the direct action against the insurer. This type of action gave rise to a lot of controversy in the context of traffic accidents and product liability. In these areas only the 1971 Hague Convention on the law applicable to traffic accidents contains a specific provision for this problem. It is the famous Article 9 of the Convention which contains a three-step rule designating the law applicable to liability: if this law is not the law of the place where the accident occurred and it does not provide for direct action, then the law of the place where the accident occurred and finally, if none of these laws provide for direct action, the law governing the insurance contract. If transposed to matters concerning violations of the environment, this solution would favour compensation of damages resulting from such violations. As such, it would also be compatible with the regulatory function we think the choice of law rule should assume.

By way of consequence, a transposition would be a good solution.[32] One last question must be examined: the intervention of public policy.

(B) Public Policy

Like in other matters under private international law, the designated law can be put aside if its application is manifestly incompatible with the public policy of the forum. However, having in mind what has been said on the function of the choice of law rule in matters relating to violations of the environment, it is easy to understand that the intervention of the public policy exception should also be orientated towards the satisfaction of goals of environmental protection. Nevertheless if the rule is well designed, the public policy exception will seldom come into play. There is however one specific question that must be raised.

It concerns punitive damages. Since work on European unification of choice of law rules relating to non-contractual obligations resumed, the question of the right attitude towards this type of damages gives rise to controversy. Previous versions of the Rome II draft contained a specific rule for punitive damages asserting that they were, as such, contrary to public policy.[33] We have, elsewhere,[34] criticized this idea. Concerning French law, a brief study of

---

32 In favour of such a solution, see C. Von Bar, above note 21 at p. 397.

33 Article 24 of the Commission's proposal of 22 July 2003; Art. 22.1, ter, of the proposal amended by the European Parliament, dated 6 July 2005.

34 O. Boskovic (2003) La réparation du préjudice en droit international privé (LGDJ), n° 408–410.

domestic law shows that the principles on which punitive damages are based are not so foreign to our legal system and should not provoke repulsion. On the other hand, one can understand the reluctance of the forum toward certain foreign awards which, although qualified as compensatory, reach millions of dollars. Hence, it appears that what is shocking to the forum is not the punitive character of the award but its exorbitant amount. In other words, public policy prohibits awards of exorbitant amounts, which cannot be explained either as compensation or as a reasonable punishment.

These are the reasons why the modified proposal published by the European Commission on 21 February 2006 was to be approved. Article 23 of that text provided that 'the application of a law that would have the effect of causing non-compensatory damages to be awarded that would be excessive' may be considered as contrary to the public policy of the forum. It follows obviously that the punitive character in itself does not suffice for the public policy exception to come into play.

PART 3

Product safety

7. Product safety, private standard-setting and information networks

Fabrizio Cafaggi

NEW REGULATORY STRATEGIES IN PRODUCT SAFETY: CONTROLLING PRIVATE STANDARD-SETTING AND PROMOTING SAFETY IN INTER-FIRM NETWORKS[1]

Legal reforms concerning European product safety are under careful scrutiny.[2] The European system, encompassing a liability (Directive 374/85/EC,[3] hereinafter 'PL directive') and a regulatory system (Directive 95/2001/EC,[4] hereinafter 'GPSD'), has made important progress towards increasing safety levels and ensuring relative uniformity. The product safety regime has recently undergone a review[5] (the first report on the GPSD was published in January

1 This chapter is part of a larger project focusing on a comparative analysis concerning product safety between the EU and US. It was first presented at the Comparative Law and Economics (CLEF) workshop, Florence, February 2008. I thank the participants for comments. Responsibility is my own.

2 See the package of measures adopted in August 2008, that includes also the Regulation (EC) n° 765/2008 of the European Parliament and of the Council setting out the requirements for accreditation and market surveillance relating to the market of products, OJEU 13.08.2008, L218/03.

3 Council Directive 374/85/EEC of 25 July 1985 on the approximation of the laws, regulations and administrative provisions of the Member States concerning liability for defective products, OJ L 210, 7.8.1985, p. 29.

4 Directive 95/2001/EC of the European Parliament and of the Council of 3 December 2001 on general product safety, OJ L 11, 15.1.2002, p. 4.

5 Regulation (EC) n° 765/2008 setting out the requirements for accreditation and market surveillance relating to the marketing of products, above n. 2. The recent resolution of the European Parliament, of 20 May 2007 on EU consumer policy strategy 2007–2013 provides further indication, in particular, 'calls on the Commission to work with Member States to ensure that existing legislation is properly implemented and fully enforced by the Member States including by assessing the possibility of reviewing Directive 2001/95/EC on general product safety; recalls that the CE marking can be wrongly interpreted as a general indication of third-party testing or a mark of origin, but also that the Commission has been requested to present an in-depth analysis in the field of consumer safety markings, if necessary followed by legislative proposals'. See

2009), while the third report on the product liability directive was published in 2006.[6]

Comparative research – though not covering the 27 member states – shows that administrative practices in product safety regulation are significantly different.[7] Policy reform has been focused more on market surveillance than standard-setting, moreover, in its review, the Commission underlined the need to improve market surveillance by reinforcing and extending existing instruments such as those defined in GPSD.[8] The annual report on the rapid alert system for non-food consumer products (Rapex) shows an increased number of notifications, and suggests that cooperation between industry, national authorities and the European Commission is growing.[9]

Important changes in the standard-setting process concerning product design have taken place without adequately considering the structure of the industrial chain and its internal decision-making process.[10] In this chapter, along the lines of the overall project, I consider the interaction between private

---

par. 13, the complete text is available at http://wwweuroparl.europa.eu/sides/getDoc.do?pubRef=-//EP//TEXT+TA+P6-TA-2008-0211+0+DOC +XML+V0//EN&language=EN.

6 See Third report on the application of Council directive on the approximation of laws, regulations and administrative provisions of the Member States concerning liability for defective products, COM(2006)496 final. See D. Fairgrieve and G. Howells, 'Rethinking product liability: A missing element in the European Commission's Third review of the European Product Liability Directive', in (2007) 70 Modern Law Review, pp. 962 ff., part. pp. 972 ff.

7 In some countries, like Germany, administrative discretion in risk assessment and control prevails over technical approaches. On the contrary, in Scandinavian countries a more technical approach prevails. See H.W. Micklitz, T. Roethe, *European Product Safety Legislation – A comparative study of legal frame and practice in Germany and Baltic Sea States*, pp. 114 ff.

8 See Commission proposal for the Regulation setting out the requirements for accreditation and market surveillance, SEC (2007) 37 final: 'The proposals, following the Council's Resolution of 10 November 2003, have the objective to provide a common framework for the existing infrastructures for accreditation for the control of conformity assessment bodies, and market surveillance for the control of products and economic operators, by reinforcing and extending what exists and not weakening existing instruments such as the General Product Safety Directive which is very successful and effective.' (p. 2).

9 See Keeping European Consumers Safe, 2007 Annual Report on the operation of the Rapid Alert System for non-food consumer products, available at http://ec.europa.eu/consumers/safety/rapex/docs/rapex_annualreport2008_en.pdf.

10 But see the Resolution of the European Parliament on consumer policy strategy 2007–2013, above n. 5, where the EP 'Calls for measures to improve dialogue at EU level between consumer organisations and industry, to include all actors in the value chain; takes the view that a good dialogue, including the sharing of best practices, could reduce problems in the internal market'.

law and regulatory dimensions from two relatively under-investigated angles. I will examine (a) one hypothesis of private law influence on regulation, in particular the case of contracting over standard-setting, and (b) one aspect of regulation affecting the structure of industry, in particular the formation of vertical networks along production and distribution chains.

Firstly, I shall address the effects of private (particularly contractual) standard-setting on the definition of 'defective product' in the liability domain and that of 'dangerous product' in the regulatory domain. Changes in regulation, specifically the increasing use of self-regulation and co-regulation promoted by GPSD in relation to technical standardization, imply a greater participation of private actors in standard-setting. But how should their activity be performed? To whom should they be accountable? These changes do not only affect the regulatory but also the liability dimension to the extent that the standards employed to define a dangerous product may constitute a reference for defectiveness.[11]

Two possible schemes can be defined:

(a). acceptance of the influence of regulatory standards in the liability domain, including those privately defined, or
(b). rejection of this influence and promotion of the separation between liability and regulation, claiming that functional complementarity can allow different standard-setting procedures affecting each other over and beyond the necessity for coordination.

Secondly, I look at the product safety directive, in particular the information duties and show that compliance with them implies the creation of inter-firm networks. These networks may take different forms and be designed according to the specific structure of the industry. The aim is not only descriptive but also normative. Not only do I claim that safety regulation has a significant effect on the creation of networks among firms and indirectly on organizational forms, but I also advocate that this model should be expanded to include other features of risk control and management, thereby transforming an artificial hierarchical model into a more effective network model.

The chapter proceeds in the following way. Section 1 is devoted to a general illustration of current debate about product safety regulation at EU level. Section 2 examines the role of private standard-setting on regulatory and

---

[11] On the complementarity of regulation and liability, see F. Cafaggi, 'A coordinated approach to regulation and civil liability: Rethinking institutional complementarities', in F. Cafaggi (ed.), *The institutional framework of European private law* (OUP, 2006), pp. 191 ff. See also G. Spindler, 'Interaction between product liability and regulation at the European level', Chapter 8 below.

liability strategies and their interplay. Section 3 analyses the effects of regulatory strategies concerning information on the creation of networks, their shape and scope. Concluding remarks follow in section 4.

1. PRODUCT SAFETY IN THE FRAMEWORK OF REGULATORY INNOVATION

Before embarking on a detailed analysis, it is useful to propose a brief survey of the main institutional and substantive changes recently considered at European level. On the one hand, the EU has stressed the need for a more complex yet shared legislative process advocating the expansion of the Lamfalussy architecture.[12] On the other hand, it has advocated the broader use of alternatives to legislation distinguishing between binding and non-binding instruments.[13] The general strategy aims at developing a new approach to better regulation by combining the legitimacy demand, which triggered the White Paper on governance,[14] and the effectiveness demand, which together

---

12 See the Commission staff working document – Instruments for a modernised single market policy – Accompanying document to the Communication from the Commission to the European Parliament, the Council, the European Economic and Social Committee and the Committee of the Regions – A single market for 21st century Europe, COM(2007) 724 final, SEC(2007) 1518, pp. 8 ff. (hereinafter 'Instruments for a modernized single market').

13 See Instruments for a modernized single market, above n. 12, pp. 11 ff. 'Four types of non-binding instruments can be distinguished:

(a) Measures aiming at preparing policy action (legislative and non legislative) such as Green Paper and White Papers, other consultation documents (e.g. those prepared for internet consultations and Communications to gather views from stakeholders in preparation of initiatives
(b) Measures aiming at clarifying the law and ensuring that EU rules are properly applied on the ground without changing the EU Acquis (technical guidelines, technical handbooks, interpretive communications)
(c) Measures that contain normative elements such as Recommendations – specifically referred to by the EC Treaty and defined by the ECJ as measures adopted by EU institutions when they do not have powers under the Treaty to adopt binding measures or when they consider that is not appropriate to adopt more mandatory rules
(d) Self-regulation and co-regulation instruments, such as Codes of conduct whereby the Commission asks industry to come up with solutions provided these do not contradict EU law and the Commission's policy objectives. Voluntary standard-setting can also be comprised in this category.'

14 White Paper on European Governance, Brussels, 25.7.2001, COM(2001) 428 final.

have driven the 'Better law making/Better regulation' policy.[15] General principles concerning better regulation have been defined at national level but so far have had little impact on sector specific regulation.[16] The role of private regulators has increased.[17] This is not primarily the effect of a transfer of regulatory power from public to private, rather it is part of a process of a new architecture where new regulatory powers have emerged and old ones have been redistributed.[18] This change suggests that the analysis should not be predominantly focused on the public/private divide but within private law devices between (private) regulation and liability, and particularly on the forms of their institutional complementarities. The theoretical challenge is to analyse private regulation and liability, in this chapter civil liability, as concurring tools for risk regulation and risk management.

Safety of products is part of a broader strategy concerning risk regulation. The link between the principles of better regulation and its implementation for risk regulation has not been the pillar of EU policy. The EU has not followed the path of institutional complementarity. There is no coordination between the regulatory and liability regime. The definitions of a safe product and product defect follow different logics that can hardly be explained in the framework of institutional complementarity. While the conventional view is that regulation defines minimum standards and liability increases safety standards, the definitions suggest that the opposite is true. Safety is defined as absence of risk or existence of minimum risk.[19] Defect is defined on the basis of

---

15 See Instruments for a modernized single market, above n. 12.

16 See for example in the UK the Principles of Good Regulation drafted by the Better Regulation Task Force, available at http://archive.cabinetoffice.gov.uk/brc/publications/principlesentry.html.

17 See also the report on *Self-regulation practices in SANCO policy areas*, P. Van der Zeijden and R. Van der Horst, Zoetermeer, February 2008, where the current cases for self-regulation and co-regulation are presented, indicating also their effectiveness in terms of monitoring and compliance, pp. 32 ff.

18 See B. Hutter, 'The role of non state actors in regulation', in F. Schuppert (ed), *Global governance, and the role of non state actors* (Nomos, 2006); C. Scott, 'Self-regulation and meta-regulatory state', in F. Cafaggi, *Reframing self-regulation in European private law* (Kluwer, 2006), p. 131; J. Black, 'Tensions in the Regulatory State' (2007) Public Law, p. 58; R. Baldwin and J. Black, 'Really Responsive Regulation' (2008) 71 Modern Law Review, p. 59; F. Cafaggi, presentation at the European Economic and Social Committee, public hearing on *The Current State of European Self- and Co-Regulation*, 31 March 2008.

19 See Art. 2 of GPSD, which defines as 'safe product': 'any product which, under normal or reasonably foreseeable conditions of use including duration and, where applicable, putting into service, installation and maintenance requirements, does not present any risk or only the minimum risks compatible with the product's use, considered to be acceptable and consistent with a high level of protection for the safety and health of persons'.

consumer expectation and is generally associated with some rudimentary risk-utility analysis, at least for design defect.[20]

The reform path proceeds along parallel, yet independent, lines.[21] The current approach is that while the PL directive has general application, the GPSD only applies when no specific regime concerning product safety is in place. No coordination exists as to the definition of safe and defective product, thereby generating different standards; the same is true in relation to remedies, even if it is clear that the PL regime focuses on compensatory remedies, while the GPSD focuses on injunctive or interim remedies (such as product withdrawal and product recall). Even more difficult is the interaction in relation to information duties and post-sale duties.

Both in the field of product safety and liability, a separate strategy for trans-European groups and networks of firms and purely national ones does not emerge. No specific links are made to the private international law regime in the Rome II regulation.[22]

The uncoordinated approach to product safety and product liability has prevented the definition of a coordinated strategy, aimed at improving institutional complementarity. This is particularly relevant for strategies of market surveillance where the focus seems to be entirely on regulation, while the potential effects on the liability regimes have not been sufficiently investigated. The absence of different regulatory approaches for purely national and trans-national groups and networks has created inefficiencies. Differences in regulatory regimes and practices may severely affect the ability to select one regime. This chapter tries to show the importance of considering the interplay between regulation and civil liability especially in the context of pan-European networks.

The European Commission has devised a new general strategy to complement the specific measures concerning product safety and market surveil-

---

[20] See Art. 6 PL directive, that provides: 'A product is defective when it does not provide the safety which a person is entitled to expect, taking all circumstances into account, including:

(a) the presentation of the product;
(b) the use to which it could reasonably be expected that the product would be put;
(c) the time when the product was put into circulation'.

[21] For a deep analysis of the interaction between the two aspects see S.Whittaker, *Liability for Products – English law, French law and European Harmonisation* (OUP, 2005), and F. Cafaggi, 'A coordinated approach to regulation and civil liability', above n. 11, pp. 191 ff.

[22] Regulation (EC) No 864/2007 of the European Parliament and of the Council of 11 July 2007 on the law applicable to non-contractual obligations (Rome II), OJ L 199, 31.07.2007, p. 40.

lance.[23] A new regulation has been recently adopted.[24] One of the main purposes is the introduction of a complementary system of market surveillance based on national accreditation bodies empowered to assess conformity. The system envisaged defines national accreditation bodies; their nature and governance system. It also defines the relationship between accreditation and conformity assessment bodies. Finally it complements the measures of market surveillance designed by GPSD.

In relation to the accreditation of bodies concerned with conformity assessment, there are some features worth analysing: (a) their non-profit nature and (b) the introduction of an express principle of non-competition. The accreditation body, if not directly operated by public authorities, should be accredited as a public authority, operate on a not-for-profit basis, and should not perform activities or services usually provided by conformity assessment bodies.[25] In other words, according to the non-competition principle, accreditation bodies cannot compete among themselves and with conformity assessment bodies.[26] European legislators explicitly want to avoid that any regulatory competition system will take place. Thus, they promote a cooperative model of mutual recognition.

In relation to the market surveillance system, the description of the different measures is aimed at reinforcing the mutual recognition approach and the cooperation among national authorities, while little attention is paid to modes of market surveillance and information gathering about serious risks concerning products already in the market. Furthermore, little is said about the relationships between the conformity assessment body and the enterprises, producers and distributors charged with monitoring and information duties. There is a serious risk that the new system will increase the costs of control without improving its effectiveness or, worse, that it might overburden certifiers and conformity assessment bodies with accreditation costs that will not produce any real effects on consumer protection against unsafe and dangerous products.[27]

---

[23] Regulation n° 765/2008 setting out the requirements for accreditation and market surveillance relating to the marketing of products, above n. 2.

[24] See Regulation n° 765/2008, above n. 2.

[25] See Art. 4 Regulation on Market surveillance, General principles, above n. 2.

[26] See Art. 6 Regulation on Market Surveillance, Principle of non competition: '1. National accreditation bodies shall not compete with conformity assessment bodies 2. National accreditation bodies shall not compete with other national accreditation bodies.'

[27] See the step forward towards a better coordination indicated in *Questions and answers: Product safety activities and follow up to the 2007 stocktaking exercise*, Memo/08/251, Brussels, 17.04.2008, where the safety pact with industry has been

2. THE EFFECTS OF PRIVATE ACTIVITY IN REGULATION AND CIVIL LIABILITY

2.1 The Role of Standard-setting in Regulation and Civil Liability

Product safety should be conceived as an integrated strategy, combining regulation and liability.[28] In a previous contribution I have tried to answer more general questions concerning the desirable complementarity between the two:[29] how do these two strategies (regulation and liability) interact when standards are set? As an empirical matter, do they constitute completely separate spheres or do they overlap? Normatively speaking, if they already interact, is the coordination satisfactory or should it be improved?

In this chapter, I focus on some specific questions concerning the influence of private regulation in standard-setting on civil liability and regulation.[30] Standard-setting in both product safety and liability should be conceived as a process not as a product. Standard-setting concerning product safety is linked

---

proposed, which is a 'voluntary agreement with the toy sector to boost product safety by following certain guidelines. These will include *sharing expertise*: in particular participating in the Commission's evaluation of business safety measures in the toy supply chain with a view to investigating ways in which safety measures can be enhanced and continued cooperation regarding the implementation of such improvements; [...] *cooperation with national authorities*: working together to ensure that dangerous goods, and in particular counterfeit goods, can be identified and intercepted in time to ensure a high level of consumer safety.'

[28] The debate concerning the regulatory functions of private law in general, and specifically on civil liability is in place. Different streams of scholarship advocate such a function. Typically this is the approach of law and economics, see G. Calabresi, *The Costs of Accidents* (Yale University, 1977); S. Shavell, 'Liability for Harm versus Regulation of Safety', (1984) J Legal Studies 357; id., 'A Model of the Optimal Use of Liability and Safety Regulation' [1984] Rand J Econ 271 ff.; id., *Economic Analysis of Accident Law* (Harvard University Press, 1987); J. Landes and R. Posner, *The Economic Structure of Tort Law* (1987); S.R. Ackerman, 'Tort Law in the Regulatory State', in Schuck (ed.), *Tort Law and the Public Interest: Competition, Innovation, and Consumer Welfare* (1991), at 80 ff. This approach has also been endorsed by the socio-legal studies movement, see H. Collins, *Contract Law* (Lexis Nexis, 2004); C. Parker, C. Scott, N. Lacey, and J. Braithwaite, *Regulating Law* (2004). Critiques of this approach are made by some tort scholars. See, e.g. J. Stapleton, 'Regulating Torts', in J. Braithwaite (ed.), *Regulating Law*, at pp. 122 ff.

[29] See F. Cafaggi, 'A coordinated approach to regulation and civil liability', above n. 11, pp. 191 ff.

[30] On the definition of private regulation see F. Cafaggi (ed.), *Reframing self-regulation in European private law* (Kluwer, 2006). For a governance perspective on product standards, see H. Schepel, *The constitution of private governance: product standards in the regulation of integrating markets* (Hart, 2005).

to risk assessment which should be determined according to the available technical and scientific knowledge, given the uncertainty about risks associated to products. The same product may be deemed safe at time 0 and become unsafe at time 1. In the case of liability, there is a time dimension. The defect has to exist before the product is put into circulation.[31] No liability, under the directive, can be found if the defect could only be discovered after the product was put into circulation. The development risk defence under Article 7(e) of the PL Directive allows the producer to plead exclusion of liability if the defect could not have been discovered before the product was put into circulation.[32] It should be pointed out that the state of scientific and technical knowledge does not correspond to that used in the industry, but more broadly that available in the scientific community. The reference point is the scientific not the business community.

This approach has several consequences to choose the effective regulatory strategy: it emphasizes the dynamic structure of standard-setting and the need for responsiveness, it implies a liability system for defective standard-setting different from that to be used for a defective product. Standard-setting should be scrutinized according to specific criteria. A defective standard, thus, should not be evaluated similarly to a defective product.

In product safety, Europe has moved from input or design standard to performance or output standard.[33] The former are still used in specific fields such as drugs and food. This change has contributed to partial convergence between regulation and liability. In product liability, the definition of defective

---

[31] On the differences between the two directives see F. Cafaggi, 'A coordinated approach to regulation and civil liability', above n. 11, pp. 191 ff.

[32] See *Commission v. England*, Case C-300/95, ECR I-2649:
'In order for a producer to incur liability for defective products under directive 85/374, the victim does not have to prove that the producer was at fault; however, in accordance with the principle of fair apportionment of risk between the injured person and the producer set forth in the seventh recital in the preamble to the directive the producer has a defence if he can prove certain facts exonerating him from liability, including that the state of scientific and technical knowledge at the time when he put the product into circulation was not such as to enable the existence of the defect to be discovered. Whilst the producer has to prove that the objective state of scientific and technical knowledge, including the most advanced level of such knowledge, without any restriction as to the industrial sector concerned, was not such as to enable the existence of the defect to be discovered, in order for the relevant knowledge to be successfully pleaded as against the producer, that knowledge must have been accessible at the time when the product in question was put into circulation.'

[33] For this distinction, see A. Ogus, *Regulation: Legal Form and Economic Theory* (Oxford, 2004), pp. 168 ff.

product is based on consumers' expectations.[34] No specific references are made to private standard-setting and expectations that can arise. The debate has focused more on the role of alternative designs than on the safety expectations of consumers coming from privately defined standards developed through codes of conduct.[35] There is a clear divergence between the definition of dangerous product and that of defective product in this respect.[36]

The regulatory approach adopted in GPSD is framed under the proportionality principle and favours the adoption of codes of practice both at European and national level.[37] The use of private standard setters, especially in relation to technical standardization, is promoted and its interplay with market surveillance has recently been revised.[38] The framework is to be completed by reference to technical standardization and the new approach which has given significant importance to mutual recognition of safety standards.[39]

As to the interaction between standard-setting in regulation and civil liability at least two general points should be made. The first is concerned with the role of regulatory compliance as a 'coordination mechanism' between civil liability and regulation.[40] The second is related to the impact on civil liability of private regulation either as an alternative or as a complement to public regulation.[41]

---

34 See Art. 6 PL directive which provides:
'1. A product is defective when it does not provide the safety which a person is entitled to expect, taking all circumstances into account, including:
(a) the presentation of the product;
(b) the use to which it could reasonably be expected that the product would be put;
(c) the time when the product was put into circulation.
2. A product shall not be considered defective for the sole reason that a better product is subsequently put into circulation.'
See S. Whittaker, *Liability for Products*, above n. 21; C. Castronovo, 'La responsabilità civile', in C. Castronovo and S. Mazzamuto (eds.), *Manuale di diritto privato europeo* (Giuffré, Milano, 2007), pp. 213 ff. part. pp. 226 ff.

35 In the Third report the Commission has drawn attention to different interpretations of defect given by national courts. On these questions see D. Fairgrieve (ed.), *Product liability in comparative perspective* (Cambridge University Press, 2005).

36 See F. Cafaggi, 'A coordinated approach to regulation and civil liability', above n. 11, pp. 191 ff.

37 See Arts. 4, 8, 11, 12, 13 of GPSD.

38 See G. Spindler, 'Interaction between product liability and regulation at the European level', Chapter 8 below.

39 See M. Audit, 'Impact of the mutual recognition principle on the law applicable to products', Chapter 9 below.

40 In general regulatory compliance is seen more as an enforcement than as a coordination device, concentrating on the question of whether compliance with administrative regulation is sufficient to exclude liability.

41 While here I am focusing on the definition of defect, in particular design defect, the potential impact of private regulation is much broader.

When standards of manufacturers' conduct are defined by administrative entities they certainly influence the standards employed in civil liability. Often, analogous principles operate for strict liability and for negligence, although judges tend to be stricter with non-compliance in strict liability and less severe with non-compliance in negligence.

The general rule, common to most legal systems, is that compliance with administratively defined standards does not exclude liability while a violation generally implies liability.[42] This is also the approach at EU level, both in relation to specific products and to general product liability.[43] These principles have been hotly debated, suggesting that regulatory requirements should become the civil liability standards thereby introducing a regulatory compliance defence.[44] The introduction of a regulatory compliance defence may move the litigation from producers to regulators, if safety standards were

---

[42] See for the UK, General Product Safety Regulations 2005 (SI 2005/1803), on which see D. Fairgrieve and G. Howells, 'General product safety – a revolution through reform?', 69 Modern Law Review, p. 59; P. Cartwright, 'The regulation of product safety', in G. Howells (ed), *The law of product liability* (Lexis-Nexis, 2007), pp. 695 ff. For France, see Art. 1386-10 of the French Civil Code, 'A producer may be liable for a defect although the product was manufactured in accordance with the rules of the trade or of existing standards or although it was the subject of an administrative authorization'; see B. Cazeneuve, *La responsabilité du fait des produits* (Dunod, 2005), p. 78; J.S. Borghetti, 'Contrats et responsabilité. La responsabilité des fournisseurs du fait du défaut de sécurité de leurs produits' (2006) *Revue des contrats*, p. 835. For Italy, see F. Cafaggi, *La responsabilità del produttore* (Cedam, 2003), p. 995. For the case law concerning drugs see Cass. N. 8069, 20 luglio 1993, and Cass. n. 1138, 1 February 1995: 'le imprese farmaceutiche le quali intervengono nel ciclo produttivo di gammaglobuline umane, sono responsabili per colpa grave dei danni derivati in caso di contagio conseguite all'uso del farmaco ove, pur avendo ottemperato alle disposizioni normative vigenti non dimostrino di avere impiegato ogni cautela idonea ad impedire l'evento'. For the US see Third Restatement on Products Liability § 402 (a).

[43] See C. Hodges, *European regulation of consumer product safety* (OUP, 2005), pp. 21 ff. See for pharmaceutical products, M. Mildred, 'Pharmaceutical products: the relationship between regulatory approval and the existence of a defect' (2007) European Business Law Review, pp. 1267 ff.

[44] In Europe see the third report, COM (2006) 496 final, 14.09.2006, p. 11. In the US the Supreme Court has recently issued a judgment, *Riegel* v. *Medtronic INC*, 06/179, WL 440744, 20 February 2008, reviewing the relationship between administrative regulation and tort law; see on these questions C. Sharkey, 'Products liability pre-emption: an institutional approach', 76 George Washington LR, pp. 449 ff.; S. Issacharoff and C. Sharkey, 'Backdoor federalization', 53 UCLA L.R., pp. 1353 ff. For earlier significant contributions to the regulatory compliance debate see R. Rabin, 'Reassessing regulatory compliance' (2000) 88 Geo LJ p. 2049; R. Stewart, 'Regulatory compliance preclusion of tort liability: Limiting the dual track system' (2000) 88 Geo LJ, p. 2167.

lowered or inappropriate.[45] But the current divergences among member states in relation to state liability for defective standards are much wider than those harmonized in the PL directive.[46] In addition, public regulators, if bearing the overall liability burden, may become sensitive and over regulate, thereby hindering product innovation. The rejection of the defence of regulatory compliance is perfectly defensible under the institutional complementarity approach; less defensible if liability and regulation are considered functional equivalents rather than complements.

Somewhat similar though not identical rules are used for technical standards, publicly produced. Compliance with technical standards does not exclude liability.[47] Non-compliance with standards, imposed by legislation or by regulators constitutes a violation, often of dual, civil and criminal, character.[48]

A different rule concerns technical standards when they have been privately produced without the approval of a public authority or within a co-regulatory process.[49] The function of private bodies in technical standard-setting is not only to ensure that the best available scientific and technical knowledge is

---

45 See on state liability for defective products mainly in relation to health related injuries such as blood infection, S. Whittaker, *Liability for Products*, above n. 21 pp. 305 ff. In Italy see Cass. n. 11609, 31 May 2005 on which N. Coggiola, The Italian Ministry of Health held liable for the damages arising out of contaminated blood and blood products, ERPL, 2007, pp. 451 ff.

46 For a detailed examination of England and France, see S. Whittaker, *Liability for Products*, above n. 21 pp. 305 ff.

47 See for example in UK, *Balding* v. *Law Ways Ltd* (1995) QBLR 314 where the judge held that compliance with technical standards does not amount to due diligence under Consumer Protection Act 1987. See C. Scott and J. Black, *Cranston's Consumers and the Law*, 3rd edn (Butterworths, 2000), p. 331.

48 See the national implementation of the GPSD. As to the UK, 'Non-compliance with standards imposed by legislation is a different matter. It will typically constitute a criminal offence, and there may also be a civil remedy for breach of the statutory duty or, as it is termed in some jurisdictions, in respect of negligence per se. In some statutes the position with respect to civil remedies is stated clearly (as in CPA). Where it is not, one is called on to discover legislative intent both as to the existence of the remedy and as to the types of damage or loss covered', see C.J. Miller and R.S. Goldberg, *Product Liability*, 2nd edn (Oxford University Press, 2004), p. 612.

49 As to the UK, see C.J. Miller and R.S. Goldberg, *Product Liability*, p. 612: 'Non-compliance with standards produced by a body such as the British Standards Institute is broadly comparable to non-compliance with general industrial standards. The main difference is that, being written and formulated by experts, such standards are more precise and authoritative. Consequently, it is that much less likely that non-compliance will be seen as consistent with reasonable safety.' For a critique of the approach that does not distinguish between technical and industry produced standards see below text pp. 226 ff.

used to define the most updated standard, but also to foster innovation. The incentives to promote innovation in safety standards come from different sources but the liability of these bodies for negligent standard-setting is a potential engine for innovation scarcely used by consumers in litigation.[50] Compliance with technical standards is voluntary. Producers have to meet the essential requirements of safety. If they comply with technical standards they will be freed from the burden of proving that their products are safe. If they deviate, the burden of proof will be on them.[51]

When is a private standard violated? In particular, should alternative product designs that do not follow the technical standards defined by private bodies be deemed violations? The answer is negative. An examination of the deviation is needed. A rule which would consider every deviation as violation would be questionable under Article 28 of the EC Treaty but would also hinder product innovation by forcing manufacturers to comply only with one technical standard.[52] Violations of standards privately defined, for example through self-regulation, do not always constitute negligence or at least *negligence per se*.[53] Often there is a presumption of negligence that can be rebutted if the tortfeasor can prove the obsolescence of the technical standard.[54]

---

50 See F. Cafaggi, 'Rethinking self-regulation in European private law', n. 11.

51 See Art. 3.2 GPSD. On the interpretation see G. Spindler, 'Interaction between product liability and regulation at European level', Chapter 8 below.

52 See G. Spindler, 'Interaction between product liability and regulation at European level', Chapter 8 below.

53 The legal status of private standard-setting varies even within each legal system. In some cases it is equated to custom, in other cases it is qualified as non-statutory standards, or it is qualified as private regulation and equated to administrative regulation. Divergences also depend on the reference to general clauses or to specific rules. Legal systems that apply general clauses, like France or Italy, confer on judges the power to define the relevant elements to identify due care, among which privately set standards are considered. Common law systems have a different approach. For US, *Spearman* v. *Georgia Building Authority* 482 SE 2d 465 (GA App. 1997); for UK, *Ward* v. *Ritz Hotel* [1992] PIQR 315.

54 The ECJ has interpreted Art. 7(e) of the PL Directive stating that 'the clause providing for the defence in question does not contemplate the state of knowledge of which the producer in question actually or subjectively was or could have been apprised, but the objective state of scientific and technical knowledge of which the producer is presumed to have been informed. However, it is implicit in the wording of Article 7(e) that the relevant scientific and technical knowledge must have been accessible at the time when the product in question was put into circulation. It follows that, in order to have a defence under Article 7(e) of the Directive, the producer of a defective product must prove that the objective state of scientific and technical knowledge, including the most advanced level of such knowledge, at the time when the product in question was put into circulation was not such as to enable the existence of the defect to be discovered.' See Case C-300/95, *Commission* v. *UK* [1997] ECR I-2649. See also,

Compliance with self-regulation does not exclude liability but it may constitute evidence of due care. In many legal systems, privately defined standards are conceived to be minimum standards to the extent they reflect the state of the art.[55] Violation of private standards is often held to be relevant though not always conclusive evidence of product defectiveness.[56] It should however be pointed out that legal systems, within the European Union, diverge quite significantly in relation to the factors constituting breach of a regulatory standard and the relationship it bears to the notion of defect.

Technical standards should be differentiated from custom and from standards privately defined by industries. They are presumptively produced by 'impartial' technical experts. However, looking at the composition of governance bodies of technical standards this conclusion could be seriously questioned.[57] Consumer interests' representation in technical standardization is an open issue both at European and international level.[58] In self-regulation, standards are often unilaterally produced by manufacturers. In this case, clearly there cannot be presumption of impartiality. When they are negotiated with other constituencies, sufficiently representative of conflicting interests, these standards can be differentiated from custom.[59] But representativeness is not the only issue; procedural rules that characterize public standard-setting such as public hearings and duty to give reasons should be applied to private

---

for a critical evaluation of the relationship between the definition of defective product and development risk defence, J. Stapleton, 'Products Liability in the United Kingdom: The Myths of Reform' (1999) 34 Tex Int LJ, p. 50 at p. 53.

[55] See for the Italian system, F. Cafaggi, *Profili di relazionalità della colpa* (Padova, Cedam, 1996). For the German system, B. Markesinis, *The German Law of Torts*, 3rd edn, p 562; G. Spindler, 'Market Processes, Standardisation and Tort Law' (1998) 4 European Law Journal, pp. 316 ff. and p. 320 and id., 'Interaction between product liability and regulation at the European level', Chapter 8 below . See for a comparative analysis H. Schepel and J. Falke, *Legal aspects of standardisation in the Member States of the EC and EFTA*, Volume 1 Comparative Report (Luxembourg, 2000), pp. 233 ff.

[56] In Germany, C. Von Bar, *The Common European law of torts* (OUP, 2000), 421; B. Markesinis, *The German Law of Torts*, above n. 55, p. 99, S. Lenze, 'German product liability law between European directives, American restatements and common sense', in D. Fairgrieve (ed.), *Product liability in comparative perspective*, above n. 35 p. 106. In Italy, F. Cafaggi, 'La responsabilità dell'impresa per prodotti difettosi', in N. Lipari (ed.), *Trattato di diritto private europeo* (Cedam, 2003), p. 996.

[57] In the area of technical standards see the agreement between CEN and CENELEC and the Commission 2003 (General Guidelines for the cooperation between CEN, CENELEC and ETSI and the European Commission and the European Free Trade Association, 28 March 2003, (2003/C 91/04)).

[58] See H. Schepel, *Constitution of private governance*, above n. 30; I. Ramsay, *Consumer law and policy*, 2nd edn. (Hart, Oxford), 2007 pp. 711 ff.

[59] See below text and footnotes pp. 229 ff.

standard-setting as well to ensure that the rule-making process is sufficiently accountable.[60]

Moreover, in different legal systems, courts do not often explicitly distinguish – for the purpose of establishing civil liability – between purely private standard-setting and standard-setting by private bodies within a framework of co-regulation or delegated self-regulation.[61] This distinction is certainly relevant for judicial review purposes, but, so far, it has not been considered fundamental to the definition of civil liability for non-compliance.[62]

An integrated approach to regulation and civil liability should allow differentiating modes of regulatory standard-setting and their influences on the definition of negligence and strict liability.[63]

The possibility for judges to evaluate injurers' and victims' conduct, beyond compliance with regulatory standards, has been justified in different ways. The most common interpretation is that administrative rules define minimum standards while civil liability can increase the required level of due precaution.[64] The principle that regulatory compliance does not exclude liability shows the

---

60 The question of consumer representation in technical standard-setting has been one of the main preoccupations of the European Commission. See the results of the Consultation on the review and extension of the new approach, available at http://ec.europa.eu/enterprise/newapproach/review_en.htm.

61 For this distinction see F. Cafaggi, 'Le rôle des acteurs privés dans le processus de régulation: participation, autorégulation et régulation privée', in *La Régulation, Nouveaux modes? Nouveaux territoires?* (2004) 109 *Revue française d'administration publique*, p. 23; and 'Gouvernance et responsabilité des régulateurs privés' (2005) *Revue Internationale de Droit Economique*, 111.

62 It is important to differentiate between standards that are purely private and binding only on those who consented to them and standards that are enacted in the context of co-regulation, delegated private regulation and ex post recognized self-regulation. See F. Cafaggi, *Contractualizing standard-setting in civil liability*, on file with the author.

63 See G. Howell, 'Product Liability A History of Harmonization', in A. Hartkamp, M. Hesselink, and E. Hondius *et al., Towards a European Civil Code* (Kluwer Law International, 2004), at 645; S. Whittaker, *Liability for Products*, above n. 21. See also M. Reimann, 'Product Liability in Global Context: the Hollow Victory of the European Model' (2003) *European Review Private Law*, p. 132, '[j]urisdictions joining the product liability bandwagon have uniformly cast their special regimes in statutory form rather than relying on judicial decisions, restatements, or the like. This is no wonder in countries belonging to the civil law orbit, e.g., in continental Europe, Latin America, most Asian nations, and Quebec. But it is also true in several common law jurisdictions, namely United Kingdom, Ireland, and Australia. As a result, the field now has a legislative centrepiece in the vast majority of legal systems recognising it as a special subject. In fact, the only country where product liability is clearly established as a field with its own rules and principles (such as strict liability), but still remains a matter of case law, is the United States.'

64 For an evaluation of regulatory compliance in the US setting, see R. Rabin,

adoption of an approach based on the complementarity between civil liability and regulation. Such complementarity reflects the idea that regulation only defines minimum standards while civil liability can set higher standards.[65]

A slightly different approach is taken in the area of regulation. No specific recognition of the relevance of civil liability as a complementary strategy occurs in this area.[66] Regulatory schemes do not seem explicitly to acknowledge the existence of an underlying civil liability system. However, in the area of product safety, as we shall see, compliance with safety standards may be sufficient to shield manufacturers from criminal liability, but does not exclude the imposition of duties if the dangerous nature of the product becomes known after sale.[67]

2.2 Contractualizing Standard-setting

The second point is concerned with the role of private actors in standard-setting. By private actors I refer to two main modes of participation in standard-setting: (1) through trade associations, (2) through market contracting.[68] In both cases often there is a plurality of regulators aimed at achieving some level of competition in standard-setting. The degree and effectiveness of competition among private standard setters is scrutinized by competition law.

'Reassessing regulatory compliance', above n. 44, 2049; J. Stapleton, 'Regulating Torts', in C. Parker *et al.*, *Regulating Law*, above n. 28 at 122.

65 For the definition of private regulatory standards as minimum standards, see G. Spindler, 'Interaction between product liability and regulation at the European level', Chapter 8 below.

66 The role of civil liability and judicial review should be very important for the content of regulatory activity and standard supervision. See below pp. 233 ff.

67 For the debate on product liability and the role of scientific knowledge see *Restatement of the Law Third, Torts: Products Liability*, s. 402(A) (American Law Institute, 1998), and *Restatement Third on the Law of Torts: Liability for Physical Harm*, Proposed final draft, N1 (2005), in particular in relation to burden of proof in causation, at 477 ff. Specifically on the risk development defence, see J.-S. Borghetti, *La responsabilité du fait des produits. Étude de droit comparé* (2004) LGDJ, at pp. 59–62 and reference to the vast case law there contained. The role of scientific knowledge in relation to product liability regimes also concerns possible defects which may depend on the projectual phase of the product rather than on the very manufacturing activity: for the German system see again Borghetti, ibid., at pp. 125–127. If para. 823 BGB provides a principle of negligence liability for project defects, different solutions may be reached when there are European, national, or international provisions establishing safety standards (at p. 127). The problem is at the very core of the risk development defence. See *A and Others* v. *National Blood Authority and Others* [2001] 3 All ER 289.

68 For a detailed analysis concerning contract law, see F. Cafaggi, 'Self-regulation in European contract law' (2007) *European Journal of Legal Studies*, 1, available at www.ejls.eu.

Most of the 'advantages' of private regulation, however, may be lost if the private regulator is a monopolist.[69] Private regulation should thus be distinguished from technical regulation by a private body of 'independent' experts'.[70] In practice this is a difficult distinction given the risks of capture of experts by the industry. This difficulty, however, should not lead to eliminating the differences between expertise and interest-based regulation. On the contrary, they should reinforce the necessity to identify clear boundaries between independent and non-independent private regulation. A second question is related to access to standards. Private regulation often implies sale of technical standards to a greater extent by independent regulatory bodies than by private regulators representing the industries. How does the market for standards affect the level of safety? Does it increase it or decrease it? Empirical studies are needed to answer this question and to clarify the effects of the participation of private actors in the process of standard-setting concerning product safety.

To what extent do private actors participate in standard-setting in civil liability and regulation? Are there differences in the two domains? How do the new models of regulation, broadening the participation of relevant stakeholders, affect standard-setting in civil liability?

In this section, I focus on the influence of private standard-setting in product safety and defectiveness and the consequences for violations of these standards by producers and distributors. I do not address the related question of the liability of the standard setters and how it changes when a transfer from public to private has occurred.[71] Of course especially in the case of private standard-setting by market players the two questions are strictly inter-related.[72]

Standards are, in this context, related to product safety (dangerousness) and defectiveness. Part of the definition of a safe or non-defective product is related to the level and adequacy of information provided by producers and distributors. I will deal mainly with product design standards in this section

---

[69] See O. Hart, A. Shleifer and R. Vishny, 'The proper scope of government: theory and application to prisons' (1997) 112 Quarterly Journal of Economics, 1127; F. Cafaggi, 'A coordinated approach to regulation and civil liability', above n. 11 p. 191.

[70] Art. 3.3 of GPSD includes different types of private regulation to assess general safety requirements without distinguishing criteria. Under letter (a) it mentions voluntary national standards transposing relevant European standards, under letter (d) product safety codes of good practice in force in the sector concerned under letter (e) the state of the art and technology.

[71] I have addressed this issue in 'La responsabilité des régulateurs privés', cit., p. 111; and 'La responsabilità dei regolatori privati' (2006) Mercato Concorrenza e Regole, pp. 1 ff.

[72] For a detailed analysis of these aspects, see S. Whittaker, *Liability for Products*, above n. 21 pp. 305 ff.

and focus on information standards in the next section. The definition of defect, introduced with the PL directive, does not specifically refer to regulatory standards but to the exclusion of liability if the defect is due to compliance with legislative mandatory rules. The general rule, with different applications across member states, states that compliance with regulatory standards can have relevant but not conclusive evidentiary weight. This leaves the judges discretion to hold liable producers who have fully complied with regulatory standards. Regulatory compliance is not a full defence.[73] Does the existence of a regulatory standard affect the definition of what is a defective product, given that compliance with standards according to the GPSD constitutes a rebuttable presumption of safety? Should the regulatory standard have some influence in the definition of consumer expectation according to Article 6?

The regulatory standard contributes to define the minimum level of consumer expectation but certainly does not coincide with the expectation itself which is based on several factors, some legal some factual. Objectively defined consumer expectation may be higher than the regulatory standard or simply different. Thus, a safe product can be defective and a dangerous product might not be defective. Product safety and product defectiveness are not mutually exclusive because regulation and liability have complementary functions.[74]

Traditionally, in civil liability the role of private parties as standard setters has been neglected or denied but for technical standardization. Given that civil liability is a domain of mandatory rules, the role of private parties in the definition of due care standards has generally been rejected. Standards of due care and strict liability have been the exclusive domain of legislators and judges for a long time. The rise of the regulatory state has added public regulators, that is, government or administrative agencies to the traditional institutional landscape.

---

[73] See S. Whittaker, *Liability for Products*, above n. 21 p. 483.

[74] See F. Cafaggi, 'Rethinking institutional complementarities', above n. 11 p. 191. See in Italy, Corte di cassazione, n. 6007, 15.03.2007, which states: 'Senonchè, l'art. 5 della legge definisce difettoso non ogni prodotto insicuro ma quel prodotto che non offra la sicurezza che ci si può legittimamente attendere in relazione al modo in cui il prodotto è stato messo in circolazione, alla sua presentazione, alle sue caratteristiche palesi alle istruzioni o alle avvertenze fornite, all'uso per il quale il prodotto può essere ragionevolmente destinato, ed ai comportamenti che, in relazione ad esso, si possono ragionevolmente prevedere, al tempo in cui il prodotto è stato messo in circolazione.
Il difetto del prodotto non si identifica, dunque, con la mancanza di una assoluta certezza o di una oggettiva condizione di innocuità dello stesso, ma con la mancanza dei requisiti di sicurezza generalmente richiesti dall'utenza in relazione alle circostanze specificamente indicate dall'art. 5 o ad altri elementi in concreto valutabili e concretamente valutati dal giudice di merito, nell'ambito dei quali, ovviamente, possono e debbono farsi rientrare gli standards di sicurezza eventualmente imposti dalle norme in materia.'

Contract law has been considered to limit the freedom to contracting out publicly defined standards. In the traditional perspective, individual parties can modify legislatively defined liability standards on a contractual basis but only in a limited way. This is certainly true for contractual liability, but sometimes it is extended to extra-contractual liability.[75] Parties however, cannot exclude civil liability between themselves and towards third parties.[76]

In national legal systems, the possibility to modify standards of contractual liability has always been recognized at the individual level, so that the potential injurer and victim could negotiate, within certain limits, on the liability regime and on the level of compensation.[77]

Limitations of contractual and extra-contractual liability are however scrutinized under unfair contract terms legislation.[78] In those legal systems where unfair contract terms are scrutinized in relation to business-to-consumer (BtoC) relationships, the ability to exclude liability for product defectiveness is almost non-existent,[79] so that only a valid clause can limit injurers' or victims' extra-contractual liability. In those countries where unfair terms are scrutinized in both business-to-business (BtoB) and BtoC the right to exclude liability is very limited.

The Draft Common Frame of Reference (hereinafter DCFR) takes a relatively strict position, prohibiting exclusion or limitation for intentional and reckless misconduct and for personal injuries, even in negligence.[80] It allows

---

75 See *Study on property law and non contractual liability as they relate to contract law*. Submitted to the EC Health and Consumer Protection directorate general, Sanco B5-1000/02/000574 by C. Von Bar and U. Drobnig (hereinafter the Study on non contractual liability), available at http://ec.europa.eu/consumers/cons_int/safe_shop/fair_bus_pract/cont_law/study.pdf.

76 See the Study on non contractual liability, above n. 75 pp. 164 ff. In relation to the English and French system, see S. Whittaker, *Liability for products*, above n. 21 pp. 93 ff. and pp. 260 ff.

77 Member states' legal regimes differ quite significantly, but they all allow some possibility. See the Study on non contractual liability, above n. 75 pp. 164 ff. For the French system see M. Fabre Magnan, *Les obligations* (PUF, 2004), pp. 586 ff. For the English system, see E. McKendrick, *Contract Law* 7th edn (Palgrave Macmillan, 2007), p. 230.

78 See Research Group on the Existing EC Private Law (Acquis Group), *Principles of the Existing EC Contract Law (Acquis Principles) – Pre-contractual Obligations, Conclusion of Contract, Unfair Terms Contract I* (2007) European Law Publisher.

79 See Art. 12 Dir. 374/85 EC.

80 See *Principles, Definitions and model Rules of European private law*, Draft Common Frame of Reference, available at http://webh01.ua.ac.be/storme/DCFRInterim.pdf. In particular, see book VI Art. 5:401, 'Contractual exclusion and restriction of liability':

'Liability for causing legally relevant damage intentionally cannot be excluded or restricted

exclusions or limitations only in relation to economic interests.[81] When lawful clauses are introduced, they will be scrutinized under the fairness test and will be declared valid if they do not create a disproportionate ratio of rights and duties. It is important to point out that exclusions or limitations are prohibited when 'otherwise illegal or contrary to good faith and fair dealing'.

Product safety regulation reveals a slightly different picture. The role of private actors in regulation has been debated for the last 20 years but their increasing relevance cannot be questioned.[82] Changes have occurred both in relation to the definition of private regulation and private regulators affecting the boundaries of the private-public divide.[83] Private regulation in this area takes different forms, but co-regulation and delegation largely prevail over pure self-regulation.[84] The use of private regulation is often framed within a cooperative approach aimed at increasing accountability of the regulatory process.

Traditionally private parties are unable to change or deviate from the standard of product safety and product defectiveness. Thus, pure self-regulation unlike co-regulation and delegated regulation has little role in the field.

My claim is that the influence of private regulation in product and service safety, in particular contractualization of standard-setting – but to some extent even of monitoring – has entered the field of product liability through that of product safety. Changes in the regulatory regimes affect the operation of product liability and the tort system. The interplay between the two areas is bringing about a higher degree of contractualization, even if rules about compliance are still kept differently in administrative regulation and product liability. An open question which requires empirical research is which changes this

---

(1) Liability for causing legally relevant damage as a result of profound failure to take such care as is manifestly required in the circumstances cannot be excluded or restricted:
  (a) in respect of personal injury (including fatal injury), or
  (b) if the exclusion or restriction is otherwise illegal or contrary to good faith and fair dealing.'

81 This can be inferred from the last part of the article where it is stated that 'Other liability under this Book can be excluded or restricted unless statute provides otherwise', DCFR VI-5:401(4).

82 See J. Black, 'Tensions in the Regulatory State' (2007) Public Law, p. 58; R. Baldwin and J. Black, 'Really Responsive Regulation' (2008) 71 Modern Law Review, p. 59.

83 See J. B. Auby and M. Freedland (eds.), *The public-private law divide: Une entente assez cordiale?* (Oxford, Hart, 2006).

84 Delegation occurs when a public body transfers its law making power to private bodies or when it shares it. See C.M. Donnelly, *Delegation of governmental power to private parties – A comparative perspective* (OUP, 2007); and F. Cafaggi, 'Rethinking Private Regulation in the European Regulatory Space', in F. Cafaggi (ed.), *Reframing self-regulation in European private law* (Kluwer, 2006), p. 3.

contractualization has brought in relation to the type of standards. On the one hand, one could expect that private actors would move from design to performance standards, leaving more discretion to producers. On the other hand, incentives to reduce competitiveness on safety may induce the use of more design than performance standards. The Commission has provided detailed guidelines concerning technical standardization to prevent anticompetitive standardization but there are no specific references to the preferability of performance standards.[85]

The interaction between regulation and civil liability poses new challenges if we consider the role of private regulation.[86] Here the reference is to private regulation as normative not technical standard-setting.[87] When industries self-define the standards of product safety or environmental protection, can the binding contractual arrangements they apply affect the standard of defectiveness in product liability? Should the limits of this private regulatory power be defined by the rules concerning contractual exclusion of liability or should they be defined according to different criteria, given the regulatory nature of the contract?

Possible alternative answers to this question are:

(1). to consider self-regulation and co-regulation as a form of regulation and apply the rules developed for administrative regulation to the interaction between self-regulation and civil liability; or

(2). to apply the rules of contractual limitation of contractual liability.[88]

The two aspects just examined reveal different relationships between regulation and civil liability. While potential injurers cannot escape liability even if they comply with administrative regulation, in the case of private parties who have contracted limitations of liability, judges are bound to apply the contractual

[85] See Guidelines on horizontal cooperation 2001, in particular Art. 6 on standard agreements: 'Standardisation agreements have as their primary objective the definition of technical or quality requirements with which current or future products, production processes or methods may comply. Standardisation agreements can cover various issues, such as standardisation of different grades or sizes of a particular product or technical specifications in markets where compatibility and interoperability with other products or systems is essential. The terms of access to a particular quality mark or for approval by a regulatory body can also be regarded as a standard'.

[86] For an overview, see F. Cafaggi, 'Rethinking Private Regulation in the European Regulatory Space', above n. 84, p. 16.

[87] See on the distinction between private normative and technical standard-setting, pp. 229 ff.

[88] On the role of self-regulation in civil liability and in particular in standard-setting, see F. Cafaggi, *Contractualizing standard-setting in civil liability*, above n. 62.

arrangement even if it lowers the standards of protection, unless the clause is unfair.

While the principles developed in contract law for the exclusion of liability might be considered a starting point, a different account is needed for standard-setting defined through contractual arrangements, that is to say codes of conduct enacted by private actors in the field of product safety and environmental protection. The possibility that self-regulatory normative standards can be considered minimal should be preserved; therefore the judge, when evaluating injurers' liability, should be able to hold an injurer liable even if he or she complied with standards defined by the private regulatory body. The use of private autonomy as a shield from liability would undermine the acceptability of private regulation as a complementary regulatory device. If private regulators could set standards that exclude or reduce potential injurers' liability without limits, the credibility of private regulation would be severely affected. If it is accepted that regulatory compliance related to administrative regulation is not a defence then, *a fortiori*, regulatory compliance related to private regulation should not be considered decisive.[89]

The influence of private regulation on the level of consumer protection may also be indirect. If private regulators set standards that would reduce competition and these standards are internalized by the civil liability system, then negligence or strict liability may become anti-competitive devices that reduce the level of protection.[90] A pro-competitive system of civil liability should encourage the adoption of alternative safer standards, promoting innovation.

---

89 See F. Cafaggi, *Contractualizing standard-setting in civil liability*, above n. 62.

90 See F. Cafaggi, 'Self-regulation in European Contract law', above, n 68. Agreements among firms that perform standard-setting functions are generally scrutinized under antitrust rules. See Commission notice of 6 January 2001, *Guidelines on the applicability of Article 81 of the EC Treaty to horizontal cooperation agreements*, OJ C 3 06.01.2001, p. 167. 'The existence of a restriction of competition in standardisation agreements depends upon the extent to which the parties remain free to develop alternative standards or products that do not comply with the agreed standard. Standardisation agreements may restrict competition where they prevent the parties from either developing alternative standards or commercialising products that do not comply with the standard. Agreements that entrust certain bodies with the exclusive right to test compliance with the standard go beyond the primary objective of defining the standard and may also restrict competition. Agreements that impose restrictions on marking conformity with standards unless imposed by regulatory standards may also restrict competition.' See also General Guidelines for the cooperation between CEN, CENELEC and ETSI and the European Commission and the European Trade Association, above n. 57, 'With regard to possible restrictions to competition caused by horizontal cooperation agreements between companies operating on the same market level(s) the Commission published a notice on the applicability of Article 81 of the EC

To conclude: standards concerning safety of products are generated both within the civil liability and the regulatory systems. Coordination between these two activities is poorly defined both at national and at European level in relation to the traditional framework that compares administrative regulation and civil liability. New challenges to this interaction are posed by changes occurring in the field of regulation with the consolidation of the role of private regulators and the introduction of new regulatory schemes. An integrated system of civil liability and regulation requires coordination mechanisms that go beyond regulatory compliance.

Legislative intervention to coordinate the liability for defective products and safety regulatory regime is needed. This intervention should not eliminate the specificities of the two approaches, but it should define better coordination devices between the two regimes in relation to both deterrence and compensation. The preliminary step is to have a clear distinction among different types of regulatory strategies. Private standard-setting may be categorized as (1) custom, (2) negotiated standardization and (3) standardization by independent bodies. These differences should affect the influence of self-regulation on standard-setting in civil liability and should be differentiated between their impact on fault and on strict liability. Custom and unilateral standardization should be considered only for evidentiary purposes. Negotiated standardization, in compliance with clear procedural rules concerning openness, transparency and accountability, and independent standardization could give rise to a rebuttable presumption of safety when there is compliance with the technical standard. Negotiated standardization without procedural guarantees should be treated as unilateral standardization and produce only evidentiary effects.

Treaty. In this notice standardisation agreements are considered to be a type of horizontal cooperation agreement, either concluded between private undertakings or determined under the aegis of public bodies or bodies entrusted with the operation of services of general economic interests, such as the standard organisations recognised under directive 98/34/EC. The notice also states that in principle standardisation agreements do not restrict competition if the standards are adopted by recognised standard organisations, based on non discriminatory open and transparent procedures.' On the relationship between standard-setting by private organizations and competition rules, see F. Cafaggi, *Contractualizing standard-setting*, above n. 62.

3. THE EFFECTS OF REGULATION ON THE PRIVATE LAW DIMENSION: THE CREATION OF INDUSTRY NETWORKS TO PROMOTE AND CONTROL PRODUCT SAFETY[91]

The information flow towards consumers is defined by three different bodies of law at EU level: contract (sale of goods directive 99/44/EC), civil liability (PL directive), and GPSD. The three systems, not well coordinated, impose duties to inform on the producer, the distributor and the final seller. They define different liability regimes which affect the incentives to produce information, but most importantly impact upon the incentives to monitor product safety and defectiveness once the product has been marketed. Information duties play different functions depending on the level and nature of risk but also on the identity of the addressee, buyer, user and bystander to whom the information is conveyed.[92] (1) They reduce the level of risk by conveying information about the risks of the product and the modes of assessment by the consumer, (2) they allow consumers, buyers and users, to make informed choices about purchase and use of the product once it has been bought. In this context, I focus on information concerning safety leaving aside quality. Information may contribute to risk assessment when consumers have to make a choice, which is not always the case as the example of bystanders shows. Information can also contribute to risk management, if the risk is known and only partially avoidable with the cooperation of consumers or third parties.

Information duties are owed before the product is sold, when it is marketed, but also after sale, when they interact with the duty to monitor product safety. Post-market surveillance has become a central issue in the current debate. Duties to inform are thus related to sale and post-marketing. They cover the whole life of the product. Thus, their relationship with monitoring becomes

---

[91] This part summarizes the results of a broader project which I am currently working on: 'Creating safety networks. Moving away from hierarchy in product safety and liability'. See F. Cafaggi, *The divergences between real industrial organisational forms and regulatory strategies concerning product safety. When theory departs from reality in institutional design*. Unpublished manuscript.

[92] The issue becomes even more difficult in relation to liability for defective drugs where information has to be conveyed to doctors who prescribe the drugs as well as to potential users. The matter is regulated at EU level by directive 2001/83/EC and subsequent amendments. Under the directive the holder of market authorization has to conduct pharmacovigilance of the products and to report adverse reactions to the competent authority. See M. Mildred, 'Pharmaceutical products: the relationship between regulatory approval and the existence of a defect', above n. 43 p. 1269.

extremely relevant. The debate about the liability standard which gives optimal incentives to inform is still open.[93]

The GPSD takes a different approach from the PL and the sale of goods directives, but also from sector specific regulatory regimes. It must be recalled that the GPSD is residual and it only applies to consumer products whose safety is not specifically regulated. The analysis will focus on this regime and only occasional references to food and drug safety regimes will be made, in particular apropos to Regulation 178/2002.[94] The GPSD defines the industrial chain by distinguishing suppliers and distributors. The former, according to the directive, are those who can affect the safety of the product, the latter are those who cannot.[95] While placing the burden of safety obligations on the producer it allocates information duties along the chain with some emphasis on the distributors and retailers.

Before examining the structure of information obligations and their implication for the network it is necessary to focus on the definition of the distributor. The distributor is defined in a quite peculiar way for at least two reasons:

(1). It is negatively defined as being unable to affect the safety, thus adopting a very abstract and old-fashioned idea of the decision-making power between producers and distributors. It is evident how relevant big distributors are for the definition of product safety, not only in the case of private labelling. For reasons concerning market reputation and costs associated with withdrawal and recall, distributors impose on producers safety and quality control systems that can affect safety.

(2). It leaves unclear whether the expression 'cannot affect safety' refers to technological or contractual constraints. In the latter case the parties would be able contractually to allocate the regulatory burdens in ways that may not be the most efficient because driven by asset instead of real ability to control safety (that is to say the producer is the small firm that can only be liable for a limited amount while the big and powerful

93 For a recent analysis related to the US system, see K. Spier, 'Product safety, buybacks and the post-sale duty to warn', Harvard Law and Economics Discussion Paper No. 597, available at http://ssrn.com/abstract=1023125, and, from a different perspective, A.M. Polinsky and S. Shavell, 'Mandatory versus Voluntary Disclosure of Product Risks', Stanford Law and Economics Olin Working Paper No. 327, available at http://ssrn.com/abstract=939546. For an earlier influential contribution on these matters, see G. Hadfield, R. Howse, M. Trebilcock, 'Information based principles for rethinking consumer protection policy' (1998) 21 *Journal of Consumer Policy*, 131.

94 The food regime imposes on the food business operator the responsibility to ensure that requirements of food law are met within the food business under their control (see Art. 3(3) Regulation 178/2002).

95 See Art. 5.3 of GPSD.

distributor does not have any safety obligation whilst being better equipped to be in charge of safety precautions).

This definition of distributor is in tension with other rules of the directives requiring distributors' participation in monitoring, and recognizing their importance in producing, collecting and transmitting information to the consumer and the producer.[96] Compliance with these duties can contribute to make the product safe. On the contrary, violation of these duties may make the product dangerous.[97] National authorities can require enterprises to warn consumers when there are reasonable grounds that a product can pose risks to all or certain categories of consumers.[98]

I turn to an examination of the potential effects of 'duties to inform' on the supply and distribution chain and the potential implications for a more general institutional design aimed at making information discovery and flow more effective.

A product can be deemed dangerous or unsafe if information is not adequately provided to consumers.[99] GPSD imposes duties to inform not only on producers but also on distributors to final consumers.[100] It also imposes

---

96 See Art. 5.2 of GPSD.

97 To solve this contradiction a review of the Directive is needed to rephrase the definition of distributor. Before then a functional approach should qualify as producers those who are generally considered distributors from an economic perspective whenever they are in the position to monitor products' safety.

98 See in General Product Safety Regulations 2005 (SI 2005/1803) reg. 13(1): 'Where an enforcement authority has reasonable grounds for believing that a product is a dangerous product in that it could pose risks for certain persons, the authority may serve a notice ("a requirement to warn") requiring the person on whom the notice is served at his own expense to undertake one or more of the following as specified in the notice:

(a) where and to the extent it is practicable to do so, to ensure that any person who could be subject to such risks and who has been supplied with the product be given warning of the risks in good time and in a form specified in the notice,
(b) to publish a warning of the risks in such a form and manner as is likely to bring those risks to the attention of any such person,
(c) to ensure that the product carries a warning of the risks in a form specified by the notice.'

99 See P. Cartwright, 'The regulation of product safety', in G. Howells, *The law of product liability* (Lexis-Nexis, 2007), pp. 734 ff; F. Cafaggi, 'Rethinking institutional complementarities', above n. 11, p. 214; S. Weatherill, *EU Consumer law and policy* (Edward Elgar, 2005), pp. 216 ff.

100 In relation to producers Art. 5.1 of GPSD correlates information duties and consumers' risk assessment and deterrence: 'Within the limits of their respective activities producers shall provide consumers with the relevant information to enable them

coordination mechanisms between parties operating in the chain and especially between producers and distributors.[101] Distributors are bound to gather information and transmit it to producers; producers are bound to inform distributors.[102] Both are obliged to inform the competent national authorities about risks concerning the safety of the product to be processed through the RAPEX system.[103] Uncertainty about who takes main responsibility may bring about coordination problems which are in some legal systems addressed by national authorities through their guidelines.[104] One of the most relevant questions is when a duty to inform the competent authorities arises and whether there is coincidence between this duty and the post-sale duties to inform regulated by the civil liability system and by contract rules.

Regulators have tried to define guidelines as to when information is to be transferred to combine the need to have a manageable system and that of protecting consumers as soon as risks become known.[105]

---

to assess the risks inherent in a product throughout the normal or reasonably foreseeable period of its use, where such risks are not immediately obvious without adequate warnings and to take precautions against those risks.' In relation to distributors Art. 5.2 of GPSD states 'Moreover, within the limits of their respective activities, they shall participate in monitoring the safety of products place on the market, especially by passing on information on product risks, keeping and providing documentation necessary for tracing the origin of products, and cooperating in the actions taken by producers and competent authorities to avoid the risks.'

101 Art. 5.2 of GPSD: 'Within the limits of their respective activities they shall take measures enabling them to cooperate efficiently.'

102 See again GPSD Art. 5.1 for producers and 5.2 for distributors.

103 See Art. 8 of GPSD.

104 See for example in the UK, DTI Guidance for business, consumers and enforcement authorities, August 2005, available at http://www.berr.gov.uk/consumers/Safety/products/index.html, para. 7.4.

105 'Producers and distributors should analyse the information collected and decide whether a particular hazardous situation should be notified to the authorities taking into account:

The gravity of the outcome of the hazard, depending on the severity and probability of the possible health and safety damage. Combining the severity and probability gives an assessment of the gravity of the risk. The accuracy of this assessment will depend upon the quality of the information available to the producer or the distributor.

The severity of health/safety damage for a given hazard should be that for which there is reasonable evidence that the health and safety damage attributable to the product could occur under foreseeable use. This could be the worst case from health and safety damages that have occurred with similar products.

The probability of health and safety damage for a normal user who has an exposure corresponded to the intended or reasonably expected use of the defective product has also to be considered as well as the probability of the product being or becoming defective.

The decision to notify should not be influenced by the number of products on the market or by the number of people who could be affected by a dangerous product.

There is not a necessary coincidence between the duty to inform consumers and the duty to report to the competent authority. Often the type of information and the ways to inform might have to be defined in a coordinated way and it might be advisable to report to the authority first and then decide which information is to be given to the public and how to define the appropriate means.

Monitoring techniques may differ according to each product.[106] They also depend on the qualification of 'dangerousness' provided by Article 8 of GPSD.[107]

These factors may be taken into account in deciding on the type of action to be taken to solve the problem.' See Commission Decision, 14.12.2004, laying down guidelines for the notification of dangerous consumer products to the competent authorities of the Member States by producers and distributors, in accordance with Article 5(3) of Directive 2001/95/EC of the European Parliament and of the Council, OJ L 381, 28.12.2004, p. 63.
Compare the elements listed in Europe by the Guidelines enacted by the European Commission in the framework of the Rapex system established with the GPSD with those defined by the Consumer Product Safety Commission in the US in the Recall Handbook (Recall Handbook, A Guide for Manufacturers, Importers, Distributors and Retailers on Reporting under Sections 15 and 37 of the Consumer and Product Safety Act, section II Identifying defect). 'In determining whether a risk of injury associated with a product could make the product defective, the Commission considers the following:

1) What is the utility of the product? What is it supposed to do?
2) What is the nature of the injury that the product might cause?
3) What is the need for the product?
4) What is the population exposed to the product and the risk of injury?
5) What is the Commission's experience with the product?
6) Finally what other information sheds light on the product and patterns of consumer use?'

Available at http://www.cpsc.gov/businfo/corrective.html.

[106] See C. Hodges, *European regulation of consumer product safety*, above n. 43 p. 129 ff.

[107] Art. 6 GPSD identifies six different categories:

a) any product
b) any product that could pose risks in certain conditions
c) any product that could pose risks for certain persons
d) any product that could be dangerous
e) any dangerous product
f) any dangerous product already in the market.

See for example in the UK, General Product Safety Regulations 2005 (SI 2005/1803) reg. 9:
'(1) Subject to paragraph (2) where a producer or a distributor knows that a product he has placed on the market or supplied poses risks to the consumer that are incompatible with the general safety requirement, he shall forthwith notify an enforcement authority in writing of that information and –

(a) the action taken to prevent risk to the consumer; and [...]

This web of duties to inform implies the design of an informational network that would process information in a rapid and effective way. In some legal systems it has been suggested that an internal coordinator in relation to product recall might be created.[108] It is important to point out the scope of these duties to inform. Not only do they refer to ex ante known risks but, and perhaps more importantly, they provide further incentives to the discovery of new risks and fast information processing.[109] It is mainly in relation to post-marketing 'duties to inform' that the creation of an efficient network becomes important.

GPSD focuses on the activity and does not address the means through which individual enterprises and the chain as whole should comply. When compliance with these duties is evaluated by judges it becomes clear that the inquiry moves to the mechanisms put in place to collect and transmit information.[110] It becomes necessary to explore the structure of the chain to evaluate how individual enterprises cooperate to ensure that duties to monitor and to inform are complied with.

A preliminary distinction, related to information production and transmission, concerns groups and networks.[111] In pyramidal groups, ownership control requires the adoption of an organizational structure that encompasses information production and transfer among the different participants. Unlike groups, networks – especially contractual ones – may lack an organizational form with ownership control.[112] This is more true for the production chain

---

(2) In the event of a serious risk the notification under paragraph (1) shall include the following

(a) information enabling a precise identification of the product or batch of products in question
(b) a full description of the risks that the product presents
(c) all available information relevant for tracing the product, and
(d) a description of the action undertaken to prevent risks to the consumer.'

108 See in the US the Handbook on Recall issued by the Consumer Product Safety Commission, above n. 105.

109 See Art. 5.3 of GPSD.

110 See C. Hodges, *European regulation of consumer product safety*, above n. 43 pp. 132 ff and 191 ff., describing the different criteria for evaluating post-marketing obligations of producers and distributors.

111 See for an introduction, E. Todeva, *Business networks* (Routledge, 2006), part. pp. 85 ff.; A. Grandori (ed.) *Inter-firm networks* (Routledge, 1999). For a more general framework see J. Zeitlin, 'Industrial districts and regional clusters', in J. Zeitlin, *Handbook of business history* (OUP, 2007); from a different perspective, M. Granovetter, 'Coase revisited: business groups in the modern economy', in G. Dosi, D. Teece, J. Chytry, *Technology, organization and competitiveness* (Oxford, 1998), pp. 67 ff.

112 On the definition of contractual networks, see F. Cafaggi, 'Contractual networks and the Small Business Act: towards European principles?', EUI working paper 2008/15.

(that is, subcontracting), less true for the distribution chain, where the contractual nature of the network implies a higher level of coordination, as in franchising and dealership.[113] I discuss the relationship between the decision-power allocation along the supply and distribution chain and product safety elsewhere.[114] In this context, I would only like to suggest that the organizational form of the chain affects (or should affect) the regulatory design concerning product safety, in particular duties to inform consumers and competent authorities, but symmetrically the regulatory design will influence the business model. The relevant question is whether the regulatory design should operate irrespective of the different business models or should be tailored to them, that is to say, are business models a relevant variable to define effective information systems about product safety?

The current approach of GPSD seems to ignore the differences among business models and apply to industrial chains which operate very differently. I suggest that business networks should be designed to ensure effective monitoring in product safety, thus taking into account the different organizational structures, distinguishing between big, medium and small enterprises. A specific policy for product safety in small and medium-sized enterprises (SMEs) may require different organizational networks from those operating for big multinationals.

It is important to distinguish between production and information transfer within different links in the chain and information networks aimed at communicating with the public. Firms have created various informational networks to ensure that information about safety products is produced and transferred in effective ways. Individual enterprises have to take measures enabling them to monitor the safety of the product. While no specifications are made in the directive about size of enterprises and especially in relation to distribution between wholesale and retail, national legal systems have recognized that differences may affect the expected standard and the type of internal organization set up to monitor product safety.[115]

---

113 For a comparison between networks and groups, see F. Cafaggi, *Reti di imprese tra regolazione e norme sociali* (Il Mulino, 2004). For a broad analysis of business networks, E. Todeva, *Business networks*, above n. 111 passim.

114 See F. Cafaggi, *The divergences between real industrial organisational forms and regulatory strategies concerning product safety. When theory departs from reality in institutional design*, unpublished manuscript.

115 In the UK these differences have been acknowledged by DTI Guidance suggesting agreements along the chain on who should make the notification. See DTI Guidance for businesses, consumers and enforcement authorities, above n. 104 p. 6.6. See also P. Cartwright, 'The regulation of product safety', above n. 42 pp. 738 ff.

In relation to the shape of networks aimed at producing and generating information within the chain, two main models can be identified:[116]

(a) hierarchical network
(b) horizontal network.

In the hierarchical network information gathered at different levels is all passed on to the producer who then conveys it to the relevant actors, both consumers and competent authorities. The hierarchy is relevant to decide which information should be transmitted, when the product-related risk is such that dissemination of information takes place within the group, and, in the case of multinationals, this can also be independent from any administrative action. Competent authorities proceed through a parallel process to gather and disseminate information about product risks. The relevant decision-making power to define which information should be disclosed and at what speed is left to the producer.

3.1 Hierarchical Network

Let us take the example of franchise. The information flows from the franchisees to the franchisor and then back to the franchisees; see Figure 7.1.

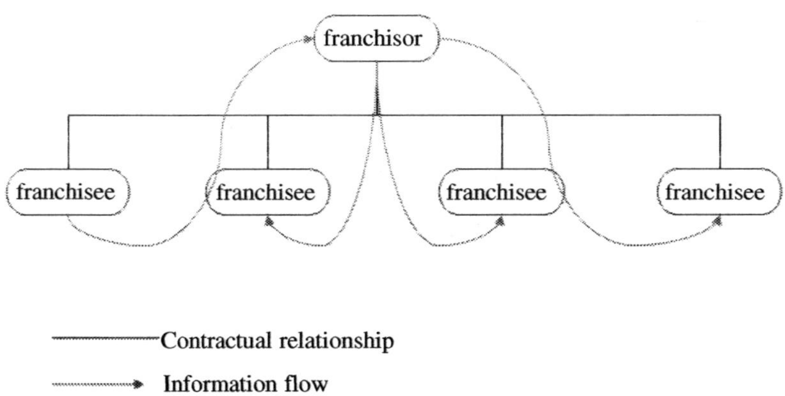

Figure 7.1 Hierarchical structure in franchising network

116 For a summary concerning different network configurations, see E. Todeva, *Business networks*, above n. 111 pp. 130 ff.

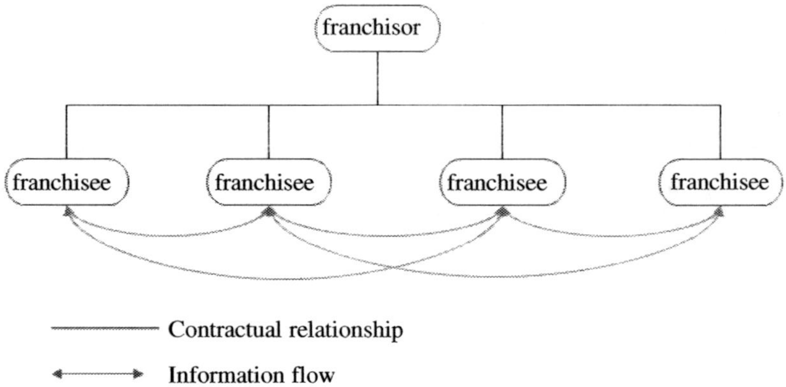

Figure 7.2 Horizontal structure in franchising network

3.2 Horizontal Network: Again the Example of Franchise

The information is exchanged directly among franchisees not necessarily after intermediation by the franchisor.

In the horizontal network data are shared by the different knots. For example in franchise, the franchisees communicate directly without the mediation of the franchisor. In a dealership organized as a horizontal network, the dealers communicate among themselves without the hierarchical intervention of the producer who may simply participate in the process.

3.3 Hierarchical and Horizontal Networks Considered

These networks are aimed at generating information, providing each enterprise along the chain with incentives to collect information and to define tools to detect new risks and assess known ones. The search for the most effective information producer can place higher burdens on one particular knot which, however, does not necessarily mean that it will bear the entire cost. Certainly, the structure of the GPSD suggests that producers may bear the higher costs of producing and distributing information.

The decision about the structure of the information network is driven by several interrelated factors. One is the liability regime if no information is collected and communicated, but others are related to the form of the chain and the decision-making power allocated along the chain. If market and contractual power is strongly asymmetric along the supply and distribution chain, it is likely that it would generate a hierarchical information network.

Conversely, if power is distributed relatively evenly, chances for a horizontal network to arise are relatively higher.

The main policy question for product safety is the extent to which these networks, contractually organized, should either only mirror the regulatory structure or enjoy some level of discretion internally to allocate burdens and costs so as to improve the final results: that is to say, effectiveness in producing and transmitting information about risks. In other words, should legislators and regulators define the shape of the network or should they only define their aims and leave parties the freedom to organize them?

The desirable policy is to define the goals and, accordingly, the liability system for non-compliance of information duties on producers and distributors, while leaving parties discretion to choose the most appropriate organizational form. To leave enterprises discretion does not mean that compliance evaluation should not take into account the adopted organizational model, how the network performed and which improvements can be made. The producer or the distributor could never use compliance with the chosen organizational model as a defence if information was not produced or effectively transmitted. Scrutiny of the organizational model to gather information should thus be allowed.

The current regime should thus introduce default rules concerning the network forms to be adopted to comply with information duties related to product safety.

The example of information networks in product safety shows how a specific regulatory strategy that imposes coordination to produce and transfer information about product risks, may affect the industrial structure and promote vertical and horizontal cooperation concerning safety matters. GPSD places the most relevant safety burdens on producers but imposes on distributors a fault-based duty to act when they know or should know that the product can be dangerous or unsafe.[117]

This organizational form is very important for networks where the product is manufactured and sold in Europe but may have relevant implications for transcontinental safety networks where production is partly developed outside Europe (Far East or South America) and thus safety control may be defined by different legal regimes and the importer would bear the costs of verifying compliance with European standards.

[117] See Art. 5.2 of GPSD: 'Distributors shall be required to act with due care to help to ensure compliance with the applicable safety requirements, in particular by not supplying products which they know or should have presumed, on the basis of information in their possession and as professionals, do not comply with those requirements.'

Following the toy recalls in summer 2007, the European Commission engaged in a wide-ranging stocktaking review on product safety and an audit of the business safety measures in the toy supply chain.[118]

The creation of these networks implies a relatively high investment, albeit not necessarily information-specific. Thus, the possibility of expanding the scope of the network for pure information collection and transfer to other safety aspects concerning risk-control should be explored.

The adoption of a network model for safety precaution would generate important benefits for the final consumer but also important positive externalities. To promote these networks may imply regulatory reforms. A change in both directives, PL and GPSD, should be made, reallocating the burden of safety control and risk detection among different actors through the definition of information networks.[119] This should occur by introducing default rules that design these safety networks and leave parties free to reallocate the burden in a more hierarchical way, concentrating the burden on few specific actors with some constraints if they so wish.

The freedom to use contracts in order to distribute burdens among parties should not lower the level of safety for the final consumers. Standards related to the network should thus be defined when the network form is adopted. These standards, which may include joint and several liabilities, should identify minimum rules that parties can specify through contracting.

To summarize, the general principle should define the safety and information duties while default rules can design the means to organize network forms tailored to different business models. The current stress on producers can be left in the text of the directive, but the artificial hierarchical model, implicitly stemming from the current text, should be corrected by introducing a more generalized horizontal network model including distributors and reflecting the different business forms of industrial chains. A default rule should introduce the concept of a safety network to allocate contractually control and information, leaving the enterprises belonging to the network the power to allocate the costs of detecting and controlling the risks. Participation in the product safety network will be defined by the structure of the chain and the contractual links among enterprises related to the product circulated in the market. The bound-

---

[118] See the speech of Commissioner for Consumer Protection, Meglena Kuneva 'Outcome of stocktaking review on consumer product safety', of 22 November 2007 available at http://europa.eu/rapid/pressReleasesAction.do?reference=SPEECH/07/741& format=HTML&aged=0&language=EN&guiLanguage=en.

[119] On these questions beyond the specific issue of product safety, see C. Sabel, 'A real time revolution in routines', in C. Heckscher and P. Adler, *The Firm as a Collaborative Community* (OUP, 2006), p. 106.

aries will thus be designed according to the product and the process of production and distribution.

The advantages of the network model primarily concern the possibility of defining incentives along the chain to produce and transfer information about product related risks, instead of placing the entire burden on the producer regardless of the real allocation of decision-making power. The current allocation, on the one hand, does not descriptively represent many current modes of allocating decision-making power; on the other hand, it may not efficiently allocate incentives to generate new information and to detect new risks to protect consumers effectively.

4. CONCLUDING REMARKS

This chapter has dealt with product safety and liability, looking in particular at the interaction between regulation, contract and civil liability. The main aim has been to suggest that risk definition, assessment and management in product safety has changed in the last 20 years and that a well-recognized role is played by private actors both in standard-setting, in monitoring and risk management concerning post-sale duties. Post-market surveillance has become a crucial part of the risk management strategies but the regulatory dimension has not been sufficiently linked with that of governance.

In the first part I have examined the current review of product safety at EU level with the proposed regulation on market surveillance and its relationship with the broader debate concerning better regulation.

In the second part, I have shown the increasing contractualization of standard-setting concerning safety and product defectiveness, which influences both regulation and civil liability systems. In both cases, however, insufficient attention has been given to the implications of such a contractualization for liability standards. Two sets of issues have been underlined:

(1). the lack of accountability of private regulators when defining technical and non-technical standards and the difficulty of subjecting this activity to the scrutiny of judicial review;
(2). the complementarity of regulation and liability is often not well designed. It is unclear when the standards are defined by private bodies how they should affect the definition of defect or when that of negligence and/or strict liability is not applicable.

Standard-setting may have different functions in the two fields due to institutional complementarity. However, often this differentiation is not well designed and it only emerges in its quantitative dimension: regulation defines minimum standards, liability may increase the standard, mainly for the purpose of compensating the victims.

I then moved on to information duties in product safety and product liability and claimed that business models of the supply and distribution chain may be affected by the regulatory design concerning product safety. I contended that a reform of the GPSD and PL directives should promote the creation of more structured information networks, aimed at making information production and transmission concerning product safety more effective. Enterprises should be constrained by the safety goals, but they should enjoy discretion in choosing organizational models that best fit with their business models. In particular the distinction between hierarchical and horizontal networks should be fruitfully employed to design default rules organizing the information safety network. This would be particularly important for pan-European networks which have to coordinate enterprises operating in different legal systems with different institutional frameworks. I propose that default rules be introduced concerning information networks that parties can adjust to their specific business models.

In this chapter I have shown that private law and regulation interplay in the field of product safety. Not only does it happen between administrative regulation and civil liability, as has long been recognized, but also with contract law, given the increasing contractualization of standard-setting and the necessity to build contractual networks to implement monitoring of product safety in modern market economies. These examples suggest that the current approach to harmonization of European private law is limited and does not reflect the necessity to coordinate different instruments to pursue unitary policy objectives: producing higher and more effective product safety in Europe at reasonable costs.

8. Interaction between product liability and regulation at the European level

Gerald Spindler

The chapter deals with types and modes of product safety regulation on the European as well as on national levels, demonstrating that on each level similar modes have arisen in the European Community. These governance structures make use of a mixed state-private norm approach which in fact mostly relies upon technical regulations enacted by competent private national or European standards organizations (for example German Institute for Standardisation (DIN); Association of German Engineers (VDI); European Committee for Standardisation (CEN); and European Committee for Electrotechnical Standardization (CENELEC)). In general, these regulations have a severe impact on product liability since they are considered as the minimum standard of care in terms of tort law.[1] However, courts are not bound by private set standards as they have no force of law.[2] Courts may demand higher standards than those laid down in private regulations and sometimes openly deviate from these standards.[3] Thus, a complex interaction between standards

---

1 Bundesgerichtshof of 18.5.1999, VI ZR 192/98, *Neue Juristische Wochenschrift (NJW)* 38 (1999), p. 2815 (2816); Spindler, Gerald (2003), in Bamberger, Heinz Georg and Roth, Herbert (eds), *Kommentar zum Bürgerlichen Gesetzbuch*, Munich, § 823, sec. 251; Wagner, Gerhard (2004), in Rebmann, Kurt, Säcker, Franz Jürgen and Rixecker, Roland, *Münchener Kommentar zum BGB*, Munich, § 823, sec. 272; Hager, Johannes (1999), in Staudinger, *Kommentar zum Bürgerlichen Gesetzbuch, Zweites Buch, Recht der Schuldverhältnisse*, Berlin, § 823, sec. G 34.

2 Bundesgerichtshof of 10 March 1987, VI ZR 144/86, *Neue Juristische Wochenschrift (NJW)* 36 (1987), pp. 2222, 2223; Vieweg, Klaus (2003), 'Produkthaftung', in Schulte, Martin (ed), *Handbuch des Technikrechts*, Berlin, Heidelberg, New York, p. 360; Spindler, Gerald (2003), in Bamberger, Heinz Georg and Roth, Herbert (eds), above n. 1 § 823, sec. 255.

3 Bundesgerichtshof of 12 November 1996, VI ZR 270/96, *Neue Juristische Wochenschrift (NJW)* 9 (1997), p. 582 (583); Bundesgerichtshof of 28 April 1987, VI ZR 127/86, *Neue Juristische Wochenschrift (NJW)* 1-2 (1988), p. 48 (49); von Bar, Christian, 'Entwicklungen und Entwicklungstendenzen im Recht der

as defined by courts and private set rules takes place. Intervention by European agencies is rare due to scarce resources and capacities to monitor in general different production sectors. However, in economic sectors which are not yet regulated we observe severe market failures, such as for IT-products. The specific framework and pitfalls of these markets will be analysed more in depth in this chapter, offering new insights as well as policy recommendations for IT-security and IT-regulation. In more general terms, the differences between sectors which are regulated by product safety and those which are not are highlighted, analysing the role which product liability can play in substituting (or not) product safety regulations.

I. INTRODUCTION

The interactions between product safety and product liability regulations on the European level have a long record, and much has been written about the different aspects of product safety regulations (and directives) as well as product liability directives. Hence, there seems to be no need to add just another publication to this vast amount of analysis as it is difficult to perceive at first glance which aspect could have been neglected so far.

However, not withstanding this bulk of highly intriguing articles, it is surprising that both sectors – product safety (public law) and product liability (private law) – are not closely interlaced. Interactions between both sectors are hardly discussed, impacts of standardization are scrutinized only separately. Thus, repercussions of one sector on the other are widely ignored. Moreover, it is striking that – as far as we can see – Europe still lacks a general approach for a comprehensive regulation scheme for both product safety and product liability, for example on the basis of economic analysis. Whereas American doctrine has developed some approaches that cover both public and private product safety/liability issues, the European version of interaction between these sectors obviously is still waiting for in-depth analysis.

This chapter intends to provide a tentative approach to this interrelationship (and interaction), in particular focusing on IT-products which are crucial for any developed economy today. We will identify the incentives for producers, IT-intermediaries, and consumers to care for safety measures and improvements of their products, thus showing pitfalls of the current regulations and of the interaction between public product safety and product liability regulations.

Verkehrs(sicherungs)pflichten', *Juristische Schulung (JuS)* 3 (1988), p. 169 (172); Hager, Johannes (1999), in Staudinger, above n. 1 § 823, sec. G 34; Spindler, Gerald (2003), in Bamberger, Heinz Georg and Roth, Herbert (eds), above n. 1 § 823, sec. 255.

II. PRODUCT SAFETY REGULATIONS – THE STATE OF THE ART

On a national level, product safety has been regulated in public law like the German 'Gerätesicherheitsgesetz'[4] for a long time. In general, these norms provided a set of rules for all producers regarding product safety, supplemented by technical standards for specific products set by hybrid state-private bodies. On the European level the European Commission soon realized that diverging technical standards and regulations in Member States meant a barrier to trade. In an effort to improve free movement of goods as stipulated in Article 30 of the Treaty establishing the European Economic Community (EEC Treaty, now Article 28 EC Treaty), the European Community initially followed a concept of full harmonization of all requirements relevant to a particular type of product. But soon the Commission realized that this way of proceeding could not succeed due to the inflexibility of European legislation which could not keep up with technological progress and changes. The concept of full harmonization failed. Following the ruling of the European Court of Justice in the 'Cassis de Dijon' case,[5] the Commission developed the principle of mutual recognition of national regulations which finally resulted in what is known today as the 'New Approach'.[6] The New Approach should soon become the predominant concept for product safety regulations.

1. European Harmonized Sector – the 'New Approach' of the 1980s

Following preliminary consultations, the European Commission introduced the so-called New Approach to technical harmonization and standards in the mid 1980s. This new regulatory technique and strategy – in a nutshell – is based on hybrid regulation:[7] essential requirements of product safety that are of public interest are harmonized in EU directives, unique requirements, however, are specified in technical standards (harmonized standards) set by

[4] Gesetz über technische Arbeitsmittel (Gerätesicherheitsgesetz) of 24 June 1968, *Bundesgesetzblatt I*, p. 717.

[5] Judgment of the Court of 20 February 1979, C-120/78, European Court Reports 1979, p. 649.

[6] Council Resolution of 7 May 1985 on a new approach to technical harmonization and standards, OJ C 136, p. 1; see also EC Commission, Guide to the Implementation of Directives based on the New Approach and the Global Approach, 2000, http://ec.europa.eu/enterprise/newapproach/legislation/guide/document/1999_1282_en.pdf, accessed 30 June 2006.

[7] In detail, EC Commission, Guide to the Implementation of Directives, above n. 6 .

private European standards organizations (CEN,[8] CENELEC,[9] ETSI[10]) which are officially mandated by the Commission. The harmonized standards are transposed into national standards by national standards organizations like 'Deutsches Institut für Normung e.V.' (DIN).[11]

Products manufactured in compliance with harmonized standards benefit from a presumption of conformity with the corresponding essential requirements.[12] Thus, conformity with these technical standards will relieve the producer of the burden of proof that his product meets all product safety demands. But technical standardization is no binding determination of product safety requirements. The application of harmonized standards remains voluntary. Only the essential safety levels aimed at in directives are mandatory and legally binding. For consumer protection purposes it is sufficient if producers attain this level of safety in deviation from technical standards. Therefore producers are free to deviate from harmonized standards as long as they meet the essential safety requirements as laid down in the directive. But if they do so, they carry the burden of proof for compliance with the directive's essential requirementss, because only manufacturing according to harmonized standards grants the presumption of conformity.[13]

The New Approach is completed by the Council Resolution on the 'Global Appoach to certification and testing' of 15 June 1989[14] which was transposed and updated by Council Decision 93/465/EEC of 22 July 1993.[15] Producers who make use of a certified quality management system benefit from a presumption that their products comply with all requirements of technical standards and the product safety directive.[16]

---

8 European Committtee for Standardization = Comité Européen de Normalisation, http://www.cenorm.be/cenorm/index.htm, accessed 30 June 2006.

9 European Committee for Electrotechnical Standardization = Comité Européen de Normalisation – Electrotechnique, http://www.cenelec.org/Cenelec/Homepage.htm, accessed 30 June 2006.

10 European Telecommunications Standards Institute, http://www.etsi.org/, accessed 30 June 2006.

11 http://www2.din.de/, accessed 30 June 2006.

12 See § 4 I Gesetz über technische Arbeitsmittel und Verbraucherprodukte (Geräte- und Produktsicherheitsgesetz – GPSG) of 6 January 2004, *Bundesgesetzblatt I*, p. 219, which implements Art. 3 II 2 of Directive 2001/95/EC of the European Parliament and of the Council of 3 December 2001 on general product safety, OJ L 11, p. 4.

13 Spindler, Gerald (2001), *Unternehmensorganizationspflichten*, Köln, Berlin, Bonn, München, Carl Heymanns, p. 160.

14 OJ C 267, p. 3.

15 OJ L 220, p. 23.

16 Spindler, Gerald (2001), see n. 13 above, p. 159.

2. The Non-harmonized (National) Sector – Old Rules still Prevailing

In contrast to the harmonized sectors, most national non-harmonized regulations do not solely rely on technical standards which are set by private bodies rather on standards drafted by mixed bodies which are composed both of industry and state representatives. German product safety in the non-harmonized sector still focuses on such standards ('Technische Regeln') which are adopted in a formal way by these standard-setting bodies.

The German 'Geräte- und Produktsicherheitsgesetz' of 6 January 2004[17] partially pursues a new regulative pattern on the national level that in a way conforms to the New Approach of the European Commission. A product in the non-harmonized sector is presumed safe concerning a particular safety requirement, if it complies with national technical standards drawn up by the Commission on technical work equipment and consumer products (Ausschuss für technische Arbeitsmittel und Verbraucherprodukte[18]) and published in the German Federal Gazette (Bundesanzeiger) by the Federal Agency for Employment Protection and Occupational Medicine (Bundesanstalt für Arbeitsschutz und Arbeitsmedizin[19]).[20] Following the European usage this concept is justifiably named the 'National New Approach'.[21]

However, the bulk of product safety related standards are still not linked formally to product safety regulations like those on the European level. Nevertheless, courts usually make use of technical standards as basic evidence for minimum safety standards.

Norm setting procedures and state involvement

Whereas this short glance at different approaches to standard setting suggests a clear and sharp distinction between private standard drafting and governmental bodies, the reality is far more complex: even if standardization is left to private organizations,[22] states like Germany have an interest in influencing

---

17 Gesetz über technische Arbeitsmittel und Verbraucherprodukte (Geräte- und Produktsicherheitsgesetz – GPSG) of 6 January 2004, *Bundesgesetzblatt I*, p. 219.

18 § 13 Gesetz über technische Arbeitsmittel und Verbraucherprodukte (Geräte- und Produktsicherheitsgesetz – GPSG) of 6 January 2004, *Bundesgesetzblatt I*, p. 219.

19 §§ 2 No. 14, 12 Gesetz über technische Arbeitsmittel und Verbraucherprodukte (Geräte- und Produktsicherheitsgesetz – GPSG) of 6 January 2004, *Bundesgesetzblatt I*, p. 219.

20 Klindt, Thomas, 'Das neue Geräte- und Produktsicherheitsgesetz', *Neue Juristische Wochenschrift (NJW)*, 8 (2004), p. 465 (467); Wilrich, Thomas (2004), *Geräte und Produktsicherheitsgesetz (GPSG)*, Berlin, § 4 sec. 43.

21 Klindt, Thomas, above n. 20, p. 465 (467).

22 The major standards organizations in Germany like 'Deutsches Institut für Normung e.V.' (DIN), ' Verband Deutscher Elektritechniker e.V.' (VDE) and 'Verband

the standardization process. Although standards organizations are organized in private forms, they execute versatile and tangible influence on the interests of the general public as technical standards – among other criteria – mould common safety expectations and ultimately concretize due diligence in civil law and act as guidelines for administrative decisions. Furthermore, the national interest follows from the need to provide for an adequate level of product safety and consumer protection as well as undisturbed competition. From a European perspective the need for governmental influence on standards can be derived from the obligation to reduce restrictions or measures having equivalent effect on the free movement of goods (Articles 28, 30 EC Treaty). Therefore it is accepted that there is a need for government influence on standardization,[23] which is executed by sending state representatives to standardization boards and suggesting certain product areas for standardization.[24]

III. PRODUCT SAFETY LAW, STANDARDS, AND TORT LAW

The picture of interaction between legal regulations and private standard settings gets even more complex if we take into account private law, in particular tort law.

First, public product safety law can enable product users and bystanders to claim for damages on grounds of infringement of a protective statute. Product safety law can be qualified as legal norms envisaging the protection of individuals. In Europe, some jurisdictions, that do not follow the French approach of a general clause,[25] grant specific tort actions for unlawful violations of legal provisions aimed at the protection of other indiviuals.[26] Examples of this regu-

Deutscher Ingenieure e.V.' (VDI) are organized as private registered associations ('Eingetragener Verein', e.V.). See in extenso, Marburger, Peter (1979), *Die Regeln der Technik im Recht*, Köln, Berlin, Bonn, München, pp. 195 ff.

[23] Marburger, Peter (1979), above n. 22, p. 588 ff.

[24] For alternative approaches, see Marburger, Peter (1979), above n. 22, pp. 603 ff.

[25] See Arts. 1382 and 1383 French Code civil and corresponding Arts. 1382, 1383 Belgian Code civil and Arts. 1151, 1152 Italian Codice civile.

[26] The German product safety legislation is generally characterized as protective law. For the Gesetz über technische Arbeitsmittel und Verbraucherprodukte (Geräte- und Produktsicherheitsgesetz – GPSG) of 6 January 2004, *Bundesgesetzblatt I*, p. 219, which implements Directive 2001/95/EC of the European Parliament and of the Council of 3 December 2001 on general product safety, OJ L 11, p. 4, see Potinecke, Harald, 'Das Geräte- und Produktsicherheitsgesetz', *Der Betrieb (DB)* 1 (2004), p. 55 (60); Spindler, Gerald, 'IT-Sicherheit und Produkthaftung – Sicherheitslücken, Pflichten der Hersteller und der Softwarenutzer', *Neue Juristische Wochenschrift*

lative concept are the tort laws of Germany[27] and Portugal.[28] Although product safety law primarily aims at administrative procedures and powers to enforce product safety and therefore serves the public interest, it also envisages the protection of individuals.

In default of legislative power of standards organizations, privately set technical standards cannot be seen as legal norms.[29] Thus a violation of technical standards is not tantamount to a violation of protective law. But technical standards may be of relevance for claims based on the violation of protective statutes, as far as legal norms refer to a particular standard.[30] Even then technical standards remain a kind of mere recommendation[31] for the manufacturing of products, without any legal force.[32] But the technical standards referred to are qualified for substantiating the requirements laid down in the protective statute.[33] A producer whose products comply with these technical standards benefits from advantages within the realms of burden of proof, as compliance indicates that a product meets all the statute's safety requirements. However, a reference to technical standards in public product safety law does not necessarily mean a ban on alternative manufacturing solutions. The producer may well deviate from the specifications in technical standards and apply other specifications as long as the product meets all safety requirements as regulated in public product safety law. In individual cases, public product safety law may force particular safety measures. This means that a

---

(NJW) 44 (2004), p. 3145 (3149). For § 3 Gerätesicherheitsgesetz, which was replaced by the Geräte- und Produktsicherheitsgesetz; see Bundesgerichtshof of 28 March 2006, VI ZR 46/05, *Versicherungsrecht (VersR)* 15 (2006), pp. 710–712 and Bundesgerichtshof of 18 January 1983, VI ZR 270/80, *Versicherungsrecht (VersR)* 14 (1983), p. 346 (347).

27 § 823 II Bürgerliches Gesetzbuch.

28 Art. 483 I Código civil.

29 Bundesgerichtshof of 10 March 1987, VI ZR 144/86, *Neue Juristische Wochenschrift (NJW),* 36 (1987), p. 2222 (2223); Vieweg, Klaus (2001), 'Produkthaftung', in Schulte, Martin (ed), above n. 2, p. 363; Marburger, Peter (1979), above n. 22, p. 475; Jürgens, Andreas (1995), *Technische Standards im Haftungsrecht*, Göttingen, p. 67; Spindler, Gerald (2003), in Bamberger, Heinz Georg and Roth, Herbert (eds), above n. 1 § 823, sec. 152; Wagner, Gerhard (2004), in Rebmann, Kurt, Säcker, Franz Jürgen and Rixecker, Roland, above n. 1 § 823, sec. 326.

30 In detail Marburger, Peter (1979), above n. 22 pp. 379 ff., 475 ff.

31 Bundesgerichtshof of 14 May 1998, VII ZR 184/97, *Neue Juristische Wochenschrift (NJW)* 38 (1998), p. 2814 (2815); Hager, Johannes (1999), in Staudinger, above n. 1 § 823, sec. G 13.

32 Marburger, Peter (1979), above n. 22 p. 476.

33 Vieweg, Klaus (2001), 'Produkthaftung', in Schulte, Martin (ed), above n. 2 p. 363; Foerste, Ulrich (1997) in Graf v. Westphalen, Friedrich, *Produkthaftungshandbuch,* Volume 1, 2nd edition, § 32 sec. 3; Marburger, Peter (1979), above n. 22 p. 476.

producer can comply with safety requirements only by applying the manufacturing standards referred to in the legal norm.[34] On the other hand, the producer is relieved from the allegation of having violated the duty of care even if the technical standard is outdated. A legal order cannot hold an act unlawful that is governed by legal norms.

Second, the interactions between product safety (and private standards) and private law are not limited to the qualification of public legal regulations as norms relevant for tort claims. Product safety regulations and private standards are commonly qualified as a *de minimis* standard whose violation constitutes per se negligent behaviour.[35] Although the producer may in theory provide evidence that he or she has opted for other solutions which are equivalent from the perspective of product safety, courts often rely upon private standards as representing the minimum standard. Thus in practice courts tend to hold producers liable if producers have failed to comply with these technical standards. Even if product liability does not refer to notions of negligence rather than to strict liability, courts make use of private standards in order to specify the expected level of safety.[36] Thus, private standards have a double role in product liability, denoting the required level of safety as well as of care.

However, civil courts usually claim that they assess independently the appropriateness of privately set standards to specify safety minimum standards without being bound by administrative legal regulations or private standard-setting procedures. Thus, even if producers prove compliance with private standards, judges may consider these standards inadequate for several reasons:[37]

---

[34] Foerste, Ulrich (1997), see n. 33 above § 24 sec. 45 f.

[35] Bundesgerichtshof of 17 January 1984, VI ZR 35/85, *Versicherungsrecht (VersR)* 11 (1984), pp. 270, 271; Vieweg, Klaus (2001), 'Produkthaftung', in Schulte, Martin (ed), above n. 2 p. 361; Foerste, Ulrich (1997) in Graf v. Westphalen, Friedrich, *Produkthaftungshandbuch*, Volume 1, § 24 sec. 39; Wagner, Gerhard (2004), in Rebmann, Kurt, Säcker, Franz Jürgen and Rixecker, Roland, above n. 1 § 823, sec. 326.

[36] See § 3 I Gesetz über die Haftung für fehlerhafte Produkte (Produkthaftungsgesetz – ProdHaftG) of 15 December 1989 and Art. 6 Council Directive 85/374/EEC of 25 July 1985 on the approximation of the laws, regulations and administrative provisions of the Member States concerning liability for defective products; Jürgens, Andreas (1995), above n. 29 pp. 72 f.; Vieweg, Klaus (2001), 'Produkthaftung', in Schulte, Martin (ed), above n. 2 pp. 363 f.; Graf von Westphalen (1999) in Graf von Westphalen, Friedrich, *Produkthaftungshandbuch*, Volume 2, § 74 sec. 14.

[37] In detail Vieweg, Klaus (2001), 'Produkthaftung', in Schulte, Martin (ed), above n. 2 p. 360.

- First, the standards may be outdated as they are overtaken by recent scientific developments[38] or because they had been mainly interest driven, giving (some) producers unjustified privileges by stating obsolete technical standards.[39]
- Second, standards may not cover all potential scenarios which could endanger third parties.[40]

Thus, courts often impose additional obligations upon producers, in particular to supervise the development of technical progress affecting their products and to analyse the specific dangers which may arise from the specific use of their products by third parties. In consequence, even if private standards are officially acknowledged by the European Commission, civil courts may qualify the compliance of a producer with these private standards as insufficient.

In sum, the interaction between product safety and private standards on one hand and civil law on the other hand, in particular product liability, is complex and not one-sided. The judgment of a civil court concerning a private standard as not being representative of minimum standards may soon lead to a review of such a standard. Producers cannot restrict their actions to compliance with private standards; rather they have to conduct research and to observe markets and to monitor their products for subsequent dangers.

So far, the picture of interactions between product safety and product liability corresponds to the traditional outlines: public law denoting the minimum level of safety, private standards specifying them, civil (tort) law looking into the particular circumstances and fine tuning the obligations of producers. Also, from a more economic perspective the incentive structures seem to be well balanced:

- Public law is restricted to formulate the basic requirements, administrative procedures are limited to the protection of most crucial public or individual goods such as life and health, given the limited resources of public authorities to enforce general public safety regulations.
- Technical standard-setting is left to private agencies with a right to veto for public authorities, thus preventing evident interest capturing activities, whereas in principle standards could be more easily adapted to recent developments as well as to specific needs.

---

38 Ibid.

39 Spindler, Gerald (2003), in Bamberger, Heinz Georg and Roth, Herbert (eds), above n. 1 § 823, sec. 255; Vieweg, Klaus (2001), 'Produkthaftung', in Schulte, Martin (ed), above n. 2 p. 360.

40 Vieweg, Klaus (2001), 'Produkthaftung', in Schulte, Martin (ed), above n. 2 pp. 360 f.

- Civil law fine tunes the balance between producers and third parties filling in the gaps left by public law and technical standards and establishing incentives for producers to take care of dangers themselves.

At first glance, this structure obviously covers all the needs of economy and society to provide for a sufficient level of product safety. However, this balance assumes that product safety and product liability regulations cover all relevant damages and dangers, thus complementing each other. Whereas for most products this assumption is true, it fails for some crucial products, such as software which rules all sectors of life today.

IV. PITFALLS FOR PRODUCT SAFETY: THE IT-SECTOR

The actual relevance of IT-products is obvious: there is scarcely any sector of life which is not controlled or managed with the help of IT-products. Be it the control of highway traffic or hospital operations, be it exams at the university or financial transactions, all are managed by means of IT-products. On the other side, due to the Internet and to open networks IT-products are today a vulnerable target for any sort of malicious attacks, ranging from denial-of-service attacks to viruses and worms.

Hence, safety of IT-products plays a dominant role in the economy, comparable to energy or finance sectors. Therefore, due to the overall public interest in safe software we should expect a considerable part of IT-products to be governed by product safety regulations; however, things look different as there are scarcely any product safety regulations at all. What is more, product liability fails largely to cover the gaps left by public law.

1. (Non-) Regulation of Product Safety in the IT-Sector

A short glance at regulations on the European level reveals that there are hardly any specific regulations at all. Notwithstanding so-called embedded systems which are used in robotic machines and specific areas such as medicine products, IT-products are not specifically dealt with by European regulations. This might be no surprise as IT-products are multifunctional, whereas the bulk of European regulations concentrate on specific areas or products with well-defined usages. However, even for specific purposes regulations are scarcely to be found. Regarding the regulation of specific activities such as the banking or insurance sector, IT-specific requirements are still the exception.

Even national regulations seldom address the issue of IT-product safety. As far as we can see for Germany there are hardly any product safety regulations to be found that refer to IT-products. The situation does not seem to alter much for other member states such as Austria, Sweden, or the UK. Only for specific activities or sectors like banking are there some hints as to IT-product safety requirements or IT-related organizational duties such as IT-risk management according to ISO 27001.

Finally, general product safety regulations such as Directive 2001/95/EC[41] do not refer to IT-product specific risks or damages. Moreover, this directive is limited to particular damage such as life, health, or property related damage (for consumers), so that the bulk of damage caused by IT-products – 'pure' economic losses – is seldom covered.[42] In particular, it is still being debated whether the notion of 'property' encompasses intangible goods such as personal data or data in general.[43]

In sum, producers of IT-products in principle do not have to comply with specific product safety regulations. Only in some specific cases, such as banking or the insurance industry, are there some more or less general allusions to IT-specific requirements for safety.

2. Sufficient Incentives by Product Liability?

Given these weak incentives by public law and the weak public controls over IT-production, we should expect product liability to step in as the fine tuning tool to guarantee sufficient product safety levels. However, with respect to IT-products we are again faced with a narrow range of product liability norms. Most European jurisdictions restrict the application of torts to injuries of certain goods which are the object of legal protection such as life, health, or property.[44] Even jurisdictions which follow a more general approach like the French system and make use of a general clause, finally restrict tort claims to such injuries by other means.[45] The German system might be considered to be representative of the other systems (like Austria, Sweden, Belgium etc.).

The crucial issue for product liability in the digital age concerns the qualification of property and related innominate rights/goods. If we can treat data as an emanation of property[46] then there are good reasons to allow tort claims against IT-producers in the case of failing software. However, even then we

---

41 Directive 2001/95/EC of the European Parliament and the European Council of 3 December 2001 on general product safety, OJ L 11, p. 4.

42 Wilrich, Thomas (2004), above n. 20 sec. 4 and sec. 6.

43 A summary of the discussion is provided by Spindler, Gerald (2003), in Bamberger, Heinz Georg and Roth, Herbert (eds), above n. 1 § 823, sec. 93 f.

44 See for example the main provision concerning torts in Germany, § 823 BGB.

45 von Bar, Christian (1998), *The Common European Law of Torts*, Volume One, Munich, sec. 14.

46 Most German authors consider only the storage medium as a part of property, e.g. Hager, Johannes (1999), in Staudinger, above n. 1 § 823, sec. B 60 and B 192.

could not tackle simple malfunctions of software that can lead in the end to a complete shut down of plants (or traffic etc.). Such damage is still treated by most jurisdictions as pure economic loss for which there is no relief outside contract law.[47]

Moreover, in order to distinguish tort law from contract law, obligations under tort law are restricted in principle to saving the customer from risks by simply warning and instructing him or her.[48] It is difficult to conceive a claim on the grounds of tort law which addresses expenses and costs of repairing malfunctioning software; these claims are usually based on contractual obligations. Hence, there is in principle no obligation on IT-producers to provide the usual patches for software for the customer as these are related to 'Softwarepflege' the usual software support.

On the other hand, contractual liability does not provide incentives for IT-producers as usually only contracting parties, in this case retailers, could be held responsible for damage resulting from failing software. Most jurisdictions, however, require for these damage claims that the retailer acted negligently;[49] but as most retailers do not have the knowledge to assess the quality of software codes and their proper functions it would not be easy to file such a suit. Indeed, in practice we rarely observe damage claims against retailers.[50] Only if software has been developed individually for a customer are there some cases which allow damage claims by the customer.[51]

In sum, with respect to product liability IT-producers also have few incentives to provide sufficient product safety in their products such as software.

---

[47] For Germany: Hager, Johannes (1999), in Staudinger, above n. 1 §§ 823 ff., sec. 20, sec. B 53 and sec. B 192; Larenz, Karl (1987), *Lehrbuch des Schuldrechts*, Band I Allgemeiner Teil, 14th edition, Munich, § 9 I c, § 24 I a; Larenz, Karl and Canaris, Claus-Wilhelm (1994), *Lehrbuch des Schuldrechts*, Volume II/2 Besonderer Teil, 13th edition, Munich, § 75 I 3 b; Picker, Eduard, Positive Forderungsverletzung und culpa in contrahendo – Zur Problematik der Haftungen "zwischen" Vertrag und Delikt', *Archiv für die civilistische Praxis,* 183 (1983), p. 369 (470 ff). Concerning Portugal: von Bar, Christian (1998), above n. 45, sec. 22-23. Greece: von Bar, Christian (1998), above n. 45 sec. 19. Italy: von Bar, Christian (1998), above n. 45, sec. 20-21. Netherlands: von Bar, Christian (1998), above n. 45 sec. 24-25. France: von Bar, Christian (1998), above n. 45 sec. 14.

[48] In German tort law, these obligations are called *Verkehrspflichten* or *Verkehrssicherungspflichten.* A detailed view of these obligation is given by Hager, Johannes (1999), in Staudinger, above n. 1 § 823, sec. E; Spindler, Gerald (2003), in Bamberger, Heinz Georg and Roth, Herbert (eds), above n. 1 § 823, sec. 23 to 25, 510 to 520.

[49] In German contract law § 280 BGB stipulates this fundamental rule.

[50] One of the rare examples in German jurisdiction is Landgericht Bonn of 27 February 2004, 10 O 618/03.

[51] An example in the German jurisdiction is Oberlandesgericht Köln of 10 March 2006, 19 U 160/05.

One consequence which can be observed in practice are 'Softwarepflegeverträge', contracts about software support, in order to adapt software to new risk potentials or new developments in its environment.

3. The Role of Standards

What then is the role of standards in this scenario? As we have already seen private standards often are the missing link between fundamental product safety and liability regulations, specifying the necessary level of safety as well as of care. However, it is striking that even on the level of private standards there is little to be reported of standards which could govern IT-product safety. Whereas most sectors of the economy are covered by a wide range of private standards for all kinds of products, software is seldom regulated by private standards. To be sure, some standards have evolved over time; however, their character differs widely from the traditional standards as they consist in general of two parts: first, generally accepted procedures to evaluate the security of a software, the so-called 'Common Criteria', second, individually shaped 'Protection Profiles' that describe the specific usage of the software. Only by the combination of both standards can software be 'standardized' and in consequence certified. This highlights the fundamental dilemma of software products: in contrast to most other products they are usually multifunctional so that it is difficult to define a minimum safety standard. Whereas 'normal' private standards may be used to define the minimum level of care or of product safety, IT-standards could seldom be used without assessing the individual risks of the customer/user. Hence, it is difficult for courts to conceive these standards as setting specifications of a general nature.

On the other hand, we observe trends to incorporate IT-risks into standardizations of risk management, such as the recently adopted ISO 27001 as a fundamental standard for IT-risk management. However, these standards are usually applicable on the customer's side and part of their overall risk management obligation; they do not solve the dilemma of multifunctional software.

4. Who Should be Held Liable?

IT-products are complex. Sometimes it has even been argued that product liability could not be applied to IT-products as today there is no chance of producing IT-software without any bugs.[52] Hence, IT-producers would not

[52] See e.g. Gorny, Peter (1985), 'Fehlerhafte Software – Einige Gedanken aus Sicht der Informatik', in Gorny, Peter and Kilian, Wolfgang (eds), *Computer-Software und Sachmängelhaftung*, Stuttgart, p. 15. German jurisdiction and doctrine also accepts the inevitability of software bugs, e.g. Bundesgerichtshof of 4 November 1987, VIII

face any or only a restricted liability for their products. However, waiving any liability for producers would go too far and would not correspond to the sophisticated system of product liability which is based on negligence and can be adapted to specific situations and products.[53]

On the other hand, flaws in IT-products may induce dangers anywhere in the IT-network such as hacker attacks on an IT-provider platform. In other words, issues of liability (and responsibility) cannot be reduced to the simple question as to whether the producer is the one to be held liable rather than splitting up liability along the value chain of IT. Whereas IT-producers are being held liable for construction faults and for shortcomings concerning the use of their products, IT-providers have to provide a sufficient level of safety in their operating networks. In other words, IT-providers have to supervise their systems in order to detect any flaws of the IT-products in use; they have to enhance their safety measures according to the rise of new dangers.[54]

Last but not least customers are not exempted from all obligations: depending upon their knowledge and capacities they are obliged to take measures to protect themselves against well-known dangers. Of course, private customers may not be obliged to install highly complex defensive systems rather than widely used software such as virus-scanners.[55] On the other side, highly sophisticated users like banks can employ vast resources to cope with IT-problems, for instance by establishing IT-departments or contracting for

---

ZR 314/86, *Neue Juristische Wochenschrift (NJW)* 7 (1988), p. 406 (408); Oberlandesgericht Düsseldorf of 18 October 1990, 6 U 71/87, *Computer & Recht (CR)* 12 (1992), p. 724; Oberlandesgericht Hamburg of 9 August 1985, 11 U 209/84, *Computer & Recht (CR)* 2 (1986), p. 83 (84); Köhler, Helmut and Fritzsche, Jörg (1993), 'Die Herstellung und Überlassung von Software im bürgerlichen Recht', in Lehmann, Michael, *Rechtsschutz und Verwertung von Computerprogrammen*, 2nd edition, Köln, Otto Schmidt, p. 513 (556).

53 See Oberlandesgericht Stuttgart of 6 May 1994, 2 U 275/93, *Computer & Recht (CR)* 5 (1995), p. 269; Bydlinski, Peter (1998), Der Sachbegriff im elektronischen Zeitalter: zeitlos oder anpassungsfähig?', *Archiv für die civilistische Praxis* 198 (1998), p. 287 (323); Marly, Jochen (2004), *Softwareüberlassungsverträge*, Munich, C.H. Beck, sec. 840.

54 For contract liability of Internet Service Providers, see Spindler, Gerald (2004), 'Vertrag mit dem Endkunden', in Spindler, Gerald (ed.), *Vertragsrecht der Internetprovider*, Köln, pp. 239–512.

55 For the obligation to take measures against dialler software, see Bundesgerichtshof of 4 March 2004, III ZR 96/03, *Neue Juristische Wochenschrift (NJW)* 22 (2004), 1590; for further details concerning obligations of private users, see also Koch, Robert, 'Haftung für die Weiterverbreitung von Viren durch E-Mails', *Neue Juristische Wochenschrift (NJW)* 12 (2004), pp. 801–807; Libertus, Michael (2005), 'Zivilrechtliche Haftung und strafrechtliche Verantwortlichkeit bei unbeabsichtigter Verbreitung von Computerviren', *Multimedia und Recht (MMR)* 8 (2005), pp. 507–512.

experts outside the company. In other words, we could expect far more protective measures from a bank than from a private customer.[56]

Hence, in a nutshell, we are facing a complex system of interacting obligations and responsibilities which should match each other in order to guarantee 'at the end of the pipeline' a sufficient level of safety for the whole IT-network. Such a distribution of responsibilities and obligations along the IT-chain would also reflect the widely accepted principle of economic analysis of law that the cheapest cost avoider should take the risks and obligations. The obligations are specified and distributed according to the ability of each producer to control production, operating systems, or the specific use of an IT-product.

However, as we have demonstrated already, incentives by product liability and safety regulations are not strong enough for IT-producers; this is made even worse if we take into account IT-providers as they benefit largely from legal exceptions or privileges concerning liability for any damages occurring due to flaws of their operating systems.

V CONCLUSION: SUB-OPTIMAL LEVEL OF PRODUCT SAFETY INCENTIVES

If we turn again to the overall picture of product safety and liability, we have to assert that incentives to provide for sufficient safety are still restricted to injuries and damage related to life, health, and property. However, a vast majority of products and services today are based upon IT-products; thus, deficiencies in the safety of IT-products directly affect safety and the proper function of other value chains in the economy. According to this eminent role of IT-products we should then expect sufficient incentives for all players involved in the IT-chain. However, we note that most of these players, like IT-producers and IT-providers, do not face strong incentives from liability rules or safety regulations to care for product safety, as in most cases only economic loss could be claimed which is not addressed by product liability rules. Moreover, contractual liability often fails to provide incentives for IT-producers or IT-providers as they benefit from contractual or even legal liability disclaimers.

How could this pitfall be addressed by an interaction between product liability and product safety? If we accept that IT-security is a publicly accepted

56 For the financial sector there are several special obligations. According to § 25a Kreditwirtschaftsgesetz (KWG) and § 31 Wertpapierhandelsgesetz (WpHG) banks have to take adequate safety measures for their IT-systems.

goal and necessary for the national economy and if we do not want to change tort law in general (by incorporating economic losses in principle), we have to turn to product safety regulations. By means of setting basic product safety standards IT-security may even cover economic losses. As these regulations could be qualified as norms protecting individuals, they could act as well on the public legal level as on the civil law level (tort law). Thus, by interaction between both European regulation areas incentives might be set appropriately, also avoiding enforcement problems which reveal themselves if a regulation is left solely to public law.

9. Impact of the mutual recognition principle on the law applicable to products

Mathias Audit

I. INTRODUCTION

In the main legal tradition, there is a border that is nearly impassable between the fields of public law on the one hand and private law on the other. This strict separation occurs in the theory of private international law. Scholars traditionally consider that the conflict of legal rules[1] only concerns the field of private law. At a pinch, a specific public law rule would be considered as a mandatory rule within a private law dispute.[2] But it is widely accepted that there is no conflict of laws between the public law rules of different states.

However, this traditional point of view is now contradicted by facts, due to the particular angle of EC law. One of the main goals of European legal rules is to build an integrated market within the European territory, allowing in particular goods to move freely between the member states. This free movement of goods is supposed to promote efficiency in production because it will permit producers in different countries to compete directly with each other. From that specifically economic angle, the distinction between public and private law that exists in the national legal systems of the member states is partially, if not totally, irrelevant. National legal rules of member states are subject to the edification of the internal market, wherever they belong to one branch or the other of the so-called *summa divisio* between private and public law.

Products are a perfect example of this challenge to the public/private law distinction within the private international law field, as an effect of EC rules

1 See, eg, Audit B. (2006), *Droit international privé*, Paris, France: Economica, p. 110; Mayer P. and Heuzé V. (2007), *Droit international privé*, Paris, France: Montchrestien, p. 100.

2 Muir Watt H. & Radicati di Brozolo L.G. (2004), 'Party Autonomy and Mandatory Rules in a Global World', *International Law FORUM du droit international*, 2 (6), 90–96.

on the free movement of goods. To understand it, it should be recognized that in every member state of the European Union, two different branches of law deal with products. The first is essentially about rules of public law: they deal with safety regulations, administrative authorizations, prudential supervision or product quality. The second one is more about private law rules: they deal with tort in general and product liability in particular.

But, at the end of the day, those two types of legal rules share the same goal: the safety and satisfaction of consumers. They aim to avoid dangerous or inappropriate products being sold to consumers. Their economic impact for the producer is also quite similar. Cost prices of products have to include charges incurred by the enforcement of the public law rules mentioned above, such as safety regulations for example. From a certain point of view, these cost prices might also take account of the eventuality of liability proceedings and their financial consequences.

It is obvious that this economic impact is less certain for the producer than the one resulting from the enforcement of public law regulations. For producers, it is compulsory to respect legal provisions in matters of safety regulations or product quality, if they wish to sell their items in all legality. This expense cannot be spared without acting unlawfully. But, regarding tort legal actions, producers can bank on the lack of legal proceedings. However, as product liability has gained prominence over the past 50 years, this could prove a very risky gamble. The US experience shows that the liability risks have been included in American firms' transactions costs for a long time,[3] even though the punitive damages system that does not exist in Europe increases the financial risk on the other side of the Atlantic. It is even said that liability risk associated with the punitive damages system is burdensome for the American economy.

For a European producer, something else is at stake: the diversity of national legal systems. Producers and manufacturers selling in their own country have only to take account of their own national public law rules and their own national tort law rules. But when they are selling throughout Europe or to other EU member states, their transaction costs rise. They should include information and enforcement charges on as many public law regulations and tort legal rules as the number of European countries in which their products are available.

This situation contradicts the edification of an integrated market within the European territory, which is one of the main goals of the European Union. As mentioned by Article 3(1)(c) of the Treaty establishing the European

[3] Silva F. & Cavaliere A. (2000), 'The Economic Impact of Product Liability: Lessons from the US and the EU Experience' in G. Galli and J. Pelkmans (Eds.), *Regulatory Reform and Competitiveness in Europe*, Cheltenham, UK: Edward Elgar.

Community, the internal market is 'characterized by the abolition, as between Member States, of obstacles to the free movement of goods, persons, services and capital'. Article 14(2) reiterates that 'the internal market shall comprise an area without internal frontiers in which the free movement of goods, persons, services and capital is ensured'.

But because of the coexistence of diverse national legal systems within the European Union, selling products in the member state where they have been produced and selling them in another member state do not generate the same cost prices for manufacturers and producers. Prices of exported products should include charges arising from information about the host member states' public law regulations and tort law and their enforcement. Therefore, from this point of view, the European market is not totally equivalent to a national market. There is a market failure due to distorted competition between local producers and those based in other member states.

As this situation is not acceptable with regard to the edification of a European integrated market, a solution to this situation has been founded in the idea that an economic activity developed under the auspices of a member state must be able to be deployed throughout the internal market under the governance of the legal rules imposed by its state of origin.[4] In particular, the free movement of goods principle laid down by EC rules would imply an identical movement of certain legal rules of the member state from which they emanate. As an exported product crosses the border between the state where it has been produced and the country where it will be available and sold to consumers, some legal rules will cross it as well.

A comparison can be drawn here with an old civil law theory. In this theory, some legal actions are transmitted with the sale of goods. In some ways, they are attached to the goods. French scholars speak of appurtenance to the goods ('*accessoire de la chose*').[5] With this theory, the legal action is transmitted from the seller to the buyer and, eventually, to another buyer, and so on. Regarding the free movement of goods, the important aspect is that the legal rules are attached to the goods. To draw an analogy between this old civil law theory and the selling of products within the European Union territory, it can be considered that, with the free movement of goods, different laws from the state where the product is made are attached to it. They cross borders within the European Union as well as the product itself. They become accessories of the product being sold.

The general idea of this study is to analyse and to evaluate the relevance of

---

4 Audit M. (2006), 'Régulation du marché intérieur et libre circulation des lois', *Journal du droit international*, 133, 1333–1363.

5 Aubry C. & Rau C. (1961), *Cours de droit civil français d'après la méthode de Zachariæ, t. II: Biens*, Paris: Libr. techniques, § 176, n° 69.

this trans-border movement of legal rules between the home country of the producer or the manufacturer and the target country with regard to the edification of the internal market. As it affects international transactions and the laws applicable to them, links between this theory and conflict of laws cannot be ignored either.

II. INTRA-EU MOVEMENT OF THE HOME COUNTRY PUBLIC LAW REGULATIONS AS A FIRST STEP

As mentioned above, producers or manufacturers are subject in their home member state to different public law provisions, which regulate their activities. These provisions impose safety regulations or administrative authorizations of whatever kind upon them. But to obtain access to a targeted market of another member state, the manufacturing firm would normally have to enforce public law provisions similar to those in force in that country.

However, the construction by EC law of an internal market is based on the will to break down national trade barriers in order to facilitate access for economic operators located throughout the Community. In a way, the enforcement of safety regulations, prudential supervision or product quality by the host country could be seen as a trade barrier. It is for that purpose that the mutual recognition principle has been developed since the *Cassis de Dijon* case.[6]

In fact, initially, the public law regulations of the country where the products were produced had no real importance in establishing a solution. In this case, as in those that followed, the European Court of Justice has aimed to break down the rules of the country of destination of the products impeding access to its market. In the *Cassis de Dijon* case, it was consequently the German rule banning the sale of drinks with an alcohol content below a certain level that focused the ECJ's entire attention. In other words, it was a legal rule of the member state into which the products had been imported that was targeted. Similarly, in the *Keck and Mithouard* case, it was the French rule on '*refus de vente*' that was incriminated, in this case, again, a legal rule of the member state for which the products were destined.[7]

More broadly speaking, the numerous precedents of the European Court of

---

[6] ECJ, 20 February 1979, *Rewe/Bundesmonopolverwaltung für Branntwein*, Case 120/78 (Rec. 1979, p. 649).

[7] ECJ, 24 November 1993, *Bernard Keck and Daniel Mithouard*, Case C-267/91 and 268/91, (Rec. 1993, p. I-6097).

Justice following the *Cassis de Dijon* case originally had one single goal: identifying the rules of the member state to which goods were destined that might constitute trade barriers. But it happens that in the *Cassis de Dijon* case, the European Court of Justice did not just rule against the internal market principles in the rules of the host country of the products. Its reasoning contained a reference to the legal provisions of the products' member state of origin. The ECJ held that the prohibition of marketing drinks with an alcohol content below a certain level resulting from the German law cannot prevent the importation of goods coming from France, where they are 'lawfully produced and marketed'.

This means that if a product has been produced and marketed in a member state in compliance with local regulations, it can then be freely sold or distributed in another member state, without necessarily complying with equivalent legal rules of the latter country. In a communication in 1980 on the repercussions of the *Cassis de Dijon* case, the European Commission had stated that 'any product imported from a member state must in principle be allowed on the territory of any other member state if it is legally manufactured (i.e. if it conforms to the regulatory or manufacturing processes of the exporting country) and marketed in the territory of the exporting country'.[8]

Therefore, with the mutual recognition principle, enforcement of the public law regulations of the country of origin will make it possible to avoid the applicability of equivalent rules of the country of destination of the products. On the grounds of their compliance in their home country, manufacturing firms will not have to submit to similar rules in the member state to which their products are being exported, thus opening wider access to this member state's national market.

Metaphorically, the home country's public law rules travel with the products towards the country where they will be sold and distributed. In practical terms, the mutual recognition principle is a cost-cutting device, as charges generated by the enforcement of the public law regulations of the products' country of destination will be avoided, leading to a more integrated market within the European Union.

Yet this conclusion is not totally definitive, as the producer's home country public regulations could occasionally resurface during a tort legal action.

---

[8] *Communication de la Commission sur les suites à donner à l'arrêt rendu par la Cour de justice le 20 février 1979 dans l'affaire 120/78 (Cassis de Dijon)*, 3 October 1980, Official Journal C 256.

III. IMPACT OF HOME COUNTRY PUBLIC LAW REGULATIONS ON TORT DISPUTES AS A SECOND STEP

The conflict of legal rules applicable in the field of products has been widely studied, especially regarding tortious liability.[9] Nevertheless, a distinction has to be made. In fact, there are two different questions that can arise in 'products' matters that involve different sets of conflict of law rules.

Firstly, a consumer has bought a product that does not match what the contract of sale provides. There is a lack of conformity and it could create a conflict of laws if the consumer and the seller are not located in the same country. In this case, specific conflict of laws rules should be applied. Principally, two sets of conflict of laws rules are concerned: the Rome Convention on the law applicable to contractual obligations of 19th June 1980[10] as far as member states of the European Union are concerned and, eventually, the Hague Convention on the law applicable to international sales of goods concluded on 15th June 1955 for the states that have ratified it.

But this first issue is not specific to products. It is related to contracts in general, unlike the following second kind of question that can only arise in matters concerning products.

Secondly, damage could have been caused by the defectiveness of a product. And the consumer or, more generally speaking, the injured person will sue the producer, the manufacturer, the supplier or, even, the repairer. The former will seek the latter's liability for the defectiveness of his product. But, when the product has been manufactured in one country and sold in another, the injured person and the defendant are not located in the same state, resulting in a conflict of laws situation. Put differently, there is an injured person who is seeking to establish the liability of a producer or a manufacturer of the defective product, which caused the injury, who is located in another country. In this kind of case, the problem is that the legal action can be founded either on the

---

[9] Duintjer Tebbens H. (1979), *International Product Liability – A study of comparative and international legal aspects of product liability*, Leiden: A. W. Sijthoff; Wandi M. (1995), *International Produkthaftung*, Heidelberg: Recht und Wirtschaft. With a European perspective: Basedow J. (1995), 'Der kollisonrechtlichte Gehalt der produktfreiheiten im europäischen Binnemarket: favor offerentis', *RabelZ* 1; Fawcett J.J. (1993), 'Products in Private International Law: A European Perspective', *RCADI*, 238 (I), 9; Kadner Graziano T. (2004), *La responsabilité délictuelle en droit international privé européen*, Bâle: Helbing & Lichtenhahn; Kadner Graziano T. (2005), 'The Law Applicable to Product Liability: The present State of the Law in Europe and Current Proposals for Reform', *ICLQ*, 54, 475.

[10] Official Journal C 27, 26 January 1998, p. 34.

injured person's national law or on the defendant's (producer, manufacturer) national law.

To solve this problem, which means determining whether the legal action should be subject to the injured person's national law or to the producer's national law, the first set of conflict of law rules that are applied to product liability is a Hague Convention: the Convention on the law applicable to products liability, concluded on 2nd October 1973 which came into force on 1st October 1977. Quite a number of European countries have ratified this convention: France, Spain, Italy, Luxembourg and Belgium, for example, but not the United Kingdom.

This Convention aims to determine the law applicable to the liability of producers and manufacturers for damage caused by products, 'including damage in consequence of a misdescription of the product or of a failure to give adequate notice of its qualities, its characteristics or its method of use' (Article 3). In this case, the applicable law is in principle the law of the state of the place of injury, but only if that state is also 'the place of the habitual residence of the person directly suffering damage' (Article 4). That means that the person suffering the damage can found his or her legal action on his or her own law if the injury occurs in the country where he or she lives.

On 11th July 2009, this specific rule of conflict of law from the Hague Convention of 1973 will be superseded by a new European Union regulation. Conflict of laws rules in non-contractual obligations, which includes product liability, will be unified in all the European countries that have ratified the Amsterdam treaty. Besides other provisions, this treaty, which entered into force on 1st May 1999, aims to promote the compatibility of applicable rules in the member states concerning the conflict of laws and jurisdictions.[11]

On that basis, the European Parliament and the Council have adopted a 'Regulation on the law applicable to non-contractual obligations (Rome II)'.[12] This regulation contains a specific conflict of law rule in the field of product liability. Under Article 5 of the regulation, the applicable law is the law of the place where the person sustaining damage has his or her habitual residence. However, this solution has a condition. It is conditional on the product having

---

11 Under Article 65(b) of the EC Treaty introduced by the Treaty of Amsterdam, measures in the field of judicial co-operation in civil matters to be taken 'in so far as necessary for the proper functioning of the internal market' include 'promoting the compatibility of the rules applicable in the Member States concerning the conflict of laws'.

12 Regulation (EC) 864/2007 of 11 July 2007 on the law applicable to non-contractual obligations (Rome II): Official Journal L 199, 31 July 2007, p. 40. See Symeonides S.C. (2004), 'Tort Conflicts and Rome II: A View from Across', *Festschrift in Honour of Erik Jayme*, München: Beck, p. 935.

been marketed in that country with the consent of the person claimed to be liable.

These two texts (Hague Convention of 1973 and Rome II) lead to a mutual conclusion. In one case or the other, in a legal liability action introduced by a person resident in a European country against manufacturers or producers located in another member state, the applicable law will most of the time be the national law of the claimant. And this is obviously very protective because he or she will not have to plead on the basis of a foreign law.

But setting aside this aspect that protects the injured person, a case might occur in which the claimant wishes to invoke some non-compliance with his or her own national regulations in the field of product quality standards, for example. In other words, it is conceivable that the injured person would like to found his or her tort action on non-compliance with the local public law regulation.

From the conflict of law point of view, this raises no problem: the law applicable is that of the place of injury. But from the point of view of building an integrated market, it is more questionable. Indeed, it could obliterate what has been gained for the producer on the grounds of the mutual recognition principle. In fact, its transaction costs would still have to include the enforcement of the public law regulations of the country where the products will be distributed and sold, even if these regulations would not have been directly applicable, but indirectly through the law applicable to tort liability. But for the producer to benefit fully from market access under the conditions of the mutual recognition principle, it is essential that at no time should he or she have to comply with the regulations of the country for which the products are destined equivalent to those to which he or she has already agreed in his or her home state.

Be it in their relationships with the administration of the state of the product's destination or in their relationships with local customers, producers or manufacturers should not have to enforce the public regulations of the member state that is the destination of their products. Otherwise, their transaction costs will have to take account of this risk and, in such a case, trading in other member states will not be possible under those same conditions as prevail when trading in their own state, which implies a less integrated European market.

That is the reason why the mutual recognition principle should be taken into account in the conflict of laws theory. Consequently, two Belgian authors have developed the idea of an exception of mutual recognition integrating the principles of private international law.[13]

---

13 Fallon M., Meeusen J. (2002), 'Private international law in the European

According to this academic proposal, the principle of mutual recognition is not going to replace the existing rules of conflict of laws. More modestly, the test of equivalence inherent in the mutual recognition principle must be integrated within classical principles of private international law. Nevertheless, this integration should only occur in the presence of very special circumstances. Two conditions must be met. First of all, tort litigation should be applicable to the law of the member state where the defective product has been marketed and where the injury was suffered. Secondly, a specific public law rule of this law applicable to the case could be regarded as constituting an obstacle on the grounds that there is an equivalent rule in the country of origin of the producer concerned.[14]

Assuming that the Rome II Regulation is applicable to a specific tort action, the applicable law will most of the time be the law of the member state where the product has been marketed, which is also the place where the damage occurred. Therefore, the manufacturer of a product in a member state may be subject to liability on the basis of the law of another member state in which it has invested the market on the grounds that on that occasion a user of this product has suffered damage. In this case, if the misconduct is constituted by a breach of regulations of the destination country deemed equivalent to a rule of the state of origin of the manufacturer, the mutual recognition principle can then be invoked. On that basis, public law regulations of the destination country will be dismissed.

Once again, the implementation of the principle of mutual recognition in private international law implies at the same time that the law applicable to the tort is the law of the country of destination and that upon the occasion of a tort the producer or manufacturer will be required to comply with the rules equivalent to the ones he or she has already agreed to in his or her state of origin. If these two conditions are met, the exception of mutual recognition can be implemented.

Union and the exception of mutual recognition', *PILY*, 4, 37–66; Fallon M. (2004), 'Libertés communautaires et règle de conflit de lois', *Les conflits de lois et le système juridique communautaire*, Paris: Dalloz, 76–78; Gaudemet-Tallon H. (2005), 'De nouvelles fonctions pour l'équivalence en droit international privé?', *Mélanges Paul Lagarde*, Paris: Dalloz, 303–326; Jobard-Bachellier M.-N. (2005), 'La portée du test de compatibilité communautaire en droit international privé contractuel', *Mélanges Paul Lagarde*, Paris: Dalloz, 475–492.

14 Muir Watt H. (2006), 'Integration and Diversity: The Conflict of Laws as a Regulatory Tool' in *The Institutional Framework of European Private Law*, F. Cafaggi (ed.), Oxford: OUP, 107–148, p. 114; Muir Watt H. (2004), *Aspects économiques du droit international privé, Réflexion sur l'impact de la globalisation économique sur les fondements des conflits de lois et de juridictions*, RCADI, 307.

This implementation would avoid a side effect by which producers or manufacturers based in a specific member state would have to respect the public law regulations of all other member states where they market their products, because of the existing risk that these regulations might be applicable not directly but on the occasion of a tort action. With the exception of mutual recognition, manufacturing firms are definitely and totally protected from the potential applicability to their products of public law regulations of the country to which these products have been exported.

Consequently, the charges incurred by the enforcement of these regulations are definitively removed from the cost prices of the products concerned. However, this does not prevent producers and manufacturers from anticipating the applicability of the tort laws of the different states where their products are being distributed and sold.

IV. INTRA-EU MOVEMENT OF NATIONAL LAWS REGARDING TORTS AS A THIRD STEP?

The mutual recognition principle has an immediate effect on the edification of a more integrated European market: as long as they enforce their own national public law regulations regarding their manufactured products, producers will not have the obligation to respect all the equivalent legislation in all the member states where their items are being marketed and sold.

Because of the so-called exception of mutual recognition introduced in private international law, the enforcing of these equivalent regulations of the countries of destination of the products is even precluded in the case of a tort legal action introduced by an injured person against the producer or the manufacturer. The effect for these professionals is immediate: searching for information about these regulations and their enforcement no longer adds any supplementary burden to the cost prices of the products.

And yet specific costs for distributing and selling products throughout all the EU member states will not totally get rid of the economic impact generated by the diversity of national law systems. Even though public law regulations are out of the game, producers and manufacturers based in one of the member states still have to cope with the different private law systems of all other member states where their products are marketed. Their cost prices do have to take account of the financial consequences of likely tort legal actions on the grounds of one or the other member states' private laws. If a product has been manufactured in Poland and sold in Italy, Italian public law is not affected by the transaction, as has been previously explained. But Italian law on tort is still in the frame. An Italian consumer injured by the product could still sue the Polish producer on grounds of the *lex loci delicti*, which is Italian law.

From this point of view, selling products locally does not incur the same cost as selling abroad in another member state. A price difference still exists between doing business on the national market of a member state and doing business throughout Europe. Because of the differences remaining between national tort laws, the potential financial consequences of selling in other member states are still higher than those to which a local producer is exposed. Therefore, competition between local and foreign producers is compromised.

To avoid this consequence and to get closer to an integrated market covering the whole European Union, a new principle has emerged. This idea is that the law of the country of origin of the products must not merely be helpful in setting aside equivalent rules of the law of the country where the products are marketed, but that it will be entirely applicable to the case as a whole. With this new so-called principle of the law of origin stemming from the mutual recognition principle,[15] a new situation has been reached: it is stated that in order to benefit fully from the EC freedoms of movement, the operator installed in a member state must be able to trade across the EU only with the requirements of its law of origin. Originally, this principle appeared in academic literature with the idea of a hidden choice of laws rule.[16] Later on, it gave

15 It seems that the law of origin principle was first stated in a study by the German Ministry of Economics on the meaning of the concept of internal market under the appellation of 'Herkunftsprinzip': *Wissenschaftlicher Beirat beim Bundesministerium für Wirtschaft, Stellungnahme zum Weissbuch der EG-Kommission über den Binnenmarkt, Hektografiert*, Bonn, 22 February 1986; Steindorff E. (1986), 'Gemeinsamer Markt als Binnenmarkt', *ZHR*, 687.

16 Basedow J. (1995), 'Das kollisionsrecht Gehalt der Produktfreiheiten im europäischen Binnenmarkt: favor offentis', *RabelsZ.*, 1–54; Bernhard P. (1992), 'Cassis de Dijon und Kollisionsrecht am Beispiel des unlauteren Wettbewerbs', *Europäisches Zeitschrift für Wirtschatfsrecht*, 437; Duintjer Tebbens H. (1994), 'Les conflits de lois en matière de publicité déloyale à l'épreuve du droit communautaire', *Rev. crit. DIP*, 451–481; Fallon M. (1995), *Les conflits de lois et de juridictions dans un espace économique intégré, L'expérience de la Communauté européenne*, RCADI, 1995, 253, 9–282; Fallon M. (1993), 'Variations sur le principe d'origine, entre droit communautaire et droit international privé' *in Mélanges François Rigaux*, Bruxelles: Bruylant, 187–221; Grundmann S. (2004), 'Internal Market Conflict of Laws From Traditional Conflict of Laws to an Integrated Two Level Order' *in Les conflits de lois et le système juridique communautaire*, A. Fuchs, H. Muir Watt, E. Pataut (eds.), Paris: Dalloz, 5–29; Grundmann S. (2000), 'Binnenmarktkollisionsrecht – Vom klassischen IPR sur Integrationsordnung', *RabelsZ.*, 457; Radicati di Brozolo L. (1990), 'L'ambito di applicazione della legge del paese di origine nella libera prestazione dei servizi bancari nella CEE', *Foro italiano*, 1990, IV, 424; Radicati di Brozolo L.G. (1993), L'influence sur les conflits de lois des principes de droit communautaire en matière de liberté de circulation', *Rev. crit. DIP*, 401–424; Rossolillo G. (2002), *Mutuo riconoscimento e tecniche conflittuali*, Padova: Cedam, 2002, 335; Roth W.-H. (1991), 'Der Einfluss des Europäisches Gemeinschaftrechts auf das internationale Privatrecht',

rise to intense debate, especially during the discussion of the first version of the Directive on services in the internal market.[17]

Application of this principle implies that all the legal aspects of marketing and selling products in another member state would be submitted to the law of the member state whence the products originated. If a product is manufactured in Germany and sold in France, Italy and Spain, enforcement of this principle would imply that German law would govern injuries suffered from the use of these products. In this light, the law of origin principle sets aside the traditional conflict of law rules applicable either in contract or in tort matters. Because of the width of its scope of application, it necessarily precludes the normal rules of conflict of laws that it replaces.[18]

In fact, with the principle of the law of origin, it is a new type of conflict of laws rule that is proposed, founded on a specifically regulatory function.[19] Unlike traditional conflict of law rules, this is not to seek the closest connecting factors or to respect states' sovereignties. The law of origin is indeed a kind of conflict of laws rule, but based on purely economic logic. From this particular point of view, it certainly contributes to the edification of a more integrated internal market.

However, it raises difficulties. These are not so much that the principle of the law of the country of origin breaks with classical theories of conflict of laws being based solely on economic logic, but that it conveys a particular type of economic regulation. Beyond the different and numerous interests called into question by an intra-EU legal relationship, only one of them is taken into consideration by the principle of the law of the country of origin: the operator's interests. It could of course be argued that these interests in the final analysis coincide with those of the European Community as a whole,

---

Rabels Z., 623; Sonnenberger H. (1996), 'Europarecht und Internationales Privatrecht', *Zeitschrift für Vergleichende Rechtswissenschaft*, 3–47; Spindler G. (2002), 'Herkunftslandprinzip und Kollisionsrecht, Binnenmarktintegration ohne Harmonisierung?', *RabelsZ.*, 633–709; Wolf (1990), 'Privates Bankvertragsrecht im EG-Binnenmarkt', *Wespapier Mitteilungen*, 1941; Wilderspin M. & Lewis X. (2002), 'Les relations entre le droit communautaire et les règles de conflit de lois des Etats membres', *Rev. crit. DIP*, 1–37.

17 COM(2004)2 final, 5 March 2004.

18 de Schutter O. & Francq S. (2005), 'La proposition de directive relative aux services dans le marché intérieur: reconnaissance mutuelle, harmonisation et conflit de lois dans l'Europe élargie', *Cah. dr. eur.*, 603–660, 640 and 644–645; Mankowski P. (2004), 'Wieder ein Herkunftslandprinzip für Dienstleistungen im Binnenmarkt', *IPRax*, 385–395.

19 Muir Watt H. (2006), 'Integration and Diversity: The Conflict of Laws as a Regulatory Tool' in *The Institutional Framework of European Private Law*, F. Cafaggi (ed.), Oxford: OUP, 107–148, p. 137.

allowing greater economic development and creating more wealth within the Union, which will be beneficial to all.

However, on the one hand, this kind of an impact of the principle of the law of origin on economic growth in Europe remains to be proven. On the other hand, it establishes the satisfaction of other interests as being at least as respectable as those of the operators. Here we are talking about the interests of the operator's business partners or customers: their legal actions will be governed by foreign private laws whose application they may not necessarily have been able to anticipate. Similarly, the state of destination of the products will lose all control over legal relationships at least partially located in its territory. We can even imagine that because of the systematic application of the law of origin of the products, buyers will turn away from products manufactured in other member states, the risk of having to plead on the grounds of a foreign law being too high. In fact, the law of origin principle could have a reverse effect on the edification of a more integrated market.

V. CONCLUSION

The idea that an item produced in a particular EU state could be marketed, distributed and sold throughout the EU as a whole under the conditions imposed by the national law of this country cannot be accepted in every case. The mutual recognition principle certainly provides that all public law regulations of home states of producers and manufacturers should not be doubled by equivalent provisions of the member state to which the products have been exported. This infers the inapplicability of the public law regulations of the law of destination either directly or on the occasion of a tort legal action. But the free movement of goods and the mutual recognition principle should not interfere with private law. In particular, the existence of a new kind of conflict of law rule submitting intra-EU transactions and liabilities entirely to the law of origin of the products could not be accepted.

PART 4

E-commerce

10. E-commerce from a private law perspective

Vincenzo Zeno-Zencovich

1. TORTIOUS LIABILITY IN EU LAW

Before considering the role of the tortious provisions in Directive 2000/31, in the regulatory strategies and governance in European private law,[1] one should point out that tortious liability is only episodically considered in EU law.

A summary survey offers limited and piecemeal results: products liability[2], environmental damage,[3] aviation disasters,[4] some limited aspects of compulsory car insurance,[5] liability of public bodies in public procurement procedures,[6] data protection,[7] compensation to victims of crime[8] and

[1] The topic is examined, in a comparative perspective, by C. Rossello, *Commercio elettronico. La* governance *di Internet tra diritto statuale, autodisciplina, autodisciplina*, soft law *e* lex mercatoria, Milan, Giuffrè 2006 (especially chapter 1).

[2] Council Directive 1985/374/EEC of 25 July 1985 on the approximation of the laws, regulations and administrative provisions of the Member States concerning liability for defective products.

[3] Directive 2004/35/CE of the European Parliament and of the Council of 21 April 2004 on environmental liability with regard to the prevention and remedying of environmental damage (and previously Directives 1975/439 on waste oils, 1975/442 on waste, 1978/319 on toxic waste).

[4] Council Regulation (EC) 2027/97 of 9 October 1997 on air carrier liability in the event of accidents (now modified by Regulation 889/02 and, for the contractual provisions, by Regulation 261/04).

[5] Third Council Directive 1990/232/EEC of 14 May 1990 on the approximation of the laws of the Member States relating to insurance against civil liability in respect of the use of motor vehicles.

[6] Council Directive 1989/665/EEC of 21 December 1989 on the coordination of the laws, regulations and administrative provisions relating to the application of review procedures to the award of public supply and public works contracts.

[7] Directive 1995/46/EC of the European Parliament and of the Council of 24 October 1995 on the protection of individuals with regard to the processing of personal data and on the free movement of such data.

[8] Council Directive 2004/80/EC of 29 April 2004 relating to compensation to crime victims.

e-commerce.[9] Any lawyer familiar with the many facets of tort law easily realizes that on such scattered materials it is impossible to build a coherent EU tort law system.[10]

Such an approach however would seem to be somewhat *naïf.* The partitions of EU law do not follow traditional legal partitions (public law, private law and within the latter property, contract, tort, successions etc.) but follow an economic sectors partitioning (for example transport, financial services, telecommunications, energy etc.).

Now, if there is an area of general convergence in European private law that area is tort law: liability rules, especially when applied to businesses, tend to be similar, and differences are mostly due to factual distinctions. Moreover tort law is, in the western legal tradition, judge-made law, and this quite irrespective of whether the national systems have legislative provisions (such as in civil law countries) or broad principles distilled by the slow development of cases (such as in common law jurisdictions).

Obviously one is not questioning the wisdom of approximation through a Directive, but simply pointing out that the choice made by the EU institutions appears to express a considerable mistrust in ordinary tort law and in the role of the courts in the governance of the liability aspects of information and communications technology (ICT). Whether this mistrust is justified is highly debatable and, one must add, subjective: a lawyer with a regulatory approach would endorse the Brussels view; a private lawyer would have the opposite view and could easily point at the failure of the products liability directive.

2. LIABILITY OF ELECTRONIC COMMUNICATIONS PROVIDERS

The specific tort rules in Directive 2000/31 apparently fix a principle of relaxed liability for carrying, caching or hosting information society services. This would appear to be an exception to the growing role of tort law as a means of judicial control over business activities that are harmful to third

---

9 Directive 2000/31/EC of the European Parliament and of the Council of 8 June 2000 on certain legal aspects of information society services, in particular electronic commerce, in the Internal Market ('Directive on electronic commerce').

10 For an attempt see C. von Bar, *The Common European Law of Torts*, vol. I, Oxford, Clarendon 1998 (part 4 'Unification and Approximation of the Law of Delict within the European Union', pages 375 ff.); W. van Gerven, *The Emergence of a Common European Law in the Area of Tort Law: the EU Contribution*, in D. Fairgrieve, M. Andenas and J. Bell (eds), *Tort Liability of Public Authorities in a Comparative Perspective*, London, BIICL 2002 (pages 125 ff.).

parties. Carriers, cachers and hosts are exempted from liability provided they are not the authors of the message, do not determine the final user and do not modify the content.

If one examines the rules set out in Articles 12, 13 and 14 of the Directive, however, they seem to be an expression of the principle 'no control, no liability' which is widely acknowledged in tort law.

3. NO OBLIGATION TO CONTROL

The principle 'no control, no liability' is reaffirmed, and reinforced, by the provisions of Article 15 according to which 'Member States shall not impose a general obligation on providers, when providing the services covered by Articles 12, 13 and 14, to monitor the information which they transmit or store, nor a general obligation to actively seek facts or circumstances indicating illegal activity'.

The principle is surely novel to tort law, where the tendency is, rather, the opposite. Undertakings have a legal, and social, responsibility towards those who come into contract with their products or services. They must adopt all necessary measures to prevent damage to third parties. This tendency, which has steadily grown throughout the twentieth century, is well expressed by the principle of precaution.

Nor can one say that EU law has a general attitude of relaxed liability towards ICT. Article 23 of Directive 1995/46 on data protection sets out a rule of strict liability for damages arising from negligent personal data processing. The Preamble of the Directive does not provide any explanation of the rule.

One obvious reason is that a general obligation to monitor would have infringed the right to secrecy of communications set out by Article 8 of the European Convention on Human Rights, and the whole system of protection of personal data.

Another reason might be the cost of imposing such an obligation. It should be noted, however, that this kind of argument is not very popular with the courts (with the exception of English ones) which, in a balancing test, tend to privilege individual rights and safety over a business profit. But this is probably why this plausible explanation has remained unexpressed.

This brings us back to the starting point: to introduce a significant exception to a general rule of law (strict liability of undertakings towards third parties) through regulatory measures (such as Directive 2000/31) requires that those who are called to enforce the exception are made aware of its scope and limits. The risk, otherwise, is that it will be considered as a foreign body and rapidly rejected.

4. THE ROLE OF TORT LAW IN COMPLEX SOCIETIES

The tortious provisions in the e-commerce Directive can be read in a much wider perspective. Tort law theory, whether in civil law or in common law systems, was born in a social and economic context in which it had an important governance role.[11] The Latin expressions *neminem laedere* or *res ipsa loquitur* or *cuius commoda eius, et incommoda* or *ubi emolumentum ibi onus*, which are so common in nineteenth-century legal and legislative materials reflect the view that tort law was *the* instrument, the sole instrument, to redress what we would call nowadays 'market failures'. This idea is deeply embedded in the mentality of private lawyers who must, increasingly and since the end of the nineteenth century, face the reality: in a welfare state social and economic wrongs are redressed through legislative measures (that is to say, public law). That is quite clear starting from work accidents compensation schemes which were introduced at the turn of the twentieth century and which avoided typical tort issues such as fault and causation.[12]

Welfare state policies intervene widely in fields that originally belonged to tort law such as traffic accidents, medical malpractice, environmental disasters and so on. It should be pointed out that this trend is widespread not only in the cases of bodily harm, but also in those of purely economic damage such as protection of investors and bank depositors, liability of public bodies in public procurement and e-commerce.

On the other hand it is widely acknowledged that tort law is often public law in disguise, in the sense that the judiciary intervenes through case law in areas of extremely sensitive public choices which would be considered the realm of the legislature. This two-sided relationship has been extensively studied in US law, in which the role of punitive damages has allowed the courts to set the rules, especially in the field of products liability.

However, it should be noted that the US experience cannot easily be transposed to Europe. Although the conceptual framework of tort law is common and, at the end of the day, judgments are quite similar on both sides of the Atlantic, the different importance of the state, and in particular of the welfare state, changes the role that tortious liability has in the respective legal systems.

In a European context it would seem that when a widespread governance result is the goal, this is entrusted to the legislature and to government. Only in a second stage do the courts intervene. Therefore when we discuss the role

---

11 The topic is examined extensively by F. Cafaggi, *A Coordinated Approach to Regulation and Civil Liability in European Law: Rethinking Institutional Complementarities*, in F. Cafaggi (ed.) *The Institutional Framework of European Private Law*, Oxford, OUP, 2006 (pages 191 ff.).

12 See F. Cafaggi, cited at note 11 (at pages 193 ff.).

of tort law in European countries we cannot avoid considering that it is inextricably related to legislative choices.

5. ALLOCATION OF DAMAGES AND FUNCTIONS OF TORT LAW

This brings us to the core question: who decides how damages that have occurred must be allocated and how is it decided? Who should take precautions in order to avoid them?

In this regard, it is clear that tort law is instrumental to the result one wants to achieve. In the first place tort law is only one of the many private law solutions for shifting losses and damages and it competes with restitutions, contract law, unjust enrichment, self- and third-party insurance. In the second place, as has already been pointed out, the different private law solutions operate in a widespread legislative context, which in some cases is extremely generic – the best example is Article 1382 of the Code Napoléon: '*Tout fait quelconque de l'homme etc*' – and in other cases is extremely detailed, for example traffic accidents regulation. In the third place private law solutions are often substituted by entirely public law instruments such as compensation schemes of the most diverse nature.

The governance issue of tort law must therefore be considered taking into account all these factors.

6. A ROLE FOR INTERNATIONAL PRIVATE LAW?

It has been suggested that international private law (IPL) ould have been a better solution than that envisaged by the Directive.[13] This conclusion, grounded in a solid theoretical approach, appears, however, to be of little effect in practice. This criticism is directed to the impact of IPL on tortious liability of providers and the like, but can be extended to contractual relationships born out of e-commerce. In these last decades international private law has become an extremely complex field of law. This is so because of the enormous increase in transnational transactions and the parallel increase in number of jurisdictions involved (an example for all is the fragmentation of nation states in Eastern Europe). But this complexity is also due to an increasingly

---

[13] See e.g. S. Stalla Bourdillon, 'Re-allocating horizontal and vertical regulatory powers in the electronic marketplace: what to do with private international law', Chapter 12 below.

obscure and self-sufficient approach by international private law scholars which has brought complication rather than simplification to existing rules. IPL has become a fascinating game of chess for those specialized in the field but a real nightmare for all practising lawyers (both practitioners and judges) who get tangled in the IPL thicket.

That is not to say that IPL rules must not exist, because it is obvious that they are necessary. But it should always be borne in mind that they are instrumental to the essential goal of certainty of law, which is a value in itself. The aim of conflict of laws is to reduce those conflicts, not to turn them into a perpetual minefield. In recent decades all fields of the law have undergone a similar process towards complexity and lawyers have followed it by specializing themselves. However although this has sense for substantive law, that is not the case for procedural rules such as those of IPL. If a lawyer does not know if what he knows is of any use (because a different national law is applicable) or whether he can stand in front of the court of which he knows procedures and judges, most of the things he has learnt and is specialized in are pointless.

Increasingly IPL appears as a severe and enigmatic gate-keeper which decides if a lawyer can keep a file or must pass it over to a colleague from some other country, or if a judge, after many preliminary hearings, can decide the merits of the case or must declare that he has no competency. All this keeps the parties far away from any substantive decision, which can be further postponed if one of them can suspend the proceedings until the issue of competency has been decided by some higher court or if there is a conflict between two jurisdictions which both affirm their competency. All this brings enormous labour to very highly respected legal scholars, but is, from the parties' point of view, only a further transactional cost.

These remarks should indicate that international private law would surely have been of little help in e-commerce transactions, owing to the limited value of each transaction and the difficulty and the cost of bringing a case to court. The complexity of IPL appears to be, therefore, an incentive to adopt different approaches.[14]

No reasonable businessman (or consumer) would agree on an important contract without having met his counterpart, examined thoroughly the conditions with the assistance of a legal expert, enquired about the applicable law and the competent forum simply through a 'point and click' procedure. When it comes to over-the-counter transactions (such as those typical of e-commerce) the golden rule is that the rules on applicable law and jurisdiction

---

[14] For a list of the complexities that IPL entails in this field, see U. Draetta, *Internet e commercio internazionale nel diritto internazionale dei privati* (2nd edition), Milan, Guiffrè 2005, *passim*.

must be few, clear and modifiable by the parties in limited and non-ambiguous cases. Once applied and well settled, the market will adapt to them and the parties will rely on them as a reasonable way of behaving. If the parties – which in an e-commerce transaction are at least three: the seller of goods or services, the provider, the buyer – have to debate at length, even in the pre-contractual phase, what law applies and what jurisdiction is competent, e-commerce would have no future. To put the argument in a paradoxical way, if each of them were to seek the advice of three different and most learned scholars in international private law, the most likely result would be that no transaction would be concluded except that between them and their legal experts.

That is, put in a simple way, that certainty as to the applicable law and the competent jurisdiction – although none of them may be the best – is preferable to a legal quagmire from which they can come out only through the method used by Baron Munchausen: pulling themselves up by their bootstraps.

If one confines oneself to tortious liability it is surely preferable to know that the competent jurisdiction will generally be that of the person suffering the damage (on the basis of the simple and ancient principle of the *locus commissi delicti*) and that the applicable rules for providers and the like are unified by the Directive, while the general tort rules have been rendered uniform by case law in the last century (and the notable exception of British law does not change the outcome, it being unlikely that the restrictive attitude of English judges will be changed by IPL forcing on them German, French or Italian law).

That said, it should be noted that, on the basis of the available case law, substantive tort law does not seem, in Europe, to govern the business behaviours of providers, while a more relevant role is placed on self-imposed codes of conduct. The Directive, at Article 16, indicates that the EC and member states should encourage codes of conduct and, at Article 17, out-of-court dispute settlement. Again this is a governance approach to communication networks. But again it is outside the traditional realm of tort law which requires a legal confrontation in a court and a slow but inevitable accumulation of case law, which adapts itself to the changing times.

11. E-commerce from a regulatory perspective

Francesco Cardarelli

1. THE REGULATORY FUNCTION OF TORT LAW

Tortious liability appears to be only one of the many, possible, instruments of regulation and should be examined not within a general theory framework – which does not exist in EU law – but in its relationship with the specific regulatory framework.

This means, on the one hand, that the existing tort provisions in EU law cannot be compared among themselves, and on the other hand their coherency must be considered having in mind what the objectives of the EU law are. Although this approach may not be very appealing for a traditional legal scholar – especially if brought up in a European continental environment – it opens the way to a law and economics analysis in order to assess its efficiency.

This criterion could also be usefully applied to e-commerce regulation, comparing the tort provisions with the aims of Directive 2000/31 and verifying the economic effects of its enforcement both on e-commerce providers and on the parties that claim to have received damage.

2. COMPETING MODELS FOR LIABILITY IN ELECTRONIC COMMUNICATIONS

Having this in mind, the provisions in Articles 12, 13, 14 and 15 of the Directive should be examined considering that its aim is, essentially, that of promoting the development of information society services, and therefore of the European undertakings that offer such services. Comparative lawyers have unanimously pointed out that this is a typical example of competition between legal systems in a globalized economy. In this case the competing model is the US one. One should stress the fact that in the American legal system no preliminary authorization is required to set up an e-commerce business, and the Digital Millennium Copyright Act (DMCA) adopts a relaxed liability rule in favour of electronic services carriers.[1] The Directive was enacted only a couple of years after the DMCA: the choice of a different model would have jeopardized the competitiveness of European enterprises and encouraged them to transfer themselves – a very easy solution in the age of telecommunication networks – to a more 'friendly' legal environment.[2]

3. THE AIM OF THE DIRECTIVE

An in-depth analysis of the Directive should take into account – in the first

---

1 The DMCA amended Chapter 5 of Title 17, United States Code in the following manner:
'**§ 512. Limitations on liability relating to material online**
(a) TRANSITORY DIGITAL NETWORK COMMUNICATIONS.—A service provider shall not be liable for monetary relief, or, except as provided in subsection (j), for injunctive or other equitable relief, for infringement of copyright by reason of the provider's transmitting, routing, or providing connections for, material through a system or network controlled or operated by or for the service provider, or by reason of the intermediate and transient storage of that material in the course of such transmitting, routing, or providing connections, if—
(1) the transmission of the material was initiated by or at the direction of a person other than the service provider;
(2) the transmission, routing, provision of connections, or storage is carried out through an automatic technical process without selection of the material by the service provider;
(3) the service provider does not select the recipients of the material except as an automatic response to the request of another person;
(4) no copy of the material made by the service provider in the course of such intermediate or transient storage is maintained on the system or network in a manner ordinarily accessible to anyone other than anticipated recipients, and no such copy is maintained on the system or network in a manner ordinarily accessible to such anticipated recipients for a longer period than is reasonably necessary for the transmission, routing, or provision of connections; and
(5) the material is transmitted through the system or network without modification of its content.'
Similar provisions are added concerning system caching and information residing on systems or networks at direction of users. The resemblances to Articles 12 to 15 inclusive of the Directive are striking.

2 The point is made by several authors: see G. Ponzanelli, *Verso un diritto uniforme per la responsabilità degli* internet service providers, in S. Sica and P. Stanzione (eds.), *Commercio elettronico e categorie civilistiche*, Milan, Giuffrè 2002 (pages 363 ff.); S. Sica, *Le responsabilità civili*, in E. Tosi (ed.), *Commercio elettronico e servizi della società dell'informazione*, Milan, Giuffrè 2003 (pages 275 ff.); F. Di Ciommo, *Evoluzione tecnologica e regole di responsabilità civile*, Naples, ESI 2003 (pages 279 ff); G.M. Riccio, *La responsabilità civile degli* internet providers, Turin, Giappichelli 2002 (pages 253 ff.).

place – the explicit aims of the Directive, which are put forward in its exceptionally long preamble (65 paragraphs, for only 21 substantial articles).

One should begin with the subsidiarity principle set out in paragraph 40, according to which 'Both existing and emerging disparities in Member States' legislation and case-law concerning liability of service providers acting as intermediaries prevent the smooth functioning of the internal market, in particular by impairing the development of cross-border services and producing distortions of competition'.

4. THE INTERESTS AT STAKE

The second issue that should be considered is expressed in paragraph 41 of the Preamble: 'This Directive strikes a balance between the different interests at stake and establishes principles upon which industry agreements and standards can be based.'

The balance of interests is typical of regulation. However the lengthy Preamble does not explicitly state which these interests are, although they are implied. And stating that the Directive strikes a balance, does not necessarily mean that it has, in fact, been reached.

This can be said only in hindsight and after adequate data have been collected and analysed. This is one of the main differences between a legislative approach – in which interests are politically vested by MPs – and a regulatory approach in which the point of equilibrium is chosen by public officials following certain procedures.

The third aspect that deserves to be considered is the relationship between regulation and self-regulation.

The Preamble to the Directive repeatedly stresses the point that the EU encourages the adoption of codes of conduct. And the Directive should be read in connection with the repeated EU plans of action for a 'safe environment for the Internet'[3] which are based essentially on voluntary compliance with codes of conduct. This strategy – which is common to many other fields in which interests of the public at large are involved – requires an attentive evaluation of compliance and enforcement. Legislative measures undergo political scrutiny by constituencies and, at the end of the day, by voters. Soft law can – and must – be evaluated through facts and figures and must undergo a periodical and independent scrutiny. Incidentally it should be noted that this kind of approach is quite different from a purely private law approach, in which the

---

3 See, *ex multis*, Decision 854/2005/EC of the European Parliament and of the Council of 11 May 2005 establishing a multiannual Community Programme on promoting safer use of the Internet and new online technologies.

traditional governance model is based on a distinction between compulsory rules and default rules. Once one has abided by the first, one only has to decide if the latter must be applied or not.

5. PRIVATE LAW VS. ADMINISTRATIVE LAW

Another aspect is the relationship between what can be called the administrative provisions of the Directive and the private law provisions.[4]

As to the first, it seems quite obvious that the only effective approach can be regulatory, especially if one has to remove administrative constraints. The e-commerce Directive contains what can be considered a revolutionary principle in the European tradition – whether continental or insular – that is the explicit provision that no preliminary authorization is required to set up an e-commerce business.

There are two paradoxes in this, which are well known to those who have studied the telecoms liberalization process: first, freedom of economic activity passes through regulation. In the telecommunications sector, regulation has been used to get rid of cumbersome state monopoly, here to suppress prior authorizations. The second paradox is that what is given with one hand is taken with the other: freedom is surrounded by a multitude of obligations. As a sort of toll or ransom one has to pay to be free. Obviously the many rules which are imposed are meant to promote public interest. But the mental reservation of regulation is that there is – there must inevitably be – a market failure.[5]

6. CONTROL AND LIABILITY

Articles 12 to 15 of the e-commerce Directive suggest a model in which liability rules are used to select the operators and their *modus operandi.* They do not establish that certain conduct is against the law and that therefore those who infringe the rule will incur liability. They indicate that if certain conduct is taken – for example, select the receiver of the transmission or modify the information – the operators may be held liable if damage ensues. In this case the ordinary rules will apply.

---

[4] This is one of many examples of the difficulty in establishing, nowadays, where the private law/public law divide stands: see H. Collins, 'The Voice of the Community in Private Law Discourse' [1997] 407.

[5] This is expressed clearly by the EC Economic and Social Committee in its Opinion on 'The effects of e-commerce on the single market (SMO)' (published in OJ C 123 of 25 April 2001).

The Directive, therefore, is not meant to allocate damages but to indicate which industries may be liability-free and which instead can be held liable. By so doing, the cited provisions have a regulatory effect, in the sense that they define what the ordinary activity of a carrier, a cacher or a host should be not to incur liability. And these provisions can be easily set out in the computer programs which are used in business activity. The more automatic the whole process, the less the risk of liability.[6]

This has much to do with a policy of incentives, rather than with classical tort law, although in the past relaxed liability or limitations to liability have been extensively used in order to favour certain industries (typically transport or state owned industries). In the case of e-commerce the approach is somewhat different. One should, in the first place, take into account the peculiarities of electronic communications: one has to do with services, rendered through non-material means by ways of a trans-national network. To regulate directly the liability of access providers and similar figures would have meant establishing in detail what can and cannot be done through electronic communications networks. An unrealistic task, considering on the one side the variety of activities and on the other side the rapid evolution of digital technologies (and therefore of businesses).

Furthermore the international dimension of e-commerce would have easily frustrated attempts to regulate activity directly, favouring a race-to-the-bottom process.

7. A DIFFERENT – PUBLIC LAW – PERSPECTIVE

A public lawyer, however, might be perplexed by such a conclusion. 'Governance' is a term that implies the existence of some kind of institutional framework. In the case of e-commerce the choice, deliberately, is that of avoiding an institutional control over e-commerce.

(a). Legislation, however pervasive, has a limited effect if not supplemented by extensive regulations. The e-commerce Directive provides only general indications on the content of the information that must be given to those who access the service. Emphasis is put on self-regulation rather than on mandatory rules which are limited and expressed in broad language.

---

[6] The point is made by M. Bocchiola, *Profili di responsabilità degli intermediari dell'*e-business to consumer, in V. Franceschelli (ed.), *Commercio elettronico*, Milan, Giuffrè 2001 (pages 542 ff.).

(b). The tortious liability provisions offer a typical example of *ex post* public intervention on the market. Liability arises only if providers and similar businesses do not comply with general standards of care (they do not generate the content, nor do they modify it or control it; nor do they choose the recipients; or are aware of potential illegality of the content). Judicial control arrives generally very late (especially compared with the rapidity of e-commerce) and is haphazard.

(c). Moreover e-commerce lacks institutions which are engaged in day-to-day regulation. No 'national regulatory authority', such as those envisaged for electronic communications, are set up by the Directive and in the electronic communications Directives there is a clear distinction between services provided to end-users and e-commerce which falls out of their scope.

All this seems to point in a different direction, that of a wide private autonomy, scarcely governed by administrative bodies. This does not necessarily imply that the e-commerce Directive enhances private governance of economic processes, but it does appear to lack some of the typical features of public governance (*ex ante, ad hoc*, day-to-day regulation).

8. E-COMMERCE AND INFORMATION AND COMMUNICATIONS TECHNOLOGIES

One should also consider e-commerce within the more general framework of ICT. Traditionally public models of governance follow a top-bottom approach. There is a hierarchy not only of norms but also of institutions – mostly public – which sets out the pattern of an orderly system.

Government and governance require some form of command-and-control procedures which move from a higher level to a subordinate one. Electronic networks render this approach impracticable in as much as the various segments of the net, however limited, are at the same level and are reciprocally interdependent.[7]

In e-commerce a good example is offered by the interdependence between the (open) network through which the catalogues of products and services are displayed and from which these are chosen, and the (restricted access) network through which payments are made. None of the two 'governs' the other, but both are complementary.

---

[7] The concept has been repeatedly set out by L. Lessig in many of his seminal contributions. *Ex multis* see, 'The Architecture of Innovation' (2002) 51 Duke LJ 1783.

Governance models and procedures appear under a technological guise.[8] They are set out by network, computer and software engineers who work for private enterprises. Interoperability and compatibility are their main goals, or in proprietary models, separation from other systems. In any case dependence is not considered as an essential element. Ironically one can point out that the most hierarchically minded institution – the military – was behind the creation of the most unhierarchical infrastructure – the Internet.

Against this background e-commerce appears to be extremely flexible and with very limited barriers: it is quite common to enter an e-commerce shopping mall (a portal), move to one 'shop' and then move forward, elsewhere, through links; or browse through a list of websites selected by a search engine. Where barriers have been set up (registration, passwords) users easily back out and move elsewhere. The technical architecture of the network sets the rules which must be followed.

Non-compliance has a very effective sanction: exclusion from communication. Public government institutions are replaced by standard-setting organizations in which private entities and groups have a major role.[9]

None of this is laid out in the e-commerce Directive. However it is implied by it because, otherwise, e-commerce would not exist.

9. E-COMMERCE AND THE PUBLIC LAW/PRIVATE LAW DIVIDE

E-commerce is one of the many examples of the blurred distinction between public law and private law. It is firmly rooted in the latter because business and private consumers use it in order to sell and to buy. The legal instrument they use is contract, often in its most elementary form ('click and buy'). Public law would appear to be on the outside of the market. This market, however, covers the entire world, is ubiquitous, open 24 hours a day. It is extremely difficult for public authorities to police a market to which anybody can have access.

This mere fact requires a shift of perspective. If public law has to do with authority this would appear to be absent. But if we consider the growing

---

8 One only has to cite the Working Group on Internet Governance (WGIG) and its latest Report (Chateau de Bossey, June 2005) available at http://www.wgig.org/docs/WGIGREPORT.doc. For a less optimistic view see N.W. Netanel, 'Cyberspace Self-Governance: A Skeptical View from Liberal Democratic Theory' (2000) 88 Calif L Rev 395.

9 See J.L. Camp and C. Vincent, 'Setting Standards: Looking to the Internet for Models of Governance' (2 November 2004). Available at SSRN: http://ssrn.com/abstract=615201.

tendency to govern through contract,[10] e-commerce and its tendency towards self-regulation suggest that there may be many ways of attaining the same goal.

Public interests are fostered by encouraging the pursuance of private ones, following a theoretical model that dates back to Adam Smith.[11]

To sum all this up it would seem that once again, hidden behind apparent private law provisions, regulation has taken the upper hand.

---

10 See N.W. Netanel, 'Cyberspace Self-Governance: A Skeptical View from Liberal Democratic Theory' (2000) 88 Calif L Rev 395 (at page 398 footnote 3): 'Since its inception, the Internet domain name system has been administered by the United States government through contract. In June 1998, the Clinton Administration announced that, as part of its overall policy of promoting Internet self-regulation, it would turn over responsibility for such administration to a new nonprofit corporation.'

11 'Every individual...generally, indeed, neither intends to promote the public interest, nor knows how much he is promoting it. By preferring the support of domestic to that of foreign industry he intends only his own security; and by directing that industry in such a manner as its produce may be of the greatest value, he intends only his own gain, and he is in this, as in many other cases, led by an invisible hand to promote an end which was no part of his intention.' (*The Wealth of Nations*, Book IV, Chapter II).

12. Re-allocating horizontal and vertical regulatory powers in the electronic marketplace: what to do with private international law

Sophie Stalla-Bourdillon

INTRODUCTION

The Directive 2000/31/EC on e-commerce (ECD) is certainly the 'key instrument which ...define[s] European e-regulatory policy and harmonise[s] significant legal domains which represented major obstacles to the development of the electronic Single Market'.[1] Before going any further, it is important to pause for a moment and reflect on the precise characteristics of the ECD as a typical instrument of '*régulation*'. Indeed, under the influence of English and American Law, legal French has been enriched with the word '*régulation*' to be distinguished from '*règlementation*'. This is more than a mere updating of the vocabulary. It is important to point out that the former embodies something different from the latter: it is 'a work, consisting in introducing regularities into a social object, ensuring its stability, its durability, without setting neither all the elements nor the whole sequence, thus without excluding changes'.[2] This mutation of the law-making philosophy entails significant consequences: it affects the way statutes are conceived and, as a consequence, drafted. As a result, statutory law no longer sets up a permanent trade-off between different interests with which private actors must comply, but seeks to adapt itself to the diversity of facts, finding its legitimacy in practical achievements more than in ethereal values. In other words, it relies on heterogeneous normative powers

---

1 Edwards L. (2005), 'Preface', in *The New Legal Framework for E-Commerce in Europe*, Edwards L. (ed), Oxford and Portland, Oregon: Hart Publishing, pp. v–ix, at p. v.

2 Jammeaud A. (1998), 'Introduction à la Sémantique de la Régulation Juridique', in *Les transformations de la régulation juridique*, Clam Jean and Martin Gilles (eds), LGDJ (coll. Droit et société recherches et travaux, N° 5), pp. 47–72, at p. 53.

in terms of sources, and coordinates more than commands their respective functions. Consequently, it becomes temporary by nature, calls for regular reassessment, and opens a dialogue with private actors in order to be more effective.[3]

Yet, for reasons of competence but not only that, this is exactly what is happening with the ECD at the European level: this explains its intrinsic limits and, in some cases, its flaws. In relation to the goal that the text pursues, the Directive 'seeks to contribute to the proper functioning of the internal market by ensuring the free movement of information society services between the Member States'. [4] To achieve this, it harmonizes critical national provisions such as the establishment of service providers and the liability of three categories of intermediaries.[5] Indeed, in 1995, the Commission stated in its Green Paper on Copyright and Related Rights in an Information Society: [6] 'Service providers will be reluctant to invest in new services unless the legal systems governing them are simple and reliable. To follow the package strategy, the investor providing the package must be sure that it will be governed by one single set of easily identifiable legal rules.'[7] This statement echoed the prevailing view on the other side of the Atlantic, despite the initial cautiousness of the Working Group on Intellectual Property:[8] 'In short, Title II [safe harbours for

---

3 For a thorough description of the legislative evolution see Ost F. (1998), 'Le Temps Virtuel des Lois Postmodernes ou Comment le Droit se Traite dans la Société de l'Information', in *Les transformations*, above n. 2 pp. 423–449, at p. 436:

> In other words, the perspective has patently become instrumental. It consists less in a priori imposing a pattern (reduced to a few relevant features, but stable) than in adopting a program of actions, defined by certain general goals, within a plural and shifting conjuncture. Legislation become programmatic, so that they do not find within themselves their consistency and validity, but within the gradual achievement of the goals they set forth. Truly, the plasticity is such that soon one does not assess anymore whether the reality deflects under the pressure of the law or whether, on the contrary, the law modulates itself in relation to the resistance of facts.

This transformation makes it more difficult to distinguish between private and public law, since the legislative techniques tend to move closer to each other.

4 Article 1(1).

5 See Article 1(2).

6 The liability of ISPs was first discussed sector by sector, in other words vertically, but the underlying assumption was often the same, whatever the field at stake: immunity from liability better serves innovation.

7 Brussels, 19.07.1995, COM(95) 382 final, pp. 21–22.

8 This working group is the result of the Information Infrastructure Task Force (IITF) formed by the White House to modernize the Copyright Act of 1976 after the digital boom. Its proposals are contained in the White Paper on the National

Internet service providers] ensures that the efficiency of the Internet will continue to improve and that the variety and quality of services on the Internet will expand.'[9]

The goal of the legislative intervention was thus clearly the creation of a new market, a transitory moment in the history of the development of the Internet. Article 21, first indent, thus sets in progress a process of re-examination, which has been complied with only in part: 'Before 17 July 2003, and thereafter every two years, the Commission shall submit … a report on the application of the Directive, accompanied, where necessary, by proposals for adapting it to legal, technical and economic developments in the field of information society services … .'[10] Article 21, second indent, stresses the necessity to analyse the 'need for proposals concerning the liability of providers of hyperlinks and location tool services, "notice and take down" procedures and the attribution of liability following the taking down of content'. Moreover, 'the report shall also analyse the need for additional conditions for the exemption from liability, provided for in Articles 12 and 13, in the light of technical developments …'.

In addition, the EC legislator called for the collaboration of private actors – Internet Service Providers (ISPs) – to fill the gaps of the newly set up legal norms or at least to help implement them, in particular through the instrument of codes of conduct as suggested by Article 16. [11] Out-of-court dispute settlements were also encouraged in pursuance of Article 17.[12] To quote the words of one of the advocates of the Commission's official doctrine: 'The point of this directive does not only consist in what it prescribes, but also in the process it represents. Indeed, the directive bears witness to the ability of community law, more precisely the law of the internal market, to evolve in order to quickly

---

Information Infrastructure (NII); see http://www.uspto.gov/web/offices/com/doc/ipnii/ accessed 14 September 2006, at pp. 122–123.

9 Senate Report n°105-190, P. L. 105-304, The Digital Millennium Copyright Act of 1998, May 11 1998, p. 2.

10 See the first Report from the Commission on the application of Directive 2000/31/EC, Brussels, 21.11.2003, COM(2003) 702 final. In 2005, the Commission created the expert group on electronic commerce by Decision 2005/752/EC. The Commission can thus consult the expert group on any question related to Directive 2000/31/EC. In spite of its name, the group is a mere aggregation of the national contact points appointed under Article 19(2).

11 'Member States and the Commission shall encourage: (a) the drawing up of codes of conduct at Community level, by trade, professional, and consumer associations or organisations, designed to contribute to the proper implementation of Articles 5 to 15 …'

12 Member States must not hamper out-of-court schemes already available in national systems.

respond to the mutations of society.'[13] In 2001, the ECD therefore was sometimes seen as putting 'the Community in the way to become the most competitive and dynamic economy in the world'. [14]

While there is much to say about the ECD substantial provisions,[15] these are not the focus here. Rather I will address the question of the 'conflicts methodology'[16] used by the ECD to allocate regulatory powers, both vertically and horizontally, and gauge its appropriateness. This said, I do think that the preceding observation is particularly relevant when it comes to the question of whether the 'country of origin' principle (COP) should be pushed ahead so that its functioning resembles that of a hidden conflict-of-law rule for both public and private law. To clarify, I do not want to give another explanation of the different possible interpretations of Article 3 of the ECD referred to as the internal market clause. The literature on the connection between the COP and private international law (PIL) is already both rich and extensive.[17] Whatever

[13] Crabit E. (2000), 'La Directive sur le Commerce Electronique. Le Projet Méditerranée', Rev. droit UE 4, 749–833, at p. 752.

[14] Lopez-Tarruella A. (2001), 'A European Community Regulatory Framework for Electronic Commerce', CML Rev. 38, 1337–1384, at p. 1384.

[15] For commentaries more or less contemporaneous to the issue of the ECD, see among the rich literature on the topic, Grynbaum L. (2001), 'La directive 'Commerce Electronique' ou l'Inquiétant Retour de l'Individualisme Juridique', JCP 2001, p. 594; all the contributions in Montero E. (ed) (2001), *Le Commerce Electronique Européen sur les Rails? Analyse et Proposition de Mise en Oeuvre de la Directive sur le Commerce Electronique*, Cahiers du CRID n°19, Brussels: Bruylant; Thieffry P. (2000), 'L'Emergence d'un Droit Européen du Commerce Electronique', RTD eur. 2000, p. 649; Brownsword R. and Howells G. (2000), 'Europe's E-Commerce Directive – A too Hasty Legislative Rush to Judgement?', Journal of Law and Information Science 11(1), 77–88; Gavanon I. and Lagarde-Bellec E. (2001), 'La Directive Commerce Electronique: Quelle est la Part d'Innovation? What is New under the EC Directive on Electronic Commerce?', Revue droit. aff. europ. 2001, p. 723; Marino D. and Fontana D. (2000), 'European Parliament and Council Draft Directive on Electronic Commerce', Computer and Telecommunications Law Review 6(2), 45–48; Pearce G. and Platten N. (2000), 'Promoting the Information Society: the EU Directive on Electronic Commerce', Eur. L. Journ. 6(4), 363–378.

[16] I refer here to all the methods used to coordinate national legal orders and/or national laws. This expression is thus broader than the conflict-of-law technique.

[17] See Hellner M. (2004), 'The Country of Origin Principle in the E-Commerce Directive: A Conflict with Conflict of Laws?' in Fuchs A., Muir Watt H. and Pataut, E. (eds), *Les Systèmes de Lois et le Système Juridique Communautaire*, Paris: Dalloz, pp. 205–224, at p. 209. See also Fallon M. and Meeuse J. (2002), 'Le Commerce Electronique, la Directive 2000/31/CE et le Droit International Privé', Rev. crit. dr. int. pr. 2002, p. 435. The application of the conflict-of-law concepts to the mechanism of the four freedoms was first undertaken by German authors. See the pathbreaking work of Roth P. (1991), 'Der Einfluß des Europäischen Gemeinschaftsrechts auf das Internationale Privatrecht', *RabelsZ* 1991, p. 623. For broad considerations about the

the legal clothing, it is important to emphasize that the scheme set up by the Commission in order to guarantee that ISPs will have to comply with one single body of law, is not without pitfalls. Not only does it override the logic of mutual recognition but also that of national private law, in particular national tort laws, which tend to react progressively to technological change. While diversity of private laws may affect inter-state trade, one may legitimately wonder whether the former really does affect the latter negatively in the long run, since diversity feeds innovation. Therefore, it seems useful to assess the appropriateness of instruments alternative to the COP and appraise the potentialities of PIL as an autonomous regulatory strategy.[18] It is precisely in this direction that I will go.

Article 3 of the ECD provides that

> 1. Each Member State shall ensure that the information society services provided by a service provider established on its territory comply with the national provisions

---

relationship between EC law (the law of the internal market) and the methodology of private international law (both traditional and substantial) see, in particular, among the vast literature on the topic, various contributions in 'Mélanges en l'honneur de Paul Lagarde' (2005), *Le Droit International Privé: Esprit et Méthode*, Paris: Dalloz; all the contributions in Fuchs A., Muir Watt H. and Pataut E. (eds) (2004), *Les Systèmes de Lois*, above this footnote; all the contributions in Picone P. (ed) (2004), *Diritto Internazionale Privato e Diritto Comunitario*, Padova: Cedam; Lagarde P. (2004), 'Développements Futures du Droit International Privé dans une Europe en Voie d'Unification: quelques Conjonctures', *RabelsZ* 2004, p. 225; various contributions in Bergé J.-S. and Niboyet M.-L. (eds) (2003), *La Réception du Droit Communautaire en Droit Privé des Etats Membres*, Brussels: Bruylant; Wilderspin M. and Lewis X., 'Les Relations entre le Droit Communautaire et les Règles de Conflits de Lois des Etats Membres', Rev. crit. dr. int. pr. 2002, p. 38 and p. 289; Fallon M. (1995), 'Les Conflits de Lois et de Juridictions dans un Espace Economique Intégré – L'Expérience de la Communauté Européenne', Recueil des Cours, 253, 72; Duintjer-Tebbens H. (1994), 'Les Conflits de Lois en Matière de Publicité Déloyale à l'Epreuve du Droit Communautaire', Rev. dr. int. pr. 1994, p. 451; Radicati di Brozolo L. (1993), 'L'Influence sur les Conflits de Lois des Principes de Droit Communautaire en Matière de Liberté de Circulation', Rev. crit. dr. int. pr. 1993, p. 401; Basedow J. (1995), 'Der Kollisionsrechtliche Gehalt der Producktfreiheiten im europäischen Binnenmarkt: favor offerentis', *RabelsZ* 1995, p. 1.

18 Interestingly, S. Grundmann insists on the birth of a new conflict-of-law doctrine serving the goal of market integration. For that purpose, he distinguishes between harmonized and non-harmonized areas. In the latter the conflict-of-law rule would in part take the form of the four freedoms. As to the former, he stresses the need to deviate from the standard approach applying traditional conflict-of-law rules. See Grundmann S. (2004), 'Internal Market Conflict of Laws: From Traditional Conflict of Laws to an Integrated Two Level Order', in Fuchs A., Muir Watt H. and Pataut E. (eds), *Les Systèmes de Lois et le Système Juridique Communautaire*, Paris: Dalloz, pp. 5–29. This said, traditional PIL may be given a regulatory function as well: see section II below.

> applicable in the Member State in question which fall within the coordinated field.
> 2. Member States may not, for reasons falling within the coordinated field, restrict the freedom to provide information society services from another Member State.

While such a clause, which was conceived to go beyond ordinary primary EC law, may be legitimate to create a market and contribute to the rapid increase of the population of service providers – by lowering the regulatory burden and promising that only the law of the state where the service is established will apply – it is more and more contentious when this is the time to pass to the stage of market surveillance. This is true for two main reasons.

First, the COP, as embodied in the ECD, undermines enforcement of EC law, which should be one of the essential priorities once a market has been created. The nature of the Internet's architecture makes a centralized control difficult to undertake. Yet, decentralized control is also complicated because the victim – usually the consumer[19] – cannot rely on his or her familiar legal system once the COP is applied. The fundamental trade-off between mutual confidence and effective supervision underlying the mutual recognition mechanism is thus lost.

Second, the passage to the stage of market surveillance should reasonably mean that the balance between producers' interests and consumers' interests must be progressively refined so that an effective control of the market is established.[20] Yet, EC action tends to become obsolete very quickly. Six or even seven years after the adoption of the first EC text on electronic commerce the diagnosis is not that promising, even if anticipated. EC '*régulation*' has failed to free itself from technological biases. The phenomenon is not limited to the ECD: this holds true at least for Directive 1999/93/EC on electronic signatures,[21] for Directive 2000/46/EC

---

19 John Dickie identifies three consumers' interests which are weakened by the digital technology: fair dealing, privacy and morality. They all fall within the scope of the COP, even if B2C contractual relationships are expressly excluded. Businesses' interests are also jeopardized by this technology to the extent that the Internet eases violations of intellectual and industrial property rights. But in these cases, the COP does not apply. See Annex to the ECD and more generally Dickie J. (2005), *Producers and Consumers in EU E-Commerce Law*, Oxford and Portland, Oregon: Hart Publishing.

20 The evolution of the liability of ISPs after the enactment of the ECD is particularly telling: their role of gatekeeper is becoming more and more important in spite of the prevalence of the self-regulation/total immunity paradigm at the beginning of the millennium. See section II, §2.2, below.

21 According to Christina Ramberg,

> [E]xperience shows that it has been very difficult for the legislator not to create new

on electronic money,[22] as well as for the provisions on the liability of intermediary ISPs[23] contained in the ECD. And there is a problem when the dominant business model does not use the technology implicitly regulated by EC texts and when certain interests (for example consumers' interests) must be protected due to the existence of market failures. The very usefulness of such a form of '*régulation*' is thus doomed from the start as is legal certainty. But at the same time, national initiatives become crucial because technologies evolve so quickly that detailed regional intervention is likely to be condemned at its very birth. Therefore, in the electronic marketplace regulatory differentiation is to be promoted. To go one step further, the consideration of consumers' non-economic interests, whose contents may vary from one country to another, reinforces such a claim. Yet, in relation to this regulatory strategy, the COP is of little help. On the contrary, it is likely to thwart state actions. One thus needs to reshape the conflicts methodology. This requires overtaking traditional categories and rethinking the function of PIL within and outside the internal market.

In order to explain the rationale of the conflicts methodology of the ECD, I will proceed in two parts. I will begin by analysing the shortcomings of the COP both from the perspective of the state regulatory margin and from the

---

> legislation that is closely linked to a particular technology. The Electronic Signature Directive is a prime example. This directive turns around a particular technique for ensuring that electronic documents are not manipulated and to trace who the sender of the document is. There are many available techniques to achieve these two goals, but the E-Signature Directive – despite its ambition to be media neutral – in practice only refers to one particular technology (PKI).

Ramberg C. (2004), 'E-Commerce', in Hartkamp A. et al. (eds), *Towards a European Civil Code*, The Hague: Kluwer Law International, pp. 229–244, at p. 229.

22 'The EMI Directive seems clearly to have been drafted with smart-card technology in mind, as the dominant paradigm at the time of drafting.' Guadamuz A. and Usher J. (2005), 'The EC Electronic Money Directive 2000 – Electronic Money: The European Regulatory Approach', in Edwards L. (ed), *The New Legal Framework for E-Commerce in Europe*, Oxford and Portland, Oregon: Hart Publishing, pp. 173–201, at p. 199.

23 Taking the example of the category of mere conduit which was considered in 2000 as not being able to act appropriately against the transmission of unlawful content, Cyril Van der Net explains that today, 'Internet service providers who have entered into transmission agreements with the receivers of their services (mere conduit) are also proportionally capable of this and should therefore be obliged by law to do so. For reasons of legal certainty, technology-independent regulation, … would have been preferred.' Van der Net C. (2003), 'Civil Liability of Internet Providers Following the Directive on Electronic Commerce', in Snijders H. and Weatherill S. (eds), *E-Commerce Law – National Transposition and Transnational Topics and Perspectives*, The Hague: Kluwer Law International, pp. 49–57, at p. 54.

perspective of EC law enforcement. I will then address the potentialities of PIL as a regulatory instrument of its own, at the regional level as well as at the international level. To be sure, my claim is not that PIL is the perfect remedy to solve the problem of the '*regulability*' of cyberspace. However we are not yet at a point where it is possible to speak of a uniform Internet law and it is likely that we will never come close to it because of cultural differences. In addition, harmonization is only a partial answer. We thus still need a conflicts methodology, which is expressly admitted by the drafter of the ECD. The question is which conflicts methodology is more appropriate to reach the regulatory goal at which we aim.

I. THE SHORTCOMINGS OF THE COUNTRY OF ORIGIN PRINCIPLE

While the mutual recognition principle was originally conceived as a means both to bear in mind diversity of regulatory means and to make state enforcement more efficient, the COP is a lot more radical. It reduces the state regulatory margin and at the same time hampers state enforcement.

1. The Original *Raison d'être* of the Mutual Recognition Principle: Giving Effect to Foreign 'Public' Relationships within the Legal Order of the Forum

Under the mutual recognition principle, the legal frameworks under which products or services are manufactured or delivered in neighbouring states are considered equivalent to the legal framework where these products and services are actually hosted in order to be given access to this market, to the extent effective public control is exercised at the source, which is presumed.

1.1 Acknowledging normative equivalence

The EC treaty uses the language of mutual recognition in two provisions: Article 47 EC with regard to freedom of establishment for the self-employed through the recognition of 'diplomas, certificates and other evidence of formal qualifications', and Article 293 EC under which Member States are to negotiate to ensure the mutual recognition of companies and firms. One needs in reality to turn to the ECJ's case law to grasp the features of such a doctrine, in particular in the field of services, which offered a fertile ground for its development due to the relative shyness of the EC legislator, which was more active as regards goods. In short:

> The principle of equivalence and mutual recognition was invented by the

> Community judge to complete the action – appeared to be inefficacious – of the legislator; then it was adopted by the legislator in order to make its action more efficacious, thereby marking a turn from quantitative to qualitative legislation.[24]

Through the *Cassis de Dijon* ruling[25] and its subsequent decisions, the ECJ has set up a technique to cope with state regulatory diversity within an integrated market. In the absence of common rules, disparities between economic national laws creating obstacles to trade should stand only if they are necessary in order to satisfy mandatory requirements relating in particular to the protection of public health, the fairness of commercial transactions or the defence of consumers. This is not to say that legal diversity automatically implies an obstacle to trade, for some indistinctly applicable measures are still outside the scope of Article 28, as evidenced by the *Keck* and *Mithouard* cases,[26] which have defined the outer limit to the application of Article 28 of the Treaty. Nevertheless, the effect-based test used to identity obstacles to trade is flexible enough to encompass a large range of national measures. Under the *Dassonville* holding, 'all trading rules enacted by Member States which are capable of hindering, directly or indirectly, actually or potentially, intra-community trade are to be considered as measures having an effect equivalent to quantitative restrictions'.[27]

When it comes to services[28] and Articles 43 and 49 of the EC Treaty, the ECJ has solemnly proclaimed, in *Gebhard*,[29] *Krauss*[30] and *Svensson & Gustavsson*:[31]

> [N]ational measures liable to hinder or make less attractive the exercise of fundamental freedoms guaranteed by the Treaty must fulfil four conditions: they must be applied in a non-discriminatory manner; they must be justified by imperative requirements in the general interest; they must be suitable for securing the attainment of the objective which they pursue; and they must not go beyond what is necessary in order to attain it.[32]

---

[24] Hatzopoulos V. (1999), *Le principe communautaire d'équivalence et de reconnaissance mutuelle dans la libre prestation de services*, Brussels: Bruylant, p. 107.

[25] Case 120/78 [1979] ECR 649.

[26] Cases C-267 and C-268/91 [1973] ECR I-6097.

[27] Case 8/74 [1974] ECR 837.

[28] Craig P. and De Burca G. (2003), *EU Law, Text, Cases, and Materials*, Oxford, New York: Oxford University Press, p. 819. The *Alpine Investment* decision (Case C-384/93, [1995] ECR I-1141) confirms that non-discriminatory restrictions fall under the Treaty provisions on the freedom to provide services.

[29] Case C-55/94 [1995] ECR I-4165.

[30] Case 19/92 [1993] ECR I-1663.

[31] Case C-484/93 [1995] ECR I-3955.

[32] *Krauss*, above n. 30 at § 32.

The outer limit of the test in the realm of services is however subject to more intensive debate.[33]

Even if the term 'mutual recognition' is not pronounced, such a principle is inherent to this case-law construction. Indeed, generally speaking, the host state cannot impose a second regulatory burden and has to give effect to the home state's one, in other words, to recognize it unless it gives a legitimate justification for not doing so. Hence, the ECJ holding in the *Cassis de Dijon* case expounded upon by the Commission in its subsequent communication:[34] 'There is therefore no valid reason why, provided that they have been lawfully produced and marketed in one of the Member States, alcoholic beverages should not be introduced to another Member State.'[35]

This mechanism of market integration thus relies on a strong principle of mutual confidence. Such a premise is expressly stated by the ECJ in the *Bouchara*[36] case:

> [A]lthough Member States are not prohibited from requiring prior approval of certain products, even if those products have already been approved in another Member State, the authorities of the State of importation are however not entitled unnecessarily to require technical or chemical analyses when the same analyses or test have already been carried out in another Member State and their results are available to those authorities.[37]

---

33 See all the contributions in Andenas M. and Roth W.-H. (eds) (2002), *Services and Free Movement in EU Law*, Oxford, New York: Oxford University Press.

34 'Any product imported from another Member State must in principle be admitted to the territory of the importing Member State if it has been lawfully produced, that is, conforms to rules and processes of manufacture that are customarily and traditionally accepted in the exporting country, and is marketed in the territory in the latter. … The principles decided by the Court imply that a Member State may not in principle prohibit the sale in its territory of a product lawfully produced according to technical or quality requirements which differ from those imposed on its domestic products. Where a product 'suitably and satisfactorily' fulfils the legitimate objective of a Member State's own rules (public safety, protection of consumer or the environment, ... the importing country cannot justify prohibiting its sale in its territory by claiming that the way it fulfils the objective is different from that imposed on domestic products.' Communication from the Commission concerning the consequences of the judgment given by the Court of Justice on 20 February 1979 in Case 120/78 ('Cassis de Dijon') Official Journal C 256, 03/10/1980, pp. 2–3.

35 Ibid, § 14.

36 Case 25/88 [1989] ECR 1105.

37 Case 25/88 [1989] ECR 1105, at §18. See Hatzopoulos, V. (1999), above note 24, p. 119. See also the following cases: C-5/94 *Hedley Lomas* [1997] ECR I-2553, C-87/94 *Commission v. Belgium* [1996] ECR I-2043, Case C-390/99 *Canal Satélite Digital SL v. Administracion General del Estado* [2002] ECR I-607, C-14/02 *Altral SA v. Belgium* [2003] ECR I-4431, C-432/03 *Commission v. Portugal* [2005] ECR I-09665.

This 'upper' principle finds its roots directly in the EC Treaty, in the solidarity between Member States recognized by Article 2 EC, in the cooperation between Member States' policies found in Article 4 EC, in the principle of loyalty laid down by Article 10 EC. In other words, national rules are presumed equivalent[38] and are deemed to fulfill the same economic policy goal, so that it is possible to choose different means to reach the same objective but not to prohibit access to those already adopted by other national entities, as long as the latter are as effective as the former. If the host state is worried about an additional policy goal not already taken into account by the home state, it can regulate the cross-border relationship to the extent it gives a legitimate justification for it and tailors its measure. In theory, the list of mandatory requirements is quite extensive even if their recognition in practice depends on the degree of activism the ECJ is willing to engage in. Because measures having an effect equivalent to quantitative restrictions fall under Article 28 and more generally non-discrimination restrictions on market access fall under economic freedom provisions, the ECJ was constrained to include a rule of reason and increase the number of exceptions.[39] The list has thus been expanded several times: it goes from prevention of tax evasion to consumer protection passing via freedom of the press, protection of the environment, protection of workers, protection of intellectual property, cultural policy and so on.

This said, there is more to the mechanism of economic freedoms than the expression of trust between Member States. It has implications in terms of both horizontal and vertical allocation of regulatory powers. Implementing mutual recognition within the economic freedoms framework does not strictly mean decentralizing in a friendly environment. This institutional arrangement hides a fundamental centralizing dimension due to the presence of the true proportionality test:[40] state regulators are obliged to host within their bound-

38 The burden to allege that the national measure is justified lies with the defendant, the host state. However, it is difficult to state that, strictly speaking, the burden of proof lies with the defendant.

39 The parity between goods and services was only obtained in 1991 with Case C-353/89 *Commission v. Netherlands* [1991] ECR I-4069.

40 The ECJ balances not only competing national interests but more precisely the Community interest with that of the regulating state. It is true that the Court does not often distinguish properly between the three elements of the proportionality test, e.g. suitability (is there any connection between the national rule and the goal advanced?), necessity (could this goal be achieved by a less restrictive means in terms of intra-Community trade?), and true proportionality (cost/benefit analysis between the Community interest and the state interest); most of the time the last stage is actually included in the second one. But, as a result, 'under true proportionality the European Court of Justice, a central organ, uses the Treaty provisions on free movement, central

aries products and/or services complying with foreign laws in cases where a denial of market access would be too costly for inter-state trade.[41] In other words, it is not enough for the regulating state to allege that its policy goal is different from that of the deregulating state and that its measure is tailored to it. It may well be that its legislation as it stands has too great an effect on inter-state trade. True, this cost and benefits analysis is not often explicit but it is nonetheless inherent to the economic freedoms test.

The ECJ thus acts as the centralizing body, picking up the pro-free-trade rule among various state possibilities. Indeed, while there is a fundamental procedural dimension in the test of the economic freedoms allowing the ECJ to control whether the state policy goal is legitimate and the means tailored, there is also a substantial dimension which gives the ECJ the possibility simply to alter state preferences to boost inter-state commerce and override paternalistic policies. It is true that the content of the prevailing norm is originally set up by state power and not by EC institutions. In this sense there is a link between the mutual recognition principle and that of subsidiarity: it is enough in some cases to advance market integration through confrontation of state norms. Mutual recognition thus works as a complement to harmonization, as expressed by the Commission in its White Paper on Completing the Internal Market.[42] But at the end of the day, that out-of-state preferences have not been officially labelled majority preferences by the EC legislator does not make a big difference. They are imposed from the top.

Such a judicial activism is justified by the will to increase the offer of goods and services to European consumers within their home state without making consumers' mobility a pre-condition to market integration. It implies that consumers more than governmental bodies are the real decision-makers. Nevertheless, justifying mutual recognition in these terms becomes contentious when the preferences of consumers, as a social group with social and cultural characteristics, are altered and replaced by lower standards leading to a phenomenon of race to the bottom. Yet, such an unwanted event might occur if the preferences of the regulating state differ from those of the deregulating state. This is the reason why the substantial dimension of the test of the economic freedoms needs to be framed with care.[43]

---

rules to strike down Member State measures. Therefore, the test empowers the Community vis-à-vis Member States and has a centralising character.' Snell J. (2002), *Goods and Services in EC Law, A Study of the Relationship Between the Freedoms*, Oxford, New York: Oxford University Press, pp. 212–213.

[41] Even if reverse discrimination is not condemned.

[42] COM(85) 310 final, June 1985.

[43] It is not to deny though that other substantive considerations can affect the test of the economic freedoms, such as the protection of fundamental rights so that social

1.2 Making enforcement more efficient

It is important to note that the will to promote mutual recognition was cautiously expressed right from the beginning through the setting up of a complex equilibrium. While the distinction between public/private law rules or between regulatory/private law rules might be over-simplistic and even misleading, the ECJ's case law initially and still massively deals with regulatory law rules rather than purely private law rules, in the sense described by Antony Ogus.[44] In other words, the mechanism of mutual recognition originally implied that a centralized monitoring and enforcement system could easily be set up so that each Member State was able to supervise its market efficaciously. This is true not only for the 'judicial' mutual recognition principle but also for the 'regulatory' mutual recognition principle developed by the Commission.[45]

---

as well as economic integration is prompted. See for example Case C-60/00, *Mary Carpenter v. Secretary of State for the Home Department* [2002] ECR I-6279. But even in this case the underlying allocation of regulatory powers must be fully acknowledged and accepted by the players involved in the regulatory process because one touches upon 'internal' state preferences.

[44] Ogus A. (1994), *Regulation: legal form and economic theory*, Oxford, New York: Oxford University Press, p. 2:

> First, regulation contains the idea of control by a superior; it has a *directive* function. To achieve the desired ends, individuals are compelled by a superior authority – the state – to behave in particular ways with the threat of sanctions if they do not comply. Secondly, it is *public* law in the sense that in general it is for the state (or its agents) to enforce the obligations which cannot be overreached by private agreement between the parties concerned. Thirdly, because the state plays a fundamental role in the formulation, as well as the enforcement, of the law, it is typically centralized.

See also Rose-Ackerman S. (1991), 'Regulation and the law of torts', The American Economic Review, 81(2), 54–58, at p. 54:

> The fundamental differences between tort law and regulation center not on substantive standards, or on the distribution of benefits and harms, but on procedures. Statutory regulation, unlike tort law, uses agency officials to decide individual cases instead of judges and juries; resolve some generic issues in rulemakings not linked to individuals cases; uses nonjudicialized procedures to evaluate technocratic information; affects behaviour ex ante without waiting for harm to occur, and minimizes the inconsistent and unequal coverage arising from individual adjudication. In short, the differences involve who decides, at what time, with what information, under what procedures, and with what scope.

[45] Sun J. M. and Pelkmans J. (1995), 'Regulatory Competition in the Single Market', JCMS 31(1), 67–89.

To focus on the field of services (since digital products tend to fit more easily into the category of services than into that of goods), the foregoing can be verified both for measures regulating the access and for measures regulating the exercise of service activities.[46]

In addition, looking at the first manifestations of the COP in EC secondary legislation, the same phenomenon can be observed. To take one example, Directive 89/646/EEC on the taking up and pursuit of the business of credit institutions, amending Directive 77/780/EEC, introduced the principle of a single Community authorization, granted by a Member State to a credit institution, allowing it to pursue all basic banking business throughout the Community, either by setting up subsidiaries or by providing its services directly from the country in which it is established. It is thus up to the home Member State to carry out overall supervision of the banking institution, while the host Member State supervises branches established on its territory.[47] The link between mutual recognition and home state supervision is expressly underlined in the consolidated banking Directive 2000/12/EC:

> The approach which has been adopted is to achieve only the essential harmonisation necessary and sufficient to secure the mutual recognition of authorization and of prudential supervision systems, making possible the granting of a single licence recognized throughout the Community and the application of the principle of home Member State prudential supervision.[48]

The equilibrium set up by Directive 89/552/EEC on television broadcasting activities is similar. Under its Article 2(a)(1), 'Member States shall ensure freedom of reception and shall not restrict retransmissions on their territory of television broadcasts from other Member States for reasons which fall within the fields coordinated by this Directive'. The coordinated fields, which resemble more closely harmonized fields than anything else, encompass the promotion of European works, television advertising, sponsorship and tele-shopping and the protection of minors. A centralized supervision, be it public or even private,

---

46 See Hatzopoulos V. (1999), above note 24, pp. 133 ff. This observation is still valid for the following period (2000/2005). See Hatzopoulos V. (2006), 'The Case Law of the ECJ Concerning the Free Provision of Services: 2000–2005', CML Rev., 43, 923–991.

47 See also other related instruments such as Directive 89/299/EEC on the own funds of credit institutions, Directive 89/647/EEC on a solvency ratio for credit institutions, Directive 92/30/EEC on the supervision of credit institutions on a consolidated basis, Directive 92/121/EEC on the monitoring and control of large exposures of credit institutions. Similar solutions can be found in other fields such as financial services or insurance.

48 Recital 7.

is here often more effective because of both the nature of the architecture of the medium at stake and the very ambit of the control to be implemented.[49]

As such the mutual recognition principle is not a novelty and can be considered as an extension of a mechanism known both in public and private international law.[50] P. Picone acknowledges this and goes even further, clearly stressing the original fundamental difference between the mutual recognition principle and the traditional methodology of conflict of laws. The former instrument is not used to arbitrate between two distinct laws but rather between two different legal orders, each of them implying a package of norms and positive actions to be undertaken by the home authorities. As a result, the legal situation created in the home state (or the external elements necessary for the constitution of a legal situation in the host state) will produce effects in the host state, but within the host state's legal framework. This is an application of the '*metodo del riferimento all'ordinamento "straniero" competente*', which is presented as a complement to the PIL traditional methodology in so far as it targets legal situations which are predominantly external to the forum order.[51] Even if such an instrument may have been extended to cover private law, it was primarily devised for 'public' legal relationships.[52] Although it is difficult

---

[49] We could also evoke Directive 95/46/EC on the protection of individuals with regard to the processing of personal data and on the free movement of personal data, but the prevalence of regulatory law is already less clear. This is why one may wonder whether private enforcement should not also be encouraged in this field.

[50] See Luzzatto R. (1989), 'Il Principio del Mutuo Riconoscimento degli Enti Creditizi nel Mercato Interno della C.E.E', D.C.I, 1989, p. 183.

[51] Picone P. (2004), 'Diritto Internazionale Privato Comunitario e Pluralità dei Metodi di Coordinamento tra Ordinamenti', in Picone P. (ed), *Diritto Internazionale Privato e Diritto Comunitario*, Padova: Cedam (2004), pp. 485–525, at pp. 490–491:

> Such a method . . . presents a complementary characteristic in comparison to the classical method of conflicts of laws, so that it is usually usable for the regulation of legal situations which are mainly outside the forum order. It tends to avoid the emergence or permanence of rickety legal situations (that is to say situations which vis-à-vis two orders at issue produce some effects in only one of them and not in the other one, or vice versa).

Therefore, referring to the home state under the mutual recognition principle 'is not used to apply the law of the [home state], but to verify within the relevant order the existence of a legal situation pertaining to a good or service, which has to be considered whatever the source from which it derives is.' Ibid., p. 495. See also Picone, P. (1999), 'Les Méthodes de Coordination entre Ordres Juridiques en Droit International Privé', Recueil des cours, 276, 9–226.

[52] Picone P. (2004), above note 51, pp. 491–492: 'The hypothesis in which the method of coordination aforementioned has been mostly used is nevertheless the hypothesis in which it is used to secure with the forum the recognition of legal situations established abroad and above all through the act of a foreign public organ.'

to distinguish between public and private relationships, it is essential to grasp the original intrinsic logic of such a system of allocation of competences and to understand that once private law – to the extent the monitoring and enforcement mechanism is still mainly decentralized – is caught up in its web, difficulties arise.

As the distinction between public and private international law is becoming more and more porous and many have begun to acknowledge the applicability of foreign public laws, the mutual recognition principle has been expressed in terms of a hidden conflict-of-law rule, losing its sophistication and complexity due to its fundamental quid pro quo. This trend has been accentuated once the principle of mutual recognition was considered to apply to purely private law norms as well. Yet, this apparently innocuous theoretical exercise has fundamentally altered the characteristics of mutual recognition, giving rise to a 'sanitized' conflict-of-law rule – taking the form of the COP or for others the 'home state control' principle – which appears too simplistic in many respects. As a result, the host state's regulatory margin has shrunk considerably and decentralized enforcement is obstructed. Interestingly, this mutation took place in the arena of e-commerce with the enactment of the ECD.

2. The Evolution of the Mutual Recognition Principle into Secondary EC Law on E-commerce: Applying the Home State Law to Private Damages Suffered Within the Host State

While the COP is a further development of the mutual recognition principle, there is a fundamental difference between these two integration mechanisms. To echo K. Armstrong's words, '[f]ar from mandating a model of home state control, the judgment in *Cassis de Dijon* created a further regulatory space for host state controls through its creation of the mandatory requirements exception'.[53] On the contrary, the COP deprives the host state of any regulatory margin with regard to cross-border exchanges. Moreover, it hinders decentralized enforcement of harmonized EC law.

2.1 Shrinking the host state regulatory margin

The COP is given a broad ambit in the field of e-commerce. As mentioned above, it is not the first application of this principle in secondary legislation. Nevertheless, its implementation is problematic here because of its very scope

53 Armstrong K. A. (2002), 'Mutual Recognition', in Barnard C. and Scott J. (eds), *The Law of the Single European Market – Unpacking the Premises*, Oxford and Portland, Oregon: Hart Publishing, pp. 225–267, at p. 235.

defined in terms of an (almost) all-inclusive coordinated field,[54] including both public and private law rules. In reality, it all began with the electronic signatures Directive. Putting to one side Article 7(1), which lays down a classical mechanism of mutual recognition outside the Community, [55] Article 4(1) provides that 'Member States may not restrict the provision of certification-services originating in another Member State in the fields covered by this Directive'. At first glance, this provision might be seen as a mere duplication of EC primary law. [56] But recital 22 avers that 'certification-service-providers providing certification-services to the public are subject to national rules regarding liability'. Therefore certification-service-providers must only comply with their own national law when it comes to civil liability. This is true whether the certification-service-provider is qualified or not. As a result, certification-service-providers only have to comply with their own national law even if the liability regime has not been harmonized by the Directive.

Article 3(2) of the ECD provides that: 'Member States may not, for reasons falling within the coordinated field, restrict the freedom to provide information society services from another Member State'. The difficulty arises when one takes the definition of the coordinated field. In pursuance of Article 2(h) it encompasses 'requirements laid down in Member States' legal systems applicable to information society service providers or information society services, regardless of whether they are of a general nature or specifically designed for them'. Moreover, not only do they deal with the taking up of the activity, but they also include requirements pertaining to its pursuit, such as 'requirements regarding the quality or content of the service including those applicable to advertising and contracts, or requirements concerning the liability of the service provider'.

---

54 For an overview of the different problems raised by the EC text, see Cachard O. (2004), 'Le Domaine Coordonné par la Directive sur le Commerce Electronique et le Droit International Privé', RDAI 2, 161–179.

55 'Member States shall ensure that certificates which are issued as qualified certificates to the public by a certification-service-provider established in a third country are recognized as legally equivalent to certificates issued by a certification-service-provider established within the Community if…'

56 Article 4(2) adds that: 'Member States shall ensure that electronic-signature products which comply with this Directive are permitted to circulate freely in the internal market'. Article 6 harmonizes liability in the case of issuance of a qualified certificate to the public. Therefore, while the Directive on electronic signatures lays down minimum harmonization standards, Member States can go beyond the harmonized standard only with regard to qualified certification-service-providers established within their territory.

Once Article 3 is combined with Article 2(h) it appears that the host state should defer to an extensive section of the home state's law.[57] Such an interpretation is confirmed by the official position of the Commission as presented by E. Crabit. This author explains how the scope of mutual recognition was extended consciously to definitively wipe out borders within the single market.

> The only efficacious means to suppress borders between member states is to lay down the country of origin principle pursuant to which an operator should normally be subject to the legislation of its country of origin, be its activity local, regional, national, cross-border or pan-European.[58]

As a corollary,

> The definition (of the coordinated field) is very large because it covers all the requirements set forth by the national legislation applicable to the access to activities of information society service and to their exercise. In other words, it concerns all the material legal rules opposable to a provider for its on-line activity, be it general or specific, including national rules which are not harmonized neither by this directive nor by others.[59]

The adjunction of a coordinated field on top of the harmonized field therefore thwarts the state margin for regulating cross-border services and, by the same token, the process of minimum harmonization.[60] What is not harmonized is in reality coordinated and Member States cannot, for matters falling within the coordinated field, restrict the free movement of services, except in a limited number of hypotheses provided they have respected a certain procedure.[61] The grounds warranting a derogation from the COP are significantly limited compared to EC primary law.[62] Generally speaking, Member States can thus go beyond minimum harmonization standards but only to regulate purely internal behaviours.[63] This is why E. Crabit can add: 'This means that they

---

57 Cachard O. (2004), above note 54, pp. 164–165.

58 Crabit E. (2000), above note 13, p. 759.

59 Ibid., p. 766.

60 Generally speaking the directive does not constitute a directive of minimum harmonization. Only certain articles explicitly give member states the possibility of providing for stricter rules. This is the case of Articles 5, 6, 10 of which the wording specifies that member states shall provide that providers at least respect a certain number of information requirements.

61 See Article 3(4)(b) of Directive 2000/31/EC.

62 See Article 3(4)(a).

63 Nevertheless, this seems to be in line with the ECJ in the '*Tobacco*' case C-376/98 [2000] ECR I-8419. The court acknowledges that the Directive challenged does not ensure free movement of goods which are in conformity with its provisions because

(the Member States) can go beyond this minimum set forth in these Articles (5, 6, 7) in order to impose additional requirements to providers established on the territory and only to these ones given Article 3.' While it may make sense for limited segments of public laws, it is not so certain that such a result is appropriate for the whole realm of private law.

It should be noted, however, that requirements applicable to goods as such, to the delivery of goods, and to services not provided by electronic means are excluded from the coordinated field. Furthermore, the Annex of the Directive expressly rejects from the scope of Article 3[64] the freedom of the parties to choose the law applicable to their contract and contractual obligations concerning consumer contracts. The home state's law will therefore not be applied when the parties can benefit from the autonomy principle and where a consumer contract is at stake. In addition, consumer protective measures of the guest state may still affect the cross-border transaction if they are seen as legitimate derogations (that is to say if they meet all the requirements set by Article 3). However, apart from the fact that the ECJ tends to reject attempts to justify national restrictions on the ground of consumer protection,[65] wishing to make Member States respect the majority position in this field,[66] the existence of the procedure framing the expression of national interest inevitably condemns protective solutions progressively elaborated through case law. In other words, the very logic of private law is at stake.

---

of the very presence of Art. 5 in pursuance of which Member States retain the right to lay down, in accordance with the Treaty, such stricter requirements concerning the advertising or sponsorship of tobacco products as they deem necessary to guarantee the health protection of individuals. See §§101 to 103. Compare with Case 322/01 *Doc Morris* [2001] ECR I-488.

[64] But not of Article 2(h). Why?

[65] See, for example, C-198/89 *Commission v. Greece* [1991] ECR I-727; and C-375/92 *Commission v. Spain* [1994] ECR I-923. It is true, however, that the measures challenged restricted access to the activity rather than to the pursuit of the activity.

[66] The ground of justification for national measures has an impact on the intensity of the Court's review.

> Concerns such as public morality, public policy, public security and the related overriding reasons are primarily within Member State competence. The court may be unfamiliar with the issues and there is often no consensus, scientific or otherwise, the Court could draw on. Thus, in the field of goods the Court has shown deference to Member State measures ... This can be contrasted with a more stringent approach towards national measures purporting to protect consumers, both in the field of goods and services. Consumer protection is more closely connected in the area, and there may well be a general consensus that the Court may draw upon.

Snell J. (2002), above note 40, pp. 212–213.

Any duty or obligation imposed on an ISP, be it public or private, is thus likely to fall in the coordinated field thereby dangerously threatening state regulatory autonomy, for it makes the home state's legal regime prevail in hypotheses which have not even undergone harmonization.[67] This is not to deny that private law rules may affect free trade between states, but the equivalence between private law rules must be carefully studied before opting for the COP once and for all especially in the domain of B2C extra-contractual relationships.[68] It is thus an extremely simplified version of the conflicts methodology. This hidden conflict-of-law rule, clearly in favour of businesses, cannot be counterbalanced by unilateral mechanisms such as internationally mandatory rules.[69]

Moreover, I have already suggested that state laws are likely to be crucial in a technical environment that is evolving so quickly.[70] As the number of new activities increases very rapidly, states with the aid of private actors have to adapt or even build up liability regimes from 'scratch'. And if businesses are given incentives to relocate each time a state elaborates a stricter liability regime, a race-to-the-bottom phenomenon may take place and paralyse all regulatory initiatives. Yet, in some cases market surveillance does call for implementing stricter liability regimes rather than mere exemptions, namely where quality of the service is of the essence. The case of certification-service-

---

67 To the extent that the internal market clause works for harmonized areas, the regulatory scheme is less problematic as is the case in part for the electronic signatures Directive.

68 As for B2B contractual relationships, the hidden conflict-of-law rule is also troublesome in the sense that it does not define the regime of the autonomy principle. What if the parties have not explicitly mentioned a particular law? Should one draw a difference between international and national contracts? See for a similar discussion in the case of the service directive proposal, De Schutter O. and Francq S. (2005), 'La Proposition de Directive Relative aux Services dans le Marché Intérieur: Reconnaissance Mutuelle, Harmonisation et Conflits de Lois dans l'Europe Elargie', Cahiers de droit européen, 41(5–6), 603–660.

69 This is the reason M. Fallon's interpretation of the internal market clause should be preferred. 'The application of one provision of the designated law is set aside since within the circumstances at hand, this application would amount to a result contrary to the provisions of the law of the European Union as regards free movement of citizens, goods, persons, services and capital.' Fallon M. (2004), 'Libertés Communautaires et Règles de Conflit de Lois', in Fuchs A., Muir Watt H. and Pataut E. (eds), *Les Systèmes de Lois et le Système Juridique Communautaire*, Paris: Dalloz, pp. 31–80, at pp. 77–78. But still one may wonder whether it is at all legitimate to describe the mutual recognition principle in terms of conflict of laws. Besides, there remains the question of which regulatory function PIL must fulfil.

70 See the Introduction to this Chapter.

providers illustrates this perfectly.[71] Besides, it may be too bold to state that the Internet merely makes the consumer more powerful. Not only does the size and the borderlessness of this space jeopardize consumers' interests but its transience also makes their protection often to no avail.[72] While the offer is better, the buyer eventually loses the means to retort. Thus, if a state legislator decides to frame restrictively the liability of some categories of service providers[73] – the margin between absence of liability and strict liability as such is wide – it is likely that this will be in fact ineffective.

2.2. Undermining enforcement

It is true that a trade-off was actually set up in the electronic marketplace: the host state would refer to the home state law 'on condition' that the latter control the service provider's activity. The electronic signatures Directive states in its Article 3(3) that '[e]ach Member State shall ensure the establishment of an appropriate system that allows for supervision of certification-service-providers which are established on its territory and issue qualified certificates to the public'. There is no such a thing in the ECD. Nevertheless, one can single out Article 3(1) of the ECD which provides: '[e]ach Member State shall ensure that the information society services provided by a service provider established on its territory comply with the national provisions

71 Gobert D. (2004), 'Commerce Electronique: vers un Cadre Juridique Général pour les Tiers de Confiance, Revue du Droit des Technologies de l'information, 18, 33–56, at pp. 39–40. Taking the example of '*le recommandé électronique*' this author observes that providers often tend to limit their liability. He therefore calls for a means to distinguish quality providers from the others.

72 The very characteristics of cyberspace actually justify the states' tutelage in numerous hypotheses. See De Nayer B. (2001), 'The Consumer in Electronic Commerce: Beyond Confidence', in Wilhelmsson T., Tuominen S. and Tuomola H. (eds), *Consumer Law in the Information Society*, The Hague: Kluwer Law International, p. 117: '[T]he ideally balanced relationship between consumers and professionals is being severely threatened by the most recent developments in the field of e-commerce.' Among the factors explaining such market failures we can find mediatization, acceleration and virtualization, internationalization, parcelization and lack of transparency. See also Dickie J. (2005), above note 19.

73 It is noteworthy that such a possibility is not moot. Let's take for example the case of contractual liability – although contractual liability is not the best hypothesis to consider for B2C contractual relationships are excluded from the scope of the COP – set up by the French legislator in the electronic marketplace. Surprisingly, both B2B and B2C relationships are concerned. In any case the professional supplier is subject to a *responsabilité de plein droit*, which means that he is automatically liable if his part of the contract has not been entirely performed unless he proves: the victim's fault; the unforeseeable and insurmountable intervention of a third party; or *force majeur*. See Article 15 of '*la loi pour la confiance dans l'économie numérique*' n° 2004-575, 21 June 2004.

applicable in the Member State in question which fall within the coordinated field'. Still, one does not find any specific obligation to supervise.

However, even assuming that such an obligation is implicit,[74] it is hardly acceptable to base the extension of the COP to private law on the home state's obligation to control the activity of service providers established within its boundaries when no centralized supervision can be implemented satisfactorily due to the nature of the architecture. In other words, private actors in the host state are essential to the enforcement mechanism since they are actually 'closer' to the infringement than the home state. Yet, by systematically applying the home state private law we weaken the enforcement mechanism. We make it more difficult for private actors from the host state to act or react. True, Simon Weatherill notes:

> [H]ome State control is efficient, for the home State is closest to the trader and best able to act if the rules are violated. And home State control is undeniably conducive to driving forward market integration. However, especially (but not only) where the traders based in the home State are politically influential and where damage done by failure to police compliance with EC Directives would largely be felt by consumers in host States, it is not obvious that there are incentives for home States to act effectively to enforce the 're-regulatory bargain'. Quite the reverse – the domestic political mandate is not tied to the interests of out-of-state consumers.[75]

This said, Simon Weatherill minimizes the dark side of the picture by adding that private litigation is not a very powerful enforcement strategy, in particular when diffuse interests are injured such as consumers or the environment. Yet, the inability of consumers to act is not fatal, and consumer associations are particularly active in countries where they have standing to sue, as is the case in France.[76] Besides, the Commission has realized the importance of

---

[74] Compare with Directive 2002/21/CE on a common regulatory framework for electronic communication networks and services. The supervision of competent national regulatory authority is to be implemented as regards the Specific directives i.e. Directive 2002/20/EC (Authorisation Directive), Directive 2002/19/EC (Access Directive), Directive 2002/22/EC (Universal Service Directive) and Directive 97/66/EC.

[75] Weatherill S. (2003), 'The Regulation of E-Commerce under EC Law: The Distribution of Competence Between Home States and Host States as a Basis for Managing the Internal Market', in Snijders H. and Weatherill S. (eds), *E-Commerce Law – National Transposition and Transnational Topics and Perspectives*, The Hague: Kluwer Law International, pp. 9–26, at p. 22.

[76] See, for example, in the field of e-commerce, Tribunal de Grande Instance de Bobigny Chambre 7 Jugement du 21 mars 2006, *UFC Que Choisir v. Voyages sur mesure*; Juridiction de Proximité de Dijon Jugement du 10 novembre 2005, *UFC Que Choisir Cote d'Or v. Free*; Tribunal de commerce de Paris 1ère chambre Jugement du 05 avril 2005, *UFC Que Choisir v. Tiscali*; Tribunal de grande instance de Nanterre

consumer associations,[77] even if it has so far only put the emphasis on a procedure to allow a qualified body from one country to seek an injunction in another in the case of EC infringement,[78] and more generally on the cooperation of entities expressly defending consumers' interests.[79] Even assuming centralized control is useful,[80] why shouldn't one join both centralized and

1ère chambre Jugement du 2 juin 2004, *UFC Que Choisir v. AOL Beterlsmann Online France*; Cour de cassation, Première chambre civile, 9 mars 2004, *AOL Beterlsmann v. UFC Que Choisir et autres*. For more decisions see http://www.legalis.net/jurisprudence. php3?id_rubrique=19, accessed 14 September 2006.

[77] 'Consumer associations can make an important contribution to the proper enforcement of consumer policy measures both through their use of injunctions and their general market surveillance role.' Communication from the Commission on Consumer Policy Strategy 2002–2006, COM(2002) 208 final, at p. 25. But the Commission insists mainly on the necessity to set up training courses and involve consumer organizations in EU policies.

[78] See the Injunctions Directive 98/27/EC. The Directive does not impose any obligation on Member States to give standing to consumer associations. For a recent list of all the qualified bodies, see the Commission Communication concerning Article 4(3) of the Directive 98/27/EC on injunctions for the protection of consumers' interests, concerning the entities qualified to bring an action under Article 2 of this Directive, 2006/C 39/02. See for a presentation of the '*acquis communautaire*' in this field, Chardenoux S. and Stalla-Bourdillon S. (2006), 'L'agent de la Sanction', in Rochfeld J. and Aubert De Vincelles C. (eds), *L'Acquis Communautaire – Les Sanctions de l'Inexécution du Contrat*, Paris: Economica, pp. 67–94.

[79] Regulation 2006/2004 on cooperation between national authorities responsible for the enforcement of consumer protection law (regulation on consumer protection cooperation). The objective is to remove existing barriers to information exchange and cooperation and empower enforcement authorities to seek and obtain action from counterparts in other Member States. It seems, however, that the Commission considers here public centralized rather than private decentralized enforcement bodies.

[80] In France, the system of enforcement is actually both centralized and decentralized. Not only can consumer associations bring suits but also the administration (*la Direction générale de la concurrence, de la consummation et de la répression des fraudes* (DGCCRF) with its *Centre de surveillance du commerce électronique*) has been granted specific powers in the field of consumer protection. While it is entitled to act mainly in case of criminal infractions, it is empowered to take measures to prohibit unfair terms. This said, in its report on cyber-consumption the *Observatoire de la cyber-consommation* (launched in the framework of the *Forum des droits de l'Internet*) notes that the judiciary has been particularly active and has developed solutions protective of consumers' interests. It is however necessary to improve the mechanism of enforcement. See 'Cyber-consommation: les nouvelles tendances, Premier rapport de l'Observatoire de la cyber-consommation' (2003), http://www.ladocumentationfrancaise.fr/rapports-publics/044000142/index.shtml accessed 14 September 2006. Besides, the DGCCRF acknowledges that it principally controls websites which have been designated by consumers. See http://www.minefi.gouv.fr/DGCCRF/03_publications/actualitesccrf/internet185.htm?ru=03 accessed 14 September 2006.

decentralized enforcement means? How does one assert one's rights when one does not know the content of the law applicable to the situation at hand?

To use P. Picone's vocabulary, the objective of such a conflicts methodology is not to refer to the whole foreign legal order to give effect to a legal situation within the forum but to render more difficult actions against out-of-state actors which appear to be businesses.

It may seem, at first glance, that all this discussion does not really matter for e-commerce is basically based on contractual relationships and tort law is condemned to disappear in this marketplace. This would be explained in part by the increasing role played by intermediaries. Generally speaking, the very architecture of the digital medium makes security and authentication a primordial requirement for electronic commerce, whereas security is already built into the network design of traditional trade, be it electronic or not.[81] Intermediaries are thus often necessary to increase the security of transactions.[82] This is the reason why some can say that the 'internet's most salient characteristic is that it inserts intermediaries into relationships that could be, and previously would have been, conducted directly in an offline environment'.[83] In several cases, consumers will contract directly with them. Take, for example, the case of what could be a payment intermediary who would block the money paid by the consumer until a certain date at which the latter would receive the goods or service ordered. Such an intermediary would allow consumers to benefit in practice from the cooling-off period implemented by Directive 97/7/EC on distant selling contracts.[84]

Nonetheless, in the process of 'intermediation', contractual as well as extra-contractual relationships are likely to appear. Take this time the case of electronic-signatures-certification providers, who are not necessarily contractually related with the consumer. In some cases the consumer may have to sue directly the electronic signature provider to obtain actual redress. This is the reason why the electronic signatures Directive actually harmonizes both contractual and extra-contractual liability. [85] The same discussion could stand

---

[81] See European Commission, 'A European Initiative in Electronic Commerce', COM(1997) 157.

[82] D. Gobert insists on the importance of '*tiers de confiance*' whose role is to increase the confidence of Internet users. Gobert D. (2004), above note 71, p. 34. See also the Report drafted by L'Observatoire des Droits de l'Internet, Avis n°3, 'Pistes pour renforcer la confiance dans le commerce électronique' June 2004, available at http://www.internet-observatory.be accessed 14 September 2006.

[83] Mann R. J. and Belzley S. R. (2005), 'The Promise of Internet Intermediary Liability', Wm & Mary L Rev 47, 239–307, at p. 240.

[84] See Gobert D. (2004), above note 71, pp. 50 ff.

[85] The ground for liability is reasonable reliance, which does not necessarily imply a pre-existing contractual relationship. See Article 6(1): 'As a minimum,

for archiving service providers, whose role is likely to increase in the near future. To take but one more example, the French law on 'la confiance dans l'économie numérique'[86] has added a new contractual obligation borne by businesses:

> When a contract is entered into via electronic mail and involves a sum equal or to greater than an amount determined by decree, the supplier shall retain the document which embodies it for a period determined by that same decree and shall provide access thereto to the other contracting party whenever the latter so requests.

Businesses may be tempted to call third parties to undertake such a task.[87]

Above and beyond this, even assuming business-to-consumer relationships will usually be contractual, tort law comes back, this time by the front door, when the enforcement actor is not the individual victim anymore. Consumer associations defending a collective interest, different from the sum of individual interests, act under principles of extra-contractual liability. This seems to be true particularly at the European level. With regard to unfair terms, in 2002 the ECJ, interpreting Article 7 of Directive 93/13/EC on unfair terms, ruled[88] that a collective action to make unfair terms unlawful could be undertaken even if these terms had not been used in contracts but had only been recommended by professionals or their own associations. The contractual relationship is therefore not of the essence of the action of consumer associations. The solution adopted by the French Supreme Court, which held that a consumer association could not have standing to file a suit when the defendant had not contracted with a consumer, even if a standard-term contract had been drafted and had been used by a consumer to contract with another consumer,[89] should be abandoned. At the level of conflict of laws, this should mean that one should logically resort to connecting factors devised for extra-contractual relationships.

Member States shall ensure that by issuing a certificate as a qualified certification to the public or by guaranteeing such a certificate to the public a certification-service-provider is liable for damage caused to any entity or legal or natural person who reasonably relies on that certificate…'

86 Loi nº 2004-575, 21 June 2004, Art. 27 Journal Officiel 22 June 2004.

87 See Gobert D. (2004), above note 71, p. 44. See also Demoulin M. and Gobert D. (2003), 'L'Archivage dans le Commerce Electronique: Comment Raviver la Mémoire?', in *Commerce Electronique: de la Théorie à la Pratique,* Cahiers du CRID, n°23, Brussels: Bruylant, pp. 101–130.

88 Case C-372/99 24 January 2002.

89 Cour de cassation, civ. 1ère, 4 May 1999, Semaine Juridique édition Générale 1999, II, 10205, note G. Paisant; Dalloz 2000, sommaire 48, observation G. Paisant. Compare with Cour de cassation, civ. 1ère, 2 February 2005, Bulletin civil n°55, p. 50, Dalloz 2005, AJ p. 487, observation C. Rondey; Revue Trimestrielle de Droit Civil 2005, p. 393, n° 8, obervation J. Mestre et B. Fages; Semaine Juridique édition Générale 2005, I, 141, observation J. Rochfeld.

This consequence seems to be admitted by the EC legislator when it writes in Article 2.2 of the Directive 98/27/EC on injunctions for the protection of consumers' interests:

> This Directive shall be without prejudice to the rules of private international law, with respect to the applicable law, thus leading normally to the application of either the law of the Member State where the infringement originated or the law of the Member State where the infringement has its effect.

The language used differs from that of the conflict-of-law rule as regards contracts. Even more to the point, the ECJ went further still in 2002[90] concerning this time the conflict of jurisdictions issue. The question posed to the Court was whether an action introduced by a consumer association to prevent the use of unfair terms (under Article 7 of the unfair terms Directive) could be considered as a *delict* or quasi *delict* action under Article 5.3 of the Brussels Convention.[91] The Court answered affirmatively, considering that such an action could not fall within the limitative category of contractual actions for no contract had been concluded between the association and the defendant. The preventive nature of such an action was not conclusive. According to the Court:

> Admittedly, it is likely that the trader has already entered into contracts with a number of consumers. However, whether the court action is subsequent to a contract already concluded between the trader and a consumer or that action is purely preventive in nature and its sole aim is to prevent the occurrence of future damage, the consumer protection organisation which brought that action is never itself a party to the contract. The legal basis for its action is a right conferred by statute for the purpose of preventing the use of terms which the legislature considers to be unlawful in dealings between a professional and a private final consumer.[92]

It is therefore more than probable that such a relationship will be considered as extra-contractual when it comes to the question of the choice of the applicable law. Is it consistent to have a different conflict-of-law rule when the

---

90 Case *Henkel*, C-167/00 [2002] ECR I-8111.

91 It follows that, in order to answer the question referred by the national court, it need only be determined whether a preventive action brought by a consumer protection organisation for the purpose of preventing a trader from using terms considered to be unfair in contracts with private individuals is a matter relating to a contract within the meaning of Article 5(1) of the Brussels Convention, or in fact a matter relating to tort, delict or quasi-delict within the meaning of Article 5(3) of that convention. *Henkel*, §34.

92 *Henkel*, above n. 90 at §39.

enforcement actor differs? I do not think so. On the contrary, if consumer associations are necessary to enforce consumer law effectively given that individual consumers do not often take the initiative to sue, why not ease such an endeavour? How then could a regulatory instrument likely to obtain such a result be built?

At this stage, it is interesting to note the changes made to the Commission's original proposal for the Services Directive.[93] Initially the Commission was convinced that the COP would work better than PIL rules within the coordinated field defined as 'any requirement applicable to access to service activities or the exercise thereof'.[94] This view was heavily criticized and the former COP was replaced by a provision on the freedom to provide services. As a result the coordinated field has disappeared all of a sudden. However, while henceforth it may be seen as useless, Article 17 continues to exclude expressly from the scope of the market clause 'provisions regarding contractual and non-contractual obligations, including the form of contracts, determined pursuant to the rules of private international law'.[95]

This said, some Member States opted for the COP when they transposed the ECD. This seems to be the case for the United Kingdom even if the wording of the Electronic Commerce Regulations 2002 is not conclusive.[96]

---

[93] See first the Proposal for a Directive of the European Parliament and of the Council on Services in the Internal Market, COM(2004) 2 final/3, the Amended Proposal for a Directive of the European Parliament and of the Council on Services in the Internal Market, COM(2006) 160 final and finally the text of Directive 2006/123/EC of 12 December 2006 on services in the internal market.

[94] See Article 4(9).

[95] This exclusion was first drafted in the following manner: 'the non-contractual liability of a provider in the case of an accident involving a person and occurring as a consequence of the service provider's activities in the Member State to which he has moved temporarily.' See also the process of redrafting of Directive 2005/29/EC on unfair commercial practices as described by Micklitz H.-W. (2006), 'Minimum/Maximum Harmonisation and the Internal Market Clause', in Howells G., Micklitz H.-W. and Wilhelmsson, T., *European Fair Trading Law – The Unfair Commercial Practices Directive*, England and US: Ashgate, pp. 27–47.

[96] This is complex wording which would seem to fall short of what many may have wanted to see in the UK Regulations – a clear statement that ISSPs established in the UK must comply with UK law, and only UK law, if their activities fall within the coordinated field. One assumes from the optimistic statements by the Government, …, that [it] is the Government's view that country of origin rule as it has been implemented in the Regulations means just that: that (subject to the discussion on consumer right below) it will be the law of the place of establishment on the ISSP that is the applicable law where activities fall within the coordinated field.

Waelde C. (2005), 'Article 3, ECD: Internal Market Clause – International Private Law, Consumers and the Net: A Confusing Maze or a Smooth Path towards a Single

Luxembourg[97] and Austria[98] have adopted clearer texts in this sense. The same appears to be true for Germany[99] and France.[100] But what if PIL could do a better job? The answer to this question depends ultimately on the content of the regulatory goal being pursued.

II. THE POTENTIALITIES OF PRIVATE INTERNATIONAL LAW

To comprehend the potentialities of PIL fully, one needs to distinguish between the regional and the international level. At the regional level, it may contribute to the implementation of the subsidiarity principle, serving a high level of consumer protection. At the international level, as well as at the regional level to some extent, it can help safeguard diversity, that is to say adjusting state regulatory margins, when no supra-national authority is competent. PIL is thus twice useful.

1. At the Regional Level: Implementing the Subsidiarity Principle

At the regional level, the PIL substantial methodology may positively complement processes of harmonization.

1.1 Rediscovering the substantial methodology

It is important to begin by distinguishing between two fields of competence.[101] First, subject-matters for which the Community is competent to intervene, but not exclusively. This is the domain of the subsidiarity principle whose implementation does not strictly mean the furtherance of diversity, as an ultimate end:[102]

European Market' in Edwards L. (ed), *The New Legal Framework for E-Commerce in Europe*, Oxford and Portland, Oregon: Hart Publishing, pp. 3–29, at p. 12.

97 Loi du 14 août 2000 relative au commerce électronique, Memorial, Journal Officiel du Grand-Duché de Luxembourg, A – N° 96 du 8 septembre 2000, p. 2176, Article 2(4).

98 152. E-Commerce-Gesetz, Bundesgestzblatt 2001 vom 21/12/2001, Teil I S. 1977. Pt 6, §20(1).

99 Gesetz über rechtliche Rahmenbedingungen für den elektronischen Geschäftsverkehr, 14/12/2001, BGB1 I 2001 I, 3721.

100 Loi n° 2004-575, 21 June 2004 *'pour la confiance dans l'économie numérique'*, Article 17.

101 See Amato G. (2006), 'The Legitimacy of Private Law Making', contribution to the workshop, 'The making of European law: regulatory strategy and governance design' organized at the European University Institute in April 2006.

102 See Art. 5(2) of the EC Treaty. The subsidiarity principle remains in the hands of the Community institutions.

> In areas which do not fall within its exclusive competence, the Community shall take action, in accordance with the principle of subsidiarity, only if and in so far as the objectives of the proposed action cannot be sufficiently achieved by the Member States and can therefore, by reason of the scale of effects of the proposed action, be better achieved by the Community.

This implies that it may be sufficient to rely on Member States' initiative for the implementation of the policy goals set at the EC level. Second, in fields where the Community is not granted either exclusive competence or shared competences, Member States are competent. One thus needs here to adjust state regulatory powers so that each one is able to express its preferences freely. This is about safeguarding diversity. Not only is this true at the regional level, but also at the international level.

I will thus begin with the regional level and the implementation of the subsidiarity principle[103] according to which coordinating state regulatory powers may be more appropriate than EC direct intervention. Yet, PIL, in particular in the form of the substantial methodology, may be better suited than the COP as embodied in the ECD when it comes to the question of how to adjust national legal norms. As I have tried to show, the latter is likely to thwart state regulatory innovation and make private enforcement more difficult.

Universal PIL clauses (to be distinguished from internal market clauses) have been included in directives, as is the case in Directive 93/13/EC on unfair terms, in order to secure a certain level of consumer protection outside the Community.[104] Its Article 6(2) provides that:

> Member States shall take the necessary measures to ensure that the consumer does not lose the protection granted by this Directive by virtue of the choice of the law of a non-Member country as the law applicable to the contract if the latter has a close connection with the territory of the Member States.

The reading of this article shows that PIL should aim at preserving EC preferences in terms of consumer protection, even if the connecting factor chosen can actually be criticized.[105] But what is striking is that PIL has not been considered to advance consumers' interests within the Community, while it

---

[103] There is no doubt that consumer protection falls in the field of shared competence even after the introduction of Art. 153 EC.

[104] See also Directive 97/7/EC on distance contracts, Directive 99/44/EC on certain aspects of the sale of consumer goods and associated guarantees, and Directive 2002/65/EC on distance marketing financial services.

[105] In a recent decision the ECJ expressed its preference for a flexible connecting factor, being supposedly more protective of European consumers' interests. See Case C-70/03 *Commission v. Kingdom of Spain* [2004] ECR I-7999.

has been so considered with regard to the protection of businesses' interests. Businesses as well as consumers have their interests made vulnerable when they access the electronic marketplace. It is nowadays almost a platitude to state that digital technologies have radically improved consumers' copying capacities, creating a significant loss of earnings for intellectual property right-holders.[106] Yet when businesses' interests are jeopardized by the unlawful actions of out-of-state consumers, the majority opinion has never been that the law of the infringer should systematically apply. If one glances at the Rome II proposal, one can read in pursuance of Article 9.1: 'The law applicable to a non-contractual obligation arising from an infringement of an intellectual property right shall be the law of the country where the protection is sought.'[107] In other words, '[t]his rule, also known as the 'territorial principle', enables each country to apply its own law to an infringement of an intellectual property right which is in force in its territory'.[108] This solution has been driven by the fear that infringers will relocate to more liberal countries if the law of the country of emission systematically applies. Even if it is difficult to give a systematic presentation of conflict-of-law rules in the field of intellectual property, it is clear that the concern for the right-holder lies at the heart of the elaboration of the conflicts methodology. True, one could retort that it is not appropriate to compare CvB with BvC,[109] for there is an additional dimension in the former:

---

106 To speak only about musical work, the MP3 compression standard and peer-to-peer technologies such as Napster and many others turned the Internet into a music distribution medium through which Internet users can exchange copyrighted audio files without asking for authors' authorization and therefore paying the price for such a service. The music industry has thus initiated a copyright war by taking legal action against websites offering unlicensed song scores and lyrics. See *A&M Records Inc. v. Napster Inc* 114 F. Supp. 2d. 896 (N.D. Cal. 2000), 239 F. 3d 1004 (9th Cir. 2001); *KaZaa BV v. Vereniging Buma & Stichting Stemra* Amsterdam Court of Appeal, Case 1370/01 SKG, 28 Mars 2002; *Vereniging Buma and Stichting Stemra v. Kazaa B.V.*, C02/186HR, Hoge Raad der Nederlanden (12/19/03); *Metro-Goldwyn-Mayer Studios, Inc. v. Grokster Ltd.*, 380 F. 3d 1154 (9th Cir. 2004), 125 S. Ct. 2764, 162 L. Ed. 2d 781, U.S., (2005); *Universal Music Australia Pty Ltd v. Sharman Licence Holdings Ltd*, [2005] FCA 1242, Australia S. Ct, (5 September 2005). See also Strowel A., Thoumsin P.-Y. (2005), 'Le P2P: un Problème Pressant en Attente d'une Réponse Législative?', PI, 17, 428–434.

107 Intellectual property rights (as well as industrial property rights) are excluded from the ambit of the ECD internal market clause.

108 Proposal for a regulation of the European Parliament and Council on the law applicable to non-contractual obligations ('Rome II'), COM(2003) 427 final, p. 20.

109 It is interesting to distinguish between two kinds of B2C relationships in terms of regulatory technique used. First, situations in which consumers' interests are at stake and are likely to be infringed by businesses' actions (CvB). Second, situations in which businesses' interests deserve protection and are thus equally likely to be infringed by massive consumers' actions (BvC).

the promotion of interstate trade. However, market integration considerations are also present in the field of intellectual property. Besides, there is also a cultural dimension in the field of consumer protection.

To the extent that enforcement of EC consumer law should be enhanced and state innovation should be promoted ultimately to increase the level of consumer protection,[110] why not use the PIL substantial methodology?[111] P. Picone defines the substantial methodology in the following manner:

> Strictly understood (therefore to the exclusion of the most limitative hypotheses in which classical or traditional rules of conflict are only substantially conditioned), the substantial methodology of conflicts of laws, is the one expressed, above all within European systems of conflict, through the functioning of provisions of conflict comprising from the outset an alternative or solely subsidiary connection of several laws. These provisions of conflict compel the application of the law most favorable to the production of a specific substantial effect for the regulation of determined circumstances.[112]

True, Article 5(2) of the Rome Convention[113] is already an example of the substantial methodology. But designed for the physical world, it has shown its

---

110 Article 153(1):

> In order to promote the interests of consumers and to ensure a high level of consumer protection, the Community shall contribute to protecting the health, safety and economic interests of consumers, as well as to promoting their right to information, education and to organise themselves in order to safeguard their interests.

111 The COP can actually be seen as one expression of the PIL substantial methodology: the conflict of law rule is set to favour businesses in order to build a single European market. However, it endangers EC law enforcement as well as state innovation.

112 Picone P. (2004), above note 51, at pp. 489–490.

113 Article 5.2 of the Rome Convention provides that:

> Notwithstanding the provisions of Article 3, a choice of law made by the parties shall not have the result of depriving the consumer of the protection afforded to him by the mandatory rules of the law of the country in which he has his habitual residence: – if in that country the conclusion of the contract was preceded by a specific invitation addressed to him or by advertising, and he had taken in that country all the steps necessary on his part for the conclusion of the contract, or – if the other party or his agent received the consumer's order in that country, or – if the contract is for the sale of goods and the consumer travelled from that country to another country and there gave his order, provided that the consumer's journey was arranged by the seller for the purpose of inducing the consumer to buy.

limits when applied to cyberspace.[114] Its underlying distinction between active and passive consumers is of little help on the Internet. Assuming one really wants to further consumer protection, one could set the following conflict-of-law rules: it would be for the consumer to choose between the law of the business' establishment and the law of his residence, unless he is acting away from the country of his residence.[115] This might work both for contractual and extra-contractual relationships and would avoid artificial distinctions. Such an option given to the consumer would ensure two things. First, it is reasonable to assume that the average cyber-consumer expects his own law to be applied or at least that he lacks the means to know the intricacies of foreign laws.[116] This combination would thus allow the weakest party to defend his rights within a familiar legal framework. But if the cyber-consumer is sophisticated enough to understand that he would be better off if the law of the supplier were to be applied, he could still opt for it. The fact that businesses would have to comply with at least two different laws would force them to abide by the highest level of protection and on the whole would thus feed a race-to-the-top. Because national laws are subject to processes of harmonization, the fear of having to comply with divergent legal systems should subside. Second, state innovation is secured to the extent it aims at enhancing consumer protection because the consumer can opt for the law of his residence. In any case, if regulatory differences are too costly as regards inter-state trade, the test of the economic freedoms should be applied. But such a finding should be based on a real effects-based test. In this regard, the new amended proposal on the law applicable to extra-contractual obligations does not address specifically the problem of B2C unfair commercial practices. More precisely the quality of consumer is of no importance.[117] It is true, however, that the country where the damage arises will tend to be that of the consumer's residence.

---

[114] See Fallon M. and Meeuse J. (2002), 'Le Commerce Electronique, la Directive 2000/31/CE et le Droit International Privé', Rev. crit. dr. int. pr., p. 435.

[115] See the proposal for a regulation on the law applicable to contractual obligations. Its new Article 5.1 states that 'Consumer contracts within the meaning and in the conditions provided for by paragraph 2 shall be governed by the law of the Member State in which the consumer has his habitual residence'. See COM(2005) 0650 final.

[116] See Wilhelmsson T. (2004), 'The Abuse of the 'Confident Consumer' as a Justification for EC Consumer Law', Journal of Consumer Policy 27, 317–337.

[117] See COM(2006) 0083 final. Under Article 5.1:

> Where no choice has been made under Article 4, the law applicable to a non-contractual obligation shall be the law of the country in which the damage arises or is likely to arise, irrespective of the country in which the event giving rise to the damage occurred and irrespective of the country or countries in which the indirect consequences of that event arise.

1.2. Complementing harmonization

Refusing to include consumer protection into PIL regulatory function may be explained by the fact that consumers' interests are said to be better advanced through the use of tools different from PIL.

Despite its avowed defects, the ECD does harmonize some substantial fields such as electronic contract law (removal of requirements of forms in writing by designing an electronic equivalent,[118] regulation of information to be provided,[119] determination of the moment at which the contract is concluded[120]) but also pre-contractual law such as general information requirements,[121] and regulation of commercial communications.[122] These measures have been seen as positive improvements due to the peculiarities of cyberspace, even if their compatibility with other secondary legislation is sometimes questionable. However, it is difficult to state that it exhausts the issue of consumer protection, for it does not address, for example, the question of the role of intermediaries for the purpose of securing transactions beyond providers of certified electronic signatures. More broadly, it does not identify sanctions in the case of breach. Article 20 imposes on Member States the duty to 'determine the sanctions applicable to infringements of national provisions adopted to this Directive and … take all measures necessary to ensure that they are enforced. The sanctions they provide for shall be effective, proportionate and dissuasive.'

'Soft' harmonization had been considered two years before the enactment of the ECD: Directive 98/48/EC quickly amended Directive 98/34/EC, laying down a procedure for the provision of information in the field of technical standards and regulations, to add to its basket of rules on information society services. Recitals (11) and (12) give explanations for such an inclusion. The former[123] acknowledges the law-makers' ignorance with regard to the very architecture of the information society, rejecting the path of extensive or

---

[118] Article 9.
[119] Article 10.
[120] Article 11.
[121] Article 5.
[122] Articles 6–8.
[123] (11) Whereas, for the other still little known fields of the Information Society, it would, however be premature to coordinate national rules and regulations by means of extensive or exhaustive harmonisation at Community level of the substantive law, given that enough is not yet known about the form the new services will take or their nature, that there is as yet at national level no specific regulatory activity in this field, and that the need for, and content of, such harmonisation in the light of the internal market cannot be defined at this stage.

exhaustive harmonization. And yet, the latter[124] does not give up the goal of preserving the smooth functioning of the internal market and avoiding its fragmentation. It thus recognizes the necessity that a coordinating procedure[125] be implemented among norm-makers to secure free movement of services. Whilst Directive 98/48/EC could have been described as merely putting into practice the new approach to harmonization, its scope is definitely broader since 'rules on services' encompasses 'requirements of a general nature relating to the taking-up and pursuit of service activities … in particular provisions concerning the service provider, the services and the recipient of services, excluding any rules which are not specifically aimed at the services …'.[126] So

---

[124] (12) Whereas it is therefore necessary to preserve the smooth functioning of the internal market and to avert the risks of refragmentation by providing for a procedure for the provision of information, the holding of consultations, and administrative cooperation in respect of new draft rules and regulations; whereas such a procedure will help, inter alia, to ensure that the Treaty, in particular Articles 52 and 59 thereof, is effectively applied and, where necessary, to detect any need to protect the general interest at Community level; whereas, moreover, the improved application of the Treaty made possible by such an information procedure will have the effect of reducing the need for Community rules to what is strictly necessary and proportional in the light of the internal market and the protection of general-interest objectives; whereas, lastly, such a procedure will enable businesses to exploit the advantages of the internal market more effectively.

[125] Directive 98/34/EC establishes two types of procedures, one for standards (voluntary technical specifications) and the other for technical regulations (obligatory technical specifications) on industrial, agricultural and fishing products which was extended to cover rules for information society services by Directive 98/48/EC. Articles 2 to 7 provide for the national standardization bodies to notify the Commission, the European standardization bodies and the other national standardization bodies of any new subjects for which they have decided to prepare or amend a standard. Under Article 8(1), the Member States are required to communicate to the Commission any draft technical regulation. The notifying Member State may not adopt the technical regulation for a certain period depending on the category of the measure from the date of notification of the draft to the Commission. This standstill period allows the other Member States and the Commission to examine the notified draft and to react appropriately. In case of comments made by either other Member States or the Commission, the notifying Member State must take such comments into account as far as possible in the subsequent preparation of the technical regulation. Where the draft measure is considered by the same actors as likely to create obstacles to the free movement of goods the author must postpone the adoption of the measure and must take a responsive action detailed in an opinion. A longer standstill period is also provided for in case the Commission announces its intention to propose or adopt a binding Community act in the field concerned by the notified draft.

[126] Article 1. The first report on the implementation of the Directive for the period 1999–2000 gives example of such rules:

> measures concerning the conditions of access to an on-line activity; measures

far, it is difficult to assess the results of such a procedure,[127] the last report made by the Commission only analyses the period ranging from 1999 to 2001. Of course, the procedure has made it possible for the Commission, first, to block one national draft in the contemplation of the future ECD and, second, to check whether the Member States have imposed additional charges compared with those provided under Directive 1999/93/EC on electronic signatures and the ECD.[128] However, the ECD's own cooperation procedure (Article 19), which encourages communications between Member States, and with the Commission,[129] certainly shows that cooperation has not become part of everyday life yet, so to speak. Moreover, Article 19 is less demanding and

---

> concerning the conditions for exercising an on-line activity; measures concerning the provider of on-line services; measures concerning the provision of on-line services, measures concerning the receiver of on-line services; measures concerning de facto mandatory services (e.g. a rule referring to non-regulatory texts or a professional code of practice for the supply of services on line, compliance with which confers a presumption of conformity; a voluntary agreement to which a public authority is a contracting party and the aim of which is compliance with the rules on services; etc.). Brussels, 23.5.2003, COM(2003) 200 final.

[127] 23 drafts were notified in the field of information society services in 2000 and 25 in 2001. The same year the Commission received 505 projects concerning goods. The first report observes that:

> in the field of information society services, the notifications showed that often the Member States make the same requirements as those already fulfilled by the service provider in the Member State of origin. This was considered by the Commission as contrary to the principles of free movement of services and freedom of establishment (Articles 43 and 49 of the EC Treaty).

See the first report, above note 126, pp. 27 ff.

[128] See the first report, above note 126, p. 32. See also the second biennial report of the Commission on the application of mutual recognition within the internal market, COM(2002), 429 final.

[129] The original scheme was more ambitious and provided for the creation of a committee, gathering representatives of Member States and of the Commission to help the latter to gauge national measure in the light of Article 3 of the ECD. See the amended proposal of the ECD COM(1999) 427 final, Article 23. See also De Locht P. (2000), 'La Coopération entre Etats Membres', in Montero E. (ed), *Le Commerce Electronique Européen sur les Rails? Analyse et Proposition de Mise en Oeuvre de la Directive sur le Commerce Electronique*, Cahiers du CRID n°19, Brussels: Bruylant pp. 391–399. But on 24 October 2005 the Commission created the expert group on electronic commerce – an advisory committee composed of representatives of the Member States – whose objectives are: to enhance/facilitate administrative cooperation between Member States and the Commission, to discuss problems in the application of the Directive and to discuss emerging issues in the area of e-commerce. The first meeting was held on 17 November 2005.

the stress seems to be put on information of providers and recipients of services as much as on inter-state cooperation.[130] Along the same line, the fact that 'hard' harmonization has been felt to be necessary, as evidenced by the very enactment of ECD, is not a good sign. Besides, this process of harmonization is still one-sided: the coordinating method advances service providers' interests, not those of consumers. In any case, what the above reveals is that it is utopian wishing to eradicate regulatory diversity even by anticipating and opting for *ex ante* coordination rather than *ex post* 'hard' harmonization.

Going on with processes of 'soft' harmonization, private actors were considered from the beginning as key players of the normative process. In 1997 the Council and the Representatives of the Governments of the Member States had, through a resolution on illegal and harmful content on the Internet, invited the Member States to begin to 'encourage and facilitate self-regulatory systems including representative bodies for Internet service providers and users, effective codes of conduct and possibly hot-line reporting mechanisms available to the public'.[131] Along the same line they had requested that the Commission, to the extent of its competences, 'foster coordination at Community level of self-regulatory and representative bodies'.[132] On 18 November 1998 the Commission answered with a proposal for a legal framework aimed at regulating electronic commerce and outlining the EU conception of the regulatory strategy to be applied to electronic commerce, correctly stressing the importance of enforcement[133] and listing codes of conduct among the means to achieve this goal. The second draft of principles issued by the *eConfidence* forum[134] set up by the Commission after the adoption of the

---

130 See Article 19(4): 'Member States shall establish contact points which shall be accessible at least by electronic means and from which recipients and service providers may…'

131 Resolution of the Council and of the Representatives of the Governments of the Member States, meeting within the Council of 17 February 1997 on illegal and harmful content on the Internet (97/C 70/01), OJEC N° C 7, 10.1.1997, p. 12, § 4.

132 Ibid, § 5.

133 Rather than inventing new rules, the proposal would seek to ensure the existing EU and national legislation were effectively enforced. The development of a genuine Single Market – based on mutual confidence between Member States – is stimulated by strengthening enforcement mechanisms. The proposal would seek to do so by encouraging the development of codes of conduct at EU level, by stimulating administrative co-operation between Member States and by facilitating the setting up of effective, alternative cross-border dispute settlement systems.

'Electronic commerce: Commission proposes legal framework', Brussels 18 November 1998, IP/98/999.

134 *eConfidence* was seen as a:

common package of measures, which include as its main components the promo-

eEurope Action Plan endorsed at the Feira European Council in June 2000.[135] highlighted the key role played by codes of conduct and their standardization upstream of the stage of enforcement.

If one now considers the ECD, Article 16 expressly favours the drawing up of codes of conduct and Article 17 forces Member States to remove any obstacle likely to hamper the use of out-of-court schemes including electronic means, available under national law, in the case of a dispute arising between an information service provider and the recipient of the service. But Recital (40) is more explicit. '[S]ervice providers have a duty to act, under certain circumstances, with a view to preventing or stopping illegal activities; this Directive should constitute the appropriate basis for the development of rapid and reliable procedures for removing and disabling access to illegal information …'. This wording shows that if the drafters of the ECD might have appeared relatively lenient with information service providers (and especially with technical intermediaries), this is in part due to the state of the technical know-how at that time but also to the view that service providers 'should' have

> tion of high standards of good business practices (e.g codes of conduct, trust marks, complaint settlement procedures), as well as easy and affordable access to third-party alternative dispute resolution (ADR) systems, in particular for settling disputes arising from the expected increase in cross-border transactions over the Internet.

See the website http://econfidence.jrc.it/default/show.gx?Object.object_id=EC_FORUM000000000000000D accessed 14 September 2006. The '*core group*' of the project on principles for e-commerce codes of conduct drafted some guidelines for good quality codes. The paragraph on added value of codes of conduct is typical of the EC understanding of these documents:

> Codes should add value for consumers and code-subscribers through complementing and supplementing legal obligations. In achieving this and in particular when addressing industry-specific issues, codes may repeat, refer to or provide guidance on legal obligations to enable code-subscribers to comply with them, provided that codes do not misrepresent or purport to give authoritative interpretations and include appropriate disclaimers to that effect.

135 This action plan was part of the Lisbon strategy to make the European Union the most competitive and dynamic knowledge-based economy with improvement and social cohesion by 2010. The action was centred around three main objectives: (1) a cheaper, faster, secure Internet, (2) investing in people and skills, (3) stimulating the use of the Internet. It has been followed by the *eEurope* 2005 Action plan: An information society for all, presented for the Sevilla European Council of 21/22 June 2002 and *i2010* – A European Information Society for growth and employment launched by the Commission in early June 2005.

developed self-help mechanisms in return.[136] *De facto* harmonization was to be reached through the drawing up of codes of conduct at the Community level. For this purpose, they should have been drafted in all the Community languages and been available on-line.[137] Furthermore, their authors were invited to submit them to the Commission to determine their compliance with Community law. The EC ambition was to involve all stakeholders in the process of drafting: both businesses and consumer associations should have been involved under Article 16(2). But the 'mistake' was to rely on mere voluntary behaviour and to start from the premise that 'it is in the interest of all parties involved in the provision of information society services to adopt and implement such procedures'.[138]

Indeed, while self-regulation may have been considered as the only regulatory instrument capable of reconciling the desire to harmonize (from the bottom) and the need for a regulatory strategy flexible enough to cope with technical change and safeguard diversity, its disadvantages are increasingly pointed out. In 2006, the verdict was qualified.[139] More precisely, self-regulation as such rarely exists, since it almost always involves the state, albeit to different degrees. Generally speaking, a detailed study of codes of conduct as self-regulatory mechanisms has recently shown that 'a level of compliance needs to be ensured. Industry participants and individual users need guidance with regard to the content of codes, and an impartial arbiter needs to have an appropriate redress mechanism. Both of these variables are often absent in current initiatives'.[140] Interaction between state regulation and private regulation is thus vital.[141] While the norms incorporated in codes of conduct have inspired judges to feed legal standards,[142] a legal framework has been considered necessary for consumer

136 E. Crabit further explains that the Community was relying on another normative source comprising customs and usages. Crabit E. (2000), above note 13, p. 774.

137 Article 16(1)(c).

138 Recital 40 of the ECD.

139 See, for example, Rothchild J. (2000), 'Co-Regulating the Internet', in Wilhelmsson T., Tuominen S. and Tuomola H. (eds), *Consumer Law in the Information Society*, The Hague: Kluwer Law International, pp. 179–203; Holmes J. and Morgan B. (2003), 'The Promise and Peril of Spontaneous Order: The Role of Government in Shaping E-Commerce' in Snijders H. and Weatherill S. (eds), *E-Commerce Law – National Transposition and Transnational Topics and Perspectives*, The Hague: Kluwer Law International, pp. 93–102; Dickie J. (2005), above note 19, p. 14; Price M. E. and Verhulst S. G. (2005), *Self-regulation and the Internet*, The Hague: Kluwer Law International.

140 Price M. E. and Verhulst S. G. (2005), above note 139, p. 154.

141 The road of homologation has, however, sometimes been elected. Such a system has been fostered by the EC institutions in several domains, e. g. the protection of personal data. See Directive 95/46/EC, Art. 27.

142 In a judgment in urgent proceedings rendered on 15 January 2002 the Tribunal

protection.[143] In its amended proposal on the protection of minors and human dignity presented in 2006,[144] the Commission has finally recognized, that on the whole, self-regulation is only an effective *additional*[145] measure. Co-regulation, not easy to set up satisfactorily,[146] is preferred at both national and community level.[147] Under the French initiative, the European Internet Coregulation Network was launched on 11 December 2003.[148] In July 2005 it issued a Report on 'Internet Governance' placing co-regulation at the centre of the regulatory scheme.[149]

---

de Grande Instance of Paris, held that 'the practice of spamming considered in the milieu of Internet as an unfair practice and as seriously disturbing is contrary to the charter of good conduct': see http://www.foruminternet.org accessed 14 September 2006. It is to be noted that this decision was issued before the adoption of Directive 2002/58/EC, Art. 13 of which condemns spamming.

143 See, for example, the recommendation n° 03-01 of the French *Commission des clauses abusives* on Internet access contract:

> °3 Whereas certain standard-form contracts stipulate that the consumer commits, under the threat of contractual sanctions, to respect several codes of conducts, usages or rules of behavior presented as having been developed by the community of users of the Internet network; whereas in case the consumer does not accept the content of these rules, this clause creates an imbalance within the contractual relationship by assigning an obligation of which the object is imprecise to the user, possibly inexperienced . . .

Moreover, their binding effect is progressively accepted to the detriment of businesses. See Directive 2005/29/EC on unfair B2C commercial practices. Many commentators have however regretted the shyness of the EC legislator in relation to codes of conduct in general.

144 European Commission, Amended Proposal for a Recommendation of the European Parliament and of the Council on the Protection of Minors and Human Dignity and the Right of Reply in Relation to the Competitiveness of the European Audiovisual and Information Services Industry, COM(2006) 31 final.

145 Stressed by the author.

146 Rochfeld J. (2006), 'Les Rapports entre la Régulation et le Contrat Renouvelés par l'Internet', in Frison-Roche M.-A. (ed), *Les Engagements dans les Règles de Régulation*, Paris: Dalloz, pp. 209–220, at pp. 213–214.

147 See Poullet Y. (2004), 'Technologies de l'Information et de la Communication et 'Co-Régulation': une Nouvelle Approche?', http://www.droit-technologie.org accessed 14 September 2006, who shows that co-regulation is, generally speaking, seen as a way to implement the subsidiarity principle, whatever the field to regulate at stake.

148 'The objective of the EICN is to feed the public debate with its own vision of the notion of 'internet governance'. This vision is built on the expertise of its members in the legal and policy issues related to the internet. It is directly linked with the philosophy of regulation shared by the EICN members. It inspires recommendations or guidelines for a good internet governance.' See: http://network.foruminternet.org/article.php3?id_article=23 accessed 14 September 2006. It was created by the Commission in its decision 2002/627 [2002] OJ L 200/38.

149 A new path has to be elaborated, adapted to the specificities of the network. It

To sum-up, 'hard' harmonization is condemned to be incomplete, if not quickly obsolete, due to the speed at which technologies evolve. Likewise, 'soft' harmonization, whether centralized or decentralized, cannot stand by itself. Coordinating the national law-making process from the top is a hard task which does not eliminate differences, even if it significantly eases the transposition stage. Besides, co-regulation implies the existence of a legal framework. Therefore, allocation of state 'hard' law is necessary. Ultimately, the choice of the conflicts methodology depends on the upper value to follow, at the regional as well as the international level.

2. At the International Level (and to a Certain Extent at the Regional Level): Safeguarding Diversity

While there is some merit in setting up a dialogue between the different components of European society in order to find a way of effectively regulating the Internet, all useful means should be considered, especially when it may

must be based on a new scheme of cooperation between the public and the private actors, more balanced, more flexible, more open. This smooth procedure, associating all parties in the elaboration of the rules of the network is called coregulation. The word 'coregulation' was born in France in 1998 and it is often quoted in international texts. Nevertheless, it can describe two ways of understanding the regulation philosophy generated by the internet:

In the first meaning, coregulation stands for 'regulated self-regulation': in this form of governance, the business entities or the civil society is associated with the public authorities in order for these latter to control or frame the self-regulatory tools. It generally leads to code of conducts elaborated by a group of actors, then validated and guaranteed by the public authorities.

In the second meaning, coregulation has a wider perspective and leads to a real 'multi-stakeholder partnership'.

This approach is based on the belief of shared responsibilities between the public and private actors on internet issues. The parties have to manage their interdependencies and articulate their specific tools of regulation. It leads to open and balanced discussions between the business sector, the public authority and the civil society in order to elaborate common solutions. These solutions are combining regulatory tools and preferences at the disposal of each actor (laws and decrees, codes of conducts, technical tools, self-awareness...)

This pattern of governance involves a matter of principle: all parties concerned in the development and the uses of the Internet have a legitimate right to contribute to the definition of the rules governing them. It is also built on a matter of efficiency: many problems quite simply cannot be solved without the active contribution of all parties.

The EICN believes that this meaning of coregulation is the governance pattern best adapted to the internet.

See: http://network.foruminternet.org/article.php3?id_article=23 accessed 14 September 2006.

be difficult to reach a consensus with regard to the interests to be protected. 'Traditional' PIL is thus still of interest, but shifting from 'jurisdiction selection' to 'content-law oriented selection' may be necessary to reconcile diverging national policies through the election of an appropriate remedy. This is particularly necessary when the boundaries between public and private laws become blurred,[150] so that state interests should be considered even when private law rules are in conflict.

2.1. Re-discovering 'traditional' private international law

When speaking about the differences between the mechanism of mutual recognition and the COP, I have tried to underline the reduction of the host state's regulatory margin. The latter is not empowered to react against externalities[151] created by the application of the home state's law within its own borders. Yet, to borrow from the economic federalism school,[152] legislators can be tempted to export externalities in order to preserve their competitive-

---

[150] What to say, for example, about the protection of personal data?

[151] It is true that the concept of externalities has been presented as 'one of the most elusive in economic literature'. Scitovsky T. (1954), 'Two Concept of External Economics', Journal of Political Economy 62, 143–151. This concept can be defined in various ways. See Demsetz H. (1967), 'Toward a Theory of Property Rights', Am. Econ. Rev. 57, 347–359, at p. 349:

> Externality is an ambiguous concept. … The concept includes external costs, external benefits, and pecuniary as well as nonpecuniary externalities. No harmful or beneficial effect is external to the world. Some person or persons always suffer or enjoy these effects. What converts a harmful or beneficial effect into an externality is that the cost of bringing the effect to bear on the decisions of one or more of the interacting persons is too high to make it worthwhile, and this is what the term shall mean here.

But the idea of social cost imposed on a community which has not agreed with it, when the costs creator did not take into account such consequences when he decided to act, is essential to understand the difference between the rationale of economic freedoms and that of PIL. More simply, it should thus be possible to define externalities as 'a cost or benefit that the voluntary action of one or more people impose or confer on a third party without their consent'. Cooter R. and Ulen T. (1988), Law and Economics, New York: Harper Collins, p. 45.

[152] See Tiebout C. (1956), 'A Pure Theory of Local Expenditures', Journal of Political Economy, 64, 416–424. There is a vast literature on the Tiebout model. See for example Bratton W. W. and McCahery J. A. (1997), 'The New Economics of Jurisdictional Competition: Devolutionary Federalism in a Second-Best World', Geo. LJ 86, 201–278; Gramlich E. M. (1987), 'Cooperation and Competition in Public Welfare Policies', J Pol'y Analysis & Mgmt 6(3), 417–431; Breton A. (1998), *Competitive Governments: an Economic Theory of Politics and Public Finance*, New York and Cambridge: Cambridge University Press.

ness by lowering their standards knowing that only non-residents will suffer from this for they live in a state where the standard is higher.[153] Even more trickily, the very application of state law to its regulatees' behaviour may by definition impose costs on foreign residents because of porousness of boundaries. This is what happens on the Internet, for instance when it comes to the issue of freedom of expression. If a state has controlled freedom of expression because of its cultural and social history but its neighbour has opted for a more liberal regime and all the publications of the latter happen to be available within the former, one has a situation of cross-border externality because a social cost is created in the first state without its consent. In other words, the policy choice of the former is de facto altered. In the same vein, if one gives a too important role to private autonomy one defeats any attempt by the national entity to lay down policies. As a result, one creates a market failure due to the phenomenon of evasion which occurs when a party chooses the law of state B which does not take into account a certain category of interests of state A, although that party's activity affects that very category of interests. The result is the same if one systematically applies the home state's law.

The remedy to such cross-border externalities has traditionally been harmonization of substantial law at the federal level. However, and this is where the regulatory function of PIL may fully emerge, recent doctrinal contributions have focused on national extraterritorial regulations as a means to reduce cross-border externalities. Joel P. Trachtman insists on the strategy of regulation (as opposed to deregulation often associated with decentralization) as a response to costs' externalization by regulating states and regulatees.[154] In other words, when a state legislation creates externalities for its neighbours the latter should be allowed in some situations to respond using the tool of extraterritorial legislation, especially in cases where centralization is too costly. Not to admit this possibility would give undue consideration to the law of the state of origin. Yet, each state, be it the home state or the host state, can legitimately set up policies for its own citizens. In the language of Joel. P. Trachtman, extraterritoriality means 'the extension of jurisdiction to prescribe

---

[153] The classical example is here that of a state which adopts low environmental standards to attract firms knowing that damages will only be suffered by out-of-state citizens because of specific geographical conditions.

[154] Trachtman J. P. (1993), 'International Regulatory Competition, Externalization, and Jurisdiction', Harv Int'l LJ 34(1), 47–104, at pp. 66–67, 'First in order to limit regulatory arbitrage, especially where it involves international externalization, it may be necessary, in the absence of coordination, to apply regulation 'extraterritorially' or, beyond the generally recognized scope of regulatory jurisdiction.' See also Wai R. (2002), 'Transnational Liftoff and Juridical Touchdown: the Regulatory Function of Private International Law in an Era of Globalization', Colum J Transnat L 40, 209–274.

to conduct taking place abroad'.[155] The difficulty then lies in drawing the line between 'good' extraterritorial legislation and 'bad' extraterritorial legislation which is not proportional to its objective and affects 'too much' foreign interests. The same author therefore suggests focusing on the scope of the effect of the extraterritorial regulation in order to assess the appropriateness of its application to the foreign behaviour: 'An effects-based test for jurisdiction would be appropriate to provide congruence between regulatory jurisdiction and regulatory costs.'[156]

This approach ties up with the concern of other scholars for the preservation of diversities among national entities.[157] Every state is to be put on the same footing as long as its own laws do not defeat its neighbours' policies. This meeting of scholars coming from different backgrounds is particularly pertinent at a time when an 'avant-garde' of the European legal jurisprudence calls for a governance structure of European private law allowing diversity to be secured among Member States. The issue is therefore which legal tool, if any, is able to give life to this wish and contribute to the building of a coherent governance structure turning diversity into a value to fulfil. In US law, the issue of cross-border externalities has been traditionally tackled by the means of the Dormant Commerce Clause theory and not PIL. Jack L. Goldsmith and Alan O. Sykes' article on the realm of the Internet is a perfect example of such an exercise.[158] One possible explanation lies in the chaos of choice of law rules acknowledged by many international scholars.[159] 'Maybe because uniform federal law in the field of conflict of laws does not exist in the United States, the potential of private international law to handle the perverse effects of diversity is rarely considered.'[160] This said, various authors on both sides of the Atlantic have begun to recognize the regulatory function of PIL in the

---

155 Trachtman J. P. (1993), above note 154, p. 54 fn. 24.

156 Ibid., p. 102. To state it differently, national laws legitimately tame cross-border conducts so long as they do not create a situation of over-regulation.

157 Regan D. H. (1987), 'Siamese Essays: (I) CTS Corp. v. Dynamics Corp. of America and Dormant Commerce Clause Doctrine; (II) Extraterritoriality State Legislation', Mich L Rev 85, 1865–1913, at p. 1912; Rosen M. (2002), 'Extraterritoriality and Political Heterogeneity in American Federalism', Univ Penn LR 150, 855–972, at pp. 883–886. For a broader discussion on the relationship between federalism and diversity, see Minow M. (1990), 'Putting Up and Putting Down: Tolerance Reconsidered', Osgoode Hall L J 28(2), 409–448.

158 Goldsmith J. and Sykes A. (2001), 'The Internet and the Dormant Commerce Clause', Yale LJ 110, 785–828.

159 Juenger F. K. (2000), A Third Conflicts Restatement?, Ind LJ 75(2), 403–416; Trachtman J. P. (1994), 'Conflict of Laws and Accuracy in the Allocation of Government Responsibility', Vand J Transnat'l L 26(5), 975–1058.

160 Muir Watt H. (2004), 'Aspects Economiques du Droit International Privé', Recueil des cours, 307, 25–385, at p. 222.

market for legal products and as a result its inevitable institutional dimension.[161] Truly, the assertion of such a function is not new, but is still contentious[162] for '[m]uch of the recent law and economics scholarship of choice of law and conflict of laws, however, has focused too greatly on private interests and on the invigoration of regulatory competition, to the exclusion of governmental interests'.[163] This said, traditionally PIL actually appears particularly suited to answer the question of cross-border externalities. Apart from the fact that the mechanism of the economic freedoms is doing something different from that of the conflict of laws, as the former aims at coordinating orders and not national laws, the logic of the process of coordination fundamentally differs. This is true for at least one reason: the proportionality test to secure free movement is by definition impregnated with mutual trust as well as free trade considerations.[164] In other words, it does not balance the benefits created in the host state and the costs created within the home state but rather the benefits created in the host state and the costs created in the course of inter-state trade.[165] This is why, while the test of the economic freedoms is by

---

161 'A primary function of jurisdictional rules is similarly that of shaping governmental analysis to achieve a greater internalization of externalization among political units.' Trachtman J. P. (2001), 'Economic Analysis of Prescriptive Jurisdiction and Choice of Law', Va J Int'L 42(1), 1–80, at p. 3; 'This discipline would have the role of channeling competition between legislators, without excessively scarifying the benefits it brings elsewhere.' Muir Watt H. (2004), above note 160, p. 223; 'The basic role of private international law in addressing transnational regulatory gaps is to coordinate the process of regulation by national authorities and national laws. In particular, private international rules help to determine when parties injured by the transnational activity of actors can make complaints under national legal regimes.' Wai R. (2002), above note 154, p. 253.

162 Baxter W. (1963), 'Choice of Law and the Federal System', Stan L Rev 16(1), 1–42, at p. 22; Maier H. G. (1982), 'Extraterritorial Jurisdiction at a Crossroads: An Intersection between Public and Private International Law', Am J Int'l L 76(2), 280–320; Brilmayer L. (1987), 'The Extraterritorial Application of American Law: a Methodological and Constitutional Appraisal', Law & Contemp Probs 50(3), 11–38; Kromer L. (1991), 'Vestiges of Beale: Extraterritorial Application of American Law', Sup Ct Rev 1991, 179–224; Wai R. (2002), above note 154, p. 209.

163 Trachtman J. P. (2001), above note 161, p. 3.

164 I do not mean that the economic freedoms are not useful any more, but simply that their 'raison d'être' is different from 'traditional' PIL. They are thus complementary mechanisms. This is all the more true when the economic freedoms are used to advance upper values such as solidarity through the emergence of a European citizenship. Indeed, the strength of such a mechanism is that it can adapt to different rationales depending both on the freedom at stake and the national interests involved. But still in one way or another it is set up to make national legal orders come closer, not simply coexist.

165 J. L. Goldsmith and A. O. Sykes consider that citizens from the home state have a right to trade inter-state. If the host state rule is stricter, they automatically bear a cost.

essence a centralizing mechanism, traditionally PIL can be considered as a decentralizing one.

Going on, what is not stressed enough is that both unilateral and bilateral PIL rules are based on the same rationale. Traditional PIL, encompassing both unilateral and bilateral conflict-of-law rules,[166] aims at preserving state legislative competences, albeit with differences. Whilst the former subset seeks to reduce forum shopping and dreams of uniform conflict-of-law rules, the latter grants more leeway to states since they unilaterally decide whether their preferences are implicated by the factual settings at hand. This may lead to the simultaneous application of different laws by judges belonging to different states. But what J. Trachtman shows, drawing on the theory of governmental interests analysis, is that submitting regulatees to different laws is necessary to preserve effectiveness of state policies without automatically amounting to a situation of over-regulation. It may be less costly to force regulatees to abide by several pieces of legislation than to harmonize through a centralizing process. He thus calls for a certain degree of uniformity expressed in the terms of an effects-based test. However, this remains a unilateral methodology in the sense that states are vested with the power to decide whether their preferences are implicated or not from the very beginning, even if he moves away from the governmental interests analysis since he adds a quantitative dimension to its model, which should allow him to avoid the pitfall of over-regulation. Consequently, in the case of true conflicts the forum state must take into account the harm felt by the other affected state. It may well be that the solution entails consideration of both laws supposedly in conflict. The conflicts methodology becomes bilateral.

The question is therefore how to implement the effects-based test and calibrate it in order to avoid a situation of over-regulation, without falling into a scenario of under-regulation. The difficulty is to determine the extent to which state preferences are implicated. [167] The same author offers various parameters to gauge preferences: facultative law, mandatory law, cross-border circumstances, true conflict, circumstances where regulatory coordination produces joint gains. He insists on the fact that objective or subjective connecting factors could be used as long as they are satisfactory proxies for the distribution of effects. Besides, they would contribute to securing legal certainty from the private actors' perspective. But 'if clear entitlements do not match well

[166] P. Picone is one of the rare authors to rejoin both bilateral and unilateral methodology under the label of traditional PIL. See Picone P. (1999), above note 51, pp. 9 ff.

[167] '[T]he proper implication is not between private and public law, but in the degree to which law implicates state preferences': Trachtman J. P. (2001), above note 161, p. 21.

with the distribution of effects, then under high transaction costs circumstances, another arrangement may be preferable'.[168]

Not to be misleading, the bilateral methodology can also be corrected by unilateral mechanisms, such as mandatory international rules and rules embodying the state's international public order, which are after all the spontaneous expression of state preferences. However, it primarily relies on a 'pre-existing' allocation of legislative competences, which tends to give precedence to the 'closest' national law, without first considering its willingness to be applied,[169] to avoid the simultaneous application of different laws. The decentralization process is thus qualified.

Furthermore, the COP acting as a hidden conflict-of-law rule is not an example of traditional PIL. Truly, whilst originally the mutual recognition principle can be seen as a particular application of '*il metodo del riferimento all'ordinamento 'straniero' competente*',[170] its extension to private law has changed its nature. Henceforth it can be considered as the expression of '*il metodo materiale*',[171] according to which substantial considerations, such as the promotion of free trade, guide from the very beginning the choice of the applicable law to shrink regulating states' latitude. In this regard, one of the issues that I have raised is whether consumer protection should not instead be part of the substantial considerations which weigh on the choice of the applicable law at least in the European electronic marketplace.

2.2 Weighing the intrusiveness of national remedies

Courts within the US and even beyond tend to take into account the effects felt within the forum to assess personal jurisdiction.[172] The same seems to be true with regard to choice of law.[173] J. L. Goldsmith and A. O. Sykes show that,

---

168 Ibid., p. 77.

169 The introduction of '*renvoi*' nevertheless increases state leeway.

170 'Referring to the state of origin is not used to apply the law of the latter, but to verify the existence within its own order of a legal situation pertaining to a good or service, which must be considered whatever the source from which this legal situation stems. [T]he criterion of origin is designed within the field considered (in which the principle of mutual recognition has been affirmed for the first time) as a way to refer, from the country of destination, not to the law but to the order of the state of origin considered as a whole.' Picone P. (2004), above note 51, pp. 495–496.

171 Picone P. (2004), above note 51, pp. 489–490.

172 See Reidenberg J. (2005), 'Technology and Internet Jurisdiction', U Pa L Rev 153, 1951–1974, at p. 1955, quoting *Gator.com Corp v. L.L. Bean, Inc.*, 341 F. 3d 1072, 1078 (9th Cir. 2003), rehearing en banc granted, 366 F. 3d 789 (9th Cir. 2003); *ALS Scan, Inc. v. Digital Serv. Consultants, Inc.*, 293 F. 3d 707, 714 (4th Cir. 2002); *Panavision Int'l, L.P. v. Toeppen*, 141 F. 3d 1316, 1322 (9th Cir. 1998).

173 See Reidenberg J. (2005), above note 172, pp. 1956-1958 who makes reference to American, English and French cases. It is possible to add TGI Paris réf., 8 Juill.

indeed, the Internet is not so different from other spaces and that the allocation of state competence is both necessary and possible – even more easily in this sphere – thanks to technology.[174] They clearly stress the need to compare the scale of the harm produced within the regulating state and the effect of the remedying legislation on foreign states.[175] In other words, the conflicts methodology should not be based merely on 'jurisdiction-selection'[176] but also on 'content-oriented law selection'.[177] What the Internet teaches us, though, is that the focus should not be so much on the precise contours of the state policy but rather on the remedy used to secure such policy: to the extent that the remedy to be applied does not hamper the preferences of out-of-state citizens, the voice of the regulating state should not be shut down too quickly. If the remedy at hand calibrates efficaciously the applicable state law to the effects felt within the national market, identifying connecting factors a priori may not be necessary. Through the choice of the appropriate remedy, national laws are thus coordinated: from unilateralism one goes to bilateralism.

The *Yahoo!* case exemplifies just such a striking result.[178] A French court had enjoined (in the form of an interim order) Yahoo! to block French citizens' access to Nazi material displayed or for sale on the ISP's US site.[179] The technology made it possible to restrict the scope of the injunction so that only French users were restricted access at (presumably) relatively low costs.[180]

2005, *PMU v. Eturf, Zeturf,* and Cour d'appel de Paris, 4 janv. 2006, available at http://www.legalis.net accessed 14 September 2006.

[174] The relevant issue is that of costs and effectiveness of the measures chosen to allocate regulatory powers. Goldsmith J. and Sykes A. (2001), above note 158, p. 809.

[175] '[T]he appropriate statement of the extraterritoriality concern is that states may not impose burdens on out-of-state actors that outweigh the in-state benefits.' Therefore, judges should engage in a careful balancing test under the Dormant Commerce Clause doctrine. These authors seem however to include free trade interests in the burden imposed on out-of-state actors. Goldsmith J. and Sykes A. (2001), above note 158, p. 804.

[176] 'In traditional PIL, the choice is based exclusively on the physical contacts of the involved states ("jurisdiction-selection") and without regard to the content of their substantive laws'. Symeonides S. C. (2004), 'Tort Conflicts and Rome II: A View from Across', in Mansel H.-P. et al. (eds), *Festschrift für Erik Jayme*, München: Sellier European Law Publishers, pp. 935–954, n° 2.2.

[177] 'In contrast, in modern PIL the choice is based not only on physical contacts but also on the content of the laws of the contact state and their underlying policies ("content-oriented law selection").' Symeon C. Symeonides (2004), above note 176, n° 2.2.

[178] See Muir Watt H. (2003), 'Yahoo! Cyber-Collision of Cultures: Who Regulates?', Mich J Int'l L 24, 673–693, at p. 688.

[179] *UEJF et Licra v. Yahoo! Inc.*, Ordonnance Référé, TGI Paris, Nov. 20. 2000.

[180] A report from three experts had concluded that under current conditions approximately 70% of Yahoo! users operating from computer sites in France could be

Contrary to what the District Court of California held in a subsequent case, where Yahoo! sought a declaratory judgment that the interim orders of the French court were not recognizable or enforceable in the US, freedom of expression within the US borders was not endangered by such a remedy.[181] This was expressly acknowledged by the Court of Appeal of the ninth circuit, which ultimately refused to view the suit brought by Yahoo! as ripe for adjudication.[182] The federal judges rightly pointed out that Yahoo!'s claim amounted to granting it a 'First Amendment right to violate French criminal law and to facilitate the violation of French criminal law by others. ... The extent – indeed the very existence – of such an extraterritorial right under the First Amendment is uncertain'.[183] Because of the precise nature of the remedy awarded by the French court, it was possible both to enforce the French order applying French law and preserve freedom of expression in the US since Yahoo! did not suffer any substantial harm as a result of the interim order.[184] As the Yahoo! saga shows, parties' expectations are not conclusive to solve the issue of conflict of laws on the Internet. More precisely, they should be protected only to the extent that state policies are not undermined, as in the real world.

Going further, the actual characteristics of private law that are often forgotten at a time when regulatory law is so successful, may make civil remedies useful instruments in the search for mutual respect between national legal systems. E-commerce regulation is particularly interesting, for it explicitly combines both legal regulation and technological regulation or

identified and Yahoo! already used such identification of French users to display advertising banners in French. In addition it was possible to improve the identification mechanism on auction sites so that the combination of geographical identification of the IP address and declaration of nationality, would be likely to achieve a filtering success of rate approaching 90%.

181 *Yahoo! Inc. v. La Ligue Contre Le Racisme Et L'Antisémitisme*, 145 F. Supp. 2d 1168, 1180 (N.D. Cal. 2001).

182 *Yahoo! Inc. v. La Ligue Contre Le Racisme Et L'Antisémitisme*, 433 F. 3d 1199 (9th Cir. 2006).

183 Ibid., 1221.

184 If Yahoo! has not 'in large measure' complied with the orders, its violation lies in the fact that it has insufficiently restricted access to anti-semitic materials by Internet users located in France. There is some possibility that in further restricting access to these French users, Yahoo! might have to restrict access by American users. But this possibility is, at this point, highly speculative. This level of harm is not sufficient to overcome the factual uncertainty bearing on the legal question presented and thereby to render the suit ripe.

Besides, the court expressly noted that no financial penalty could ever be enforced against Yahoo! in the United States. *Yahoo! Inc. v. La Ligue Contre Le Racisme Et L'Antisémitisme*, 433 F. 3d 1199, 1221 (9th Cir. 2006).

lex informatica.[185] Above all, it shows that the distinction between public and private law is blurred, in terms of function, since technical choices can be constrained by private law remedies, for example *ex post* by the judge. However, some peculiarities remain: the variety and malleability of private law remedies makes it more easily neutral in terms of technological choice. After all, in the *Yahoo!* case, as J. R. Reidenberg recalls:

> He [the judge] settled for requiring Yahoo to find the technological means to prevent users from getting access to unlawful contents when they were on French territory. Without pointing to any particular technology, the French judge left all the numerous possibilities of filtering mechanisms and network architecture for Yahoo to choose among them.[186]

Nonetheless, criminalization is often seen as the best way to increase levels of compliance with legal rules. All the same, extraterritorial application of criminal sanctions should be the exception in cases where diversity prevails.

Despite the unexpected merits of the unilateral approach, identifying connecting factors a priori may be worthwhile for the sake of legal certainty or when calibration is too difficult, especially when a significant amount of damages and not an injunction is likely to be awarded. Indeed states may be tempted to try to benefit unduly from the resources accumulated by transnational private actors whose growth is sometimes more than exponential. Yet, these actors have a critical role to play in cyberspace. In other words, while their activities must be legally framed, their actual existence is crucial for taming behaviour on the net. That is to say, technological sanctions are often more efficacious in terms of both deterrence and compensation (taking into account future losses). As these intermediaries are transnational by definition, one needs to build a governance structure which would allow the development of a dialogue between states and private transnational regulators. In this regard, PIL may not be sufficient and the harmonization of private law may be necessary.

To take but one example, the harmonization of liability of ISPs at the European level[187] may be seen as aiming at creating incentives for these intermediaries to listen to state preferences and put an end to illegal activities on the Internet in a prompt and efficacious manner. Because ISPs are exempted from financial liability (on certain conditions) but not from injunctions, states can maintain their specificities. While financial liability is likely to give too

---

185 Reidenberg J. R. (2005), 'La Régulation d'Internet par la Technique et la *Lex Informatica*', in Frison-Roche M.-A. (ed), *Les Risques de Régulation*, Paris: Dalloz, pp. 81–91, at p. 81.

186 Reidenberg J. R. (2005), above note 185, p. 89.

187 Even if far from being satisfactory. See the ECD, Arts. 12 ff.

much weight to protective extraterritorial legislation as regards freedom of expression, injunctions seem to be more deferential to out-of-state interests. The recent trend towards making ISPs plainly hold their gatekeeper role under the stick of injunctions confirms this equilibrium,[188] bypassing the initial spirit of the ECD which was wary of legal regulation. Lilian Edwards observes that:

> [a]t the end of 2000, as the dust settled on Articles 12–15 of the ECD, the DMCA and the Australian government's climb down on the Broadcasting Services Act, it was a commonly held belief that global intermediary immunity had reached some kind of tentative harmony. In 2004, it now seems that this may only have been a momentary blip of consensus. For European ISSPS [information society service providers], the next two years may be a time of worrying anticipation .... In the meantime, this writer would predict that ways of circumventing ISP immunity which are already allowed under the ECD – eg the seeking of injunctive relief and demands to reveal the identity of anonymous or pseudonymous content providers – will be utilised more and more by rights-holders and other 'victims' ...[189]

While harmonization is needed in some cases, PIL remains a key element of a broad transnational governance structure combining different normative sources in the sense that it legitimizes victims' claims before transnational private regulators, such as ISPs. Private actors act in the shadow of the

---

188 According to L. Edwards, the 'self regulation/total immunity' approach based upon the belief that 'ISPs left to their own devices will, for commercial reasons, naturally take on an editorial and filtering role, if they are not afraid that by taking any kind of control of content they are putting themselves in a position of risk as publishers, distributors or the like' has failed, as shown – to a certain extent – by US case law (on the US regime for ISPs in respect of all content other than that covered by the DMCA). See Edwards L. (2005), 'Articles 12–15 ECD: ISP Liability, The Problem of Intermediary Service Provider Liability', in Edwards L. (ed), *The New Legal Framework for E-Commerce in Europe*, Oxford and Portland, Oregon: Hart Publishing, pp. 93–136, at pp. 106–107. One must bear in mind that Europe has opted for a horizontal liability regime for ISPs, whereas the US has preferred a vertical approach. The same is true in France where injunctions are used more and more even against Internet access providers. See TGI Paris, réf., 25 mars 2005, *Comm. com. électr*. 2005, comm. 118, note Grynbaum L.; TGI Paris, réf., 13 juin 2005, *RLDI* 2005/7, n° 203, p. 43, obs. *Costes* and Cour d'Appel de Paris 24 novembre 2006, available at http://www.legalis.net accessed 30 November 2006. As to providers hosting contents see TGI Paris réf., 2 nov. 2005, available at http://www.legalis.net accessed 14 September 2006; Cour d'appel de Paris 4ème Chambre, Section A, arrêt 7 juin 2006, available at http://www.legalis.net accessed 14 September 2006. Besides, a French study on 568 decisions (between 1998–2005) shows that while preliminary proceedings such as 'référé' are used more and more often, these judges tend to prefer coupling injunctions with penalty payment than awarding damages when secondary liability is at stake, available at http://www.legalis.net accessed 14 September 2006.

189 Edwards L. (2005), note above 188, pp. 93 ff.

law.[190] Rather than giving up state laws in the face of other normative systems, it might be more appropriate to use the leverage of private law and PIL as suggested by Robert Wai.[191] The originality of cyberspace is that states themselves will increasingly often have a claim to make before spontaneous private regulators using private law institutions. The very possibility of having their law applied in cross-border transactions may actually give state legislators incentives to innovate to find the least intrusive remedy capable of securing their preferences. The evolution of the regulation of online gambling in the US may be interpreted in the sense. Assuming that the US prohibition of Internet gambling[192] does not amount to indirect discrimination,[193] enacting the Unlawful Internet Gambling Funding Prohibition Act of 2006[194] could be

---

190 See Mnookin R. and Kornhauser L. (1979), 'Bargaining in the Shadow of the Law: the Case of Divorce', Yale LJ 88, 950–977; Cooter R. et al. (1982), 'Bargaining in the Shadow of the Law: a Testable Model of Strategic Behavior', J. Legal Stud. 11(2), 225–251. In the field of electronic communications, see Katsh E., Rifkin J. and Gaitenby A. (2000), 'E-Commerce, E-Dispute, and E-Dispute Resolution: in the Shadow of "eBay Law" ', Ohio St J on Disp Resol 15(3), 705–734; T. Schutz, 'eBay: un Système Juridique en Formation?', Revue du Droit des Technologies de l'Information, 22, pp. 27–51.

191 Wai R. (2002), above note 154.

192 Internet gambling activities are excluded from the scope of the ECD.

193 Which seems to be the view of the Appellate Body of the WTO: it reversed the Dispute Settlement Panel in the case brought by the island nations of Antigua and Barbuda alleging illegal restrictions on cross-border supplies of gambling and betting services on the part of the US. On 10 November 2004 the Dispute Settlement Panel had ruled against the US for the Federal Wire Act, Travel Act, and the Illegal Gambling Business Act (on top of state laws) infringed trade obligations binding upon the US. According to the Appellate Body the measures taken by the US were ultimately justified for they were 'necessary to protect public morals or to maintain public order'. See Panel Report, United States – Measures Affecting the Cross-Border Supply of Gambling and Betting Services, (10 Nov. 2004), available at http://www.wto.org/english/tratop_e/dispu_e/285r_e.pdf accessed 14 September 2006 and Appellate Body Report, United States – Measures Affecting the Cross-Border Supply of Gambling and Betting Services (7 April 2005), available at http://www.wto.org/english/tratop_e/dispu_e/cases_e/ds285_e.htm accessed 14 September 2006.

194 Section 5363 bans and section 5366 even criminalizes the acceptance of funds from bettors by operators of most online gambling websites. The operators affected are those who: (1) being engaged in the business of betting or wagering; (2) knowingly accept; (3) proceeds from credit cards, electronic fund transfers and cheques; (4) in connection with the participation of a bettor; (5) in unlawful Internet gambling, which is the sponsorship of online gambling that violates any other federal or state anti-gambling law. Nonetheless, section 5364 requires financial institutions to adopt procedures and policies designed to block the flow of prohibited funding to the operators of the affected online gambling websites. In addition section 5365 gives federal and state attorneys-general the power to seek civil remedies to help enforce the other provisions

considered as opting for a measure more deferential to out-of-state interests than prosecuting Internet gambling activities across state lines on the grounds of the Wire Act.[195]

CONCLUSION

To conclude, a conscious recombination of the traditional and substantial methodologies of PIL could therefore contribute to clarifying the originality of the European construction. The key distinction is not strictly speaking that of harmonized/unharmonized fields. The works begins upstream. One should first ask whether the EC is competent to act or whether diversity is to be furthered. In the second case, the conflicts methodology should aim at eliminating externalities. When the EC is competent it has to determine the most efficacious strategy to reach the regulatory goal set beforehand. Yet, it may be cheaper to harmonize the conflicts methodology than substantial law. In this sense, the inclusion of Title IV (Articles 61–67) in the EC Treaty marks the official acknowledgement of EC competences in the arena of PIL. Going further, the former is a necessary complement to any kind of process of harmonization.

But it is not to say that the COP should automatically be the path to follow. Such a mechanism of allocation of state powers definitely plays in favour of businesses without strengthening the supervision in the home state and makes the regulating activity of the host state futile. Therefore, serious considerations should be given to constructing the conflicts methodology to boost consumer protection. The mechanism of economic freedoms would step in at a second stage to promote mutual trust between legal orders where necessary.

At the international level this time, safeguarding legal pluralism is not only realistic but also vital. Nevertheless, decentralizing can only be undertaken in a climate of mutual respect which requires adapting PIL to be able to take into account the content of all the rules in conflict. Indeed it is not certain whether

---

of the Act. The remedies include ordering an ISP to remove access to the website of an operator who violates section 5363 or other websites that contain hyperlinks to such sites. Such remedies may only be sought as to websites that are hosted by the particular ISP. Compare with TGI Paris, 17ème chambre, 7 Juin 2005, available at http://www.legalis.net accessed 14 September 2006, which refuses to make the payment intermediary liable under Art. L.227-24 of the Penal Code which prohibits trade of pornographic messages.

195 The efficaciousness of such a strategy is nevertheless heavily criticized. See for example Weinberg J. (2006), 'Everyone's a Winner: Regulating, not Prohibiting, Internet Gambling', Sw UL Rev 35, 293–326.

on average national regulators give credit to out-of-state interests.[196] Adopting a uniform conflict-of-law body of rules giving life to the effects-based test may be a path to follow so that judges would try to qualify expressions of legal imperialism.

Finally, inadequacy of the methodology of localization does not equal uselessness of PIL. What the confrontation between the cyberspace architecture and PIL rules does, more than ever, is that it suddenly forces the international lawyer to unveil 'le but social'[197] (the social goal) of private law (including PIL), more often known under the name of the regulatory function of private law[198] in order to devise appropriate connecting factors.

---

196 See choice-of-law provisions contained in the Children's Online Privacy Protection Act (1998), 15 USC §6501(2) and in Directive 95/46/EC on the protection of individuals with regard to the processing of personal data and on the free movement of such data (Art. 4 §1(c)). For a detailed description of extraterritorial legislation, see Reidenberg J. R. (2005), above note 172, and Geist M., 'Cyberlaw 2.0', BCL Rev 44, 323–358.

197 This expressions belongs to Andreas Bucher. See Bucher A. (1993), 'L'Ordre Public et le But Social des Lois', Recueil des cours, 239, 9–116, at p. 71.

198 See Collins H. (1999), *Regulating Contracts*, Oxford and New York: Oxford University Press, pp. 7–8; Muir Watt H., 'Integration and Diversity: The Conflict of Laws as a Regulatory Tool', in Cafaggi F. (ed.), *The Institutional Framework of European Private Law,* Oxford and New York: Oxford University Press (2006), pp. 107–148.

Index